Culture, Confession, Ethnicity and Race in the Middle Basin of the Danube

By

Octavian Căpățînă

Cambridge
Scholars
Publishing

Culture, Confession, Ethnicity and Race in the Middle Basin of the Danube

By Octavian Căpăţînă

Translated by
    Nadina Vişan chapters 1-4
    Oana Frânţescu chapter 5
    Eliana Ionoaia chapters 6-16
    Ema Tămâianu Annex F
    Carmen Borbely Annex G
Text revision by Eliana Ionoaia
Final revision by Rob Tenniel

This book first published 2024

Cambridge Scholars Publishing

Lady Stephenson Library, Newcastle upon Tyne, NE6 2PA, UK

British Library Cataloguing in Publication Data
A catalogue record for this book is available from the British Library

ISBN: 978-1-0364-0874-9
ISBN (Ebook): 978-1-0364-0875-6

*To the memory of the millions of victims
of racial and religious intolerance,
of chauvinism and hatred in the
middle basin of the Danube!*

CONTENTS

CHAPTER 1

INTRODUCTION

1.1 Definitions and Abbreviations

It is essential to use the correct names of things because if the names are not correct, the meanings no longer match, and if the meanings do not match, then things will go wrong—this is an idea that is at least 2,500 years old (attributed to Confucius) and remains valid today. To facilitate the reading of this volume for those who are not familiar with the central Danube basin (covering Pannonia, the Tisa Plain, Slovakia, Banat, Crişana, Maramureş, and Transylvania) geographically and, particularly, historically, we provide some clarifications here.

The House of Basarab was the second great old family of Romanian rulers (dukes, voivodes, and princes) after that of the Asaneşti (1185-1280), first mentioned in 1241.

The Byzantine Rite, **Oriental Rite**, **Greek Rite**, or, today, the **Orthodox Rite** is the old Christian rite preserved by the Patriarchy of Constantinople and the Eastern European Churches.

A chapter (*capitlu*) is a gathering of Catholic monks or clerics from a particular region, and also the gathering place of the monks.

Comintern: the Communist International—also known as the Third International—was an international organization founded in 1919 that advocated for global communism and was led and controlled by the Soviet Union.

Cnez, knez, kenez, chinez, kinyis, etc., are forms encountered in old documents to describe a leader who had defensive, legal, and fiscal responsibilities for a village or several villages of Romanians, also called cnezates. The term comes from Sanskrit via German. 'Knez' is a different notion to 'cneaz', which is found among the Slavs. Right up until the 20th century, the form 'kinez' meant mayor in Banat.

Cuius regio, eius religio is the principle by which subjects adopt their master's religion.

Cumans/Cumaeans were a nomadic Turkic-speaking people that lived in the steppes of Central Asia and Eastern Europe during the Middle Ages. They were a subgroup of the Kipchak people.

Curuts (from the Turkish) were rebellious peasants, outlaws, or fugitives, of various ethnicities, used by the Hungarian nobility in association with Turks and Tatars against the imperialists who had expelled the Turks from Pannonia at the end of the 17th century. Geographically, the Curuts operated in the Upper Tisa region, around present-day Slovakia, Ukraine, Romania, and Hungary.

Dualism: a form of state leadership that was achieved through a personal union between Austria and Hungary (1867-1918). It was the result of the political and social crisis caused by the defeat of Austria in the war with Prussia (1866), which sought hegemony over the German states. A dualist can be a person or an institution specific to Dualism, and that supports Dualism.

Erariu (lat. *aerarium*): land administered and exploited for the public finances of the Habsburg Empire.

Robotă, clacă: free labour provided by a serf to his landlord.

Freehold land (*alodiu*, allodial): in Transylvania, this was community land, free of any charge to the king or new recipients of royalty.

The ethnonym **Hungarian** refers to the population of Pannonia and the north, east, and south regardless of the origin of that population. It seems that the Turanian nomadic tribes who came to Europe from the Urals at the beginning of 10th century called themselves 'magor' or 'moger', but the Latin monks who supported the spread of the Catholic confession east of the Germans called them 'hungarus', and thus both the Germans and the Romanians called them Hungarians. Today, the Hungarians call themselves Magyars to emphasize a presumed Central Asian descent.

Magyarized: one who has been Magyarized.

Magyarizer: one who Magyarizes others.

Magyarization: the complex set of actions taken to denationalize the Germans, Romanians, and Slavs under the power of Budapest from 1800 onwards.

Germans in this region were also referred to as Saxons, Flemings, Swabians, and Teutons.

Greek, **Byzantine**, or **Orthodox** versus **Latin** here means belonging to the Eastern Christian/Catholic denomination.

The Greek-Catholic Church took root in the middle basin of the Danube by attracting the Orthodox (Greek, Byzantine, or Eastern) bishops, through promises, to the Catholic Church, starting in 1701. This new denomination belongs *de jure* to the Vatican, but preserves the old Eastern rite.

Guard/border regiments: founded by Empress Maria Theresa in 1762 for border protection. There were three Romanian regiments: Regiment I in Orlat (Sibiu County); Regiment II in Năsăud (Bistriţa-Năsăud County); and Regiment III in Caransebeş (Caraş-Severin County). A mixed Romanian-Serbian regiment was at Biserica Albă (Serbia). They had different numbering in the Austrian army. There were three other regiments called Szeklers, which were composed of Romanians and Szeklers.

Jeler (from the German *siedler*): free peasants without land who worked on the estates of the landowners.

Jude and **judicial bench** refer both to the leader of a Dacian-Roman or Romanian community who led and resolved disputes between members of the community, and to the judicial organization, county, or court seat where several judges administered justice.

K&K: abbreviation of Kaiserlich & Koniglich, used in the army of the Austro-Hungarian Empire (1867-1918); 'Kakania' was the term that certain Viennese intellectuals used to mock the dualist empire.

Localities and names of people. For those in the geographical area under discussion, it is easy to notice when we refer to Romanian, German, and Slavic localities, and when we refer to names of people, there is usually no need for clarification except in certain circumstances. When we say the king gave to Micu, Iancu, Vlaicu, Stan, Ciot, Urdă, Cândea, Drag, Neag, Florin, Vlad, and Sandrin X, or Y, we always refer to the king of the Catholic kingdom of Pannonia and his Romanian subjects in the central Danube basin; sometimes the original document, royal or papal, provides such clarification. When we refer to localities in terms of their geographical placement, we put the geographical unit they belong to in parentheses. Regarding localities still in Romania, we indicate the county, while at other times we indicate only the region (Banat, Crişana, Maramureş, Oaş, and Carpathian Bend, etc.) or the country (Slovakia, Hungary, and Croatia, etc.). For the reader's familiarity, we have also added several helpful maps.

MADOSz: the irredentist Soviet of Hungarian Workers was set up in 1934 at Tg. Mureş and was coordinated by Moscow through Miklos Goldberger; in late 1944, the leaders of MADOSz reorganized themselves into the Hungarian National Soviet (MNSz) to reabsorb all the Horthyists.

Memorandum: a petition that the leaders of the Romanians in Transylvania wished to present to the Emperor of Austria-Hungary Franz Josef on May 28, 1892 recognizing the existence of a Romanian majority and equal rights with the Saxons, Szeklers, and Hungarians, as well as a cessation of persecution and Magyarization were requested. The authors of the Memorandum, known as *memorandists*, were sentenced to prison.

Miorița: a very old Romanian ballad, one of two myths expressing, with accomplished spontaneity, a spiritual vision of the universe and its existential value. Miorița presents the strong connection between man and nature.

Muntenia/Muntenian: is another name for Wallachia, "Țara Românească", and the name of the South Carpathian Romanians.

Ofen (*Buda* in Hungarian) is the original name of the German city on the right bank of the Danube, which united with Pest in 1873 to form Budapest.

Original democracy: a form of government established in Romania by the KGB and GRU in 1990, which mimicked democracy, but in which the former power holders appropriated national assets and remained in power.

Pashalik: an Ottoman province.

PCdR: the Communist Party of Romania (1921-1948), a Soviet structure (Comintern) made up of foreigners destined to dismember the Romanian kingdom; from 1948 the PCdR was called the Romanian Workers' Party (PRM); in 1965 it was renamed the Romanian Communist Party (PCR in Romanian, RCP in English).

Replica (translated as Rejoinder) is an answer book entitled *The Romanian Question in Transylvania and Hungary* [194]. It is a response to an ignoble document written by young Hungarians full of racial hatred, in turn a response to the intervention of university students from Bucharest in favour of the rights of Romanians from Transylvania. The first page of this book can be seen in figure 9.2.

RDMSz is the Democratic Soviet of Hungarians in Romania founded in December 1989.

Ruthenians or **Russins**: old name for the western Ukrainians located between the Romanians, Slovaks, and Poles. Russia is a new name, dating from the XVIII century, adopted by Muscovites.

Saracen: generic term for ancient, Muslim, or pagan populations.

Saxon University (*Universitas saxonica*): the decision-making forum of the Saxon community in Transylvania until 1877.

Serf (*iobagi, iobagiones*, etc.). This term has two meanings: until 1437-1514 it meant a free man with duties to defend the lord's fortress and the access roads to the fortresses (*iobagiones castri*); after 1514, serf meant movable property—*viventum rer*. A serf could be bought and sold and his obligations were included taxes, road tolls, bridge construction, the provisioning and accommodation of soldiers, several types of transport, and maintaining the priesthood, notary, as well as acting as a miller, and cowherd, to which being extorted by officials can be added. In addition, serfs had to provide arbitrary feudal labour for four to five, perhaps even seven days a week, after a whole plot or even after 1/8 of a plot, as well as an endless list of other tasks: tithes, fetching and carrying, threshing wheat, weaving, spinning, drying flax and hemp, gathering cumin, and many others [53 vol. V p.70].

Session (*sesie* in Transylvania or *delniță* in Făgăraș): a plot of land, part of a domain, over which a serf had the right of possession in exchange for rent to the feudal lord; the session could be inherited.

Slavonia: an old name used in the 10th-14th centuries for a territory in which the South Slavs lived. Today we find Slovenia, Croatia, Austria, and southwestern Hungary covering the same territory.

Slavs referring to people between the Tatra Mountains and the north of the Pannonian plain in old documents, as well as those in the west—Moravians, Bohemians (Czechs)—and those from south of the Danube. All these Slavs became differentiated over time.

Szekler (*sikili, siculi*): today, a genetically Romanian population, "descended" from a handful of warriors whose origin has not yet been identified, but who spoke a dialect that was close to Hungarian. These warriors were brought by the Catholic royalty to the Carpathian Bend to help the Romanians defend their eastern borders. These warriors were given privileges and became a local elite that the locals aspired to emulate. Genetically, they were completely assimilated by the locals, but linguistically, over the centuries, they imposed their own dialect on others. In the Middle Ages, they were the third political group alongside the nobles and Germans in Transylvania. Today, they consider themselves to be close to Hungarians.

Țara (Terra/country): followed by a geographical specification, this refers to a county with a certain geographical unity and local homogeneity. Everywhere in Transylvania, Banat, Crișana, and Maramureș, we have such countries: Bârsa, Făgăraș (or Olt), Hațeg, Amlaș, Almaj, Pădureni, Zarand, Mots, Beiuș, Chioar, Lăpuș, Năsăud, Oaș, and Maramureș, etc.

Țara de sus (Bucovina or Buchenland): the northern part of Moldavia occupied by Austria in 1774 through bribery and murder.

Țara Moților: the land of the Mots is a mountainous region of 10,000 km² that was densely populated [150 p.157] and inhabited by Romanians who called themselves Mots.

Transnistria: the land east of the Dniester River, still mostly inhabited by Romanians living in villages (2004); it was occupied by a "pacifying" Russian army in 1992 [193 p.187].

Transylvania: in a broad sense, it covers the territories north and west of the Carpathian Mountains, inhabited by the Romanians. Its popular name is 'Ardeal'. In a strictly administrative sense, it is only the territory covering the Carpathian Mountains, sometimes including Sălaj County.

Urbarium: in the Middle Ages, a register in which the ownership of land was entered.

Usque ad bene placitum principum ac regnicolarum: a text from the feudal constitution of Transylvania describing the lot of the Romanians; in other words, the Romanians could be sold or killed according to the will of the feudal lords. It is worth noting that such a thing could not happen under the Roman Empire during the time of Constantine (306-337 AD).

Voivode: a term of Slavic origin used by Romanians to refer to a leader of a country; a voivodeship could encompass anything ranging from a small area of land to a valley with villages, several cnezates, or a country, etc. Transylvania was a voivodeship and remained so even after the beginning of formal rule of Transylvania by the Catholic kingdom of Pannonia. It became an autonomous principality under Turkish suzerainty in 1540, and remained so until 1867.

Volgarians, **Vulgarians**, **Bulgarian**, and **proto-Bulgarian**. The use of the same names for the Volga Turanians and the Bulgarians of the day leads to confusion. The Turanian nomads who came from the lands around the Volga in the 7th century to south of the Danube are usually called Bulgarians, although these nomads have nothing to do with today's Bulgarian people, except that the Volgarians ruled a great khaganate (empire) during the 8th and the 9th centuries covering the same area. Today's Bulgarian people are a symbiotic unification of Romanised Dacians/Thracians and Slavs, in Slavic (religious) cultural attire. The monks who wrote chronicles further described both the native population (common people, Vulgarians) and the Turanian warrior elite using the term Vulgarians. However, the Turanian warriors were assimilated by the natives. The name Vulgarian/Bulgarian was preserved for this new synthesis. Between the letters 'b' and 'v', and between Greek and Latin there has often been confusion. Since those Turanians left no traces in today's Bulgarian people, to avoid any confusion, they will be referred to as 'Volgarians'.

Wallach, **Walati**, **Valah**, **Valach**, **Blach**, **Bloch**, **Voloh**, **Volach**, **Olah**, and **Olachos** etc., are names by which the Germans, and following the Germans the Slavs, referred to speakers of Romance languages, including the Romanians, who, from their birth through the mixture of Romans with Dacians, have retained the name 'Romanian'. The Romanians also have local (geographic) regional names, such as Misi (Moesians), Bessi,

Pannonians, Timoceans, Oltenians, Banatians, Transylvanians, Maramureşans, Muntenians, and Moldovans, etc. In addition to these names, generally consolidated under the term Romanian, in some documents, the Romanians also appear bearing the names of nomads who passed through the region, such as Cumaeans, Goths, Pechenegs, and Avars, etc.

Confusions

If we overlook the biggest hurdle of dealing with ancient and mediaeval sources, which recorded movement, but not status, and the warrior elites and not the peoples, then we have another major problem: that of denomination, of confusion between geographical names and peoples, and nomads (warrior elites), etc. There remains constant confusion in older and newer documents between the name of a region/country/population and the geographical name; between the name of the population's ethnicity and the political ruler's ethnicity. Going beyond the confusion generated, the customs of the time, and the precarious knowledge of reality, the authors also applied political and confessional filters, whether consciously or not, and so documents must be read critically and in broader context. For example, the legendary Negru Vodă, the founder of Wallachia who came from Făgăraş, appears in a work by the Ragusan Luccari, printed in 1604, as *Negro Voevoda of the Hungarian nation*; in another example in the acts of a Genoese notary from Caffa (Crimea), *Mărioara* appears as a Hungarian woman (Mărioara is the typical Romanian diminutive of the name Maria). Both cases must be read in the context of Transylvania, which was then under the rule of the Catholic kingdom in the Danube basin called Hungary [19 p.103]. Omission is another flaw of modern historiographical sources. Even in recent academic treatises when talking about Romanians in the Byzantine documents of the time, only the names of 'Mysians, Getae, Dacians, Bessi, or Frigians' are listed, leaving out the names of the Pechenegs, Bessians, Scythians, and Ausonians [194 vol. III p.9]. Using the nominative 'Auson' (Virgil's *Aeneid* or Ovid's *Exile Letters*), the Byzantine author Priscus Rhetor refers to the Dacian-Romans from Pannonia [144, p.46].

Stelian Brezeanu, an exegete of the Byzantine Empire, quotes the Lexicon of Suidas in which there are two marginal notes from a manuscript by Constantin Porphyrogenites dating from the 11th century, where we find: the Dacians, who are now called *Pechenegs* and *Dacians-Pechenegs*, and *Pechenegs who were formerly called Dacians*.

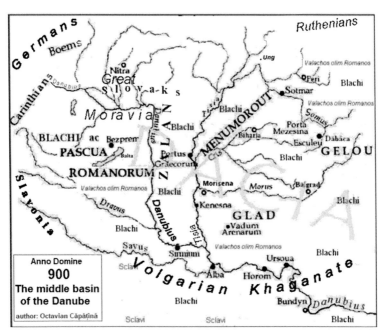

Fig. 1.1. The middle Danube basin in 900 A.D. and the Romanian duchies of Glad, Menumorout, and Gelu.

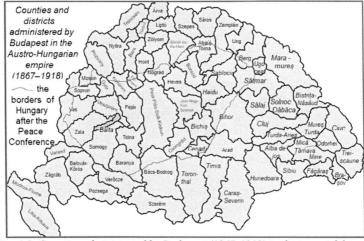

Fig. 1.2. Counties administered by Budapest (1867-1918) in the imperial frame.

Fig. 1.3. Tisa Plain, Banat, Crişana, Maramureş, and Transylvania.

The meanings of the county abbreviations in figure 1.4 are:

AB - Alba County;
AR - Arad County;
BH - Bihor County;
BN - Bistriţa Năsăud County;
BV - Braşov County;
CJ - Cluj County;
CV - Covasna County;
CS - Caraş Severin County;
HD - Hunedoara County;
HR - Harghita County;
MS - Mureş County;
MM - Maramureş County;
SJ - Sălaj County;
SB - Sibiu County;
SM - satu Mare County;
and TM - Timiş County.

Satu Mare County is sometimes referred to as Sătmar.

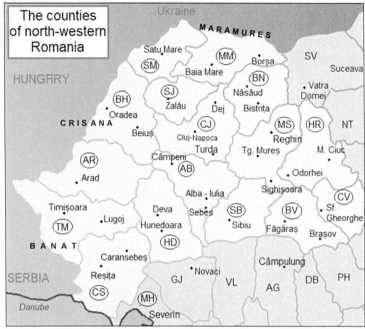

*Fig. 1.4. Today's Romanian counties of Banat, Crişana,
Maramures, and Transylvania.*

1.2 Not Just the Ignorance of the Leaders

We have gathered some fragments of papal documents, of Hungarian,
German, and Romanian research papers on race, ethnicity, denomination,
and on the extant culture behind a particular phenomenon: the policy of
Magyarization by a tiny minority of culturally superior majorities. We
have added to this linguistic evidence, material evidence, institutional
continuity, and pre-Christian traditions that have been continuously
preserved, as well as cultural evidence. We also present the culture of
hatred unveiled by Ioan Slavici and Johann Weidlein, two very important
humanists. The results of these efforts of historical synthesis have now
been confirmed by genetics. Magyarization was favoured by ignorance. It
is perhaps unknown today that Emperor Otto III (994-1002) and Pope
Sylvester III (999-1003) agreed to create two marks east of the Holy
Roman Empire of the German nation with Catholic vassals.

This is why they founded the bishoprics of Strigonius (Gran) and of Gniemo (Gnesen). In the Mark of Gran, they had the clan head, Vajk, marry a Bavarian princess, and the German monk Ascherik christened him with the name Stephen. They then equipped him with an army of *ritter* ('knights'). Stephen is sometimes referred to, by extension, as *Rex Pannoniorum*, i.e., not what he was, but what he was to become. This state had two institutional pillars, one predominantly German in relation to secular power and an Italian-French pillar that was predominantly focused on ecclesiastical power. This

Fig. 1.5. Johann Weidlein (1905-1994): the father of modern Hungarology.

construct was vested with the conversion of the locals from the Byzantine Rite to Catholicism and thus, improperly, called apostolic.

The "knowledge" or, better said, the ignorance of the German leaders since Bismarck (1815-1898), about the Pannonian area was devastating for the peoples of the Danube basin—Romanians, Slovaks, and Germans—giving wings to chauvinism and the politics of hatred. In his memoirs, Erich Ludendorff (1865-1937), fully confirms German ignorance about the field. Moreover, the contribution of the culture of hatred to the Second World War has not yet been studied, although a suggestion has been made by the British historian Wickham Steed, who considered the Hungarian policy of oppression toward nationalities as one of the main causes of the First World War, resulting in the Second World War. The refined Take Ionescu (1858-1922), referring to the way the old monarch, Franz-Joseph, ignited the First World War, described Prime Minister Stefan Tisza as *the Butcher of the Balkans* [85, p.102], considering him responsible due to his insistence on and intrigues in favour of war.

Fig. 1.6. R.W. Seton-Watson (1879-1951).

Regarding World War II, Johann Weidlein lifted the veil a little, but historiography has not yet followed up on his suggestion. Weidlein also pointed out the catastrophic consequences for Pannonian Germans and Danube Swabians due to the ignorance of German leaders in an article called *Bismarck Irrtum und seine katastrofen folgen* [183 p.10] and particularly in a collection of studies published in *Der Donauschwabe (Aal)* and *Südostdeutschen Viertel-jahresblätern (Munich)*. These studies are based on Hungarian documents that were published for the first time in the 1960s. The documents are very difficult to engage with for independent foreign researchers who do not know Hungarian history well [184; 179]. The volumes of documents that Johann Weidlein analysed to overthrow these historical prejudices, perpetuated without any scientific foundation, are found in: *The Hitler-Horthy-Mussolini Alliance* (eds. M. Adam, Gy. Juhasz, L. Kerekes, Budapest, Publishing House of the Hungarian Academy of Sciences, 1966); *A Wilhelmstrasse es Magyarorszag. Nemet diplomaciai iratok Magyarorszagrol* ("Wilhelmstrasse and Hungary. German diplomatic Writings in Hungary", eds. Gy. Ranki, E. Pamlenyi, L. Tilkovszky, Gy. Jihasz, Budapest, Kossuth Publishing House 1968); *Diplomaciai iratok Magyarorszag kulpolitikajahoz 1936-1945* ("Diplomatic writings on the foreign policy of Hungary 1936-1945", ed. L. Zsigmond, 4 vol., Budapest 1962-1970); and *Horthy Miklos titkos iratai* ("Secret writings of N. Horthy", ed. M. Szinai and L. Szucs, Budapest 1962).

With these Hungarian documents in hand, Johann Weidlein demonstrated, with evidence, that Hitler was at Horthy's mercy and not the other way around, as Horthy wrote to Stalin in September 1944 [133]. Hitler's ally had reportedly established connections with the Soviets as early as 1942 [appendix F]. The same ignorance of the German leaders informs Berlin's policy on the Danube basin to this day!

With the expulsion of the Swabians from Hungary, the Parliament of Buda spoke in 1945 of Hungarian-German enmity lasting a thousand years. Today, in the Reichstag building in Berlin, there is a bilingual

*Fig. 1.7. Ioan Slavici
(1848-1925).*

inscription that speaks of a thousand-year-old German-Hungarian friendship! The irony of this plaque has not been noticed by the German leaders who, of course, have not heard of or read Johann Weidlein, a man who lived among the Hungarians and knew their nature and culture well.

Resolution 147 of the 98th Congress of the United States (1983) offers further proof of such ignorance, highlighting how American congressmen were misled by the Hungarian and Soviet intelligence services. The resolution in question deplored the fact that 2.5 million Hungarians were left without human rights! If the 1930 census, carried out according to American standards, found 1.3 million Hungarian speakers in Romania, by 1982 they had almost doubled with 'over-rights', established by Stalin, intact—rights that no other minority in Europe had and much less, in chauvinist, racist Hungary, with a majority of Hungarians.

Finally, while the ignorance of leaders has made history, worse than this is the ignorance, cowardice, and duplicity of "experts" and "scientists". The fantastic theories of Hungarian political historiography periodically produce *histories* of Transylvania to prove non-existent historical rights. This is nothing special for those who know of the problem. What is special and remarkable about the last *History of Transylvania* (*Erdely Tortenete*, Akademiai kiado, Budapest, 1986) is not its "phantasmagorical" content, which ignores much documentary evidence, but its success in European capitals. Obviously, the applause came from the "academic" world! Going back to the content of the opus quoted above, in essence it poses the theory that the Hungarians first conquered Transylvania by the sword and, only then in the 12th and 13th centuries, did the Romanians come from the south [150 p.11] and infiltrate the area. The Western "academic world" did not even question how if the Romanians were not already settled in Transylvania, then from whom did the Hungarians conquer it? On the aberrations and falsehoods of this *pseudohistory*, we shall return with the considerations of a Cluj-Napoca survivor from Auschwitz/Birkenau, subject to the Final Solution [98].

Fig. 1.8. George Bariţiu 1812-1893.

How do they go on with such fakery and impostures without ceasing? It is not just a matter of the ignorance of the political leaders of yesterday and today, but also the mastery of such imposture. As the historian Seton-Watson observed:

No other people in Europe is able to play such a dishonest game as well as the Hungarians [64, p.258].

Worse than the ignorance of some, is the political idiocy of others! We here include the French President Fr. Mitterrand [150 p.181], even though this idiocy was "processed" for him by the eastern intelligence services, including the AVO (René Bousquet) and the KGB/GRU. They also threw gasoline on the fire and DST (the case of Charles Hernu), and our own (Nicolae Pleşiţă, the Ceauşescu family) were not only immoral and inhuman, like everyone else, but also utterly stupid, and provided grist to the Russian-French mill.

Why should we complain about the ignorance of American or German leaders concerning the history of the peoples of the middle Danube basin if our leaders do not know our own history and culture? The unequalled historian and scholar David Prodan (1902-1992), whose opponents could not dispute even the placement of a single comma in his work on Transylvania, said the *Romanians—a great people, led by a bunch of...* And how could it be otherwise, since the Romanians have won all the wars they fought in since 1859, with great sacrifice, but their leaders have never concluded a peace treaty in their favour. Not to mention the post-December 1989 period, when we had no president, no prime minister, and no minister who knew at least some of the history and culture of the Romanians, in a European context. If they did not know our history and culture, how could they have done anything for the country?

Since 1701, when the Catholics returned to Transylvania through the worldly arm of the Habsburg Empire, which had been religiously run according to Calvinism, they had only one chance—the conversion of the Orthodox Romanians to Catholicism. They ensured this conversion through the making of promises, but also through the use of cannon. In 1910, they breached all limits. If, in September 1919, even the officiant of the Metropolitanate of Blaj came to write about Magyarization through the Church as the *most vicious method* used [175, p. 46], then we wonder if this was not the same way that racial hatred and chauvinism were used to influence Pius X and the Vatican as was done by Hitler and Germany 20 years later [184]? Of course, the Metropolitanate of Blaj in 1919 was no longer blessed with the glory of the past (Innochentie Micu, Samuil Micu, Gheorghe Șincai, and Petru Maior Ioan Budai-Deleanu, etc.), but to refer indirectly to the bull of Pius X, *Cristi fidelis graeci*, from 1910 as being dastardly is something that cannot be overlooked. Since 1918, the Vatican, out of religious fundamentalism, greed, stupidity, and complete disregard for Christian truth and morals, has knowingly supported the false accusations by Catholic, Reformed and Unitarian prelates in Hungary and Romania regarding the so-called persecution of Catholics in Romania [175]. As they say, *many people, not even a Christ's nail* in so many high "servants" of the Saviour! If the high ministers of Christ had no problem supporting hate and chauvinism and willingly lying, then we have a measure of the poisonous effect that the culture of hate has had on the middle Danube basin. To break this deluge of hate, lies, Christian and Pharisaic ideas, ignorance of the laity, convenience, and prejudice, many honest scholars still have a lot of work to do in the future.

1.3 Denationalisation: A Few Examples

In 1782, noting that in the eastern part of the Habsburg Empire Hungarian was spoken by only a small minority, Emperor Joseph II proposed introducing German in place of Latin as the empire's official language. This generated anger among the empire's minorities, that is, the phenomenon of consistent Magyarization of the Romanian-German-Slovak majority. The Germans in Budapest were subject to Magyarization by violence! An important point was reached in 1848-49 when Hungarians unleashed the first genocide in modern Europe. Magyarization increased in intensity, step by step, and the new Hungarians grew ever more aggressive towards those of their countrymen who had not changed their linguistic identity. These neophytes felt obliged to prove their new Hungarian identity and became progressively more intolerant. After 1867, a threshold was crossed with a shift from the application of the Hungarian bat to discretionary Magyarization. With the start of the *Hungarian millennium*, a new stage was reached—discretionary Magyarization was no longer sufficient and the murder and massacre of Romanians and Slovaks became an everyday occurrence. Even though there were daily massacres, the 1910 census was alarming as a minority had become *the majority* on paper only. This process of Magyarization in which, as one of the exponents of Hungarian feudalism said, the others will be crushed under the heel if *they cause racial prejudice* to the homeland, proceeded to ethnic cleansing!

At the beginning of the 20th century, the method of ethnic cleansing was forced emigration combined with colonisation and Romanians were sent to the frontline in massive numbers. In the middle of the 20th century, again, mass killings and mass expulsions occurred, as well as the practice of exclusively sending non-Hungarians to the frontline and moving towards a "final solution", that is, a second genocide. The start of this second genocide against the Romanians in Northern Transylvania preceded the Holocaust, but also overlapped with it.

In 1790, the writer Samuel Decsi defined the direction of Hungarian chauvinism: through church and school *all peoples of a foreign language could be subject to Magyarization without them even being aware of it* [82 p.94].

Magyarization turned this same anger on the Swabians and Slovaks as on the Romanians. After the expulsion of the Turks from the Buda Pashalik, the Catholic Habsburgs took the initiative and persecuted all the other denominations, including the Lutherans [82 p.20]. However, they especially persecuted the Orthodox denomination and when the Romanians opposed the creation of the Greco-Catholic denomination, *divide et impera*, Maria Theresa sent General Adolf Buccow to solve the invented problem of the Romanians with "sword and cannon". Indeed, he bombed, burned, and uprooted the foundations of Orthodox monasteries and villages. As summarized by the philosopher Lucian Blaga, *the general acted without sparing anyone, threatening the Romanians with extermination* [10 p.59]. Having spoken of Austria's policy of *divide et impera*, for the purposes of balance, it is right to speak of the other side— the danger of Calvinization—which came from intolerant feudal Hungarian speakers. Here is what the author of the article *The Greek-Catholic Church*, the canonical friar Augustin Bunea, wrote in the Astra Sibiu Dictionary [197 vol. II p.609]:

> *Numerous leading Romanian families had converted completely to Calvinism and probably the complete conversion to Calvinism of the Romanians in Transylvania would have followed, had they not been saved from this by the Union with the Church of Rome, which began in 1697, as soon as Transylvania had come under the rule of the House of Habsburg.*

It is equally true that 50 years after this "union", the Greek Catholic monks, educated in Vienna and Rome, laid the foundations for the Romanian revival in the 18th century, through the well-known cultural current of *the Transylvanian School*.

In the Middle Ages, first in the name of Catholicism and then in the name of Calvinism in the Principality of Transylvania, the chauvinist elite resorted to Magyarization! The Catholic bishops and clergy of Pannonia and Transylvania supported Magyarization so fervently that even the Vatican acknowledged that the *Hungarian bishops magis politici quam catholici* ("were more political than Catholic") [82 p.66]. In *the Transfiguration of Romania*, Emil Cioran also observed that *their Catholic fervour itself is Turanism* [36]. Hungarian historian Pal Engel refers to Louis of Anjou (1342-1382) and his mother, the wife of Charles of Anjou, repeatedly using the expression *fanatics of Catholicism* [62 p.199].

A great battle was fought under Maria Theresa and Joseph II with the Hungarian landlords to destroy feudal relations in Pannonia and Slovakia [182]. In Transylvania, they did not try as hard, eventually accepting feudalism as a fact [150]. The conclusions of Emperor Joseph II (1780-1790) about Transylvania are clear:

> *Here everything is still based on the old foundations: National and religious hatred, disorder and intrigue, magistrates and authorities, then landholders who devour the subject, all this will never end* [8 p.247].

In 1848, the first genocide in the history of modern Europe occurred when more than 50,000 civilians, Romanians and Saxons, were executed in Transylvania in the most barbarous way imaginable. These murders were committed by the feudal lords, the Hungarian people's militias, the Hungarian people's movement, the "revolutionary" army, and former units of the imperial army that were on the side of the Kossuth government. There were not just mass killings in Transylvania, but also in Hungary, Slovakia, Serbia, and Croatia. In the view of those who witnessed the events of 1848/49 in Transylvania—Carl Klein, George Barițiu, and Andrei Saguna—this was clearly a war of extermination of the Romanians. In fact, Hungarians of all ethnicities—Kemeny, Kossuth, Csutak, Gabány, Esterhazi, and Czecz—directly asserted a desire for extermination.

After 1867, the situation of the majority (Germans, Slovaks, and Romanians) in the midle Danube basin deteriorated irreparably through forced Magyarization. Religion and the school proved very effective tools of Magyarization. In 1890, throughout Slovak-inhabited territory there was not a single Slovak-language gymnasium—all of them were Hungarian. The purpose of these schools was *to put young Slovaks in them only to turn them into native Hungarians* [190 p.137], as the renegade Bela Grünwald, historian and honorary member of the Hungarian Academy, wrote. R.W. Seton-Watson considered his historical writings infamous saying that:

> *...the Magyars ought to be thankful that their infamies have never been translated into any Western language* [179 p.122].

The great writer and historian of Transylvania and of the Magyars, Ioan Slavici (1848-1925), attended the German Gymnasium in Timisoara from 1856 on, during the time of Viennese absolutism. Only 5 % of the students knew Hungarian from home, the rest being Romanians, Germans, and Serbs; but all subjects were taught in Hungarian except for German literature [160 p.716]. In 1869, in the territories administered by the Hungarians, there were 1,232 German *people's schools*; by 1883 there were only 690! In Budapest, a German *opidum* a century before, by 1890 there was no longer a people's German language school for the 120,000 Germans still to be Magyarized [190 p.141].

Insulting names and stigmatization were used, not only in public institutions and schools, but also in everyday life, such as: *buta sváb* (Swabian, "stupid"); *bocskoros oláh* (Romanian, "sandal wearer"); *a tót nem ember* (Slovak, "is not human"); in reference to the Germans—*the garbage of the country* and *of the soiled dog*; and to the Swabians—*stupid and dirty* or *the graeca fides nulla fides*, and so on [82 p.5]. The result of minority chauvinism is perfectly illustrated in the protocol of the Lutheran church in Hodod village (Satu Mare County) by a quote from 1871: *Teenager Friedrich Hotz asks the teacher 'Hat, a nemet is ember?'* ("How come the German is human?") [82 p.156].

The Swabians of Ardud village (SM) complained from the very beginning about their colonisation (1728) and the hatred of the Hungarians for them. They demanded either another place of colonisation or the removal of the Hungarians, whom they could not bear! The Swabians of Ardud were vexed, *for it is impossible to dwell among these Hungarians* [82 p.36]. In 1806, a decision of the County of Bichiș mentioned how:

Fig. 1.9. PM Pal Teleki: "We will exterminate them all".

For the Hungarian language to enter the current use of the community and to gradually become the only language spoken, the praetors of the districts will persuade and compel the community to hire Hungarian teachers to learn Hungarian [166 p.17].

A typical conversation between those raised and educated by the politics of hate between Count Kolowrat and Kossuth's commissioner, General Eugen Beothy, the 1848 exterminator, is given below:

Fig. 1.10. Romanian Peasant, 1838 (drawing by St. Catterson

What have these people done? Beothy: *They are Racz. But what is their offense?* Beothy: *Isn't it enough that they are Racz? But what are you going to do with them then?* Beothy: *I'll have them all hanging. But think what you are doing, the poor devils have committed no crime!* Beothy: *No crime? They are Racz, and that is enough to be ripe for the gallows. We must wipe out the whole race* [179 p. 94].

Note that "Racz" is a Hungarian slur for Serbs. We will meet this assassin again in the first genocide in Transylvania: he instituted *blood courts, militias*, and *human hunting teams.*

This is what a foreigner (Reichs Herold, Marburg, 1889, under the title *Koloman Tisza und der magyarische Chauvinismus*) wrote about Hungarian barbarities:

In the spring of 1886, again on a party on the territory of Mogoş [Bistriţa-Năsăud], *the crowd police shot five Romanians and another ten Romanians died from their wounds... In Feldru it so happened that the inhabitants were sent a priest whom they did not want. Although the administrative agents had no right to intervene in a strictly church business, they sent crowd police to the place, and they shot 30 Romanian peasants. In the Romanian and Ruthenian lands they send crowd police that only speak Hungarian, they shout three times at them to halt and if the running peasants do not stop, the police shoot them* [190 p.108].

At the 1885 autumn congregation of Sătmar County, Count Stefan Karolyi proposed an additional 1 % tax after direct contributions to the entire population, in favour of Magyarization. As one half of the population was Romanian and the other German, Romanians and Swabians were forced to pay to be Magyarized [190 p.127].

On 9.05.1891, the Pesti *Hírlap* newspaper exulted that the Slovaks in a Slovak village being forced to listen to a sermon in Hungarian [190 p.136]. *The Siebenbürgisch Deutsches Tageblatt* (25.11.1892) wrote:

> *Even the most phlegmatic and calm Saxon* [...] *must eventually give way to anger when he reads the elucubrations of Pisti Napló or Magyar Hírlap e tutti quanti. According to their program, the dignity of the Hungarian state and of the Hungarian race is only saved when the Saxons are trampled, nudged and whipped* [190 p.143].

An additional measure was the "regulisation" of the lives of the non-Magyarized populations. Under a 1907 law promulgated by the Minister of Public Cults and Instruction, Albert Apponyi, the complete Magyarization of public education in territories administered from Budapest was ordered. The majority populations in these areas were Romanian, Slovak, German, Serbian, and Ruthenian. The desperate struggle of the non-Hungarian peoples had little wider impact on Europe, although the Norwegian writer Bjørnstjerne Bjøernson, disgusted by the duplicity of Apponyi, who presented himself at international congresses as a defender of inter-ethnic harmony, refused to attend the Munich Peace Congress in September 1907. He published a short letter that stated the basis for his refusal to participate in the congress saying that he found *himself unable to stand with the false preacher of peace* [94 p.265] who was waging war at home against children! The minister arrogantly answered that at future peace congresses he would stand with his *head up.* [94 p.265]. Bjøernson's acidic reply is given in the following:

> *Who doubts this? In the arms of this law, Germans, Romanians, Croats, Ruthenians, and Slovaks can be enslaved one by one to the Hungarian spirit. If the children left at home cannot learn Hungarian* [...] *So Hungary has the most illiterate people in Europe—what does it import? You see, Count Apponyi is holding his head held high! Empty churches—empty because the sermon is held in Hungarian—Count Apponyi fills them, alone, always with his head held high. If the Slovak people's museums are closed* [...] *On a nearby hill one can see the new protective spirit of the Hungarians: Count Apponyi—with his head held high* [94 p.266].

The crowning achievement of Apponyi's international efforts, in October 1907, was a massacre of Slovaks in Chernova, Slovakia by the police—his hatred of minorities had born fruit. With his head held high, in 1911

Apponyi undertook a tour of the United States to explain Hungarian democracy to the Americans. Unfortunately for him, however, the thousands of immigrants from the supposed kingdom of Hungary, who had moved to America for a better life, gave him such a hot welcome that this stalwart of feudalism had to shorten his visit. When journalists asked him what caused such agitation among his subjects, he answered:

> *I have the greatest sympathy for my true fellow countrymen. But against these revolutionaries, who are trying to cause racial prejudice and divide the country, I will fight until I grind them under my heel* [132 p.108].

Who could better explain to the Americans the situation of majority populations in the only country with a functioning feudal system in 20th century Europe?

***

The American professor, Larry L. Watts, deciphered the secrets of the Soviet Union and its satellite countries (particularly Hungary) during the Cold War, as well as the mental mechanisms of the US intelligence community through which its members struggled to perceive the reality of Eastern Europe [181, 180]. Providing an anatomy of the culture of hate in *Das Bild des Deutschen in der Ungarischen Literatur* [182], Johann Weidlein, doctor in Hungarian philology, gave profound, culture-based answers that are still relevant to our theme. Additionally, Ioan Slavici's studies of the Hungarians from 150 years ago remain as essential as the writings of the historian R.W. Seton-Watson from 120 years ago. With new genetic studies of European populations, we have all the cards on the table to make a neutral and informed judgment about what happened to the native peoples of the middle Danube basin and the modern-day consequences of the terrible cultural phenomenon of Magyarization.

CHAPTER 2

ETHNICITY AND DENOMINATION
IN THE MIDDLE DANUBE BASIN

2.1 Continuity Through Prehistoric Traditions
and Customs

Fig. 2.1. A pre-Christian dance that continues to this day in the Carpathians.

In addition to the evidence commonly cited, there is also linguistic, epigraphic, documentary, and archaeological evidence, which is generally Christian, as well as pre-Christian evidence. We have the traditions, customs, myths, and archaic pastoral carols that deal with the struggle against the dark and evil spirits, culminating in the rites of the winter solstice. Our folklore includes ritualistic practices concerning initiations, hunting, and pastoral and agrarian life, as well as curses, enchantments, carols, cries, ballads, doinas (Romanian grieving songs), and songs of love and play. Their origins are lost to prehistory. Obviously, some of the songs have lost their meaning and sometimes their "attire", but the skeletons remain and can give us an idea of their origin. The organization of bands, the morphology of dance, and the symbolic chaining of young hunters during such a dance, typical of pagan rituals, attest to the descent of such practices from the initiatory manifestations of the prehistoric community with its focus on the twin forces of nature. This organization into bands included girls and the tradition is still visible today in *the Dance of the Girls* from Târnave, as well as *the girdle* and the *fecioreasca* of girls from the Olt country, etc. The themes and phraseology of the songs accompanying these pre-Christian manifestations are another proof of their age. In traditional Christmas carols that were in use until 1970/80, the birth of the Saviour was mentioned only tangentially. Some carols mention, in the last lines and as a "recent" addition, that it is Christmas evening. The ancient figure, later called Christmas, has existed for a long time going back to the era of the ancestors of the Dacians. The pagan invocation of the sun's reappearance at the winter solstice has remained in various customs after the Christianisation of the Dacian-Romans and so it has been for two millennia! Even though they have been corrupted, the roots remain today. The author knows of traditional Christmas carols from the Olt country where there is no reference to the birth of the Saviour; or where there is, it occurs only as an addition at the end of the carol and is unrelated to the theme of the carol itself. Just as pastoral manifestations precede, perhaps by a millennium, agrarian customs, so do hunting customs precede pastoral ones. Each great conquest/existential passage coexists in carols with the previous stages. Mircea Eliade noticed the same thing half a century earlier:

Fig. 2.2. Another pre-Christian custom of driving away evil spirits that continues to this day.

Conversion to Christianity has given way to religious symbioses and syncretism, which often brilliantly illustrate the creativity specific to agrarian or pastoral "popular" cultures. [...] Let us note, on the other hand, that a certain number of themes and narrative motifs attested in Homeric poems are still current today in Balkan and Romanian folklore. [...] it is important to present some examples of pagan-Christian syncretism, illustrating both the resistance of traditional heritage and the process of Christianisation. I chose, for the beginning, the complicated ritual of the Twelve Days, because it has roots in prehistory. Since we cannot present it (dances and ceremonies, games, songs, cortege of ritual animal masks), we will insist on the ritual Christmas songs. They are attested throughout Eastern Europe, up to Poland. The Romanian name, "carol", derives from the Latin, from "calendae Januarii". For centuries, ecclesiastical authorities have tried to extirpate them, but without success. In 692, the Council of Constantinople reaffirmed the ban in very harsh terms. Finally, a certain number of carols were "Christianised" in the sense that they borrowed mythological characters and themes from popular Christianity [57 vol. 3 p.233].

We quote again Mircea Eliade:

It may be that a common agricultural custom of our day is more archaic than, for example, the cult of Zalmoxis. It is known that certain mythical scenarios, existing in the peasants of Central and Southeastern Europe at the beginning of the 20th century, preserved mythological fragments and rituals extinct in ancient Greece before Homer [58 p.232].

This ancient pagan "residue", which is still found in the 21st century in many traditional manifestations in the Danube basin, is proof—a direct relic of the continuity from the aborigines of prehistory to the present. It is a residue we see throughout the Thracian area. A long line of supernatural characters of Transylvanian fairy tales, such as the *Gheunoaia*, the dragon, the ogre, the monster, the brute, the werewolf, the poltergeist, the undead, "the unfathomable", the devil, the primordial wolf, the old witch, the jails, the fairies, the water fairy, the creeping serpent, the beautiful Prince, and "the bold", come from an ancient, pre-Christian, Thracian, or Thracian-Phrygian period. In relation to Transylvania, in 1800 Peter Maior wrote:

Among the people there is an old belief, and it has lasted even since the time of paganism, that there walk up, more in the evening, some fairies, who pass by, sing in the air and, especially, sleep in the fields, or in the forests and cause people much damage and evil. These fairies, as mentioned above, go under many names, that is, the beautiful, the strong, "the Windy" [48 p.58].

In the legend of Saint Friday (1580, Transylvania), we are told: *Saint Friday approaches the ogre...* [81 p.125]. On the scaffold of the Thracian ogre, the goddess Venera (Greco-Roman antiquity) first appears. Later on, in the Christian era, Venera became Saint Friday (Sânta Vineri), but still fought the Thracian ogres. Saint Friday in our stories is the primordial mother, the mother of all, and, especially, the mother of beasts (dragons, snakes, and lizards, etc.). M. Eliade and P. Caraman, and later M. Gimbutas and Ad. Poruciuc [147], wrote about these prehistoric roots. These remains come from a far distant matriarchy. It is, in fact, the history of the natives, built up layer by layer; another irrefutable proof of continuity. As Vasile Pârvan argued, the name of the Christmas holidays, Flowers and Pentecost:

> *...were at first only a mnemotechnical means of fixing the new celebrations for the pagans who from their ancestors were accustomed to other celebrations; The official church, for the purpose of necessity, also made this concession to paganism, after countless others* [129 p.110].

The use of the continuity argument through the customs, legends, and vestments of the natives is not new; this argument was also expressed at the beginning of the 19th century by Damaschin Bojinca and Eftimie Murgu [79 p.93].

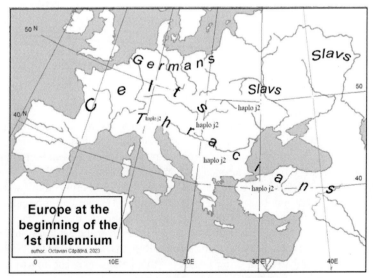

Fig. 2.3. Europe at the beginning of the 1st millennium B.C.

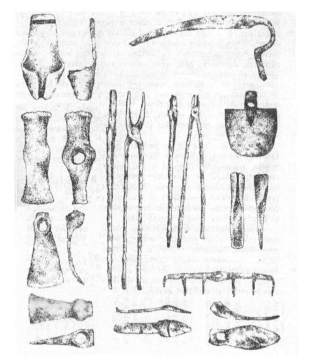

Fig. 2.4. Various Dacian iron tools.

2.2 Continuity Through Ornamentation:
From the Neolithic to the Present Day

The philosopher Lucian Blaga, in his essay *Getica* [11] published in 1943, started with a critique of the history of the religiosity of the Getae (from the *Getica* of Vasile Pârvan, 1923). The conclusions drawn by Pârvan, claimed the philosopher, did not fit the stylistic matrix and cultural topography of the Indo-European/Aryan peoples—just as with a few elements in Mendeleev's table that were intuited before they were discovered. Precisely because the written documents were few in number, the philosopher resorted to knowledge of the religiosity of the Thracians through the ensemble of stylistic potencies visible over the centuries in the intellectual creations of all kinds of Dacian-Romans. Thus, Blaga believed he had managed to outline the profile of the Thracians according to the Indo-European matrix they were part of, saying:

But for two thousand years, that is, since they were attested by direct and reconstructed testimonies, the Thracians have occupied an inner place in the Aryan space rather than an outer one. Hence our conclusion that they could not present, to the other Aryans, and especially to their neighbours at the borders, only peculiarities, which maintain them in an attenuated differentiation [11 p.76].

The Thracian mythology could not be fundamentally different from that of the other Aryans, since the Thracians occupied a central place in the Aryan space; therefore, a mythology founded on Uranus (a primordial god, conceived by Gaia and the father of the titans) cannot be attributed to the Thracians as Vasile Parvan argues. Relatively late (the 20th century), researchers in Anatolia and Central and Southeastern Europe discovered, put together, and interpreted several valuable Neolithic artifacts (dating to 6,000-3,500 BC). The function of these artifacts seems to have been ritual and sacred, a fact unanimously accepted. Hence, we come to the conclusion that the role of the "artist" was a choice of the community and possessed technical skills alongside magical or priestly functions. But how is the continuance of these forms explained here; it seems, for the time being, that we do not have an explanation? Also, what about the abundance of artifacts? Can it be accepted that magic and rites became "democratized" and penetrated the world of ordinary people of the sedentary populations in this geographical area?

Fig. 2.5. Geometric ornamentation on ceramics of the Cucuteni culture (5,800-3,200 BC).

It seems that priestly artifacts "contaminated" a significant segment of sedentary Cucuteni culture since we have such a great abundance of sacred artifacts from that era. Or were these sedentary Neolithic cultures in the Carpathians and Balkans found in considerable numbers compared to other populations at that time? The bottom images come from the Cucuteni-Turdaş culture and show their geometric styling. Among the Indo-European cultures, geometric patterns also appeared among the Celts, but in a much more attenuated form than in the Thracians, as Lucian Blaga observed [11].

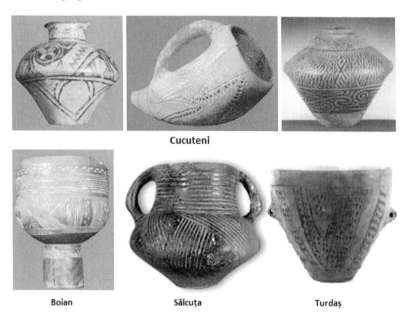

Cucuteni

Boian   Sălcuța   Turdaș

Fig. 2.6. The diversity of geometric ornaments on pottery from the Cucuteni and other Carpathian Neolithic cultures.

The stylistic topography of Lucian Blaga is presented on a map of Europe alongside the locations of Indo-European populations. The stylistic matrix of Indo-European populations that Blaga presented in his *Getica* study has been carried on, as far as the followers of the Thracians are concerned, by M. P. Nilsson's research and Mircea Eliade, as well as Maria Gimbutas and Adrian Poruciuc's research, which link to the thread coming from prehistory. The geometry of Thracian forms and the attenuated geometry of the Celts seem to come from the Neolithic culture of the Cucuteni. Indo-Europeans, Thracians, and, to some extent, Celts seem to have assimilated to varying degrees the culture of the natives of Central and Southeastern Europe, even though the Celts went further to the western edge of the continent. Up to a point, we could compare them with the Ostrogoths and Visigoths. They were all Goths, but were given different names after their last settlement, and if the Ostrogoths were to be distinguished from the Visigoths, this happened after their separation for various reasons, including their symbiosis with the sedentary peoples of Lombardy and Iberia, respectively. We thus find a local footprint on the various Aryan branches, depending on the geographical area in which the Celts, Thracians, Germans, or Slavs settled. Blaga's vision requires an update, or rather a completion, after the most recent archaeological discoveries and their new interpretations. According to Maria Gimbutas and Adrian Poruciuc, the prehistoric layer [147] was assimilated by new arrivals, Indo-European Thracians, from the locals (Cucuteni-Turdaș cultures). There was a stylistic layer that the culture of the Thracians had not lost either by the subsequent Dacian-Roman symbiosis or by the hardships of the times that followed, as we will see. *The layer of the mothers* (in Romanian mythology these are the "great-grandmothers" from whom everything sprang) also according to the great philosopher, remained, over time, unchanged. The images in fig. 2.7 are contemporary (17th-21st centuries) to the Romanians. The continued use of geometric shapes on wooden houses, tools, furniture, fabrics, and clothes is notable. The continuity of these geometrical forms speaks volumes about cultural continuity. The need to update the theory of *stylistic topography* with the new approaches (intuited by Eliade and demonstrated by Gimbutas and Poruciuc) comes from the philosopher's regard only to the result of the stylistic "production" of the Thracians and not to the roots of this "production". The fine tuning or updating of the *stylistic matrices* can be made by noting that by the Thracian Indo-Europeans presented by Blaga, one should understand there to be a symbiosis between the Cucuteni civilisation and the newcomers—the Indo-Europeans. This, in fact, reinforces Lucian Blaga's theory of stylistic topography and of the ornamentation. Obviously, the different stylistic colouring of the Thracian Indo-Europeans compared to other Indo-Europeans comes from the texture given by the local, sedentary populations—those who created what today we call the culture of Boian, Vadastra, Vinca, Turdaș, and Cucuteni. There are still some questions left: how is it that a certain geometry of forms attenuated and mixed with zoomorphism and anthropomorphism is found not only in the Celts, but also in the popular ornamentation of today's Norwegians, where also animal and anthropomorphic forms prevail? One explanation could be that the Indo-Europeans, before their march of hundreds of years towards their places of final settlement, had already lived with the sedentary inhabitants of the Carpathians for hundreds of years. This abstract geometry is also found, obviously mixed or, better said, dominated by vegetal forms, in the ornamentation of present-day Anatolia, Persia, and even around the Indus River.

Fig. 2.7. Modern-day geometric ornamentation on wood, fabric, and traditional clothing in the Carpathians.

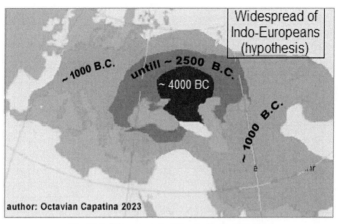

Fig. 2.8. The spread of the Indo-Europeans.

For Anatolia, the explanation would be that the Thracians who migrated to Asia Minor overlaid the creators of the Cucuteni culture after hundreds of years of coexistence in the Carpathians and the Balkans. From here in the Carpathians and the Balkans, they also occupied Anatolia, according to some historical hypotheses, as outlined on the map below. The question remains: why did they not occupy Asia Minor by making their way over the Caucasus Mountains? Being on horseback, were they forced to stop because of the mountains?

If this hypothesis of the symbiosis of the new Aryan arrivals with stronger sedentary inhabitants is not valid, then it is natural to ask: why are there such great stylistic differences between the Germans and the Celts, the Thracians and the Germans, and the Germans and the Slavs?

2.3 Continuity: Christian Material Evidence

At Sarmizegetusa, Apulum, Potaissa, Napoca and Porolissum, that is, throughout Transylvania, we find necropolises of inhumation, with built tombs or stone sarcophagi, and characteristic Christian and late Roman inventories (3rd-4th century). The numerous archaeological finds of objects of Christian character, all dated to before the arrival of the Slavs, complete the picture of Dacian-Roman continuity. A few are noted below [9].

City (county)	Objects	Century
Porolissum (Sălaj County)	Oil lamp, gemstone, pots of worship	2nd-4th
Potaissa (Cluj County)	Moan, oil lamp, inscription	2nd-4th
Apulum (Alba County)	Paleocrestine oil lamp	4th
Biertan (Sibiu County)	Donariu, inscription	4th
Sarmizegetusa (Hd County)	Oil lamp	4th
Mercheasa (Brașov County)	Oil lamp	4th
Napoca (Cluj County)	Inscription with monogram	4th
Apahida (Cluj County)	Gold fibulas, rings	5th
Someșeni (Cluj County)	Locket with cross	5th
Dej (Cluj County)	Oil lamp	5th-6th
Poian (Covasna County)	Pottery, inscription	6th
Brăteiu (Sibiu County)	Fibula, crosses, buckles	6th-7th
Rotbav (Brașov County)	Ceramics	6th-7th
Vetca (Mureș County)	Ceramics	7th-8th

The numerous monetary treasures discovered in Transylvania, predominantly small Roman copper coins from the 3rd and 4th centuries, testify absolutely to continuity. Hadrian Daicoviciu notes that immediately after the withdrawal of the Roman administration, in 306-392 A.D., Roman monetary circulation increased 50 times over in Dacia compared to the previous period [47 p.26]. The little iconographic material that follows in this paragraph will not be explained; rather to the reader we leave the pleasure of discovering the material proof, step by step, of Dacian-Roman continuity and of Christianity of Roman origin starting in the 2nd century. The fact that we do not have, so far, Christian material evidence from 64-100 A.D., does not necessarily mean that the first Christians appeared in Dacia only after 100 A.D.: research into the concept of Christiana *Minora*, a historiographical approach that seeks to assess the penetration of Christianity before written evidence from small artifacts with Christian symbols, has produced results.

An inscription on turquoise framed in a golden ring and found at Lechinta (Bistrița-Năsăud County) attests to the persecution of Christians in the middle of the 3rd century:

Ego sum flagellum Jovis contra perversos Christianos (I am Jupiter's whip against perverse Christians) [219 p.208].

For the persecution of Christians to be a problem worth revealing to one's superiors at the northern border of Roman Dacia in the middle of the 3rd century, the infiltration of Christians from the empire and the

Fig. 2.9. Gnostic symbols from Transylvania (2ⁿᵈ century).

Fig. 2.10. Evidence of early Christianity in the north of Dacia (Porolissum, 2ⁿᵈ century).

Christianisation of the natives must have taken place long before. The early Christianisation of the Dacians and the Romans in the early years of the Roman conquest, during the reign of Trajan, is indirectly attested to by Pliny the Younger. As the representative of Emperor Trajan in Bithnia and Pont (*legatus pro praetore consulari potatate*), he writes:

> *There are many people, of all ages, of all categories, men and women who will be caught in this danger. And the plague of this superstition has spread not only to the cities but also to the villages and fields* [219 p.208].

What can logically be confirmed based on documents and material objects with Christian inscriptions found throughout Dacia since the 2ⁿᵈ century, is the Christianisation of Dacians and Romans from at least the time of Trajan. The beginnings of Christianity being so early in Roman Dacia should not induce the erroneous idea that the Christianisation of the Dacians and Dacian-Romans was complete before the apostolate of Niceta of Remesiana (335-414 A.D.), since the rustics were more difficult to Christianise, hence the new Romanian meaning of the word *paganus*.

Fig. 2.11. Tombstone and inscription (Transylvania 3rd century)
[129 p.76].

2.4 Continuity Through Linguistic Evidence

From pagan times—from the time of the "gods"—expressions have been preserved in Romanian up to today such as: *grabbed God by the foot*; *behind God's back*; *God put His hand on his head*; *strikes God with an axe*; and *he wrestles with God*, etc. These are, at base, very old, pre-Christian expressions [42 p.80].

A contract written in literary Latin in 160 A.D. on a waxed board at Rosia Montana is charted by a witness as follows: Alexandra Antipatri *secodo auctor segnai* [119 p. 38]; *segnai*, that is, you signed as the *Motsi* (Romanian community in Transylvania) speak today, instead of the Latin literary form, *segnavi*!

The Italian Francesco Griselini (1717-1783), who we will meet again in Banat, expressed similar intuition, but resorted to the comparative method of the Romance languages, positing Vulgar Latin as the basis of the Italian and Romanian languages in a letter to the linguist Girolamo Tiraboschi in 1772:

> [My doubt] *concerns the origin of Italian. I live in a country where I have known a nation whose language proves that they are descendants of those ancient Roman colonists, that it is known that Nerva Trajan moved them here after the conquest of the Dacian kingdom. So, your presuppositions in*

the dissertation preceding the fourth [third] *part of your scientific paper cannot satisfy me fully. You say, with much reason, that the origin of the Italian language was hotly disputed; I have the honour to assure you that it would have been much less disputed if the Italian scholars had known the language of the Wallachians. This language has, in addition to a lot of Latinisms, many words that come close to Italian, many of which are even identical both to those used by scholars in speech and writing and to those used in the dialects of the population of the different regions of Italy; there is also no shortage of French and Spanish expressions, languages which, like Italian, were born of corrupt Latin* [43 p.77].

It is not just the Vulgar Latin used, but also the contributions of the natives that confirms the continuity of the Dacian-Romans. We find an important Thracian-Dacian heritage in the basic vocabulary of the Romanian language of about 10 %. Acording to the scientist I.I. Russu:

Semantic value, circulation, derivatives. Distinguishing the native words from the other lexical elements, one could observe how they are of remarkable importance in the lexical and in the everyday language of the popular community, being general (to the same extent as the Latin elements) throughout the Dacian linguistic territory; for example, a răbda (to endure, be patient), a (se) bucura (to have joy, be joyful), băiat (boy), leagăn (swing), zestre (dowry), vatra (hearth), gard (fence), a băga (to introduce –smt. into smt. else), a dărâma (to demolish), a mişca (to move) a rădica (to lift), a rezema (to lean against), a scula (to raise), a arunca (to throw), mare (large, sea), tare (hard), etc.; few are regional elements (as gresie (sandstone), together with Latin cute (whetstone), ghionoaie which coexists with ciocanitoare, vârdărie (woodpecker), bunget-dumbravă (meadow), mierâu-albastru-vânăt (blue), mununâ (hilltop, garland, etc.), […] *Most of them express general, fundamental notions, known everywhere, being terms of universal Romanian character and many are part of the main lexical background of the language. ... The significance of the native Romanian lexical elements in the general economy of the language is also visible in the fact that they have an intense circulation, so a relatively more frequent use than the Slavic words, of loans, which are in Romanian at least 10 times more, but of a lower frequency, out of proportion to their numerical value, and having a much lower number of derivatives* [156 p.131-132].

This Thracian linguistic inheritance cannot be explained outside Dacian-Roman continuity after the administrative departure from Dacia Felix where the native Thracian-Dacians, the Roman colonists and their offspring, the Dacian-Romans lived together. Up to 180 basic words from the Thracian-Dacian language were transmitted to Romanian, equivalent in weight to Celtic words in French, but from a qualitative and circulation point of view, the Dacian words in Romanian are superior to the Celtic words that remain in French, [219]. All the names of significant water features have Dacian origins that were taken over by the Romans: Balta, Dunărea (the Danube), Tisa, Someș, Ampoi, Cris, Mureș, Timiș, Zerna, Jiu, Motru, Olt, Lotru, Buzeu, Siret, Prut, and Dniester, etc., while only a few rivers have Latin names such as Arieș (aureus). For two rivers the native names have been preserved at the headwaters, while downstream translated ones are used: Repedea at the source and Bistrița down on the plain; and Frumoasa ("the Beauty") at the source and Sebeș down on the plain.

Many terms related to domestic industry are also Latin in origin, including: *sulă* (spear), *cămașă* (shirt), *a țese* (to weave), *bute* (wooden barrel), *cui* (nail), *scaun* (chair), *masa* (table), *cuțit* (knife), and *cunună* (girdle). Similarly, the major basic notions of trade are Latin, common both to the language spoken by the Dacians and to Vulgar Latin, or from the same Indo-European substrate: *a schimba* (to exchange), *a vinde* (to sell), *a cumpăra* (to buy), and *negustor* (merchant). This is also the case for all the essential farming words: *camp* (field), *arie* (area), *iarbă* (grass), *fân* (hay), *floare* (flower), *grâu* (wheat), *secară* (rye), *orz* (barley), *neghină* (cockle), *rapiță* (rapeseed), *mei* (millet), *pâine* (bread), *in* (flax), *cânepă* (hemp), *pai* (straw), *urzică* (stinging nettle), *măr* (apple tree), *păr* (pear tree), *prun* (plum tree), *cireș* (cherry tree), *nuc* (nut tree), *vie* (vineyard), *strugure* (grapes), *must* (stum), *vin* (wine), *lemn* (wood), *agăț* (arach), *frasin* (ash tree), *ulm* (elm), *fag* (beech), *carpen* (hornbeam), *a semăna* (to plant), *a culege* (to pick up), *a ara* (to plough), *a secera* (to reap), *a treiera* (to thresh), *a măcina* (to grind), *a aduna* (to gather), *plug* (plow), *jug* (yoke), *furcă* (fork), *seceră* (sickle), *sapă* (spade), *secure* (axe), *moară* (mill), *car* (cart), and *roată* (wheel). In Olt County, to the south of Transylvania, up to the 1960s/70s peasants still used the term *farina* for "urban" *făină* (flour), as was the case everywhere in Transylvania 60 years before that (i.e., 1900) [143]. Here, the peasants used only the Latin affirmative *ia* and not the slavic *da* (yes). *Țară* (country), *pământ* (land), *ogor* (field), *miezuină* (boundary), *pașune* (pasture), *curte* (courtyard), *casa* (house), *sat* (village), *cale* (way), *cetate* (citadel), *ușă* (door), *poartă* (gate), *fereastră* (window), and *senin* (serene) are also words of Latin origin. Pastoral or animal-related terms of Latin origin include: *ou* (egg), *lapte* (milk), *caș* (sweet cheese), *carne* (meat), *oaie* (sheep), *berbec* (ram), *miel* (lamb), *vacă* (cow), *bou* (ox), *taur* (bull), *vițel* (calf), *cal* (horse), *armăsar* (stallion), *iapă* (mare), *capră* (goat), *ied* (kid), *porc* (pig), *scroafă* (sow), *păstor* (shepherd), *păcurar* (shepherd), *turmă* (herd), *staul* (stable), *mulge* (to milk), *unt* (butter), *cheag* (rennet), *peste* (fish), *gaină* (hen), *albină* (bee), *miere* (honey), *venin* (venom), and *caine* (dog), etc. All the words referring to the family are of Latin origin: *tata* (father), *mama* (mother), *fiu* (son), *fiică* (daughter), *frate* (brother), *soră* (sister), *geamăn* (twin), *bărbat* (a married man), *om* (man), *femeie* (woman), *muiere* (married woman), *măritată* (married—for women), *însurat* (married—for men), *soacră* (mother-in-law), *socru* (father-in-law), *cumnată* (sister-in-law), *nepot* (nephew), *nepoată* (niece), *făt* (foetus), *fecior* (young man), and *prunc* (child), etc. We also find essential terms related to the human body have Latin origins: *cap* (head), *frunte* (forehead), *barbă* (beard), *cănit* (dyed) and *cărunt* (grey haired), *nas* (nose), *ochi* (eye), *păr* (hair), *ureche* (ear), *surd* (deaf), *suspin* (sigh), *piept* (chest), *braţ* (arm), *picior* (leg), *coastă* (rib), *coapsă* (thigh), *palmă* (palm), *deget* (finger), *ficat* (liver), and *fiere* (gall), etc. Calendrical terms are all of Latin origin: *an* (year), *semestru* (semester), and *trimestru* (trimester); as are the months of the year and the days of the week, except for *sâmbătă* (Saturday).

The fauna is particularly rich in Dacian terms, as well as Latin ones: *greiere* (cricket), *muscă* (fly), *purice* (flea), *somon* (salmon), *crap* (carp), *chefal* (grey mullet), *scrumbie* (mackerel), *testoase* (turtle), *viperă* (viper), *pelican* (pelican), *vultur* (eagle), *cuc* (cuckoo), *pupăză* (hoopoe), *corb* (raven), *turturică* (dove), *arici* (hedgehog), *iepure* (rabbit), *lup* (wolf), *urs* (bear), *vulpe* (fox), *hermelină* (stoat), *cerb* (male deer), *căprioară* (female deer), *leu* (lion), *tigru* (tiger), and *cămilă* (camel), etc. As for plants, and especially medicinal herbs, the Thracian terms dominate the popular lexicon.

Christianity, in Latin, spread massively and rapidly in Dacia after the first Christian persecutions with their epicentre in Rome. As one moved further away from Rome, these persecutions diminished, a fact attested to by the multitude of gems, rushlights, vessels, crosses, patterns, chandeliers, and tombstones with Christian insignia dating from the 2nd and 3rd centuries, and especially through the fundamental Christian vocabulary. Moreover, after 274 A.D., there was no more imperial authority in Dacia. All the basic Christian words of Romanian are thus Latin in origin and date to a time before the migration of the Slavs: *cruce* (cross), *Dumnezeu* (God), *creştin* (Christian), *păgân* (pagan), *sânt* (saint), *înger* (angel), *biserică* (church), *altar* (altar), *botez* (baptism), *lege* (law), *cuminecătură* (Communion), *rugăciune* (prayer), *închinare* (worship), *păcat* (sin), *preot* (priest), *părinte* (father-parent), *paresimi* (Easter Fast), *câşlegi* (the period between two fasting periods when Christians can eat anything they like), *popă* (priest), *mormânt* (grave), *sicriu* (coffin), *drac* (devil), *martir* (martyr), *martor* (witness), *împărtăşanie* (Communion), *ajuna* (fast), *căsătorie* (marriage), *nuntă* (wedding), *mărita* (marry—for women), and *însura* (marry—for men), etc. There are more than 80 Romanian words of Latin origin referring to faith [168 p.71]. What is noteworthy about this Latin-origin Christian vocabulary is that a few Latin words have no correspondence in other Romance languages, as can be seen in the table below.

Romanian	Latin root	Word in French, Italian, Spanish, Portuguese
adorarea magilor (Magi adoration)	adoratio	epiphanie, epifania, epifania, epifania
credință (faith)	credere	foi, fede, fe, fe
iertare (forgiveness)	libertare	pardon, perdonare, perdon, perdao
împărtășanie* (communion)	pars	communion, comunione, communion, comungar
lăcaș (de cult) (sanctuary)	locus	sanctuaire, santuario, santuario, santuario
suflet (soul)	sufflare	ame, anima, alma, alma
biserică (church)	basilica	eglise, chiesa, iglesia (from Greek—ecclesia)
Crăciun (Christmas)	Creatio	Noel, Natale, Navidad, Natal
colinde (carols)	calendae	Chants de Noel, canti di Natale, villancicos, cancoes de Natal

*Each worshipper receives *a part* of Christ's body and blood during Communion.

These differences present a remarkable history of the spread of the Christian faith in Europe: Romanians were Christianized through the popular apostles, from man to man, in Vulgar Latin and without the mediation of established institutions from the 1st century. Terms such as *the Epiphany* for the baptism of the Lord clearly show the cultured development of the notion, mediated by scholars and authority. Its generalization in all the Romance languages of the West shows, once again, the "institutionality" behind the notion [168 p.72]. The scientist Vasile Pârvan, writing in 1911, saw things from this perspective:

Indeed, our Christian terminology, together with certain other, profane words of our language, teaches us that we have not come as Christians from the South, but certain forms of Christianity and our Latin language could not even be formed in the South: biserică—church, sărbătoare—feast, lună—moon, pământ—earth, țară—country, etc. There are such documents, which, together with the old Christian monuments from Drobeta, prove to us, I believe, definitively, that our Roman character and Christianity are born and raised, naturally: Slowly and steadily, in

Trajan's Dacia, and have not migrated from other lands only later [129 p.201].

In another example, the word *Dumnezeu* (God), which comes from *Domine Deus*, but has a pagan ancestry, confirms the presence of early Christianity [129 p.105]. In other words, Romanians were born Christian. With widespread persecution across the empire, this province was a safe haven for Christians from the dawn of the Saviour's teachings. We have a high density of primary Christians and an original Christianity unmediated by "institutions". In the *Lord's* Prayer, which has 60 words, 56-60 are of Latin origin. Coming to the same conclusion about the spread from the beginning of Christianity from man to man among the lower classes, a specialist of the field, the historian Nicolae Gudea, writes:

> *As happened in the rest of the Roman Empire, at Porolissum, Christianity seems to have initially spread from the poor to the wealthy.* [...] *In total, for the early period of the 4th century, more Christian evidence* [is found in the north of Transylvania] *than in any other urban, rural, or military centre of the former Roman Dacians* [75 p.159].

To summarise, the persecuted Christians of Rome and other centres retreated to the periphery of the Roman Empire.

Returning to the miraculous Latin consistency of the Romanian language, we note that the specific distance (a notion from the mathematics of multidimensional spaces) between Vulgar Latin and the Thracian-Dacian language would not be great as they both come from the same Indo-European substrate and probably from the same proto-Thracian layer. This explains the easy Latinization of the Dacians, including those outside the Roman frontier. Furthermore, the specific distance between the Dacian language and Vulgar Latin is infinitely smaller than, for example, the distance between Latin and Greek or Punic.

The study of such linguistic distribution led several linguists, including Sextil Pușcariu and Emil Petrovici, as well as Romanists like K. Jaberg and Ernst Gamillscheg, to the conclusion of continuity precisely

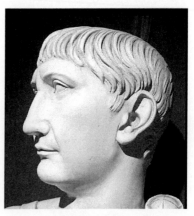

Fig. 2.12. Emperor Trajan (98-117).

because a series of Latin words such as *nea* (snow), *pedestru* (pedestrian), *june* (young man), and *cuminecătură* (Communion), etc., are spread across western Transylvania and the Tisa Plain [68 p.42]. We do not have many written documents about the period of the formation of the Romanian people, but we do have the imprint of this process in the very formation of the Romanian language. Here is the conclusion of I.I. Russu:

The chronology of the historical phonology was the first sure criterion in terms of the age and purpose of the over 160 old non-Latin words of the Romanian language. For about 70 words common with Albanian, the comparison of some showed that the Romanian forms could not have been borrowed after the process of creation of the Romanian hereditary lexical element and some of our native words retain aspects older than the Albanian counterparts: mazăre (peas), brîu (belt), pururea (forever), etc. Such a conclusion overturned any assumptions about possible neighbourhood relations ('symbiosis') between Romanians and Albanians, claimed only by hypotheses about 'lexical borrowings' in the Middle Ages (hypotheses that arose through superficial or incompetent observation of language, especially ignoring the etymological filiation of Romanian words, considered 'Albanian' or of other origin and explained as seen. [...]Thus, the spread, rooting and perpetuation of the Latin language in the territories where it was spoken in the Middle Ages and later is not due to the misunderstood fact (in the Romantic era of the Transylvanian School and by some later purist Latinists) that it has been brought and preserved for centuries by Roman colonists and veterans of Italy or provinces (to which more or less the important contribution of barbaric-local ethnic elements has been added), but by the fact that this official idiom, the Roman rule and culture was adopted by the native inhabitants and learned gradually in the course of several generations and decades or centuries, ending up being fully appropriated by the Romanised popular community.

Learning the new language must have been difficult: That sermo rusticus et provincialis generalized with many shortcomings and reductions, noticeable today in the Romance languages, but especially in Romanian, where the pre-Roman lexical substrate is stronger than anywhere, which proves that by gradually learning and speaking Latin, our native inhabitants could not suddenly

Fig 2.13. King Decebal (87-106).

forget the original idiom that fought a hard battle with the official language and from which (in the age of bilingualism) the 160 (initially of course more) words integrated into the new language of the provincial population were preserved. It bore, as Schuchhardt pointed out, the obvious seal of the replaced language, of the natives. ... The two Moesias and Dacia (possibly a part of Dalmatia and Thrace) are closer or overlap in part with the current territory of the Romanian language, the Romanian population; they experienced the long and stable Roman occupation, an intense Roman life: Military, administrative, economic, social, religious, aspects etc., mirrored in the frequent settlements (cities, castra, villages, isolated farms, etc.), abundant archaeological material, many Latin inscriptions, particularly significant traces and remains. So, in the Moeso-Geto-Dacian regions was located the country of formation, the cradle of the Romanian language together with the people who speak it, that is, the primary language (proto-Romanian—in other words, ancient Romanian), before the division of the four dialects (Dacian-Romanian, Aromanian, Megleno-Romanian, Istro-Romanian) ... The coincidence between Romanian dialects is not restricted to the phenomenon, but also to the causes and conditions as they appear, so that we find in the dialects the same "exceptions". We have, however, to deal with the same general developmental trends characteristic of our language and which, in their totality, can be considered to form the national character of the language. This linguistic unit was also observed by foreigners, who called the Romanians "Wallachians" wherever they are, in the Pind, on the Danube or in the northern Carpathians. The fact that the most typical features of the Romanian language are found in all dialects proves that in the time of language formation our ancestors had not yet separated, that among those who spoke Romanian there was a geographical community. This age, when language had not been divided into the dialects of today, when the most typical innovations had come into being, is called the proto-Romanian age. The development of dialects in the same sense presupposes a geographical community for ancient Romanian, whose language had regional differences of speech. Examining the question of the place of formation of the Romanian language, Puscariu establishes some elements of interest for the territory that stretched between the Adriatic and the Black Sea on both sides of the Danube where we must imagine the process of crystallization of the Romanian language and population [156 p.142-150].

The third theme of *Miorița*, "The Testament of the Shepherd" (see Ad. Fochi or M. Eliade), which we find to be identical among the Macedonians, proves that *the fundamental reason was known to the Romanians before their dialectical separation* and also confirms in this way the ethnogenetic space of the Romanians [58 p.241]. The philologist Vasile Bogrea remarks:

Shepherds, cart drivers, soldiers, craftsmen, besides their chief occupation
of tillage, the old Romanians manifested and affirmed themselves with
their own note, in which they excelled, in the midst and for the benefit of
neighbouring peoples, creating or transmitting elements of culture; this is
witnessed by their own languages, which show, at every step, the traces of
the role of Romanians as factors of civilisation [156 p.139].

On the Thracian-Dacian words passed from Romanian into the languages
of our neighbours, I.I. Russu summarizes:

Many of the Romanian indigenous words (as well as the Romanian-Latin
ones) borrowed in the lexicon of neighbouring peoples are obvious
evidence of an older or new cultural, economic and social influence of
Romanians on neighbouring or co-inhabiting populations over the course
of several centuries. Most of these words are found in Hungarian
(especially regional elements, in Transylvania, Szeklers), then in
Ukrainian, in Saxon, in Bulgarian, Serbian or Polish. Naturally and
necessarily, their number is proportional to the geographical proximity
and intensity of the connections between the receiving population and the
lending population of words and things, products or tools, customs,
institutions. As for the categories of borrowed words, from the native (pre-
Roman) ones, it has been noticed that—as is naturally the case—they refer
more to material-concrete things: typical Romanian products: brânză
(cheese), urdă (sweet cheese), zăr (cheese juice), etc.; generally to terms of
household and farming nature: vatră (fireplace), gard (fence), custură
(knife), caier (hank of wool), cârlig (hook), baier (hinge), strungă (ravine),
etc.; animals: vătuiu (rabbit cub), țap (he goat), mânz (foal), căpușă (tick),
etc.; plants: gorun (sessil oak), brîndușă (saffron), păstaie (pod),
măzăriche (vetch); the settlings, house, property, nature and the forms of
land: baltă (pool), măgură (hillock), groapă (pit), grui (hilltop) etc. ...
[156 p.138].

150 years ago, Hașdeu warned:

The element common to [the language of the] Romanians and Albanians—
because it is neither Latin, Slavic, nor Greek—represents the Thracian
substrate, according to the local people of the Balkan peninsula, divided
from the remotest antiquity into homogeneous tribes of Dacians, Mes,
Odris, Tribali, Frigi [81 vol. II p.43].

2.4.1 Continuity through linguistic evidence related
to Christianity

The great European scholar, Vasile Parvan, observed that Th. Mommsen,
discussing the Roman past of Europe, left out several underinhabited areas

between the Roman heartlands and the Roman provinces, with all their peculiarities. In consequence, he wrote the exceptional *Epigraphic contributions to Dacian-Roman Christianity* [129], a book so profound and rich with documentary evidence that from then up to now it has not been bettered. Since it was written, in terms of the origin and peculiarities of Romanian Christianity, the issue of continuity should have been further clarified, but the scientific world is well-settled and prone to distortions born of ignorance and politics. Pârvan also deals with a few words from the sphere of religion that have older forms than their equivalents in other Neo-Latin languages: *Dumnezeu* (God), *Duminică* (Sunday), *Crăciun* (Christmas), *drac* (devil), and *Sânziana* (a fantastic being that does evil), etc. We pause on the etymology of the word "God", as revealed by this great scholar:

> *The word god (dumnezeu) is met in this old, Vulgar Latin form, without "i", only among the Romanians; on the contrary, among the other Romance peoples "i" is preserved. ... Here is the explanation given by the epigraphy of the linguistic phenomenon. Dominus, Domina is, in its origin, an earthly title, granted to the gods only by assimilating them with human monarchies. ... On the other hand, the union of the various related cults by a common theological or moral background—post-Alexandrian Greek-Roman syncretism in the sense that the supreme God of the Semites, that of the Egyptians, and that of the Greeks would become one and the same... this process of henotheization, that is, the monotheism of ancient polytheism, leads to certain changes in the forms of worship. The name of the God becomes somewhat indifferent; the main thing is his divine, omnipotent character. Thus, a deus, with several names understood as master, monarch absolute: As the other master here on earth, the Emperor of Rome, is in this world only. It is a deus dominus. The inscriptions show us that in general in the East and especially in Dacia Traiana, this conception of the supreme deity as dominus was very widespread. ... [our note: The following are examples from the East and especially from Dacia]. There was no doubt, therefore, that the pagan invocation of the gods included Domine-deus, after which the name of the implored deity would or, often, would not follow. On the other hand, it is precisely in Dacia and Moesia that the deity Domnus (Domna), who in invocations, by her very name, was to be called Domne deus. The Christians used to say simply deus in their prayers. If they later said that the pagans dominate deus, the cause was to seek the Eastern and generally pagan influence exerted on Christianity* [129 p.101-106].

Note: Henotheism is an intermediate form between polytheism and monotheism, in which a single deity is particularly venerated.

Here is an excerpt from his conclusions on this subject:

> *For Christianity had, even when Dacia belonged to the empire, its special*
> *representatives in the province of Trajan; and then its relations with the*
> *south had been so vivid, with all the separation, that no political, religious*
> *or cultural event had taken place on the right side of the Danube, which*
> *did not immediately have its impact on the left: Enough to mention the*
> *expeditions of the emperors of the 4th century to the north of the Danube,*
> *the Christianisation and Arianism of the Goths, the uninterrupted*
> *economic relations between Pannonia, respectively the whole of Illyricum,*
> *and Dacia Traiana, etc. Indeed, our Christian terminology, together with*
> *certain other, profane words of our language, teaches us that not only did*
> *we not come as Christians from the South, but certain forms of Christianity*
> *and our Latin language could not even be formed in the South: 'Church-*
> *biserică', 'feast-sărbătoare', 'moon-lună', 'earth-pământ', 'country-țară',*
> *and so on, there are such documents, which, together with the old*
> *Christian monuments from Drobeta, prove to us, I believe, definitively, that*
> *our Romanism and Christianity are born and raised, naturally, slowly and*
> *steadily, in Trajan's Dacia, and we did not only later 'immigrate' from*
> *other lands. If, however, our Romanism and Christianity were thus*
> *developed, the reason is that we could live until the 7th century in physical*
> *and spiritual continuity with our mother, Italo-illlyric homeland, when we*
> *were therefore left in the cloak of the Slavo-Turanian barbarians; we were*
> *not children, but a vigorous people, of course still young, but fully formed.*
> *Therefore, the colonists of Trajan did not perish, but they continued and*
> *multiplied, colonizing all the countries as far as Tisa, and the sea, and the*
> *springs of the Dniester: for the Danube was never an evil enemy who*
> *separated its brethren, but was a good friend who united them* [129 p.201].

Recently, the paradigm of *Christiania Minor* has appeared, brilliantly represented in our country in the work of Professor Nicolae Gudea, who revealed through material evidence the "Christianity" of the poor and of the lower classes at least a century earlier than our historiography had previously recorded. From the outposts of Christianity synthesised in the Danube basin and permanently fixed in the 4th and 5th centuries, we see the process of Christianisation taking place over the 2nd and 3rd centuries. Obviously, many other people of culture have observed this too, including Paul Goma, from whose study we quote:

> *The penetration of Christianity was quickly, progressively, through*
> *diffusion, through individual, family consent, and using the word,*
> *Christian, the group—not by decree, as in all neighbouring peoples… That*
> *Christianisation had begun very early, that is, in full Latin, is proved by*

the whole Romanian language in which the essential terms are Latin [73 p.49].

2.5 The Natives in the Middle Danube Basin

But the thing is, we are present in the documents, Nicolae Iorga wrote [87 p.45], and what other documents are more convincing and less subject to hardships, than the living documents constituted by the people? We remind you that, chronologically speaking from the 1st to the 20th century, here we present only a few dozen documents, of the thousands of existing ones, concerning the local peoples of the middle basin of the Danube. Being all about documents, this information is not easy to assimilate, and perhaps even boring.

On the localisation of the Geto-Dacians, Strabo wrote:

The Getae are the people settled towards the sea and the East, whereas the Dacians are the ones settled to the Germans [Quazi and Marcomans] *and to the springs of the Istru* [...] *The higher parts of this river, from the spring to the cataracts (The Iron Gates) were called by them Danubius, this one flowing mainly through the land of the Dacians, and the lower parts to the sea are called Istru. The Getae speak the same language as the Dacians. Before the times of the Greeks, the Getae were better known* [95 p.12].

It seems that the endonym was *dac, daci* (*Dacian, Dacians*) and the exonym *get, geți* (*Get, Getae*), but the Latins adopted the forms *dac, daci.*

Toponymy can help us establish continuity and thus from the names of still-preserved Dacian localities, we can show that the Romans took them over [187 p.161]. A.D. Xenopol put the 68 Dacian toponyms together with the 16 Latin ones and noted that the latter also carried the Dacian name in the official name, such as Ulpia Traiana Augusta—Sarmisegetusa regia [187 p.162]. Immediately after the Roman conquest, Hadrian, the future emperor, was sent by Emperor Trajan (98-117) to Pannonia and the eastern border of Dacia to confront the Sarmatians. In Dacia, Hadrian did away with some incompetent clerks, executing the bad ones, and brought "technicians" from Italy to take their place. Later, Hadrian became emperor and legalised marriages between veterans and barbarian women, legitimising their children, and gave the veterans ownership of uncultivated land across the empire. The inscriptions from Roman Dacia show that the locals lived together with the representatives of the new Roman administration under all possible forms, including:

a) Noble Dacian families under the Romans. A tombstone of a Dacian queen bears the following Latin inscription: To the Mani Gods: Zia, the wife of Piepor, the king of Costoboci *laid by the grandsons Natoporus et Drilgisia for their grandmother 'carissimae benemerenti posuerunt'* [187 vol. I p.164].

b) Dacian families with Roman customs: *Aia of Nando lived 80 years, Andrada of Bituva lived 80 years, Bricena lived 40 years, Iusta, lived 30 years, Bedar 12. After her death, Herculan, the libert (freed slave) laid this tombstone to his patron as tribute* [187 vol. I p.163].

c) Dacian children with Roman names: *T.M. laid this stone to show his respects to Domitia of Clon* [187 vol. I p.163] (Clon is a Dacian name and Domitia, Roman).

d) Dacians enrolled in the Roman cohorts: *Iulius Secundinus evocatorum cohortae III, Salariorum qui vixit annis LXXXV, natione dacus* reads an inscription on a tombstone placed by the wife Atticia Sabina and son Julius Costas [187 vol. I p.165] (Atticia is a Dacian name and Sabina, Roman).

e) The free Dacians from outside the Roman *limes* (limit) cooperated with the Roman administration: *To Goddess Nemesis, the queen. Valerius Valentinus military consular beneficiary from Legion XIII-a Gemina, mayor of Gordian colony Napoca*, is listed for tax purposes in the region of Someş, beyond the limes *under the consulate of our lord, Emperor Marc Antoniu Gordian and Aviola* [187 vol. I p.175].

f) The endurance of the veterans in Dacia Felix after the steadfast three legions, XIII Gemina, V Macedonica, and I Adjutrix, were stationed elsewhere. According to the philologist Lazăr Şăineanu, the number of veterans must have been significantly larger for a word such as *veteran* to become *bătrân* (elder), in Dacian-Romanian [187 vol. I p.172].

In his third book, *The Ecclesiastic History*, Eusebio (260-340), Bishop of Caesarea in Palestine, the first historian of Christianity, wrote: *The saints, apostles, and the Saviour's disciples spread all over the earth inhabited by men. According to the tradition, Thomas took Partia, Andrew, Scythia, John, Asia Minor* [51 p.25]. Scythia at the time meant the northern and western areas around the Black Sea. Even if Eusebio's writings cannot be considered proof, the linguistic evidence that we have mentioned remains.

If the inscriptions found at archaeological sites in Romania attest to settlers from remote regions of the empire, such as Greece, Syria, and southern Italy, it is notable that most of them came from nearby—from Trakya, Moesia, Dalmatia, Pannonia, Noricum, the north of Italy, and Anatolia [47 p.6], that is, from the area where the Thracians had spread. From the inscriptions accounted for by Hadrian Daicoviciu, there are about 3,000 Latin, 40 Greek, and 6 Palmiran [47 p.7]. Therefore, the Romanised Thracians, as Roman colonists, Romanised Dacia—a Romanisation process that the parents or grandparents of the Thracians from south of the Danube had gone through previously.

After the bloody persecutions under Nero (54-68) and further severe ones under Domitian (81-96), when Trajan offered the citizens of the empire the option of settling in Dacia, a large number of Christians from Rome took up this offer, putting distance between themselves and Rome, which was the centre of anti-Christian persecution. Rome and, subsequently, Italy were at the time not only dangerous for Christians, but also overpopulated (considering the era) and this was why they probably supplied most of the colonists for Dacia [168 p.71]. Vasile Pârvan has also put forth arguments on the arrival of colonists from the Orient (Syria and Anatolian Trakya), who had already been "contaminated" by the new religion of redemption and salvation [129].

From the imperial diploma of Hadrian, dated 10 August 123, we learn that the military commander of Dacia, Quintus Marcius Turbo, was also supreme military chief of Dacia and Pannonia Inferior [155]. The space between Roman Dacia and Pannonia Inferior, between the middle Danube and the Tisa, was inhabited by the free Dacians together with a few tribes of Sarmatians. In the absence of any obvious economic interest, this territory was barely controlled by the empire. This unitary control is proof of a commonality in the Pannonia and Carpathian space. The imperial diploma consists of two bronze cast plates, inscribed on both sides, and was discovered in the Roman *castrum* near Gherla (Cluj County).

The archaeological and epigraphic findings prove the continuous habitation of the whole space in the entire first millennium, before the arrival of the last nomads. The paleo-Christian discoveries corroborated by the Christian vocabulary also confirm this continuity.

Tertulian (160-220), the first patristic writer, in his work *Adversus Judaeos*, written 198-203, said that the new faith had spread not only in the empire, but also in the territories inhabited by Sarmatians, Dacians, Germans, and Scythians [69 p.219]. Even if Tertulian's text is not clear, no matter if he referred to the Dacians in Dacia Trajana or to the free Dacians, the fact is that the popular apostles were undertaking

Christenings in the Carpathians *per pedes apostolorum*.

In the Roman sites Augustia, Cumidava, Praetorium, and Micia (modern-day Brețcu-Covasna, Râșnov-Brașov, Mehadia-Caraș-Severin, and Vețel-Hunedoara), where border soldiers of the empire were serving, materials from the 2nd and 3rd centuries onward have been found that are specific to the Dacians, belonging to soldiers recruited from among the local population [47 p.10]. From the same period (the 2nd and the 3rd centuries), rural settlements have been discovered inside the province, for instance at Șura Mică, Slimnic (Sibiu County), Noslac (Alba County), Soporu de Câmpie (Cluj County), Obreja (Caras-Severin County), and Morești (Mures County). All this proves that the Romans and Dacians were living together. The thoroughness and endurance of this process of Romanisation did not originate in the Dacian cities that had been taken over and developed by the Roman civilian and military administration (Dobreta, Dierna, Ampelum, Apulum, Napoca, Porolissum, Potaissa, and Tibiscum), or from the new Colonia Dacica (Ulpia Traiana Augusta Dacica Sarmizegetusa), but from the rural settlement of veterans after the end of their service, Roman colonists, and Christian refugees from Rome. Furthermore, as we have already seen, a substantial religious emigration from Rome and northern Italy wrote a unique page of history in Europe, which is proven linguistically by the presence of Latin words that are to be found only in Romanian and that are missing from the Neo-Latin word inventory of the West.

An interpreter of the Dacian language, Marcus Ulpius Celerinus, is referenced in an inscription on a sarcophagus in Brigetio (Szöny, Hungary), most likely from the first half of the 3rd century. He describes himself as *interprex Dacianorum* with Legion I Adjutrix. Judging by his name, he appears to have been the nephew of a Dacian who received Roman citizenship [124].

The Latin writer Salvianus, referring to the withdrawal of the Roman administration (274) south of the Danube wrote:

> *Not only that our brothers* [the Roman colonists] *will not run away from their parts* [Trans-Danubian Dacia] *to us* [Moesia, Mediterranean Dacia], *but on the contrary they leave us to go to them* [123 p.13].

In 325, Theofan, Bishop of Byzantium, knew that there had been priests in Dacia Trajana as early the time of Emperor Gallienus (253-268) [165 vol. I p.47].

Ulfila, a Goth, was born in Dacia and christened in Cappadocia. He was a follower of Arian and was sent out as an apostle to the Goths, preaching among them north of the Danube in the years 340-350. He also preached in Latin to the Daco-Romanians. Ulfila translated the Bible into Gothic, the *Codex Argentum*, written in Dacia about 350, using a mixture of Greek, Latin, and unknown letters.

Emperor Julian the Apostate (331-363), a learned writer and philosopher, referred to the Dacian-Romans north of the Danube also as Dacians [40 p.147]. On the territory of Roman-Dacia, thousands of Latin inscriptions have been found, more than in any other Roman province compared to their respective areas [6 vol. III p.15]. The importance of Dacia in the politics of the empire is also shown by the large numbers of representations of this province on the coins issued in the period of its annexation: about 30 % on gold and silver coins and 47 % on copper coins [110 p.68]. In a box of the Sarmizegetusa Ulpia amphitheatre, a small treasure trove consisting of imperial coins was found with the most recent dating to the time of Emperor Valentianus I (363-375). As such, it appears that Roman life continued unimpeded in Dacia Felix after the Aurelian withdrawal.

St. Paolin (354-431), Bishop of Nola (near Naples), looks in his writings, Carmen XVII and XXVII, at St. Niceta of Remesiana (366-414), whom he praised for his evangelism among the Dacian-Romans [51 p.35]. Vasile Pârvan takes the argument all the way to the contribution of St. Niceta [129 p.73]. St. Niceta of Remesiana (Serbia) is well known for the prayer *You, Lord, we praise*.

When it was rebuilt in 1758, the following inscription was found on a foundation stone in the wall of the church at Răşinari: *The year of the old church, anno Domini 420* [126 p.368].

The necropolis of Brătei (Sibiu County) in the 4th and 5th centuries (360 tombs), according to the inventory (coins, ceramics) and ritual, belongs to the Roman tradition and attests to a Dacian-Illyrian-Roman community [157 p.89].

In 448, the writer Priscus Rhetor, who accompanied General Maximin to Attila's settlement, wrote: *The Huns... are struggling to learn the language of Goths and Ausons* [144 p.46], that is of the local Dacian-Romans. If for Publius Ovidius Naso, *auson* was synonymous with Roman [122 p.188], for Priscus Rhetor, *auson* meant the *scions* of the Romans.

The Chronicle of the Salzburg Diocese (871) mentions that the Huns pushed away or pressed the Dacian-Romans, Goths, and Gepids, but some of them, the Gepids, remained there to that day: *Huni... expulerunt Romanos et Gotos et Gepidos. De Gepides autem quidam adhunc ibi resident* [183 p.16]. We cannot speak of "expulsion" in the 5th century— the nomads ruled (Herrschaft) only at the top of the hierarchy. Not only did the nomads need the local settled peoples, but they were dependent on their work, as they often used to rob them. This involved horrific murders and so the locals feared their new masters. Only the wealthy were able to seek refuge from the barbarians. These migrants, always in lower numbers, lived off the locals by plundering them. Other sources speak of the inhabitants of the cities, who withdrew for fear of the Huns, but *solis valachis remantibus*, these were mainly engaged in agriculture [82 p.54]. The Latin monk Simon of Chiza [145 p596], referring to this age of the Hunnish invasion of Panonnia, also wrote that only Blachi *remantibus sponte in Pannonia* (Romanians staying voluntarily in Pannonia).

Around 450, the historian Zozimus of Constantinople wrote about the lucky Emperor Theodosius II who defeated the "Sciri" and the Carpathian-Dacians mixed with the Huns [144 p.52]. The way the steppe nomads, the Huns, took to Constantinople was along the Danube, and therefore from Pannonia there came the "Sciri and Dacians" mixed with the Huns.

The organisation of the Church in Roman Dacia was done by the missionary Church in Illyricum, as the bishops on the right bank of the Danube had extended their jurisdiction to the left bank as well, according to *Lex Iustiniani de Ecclesiis* or *Novella 11 de Episcopis Illyrici*. This law referred to the organization of the Church in Illyricum, a region which also included Roman Dacia. The new prefecture, set up by Justinian, included Pannonia, Mediterranean Dacia, and Dacia Ripensia, under the jurisdiction of Justiniana Prima [95 p.28].

In Morești (Mureș County), of the 81 tombs dated to the 4th century, more than 10 % were found to have a rich inventory (and we do not know whether the rest had been robbed), attesting to a significant Dacian-Roman settlement and proving continuity [194 vol II p.843].

In Fizeș (Caraș-Severin County), Dăbâca (Cluj County), Ghelar, and Teliuc (Hunedoara County), ore deposits, mining tools, ovens, and iron and clay cakes dating to the 4th-7th centuries have been discovered, which proves a continuous tradition of metalwork from the Dacian era.

An inscription from Sirmium, dated 580, invokes the help of God to protect *Romania* from the invasions of the Avar [22 p.86]. Such proof of Dacian-Roman continuity we see throughout history.

The Roman emperors of New Rome knew of our origins; Emperor Flavius Mauricius (582-602) even left written proof in his work *Strategikon*. In his times, probably at about 601, General Petru defeated the Slavs north of the Danube and he mentioned that the inhabitants of the cities on the Danube considered themselves *Romans* and their territory *Romania* [86 p.35].

The "World's Chronicle" (*Weltchronik*) of Iansen Enikel, written in 1277, also describes the deeds of Charlemagne, who in the year 800 began the Christening of the Avars in Pannonia up to the land of the Romanians

[145 p.676].

Referring to *Otgerius rex Daciae* from the chronicle called *Pseudo-Turpin* dated to the 12th century, a chronicle ordered by Frederick Barbarossa I for the canonization of Charlemagne and based on *Vita et Gesta Caroli Magni* written at about 830, the Dane, Knud Togeby mentions that Pannonia was part of the region that the Romans called Dacia and as such the chief of the army could be called "the Brave of Dacia" [170].

Vita Sancti Metodii (chapter 5) mentions that Wallachian, Greek, and German (*iz Vlah, Gr'k iz Nem'k*) missionaries had contributed to the Christening of the Avars and Slavs in Moravia well ahead of the brothers Chiril and Metodiu [219 p.301], who only arrived in 862 at the invitation of Rastislav of Greater Moravia to preach Christianity on the lands under his authority. Other Blachi in the Tisa Plain were under the nominal domination of the Volgar Khaganate.

In 890, before the arrival of the Ugrian-Turanian nomads, the "Magors" as they would call themselves, Pannonia used to be inhabited only by Romanians (*Pannoniorum*) and Avars, according to the *Chronicon Saxonicum* [219 p.288].

In the 9th century, the Armenian scholar, Chorenatsi, mentions the country "Balak", that is, Blac/Vlac in his *Geography* [157 p.113].

Fig. 2.14. Part of a map of the Franks (Charlemagne) redone in 1600.

The German historian Aug. Schlözer in *Russische Annalen* [144 p.74], stated:

These Volohs [in the year 898, which is mentioned in *The Chronicle of Nestor*] *are neither Romans, nor Bulgarians, nor Wälsche, but Vlachs, descendants of the great and ancient peoples of the Thracians, the Dacians and the Getians.*

A French monk who worked as a missionary in Central Europe, was commissioned by Charles of Valois, brother to King Philip IV, the pretender to the throne of the Eastern Latin Empire, to write the treatise *Descriptio Europae Orientalis* in 1308. Here, he mentions the Romanians living between Tisa and the Carpathians before the Magyar tribes arrived in Pannonia [161 p.44]: *more than that, these people were ruled by 10 kings* [104 p.54]. The monk, who neither wrote fiction nor hagiographies for biased ears, mentions that the kingdom on the Danube used to be called Pannonia or Messia, where the Pannonians, *omnes*, were *pastores Romanorum* [146]. The Slavicist Fr. Miklosich has linguistically ascertained the presence of Romanians in Pannonia [28 p.92].

The last nomads to arrive, the Magyars, settled around the beginning of the 10th century alongside the Romanians, Slavs, and Germans. The year 896 was marked as the year of the arrival of the Magyar tribes by the Hungarian Parliament without any scientific basis, in a propagandistic manner, on the occasion of the World Exhibition! As a predatory horde or as hired mercenaries, the Magyars had already passed through Pannonia during the 9th century. In 895, they aided the Byzantines, attacking the Volgars from behind by crossing the Danube through Scithia Minor. The Magyar tribes were crushed by the Pechenegs (the Patzinaks) and by the Volgars in 896, north of the Black Sea. The battle was so fierce that the warlords of the Magyars refused the order of Constantine VII Porphyrogenitus (905-959) and would not take any part in chasing the Pechenegs away, saying:

> *We shall not attack the Patzinaks, for we cannot fight them since… they are bad people, therefore never should you urge us to quarrel with them, for such words are not to be borne* [26 p.23].

The Chronicle of Nestor confirms that, *in the year 6,406 after Genesis* (898 A.D.), the few Magors still living after the Pechenegs and Volgars had dealt with them swept up the Dnieper and stopped by Kiev, where they pitched their tents [226 p.356]. After a number of confrontations with the Ruthenians and the Cumaeans, they reached the fortress Ung (Uzhgorod, Ukraine) in the year 903. The commander of the fortress was called *duca* in the language of the locals (*qui in lingua eorum duca vocabatur*), as noted down by an anonymous author; in other words he was a Romanian [1 p.36]. Sometime after 904, the remnants of the horde took refuge on Csepel Island in the Danube [1 p.81]. Although it is likely an exaggeration, perhaps some 8,000 warriors got to the island, out of the 20,000 that had been north of Persia according to Dzaihani [135 p.72; 216 p.881]. 8,000 warriors reaching Pannonia is an overestimate, but probably reasonably close to reality. A horde of nomads could only have hundreds of warriors in order to function coherently and be properly led. If every 5-person family had provided a warrior, the total number of the people in the horde would have been 40,000. Indirect confirmation of the aforementioned number is provided by the fact that the whole of the Magyar horde settled, upon arrival in Pannonia, on an island on the Danube [1 p.81]. However, political historians often mention hundreds of thousands of Magors! Other, more reasonable historians, on the other hand, talk about one hundred thousand. Which is also impossible, since nothing in the following events can confirm such a large number. It was always the case that the nomads who arrived, Turanian-Mongolians, were

Fig. 2.15. Anonymous: Anno Domine incarnationis DCCCCIII ... [1 p.81].

few in number, which can go towards explaining their excessively bloody and violent behaviour. The number of the survivors who reached Pannonia has been indirectly confirmed by two genetic studies conducted by the Hungarian Academy (whose findings will be reproduced in §5). Had there been a hundred thousand Magyars after 903 in Pannonia, the studies of genetics could never have found only 7 % maternal Asian descendants per 1,000, nor that two centuries later there were only 16-17 clans or 108 families who could be considered Magyar during the time of Ladislaus the Cuman according to Simon of Chiza [145 p.647]. Nor would the Bishop of Naprágyi have written, in 1602, that the Hungarians were few in number, as exploiters tend to be, and that they were strangers in Transylvania [Annex A]. When discussing the arrival of the last nomadic tribes in Pannonia, the chronicle authored by *Anonymous* mentions that there were Slavs, Bolgars, and Romanians there already (*Quam terram habiterant Slavi, Bulgari et Blachi ac pastores Romanorum. Quia postmortem Athile regis terram Pannoniae ... pascebantur. Et iure terra Pannoniae pascua Romanorum esse discebatur, nam et modo Romanii pascuntur de bonis Hungariae*) [104 p.55].

Hungarian historiography with its particular political agenda, tends to consider this anonymous author valid when it describes "the feats of bravery" of the Turanian tribes, i.e., murder and pillage, while denying the validity of those passages that mention the inhabitants of Pannonia who were already there when the nomads arrived. Like most old medieval chronicles, the Anonymous Chronicle mixes some veridical data about people and places with old lore, fleshed out by the thinking of the chronicler and their times and enriched by their imagination. The Latin chronicle of Simon of Chiza, an Italian-born (according to Iorga) or Spanish-born (according to Marczali) priest at the court of King Ladislaus IV of Hungary (1272-1290), in referring to the Romanians that lived in Pannonia during the invasion of the Huns, states that they were the colonists and shepherds descended from Romans who had remained in Pannonia [161 p.43; 69 p.90]. The Chronicle of Dubnica states that the Vlachs, who were Roman *coloni* and shepherds, had willingly stayed in Pannonia [187 vol. I p.365]. It is important to remember that many old chronicles (whether Hungarian, Ruthenian, Polish, or Persian, etc.) make note of the Romanians that lived in Pannonia when the remaining tribes of Magors arrived.

The presence of Romanians in Pannonia is a fact also reflected in early mediaeval literature, starting with *Biterolf und Dietleib*, *Der Niebelungenlied*, *Die Klage*, and *La guerre d'Attila*, etc. An Anglo-Saxon chronicle from the 9th century mentions the Kingdom of Dacia, while Oğuzname, a Turkish chronicle of the 10th century, speaks of the land of the Romanians. Before the arrival of the Magyars, the Slavs in northwestern Pannonia were under the rule of King Svatopluk I of Moravia, while those in the southeast were under the rule of Voivode Zalan, a vassal of the Volgar Khaganate.

Catholic expansion in Pannonia occurred after the year 1,000—the year in which the Bishopric of Strigonium was founded (Esztergom, Hungary). After this time, Catholicism gradually gained ground among the locals—Romanian and Slovak heretics (religiously aligned with Constantinople).

Over the centuries, a very small number of nomads settled, coming under the influence of the locals, while the warrior elite continued with a few dominant clans. The Hungarian historian T. Lehoczky admits the following:

> It is doubtless that, ever since the times of the settling of the Hungarians, in the counties of Maramureș, Ugocea, and Bereg, from the northeastern border of our country, there lived Romanians of unknown origin [107 p.37].

In the 18th century, the Hungarian historian Nicolae Bethlen also noted that:

*Romanians have lived in Transylvania since time out of mind, forming
small republics, each of which was situated in a valley* [107 p.11].

In time, these Romanians, who had preserved a large lexicon of Latinate
linguistic terms related to farming, animal husbandry, and the Christian
religion, were attacked by various waves of barbarians, few of whom left
any mark. In the 10ᵗʰ century, there were "Greek" dioceses at Murisena, in
Glad's duchy; at Biharea, in Menumorut's duchy; and at Bălgrad, in
Gelu's duchy. They were Greek in the sense that they were under the
influence of Constantinople.

In 950, a century before the Schism within the Christian church, in
Bălgrad (Alba Iulia) there was a diocese under the jurisdiction of Bishop
Ieroteu that was subordinate to Patriarch Theophylact of Constantinople
[140 p.15]. It was with Ieroteu that the chieftain Gyula returned after
becoming a Christian as a foederatus of Emperor Constantin Porphyrogenitus
(905-959) of Constantinople.

We know from the Anonymous Chronicle that when the Hungarians
wished *to cross the river Timiş, they were stopped by Glad, whose
descendant is Ahtum.* We also know that Menumorut, during negotiations
with the envoys of the nomad chieftain Arpad, asked him to tell the ruler
of the Magors that *he is sorry, but since Duke Zalan conceded him a
territory, he is not going to renounce an inch of his lands, since this is his
country, inherited from his ancestor.* Zalan ruled between the Danube and
Tisa as a vassal of the Volgar Khaganate, while Menumorut was ruler of
the Romanians between Tisa and the mountains.

The Benedictine chronicler Regino of Prüm (842-915) described how:

*the most savage horde descended upon them, more savage than a wild
beast*

while a manuscript from 958, by Liudprand of Cremona (922-972) reads:

*They destroyed the cities, set fire to churches, murdered people and, to
make themselves feared, they would drink the blood of the slain* [64 p.56].

Referring to the privileges of the Archbishopric of Strigonium upon its
founding in the year 1001, King Béla IV mentions its right to collect tithes
from Romanians, wherever they might be [134 p.57; 97 p.65]. He was in
fact referring to the Romanians of Pannonia, for this was where Catholic
influence first started to take hold among the Dacian-Romanian locals of
the Byzantine Rite! It should be mentioned, at least in passing, that *censu,
tithes of any kinds, gifts of any kinds, the fiftieth part (quinquagesima), as*

well as service (servitia, robota), then *nona* together with their collection from the serfs were a very complicated thing, arbitrary and variable both temporally and geographically. Sometimes the tithes were leased and collected by the feudal authorities, but at other times the Catholic Church was already the feudal (owner), which meant that they also collected the tithes and the censu (and later the *nona*), as well as the gifts and services owed [148].

In 1020 in Constantinople, Basil II, the so-called Bulgar Slayer (in fact the Volgarian Slayer), enumerated the bishoprics of Banat and of Dibiskon/Tibiscus among the bishoprics under the jurisdiction of the Archbishopric of Ohrid.

In the legend *Vita major Sancti Gherardi*, there is mention of an Orthodox country between the Cris, the Tisa, the Danube, and the Carpathians, which, in 1025, was ruled by Ahtum, baptized at Diu (Vidin, Bulgaria) and descended from the Romanian ruler Glad [109 p.12]. According to some German historians, Ahtum may have been one of the last Gepid princes [183 p.17]. It is very unlikely that he was a Gepid prince, but the country must, indeed, have followed the Greek Rite. Ahtum erected a monastery dedicated to John the Baptist in a seat fortress, with the permission of the Greeks, as mentioned in the *Passion of Saint Gerard* [109 p.12]. Within a radius of 10 kilometres, there were other Byzantine monasteries as well at Huduș and near Nădlac (Arad County), one of which was called the Monastery of the Cnez (*kenéz monostora*). The large number of monasteries indicates that there was a numerous Byzantine-Christian population. An enamelled Byzantine cross from that time, found in the bed of the Mureș River, is exhibited in the Museum of Jula [109 p.13]. The legend of St Gerard tells us that *Ahtum*:

> *Was very proud of his strength and resistance [...] and would not bow his head to King Stephen, as he was confident that he would be protected by his strong army and the noblemen he ruled over.*

Ahtum clashed with Stephen I, after charging a fee for the cargo transported to the inhabitants living across the Tisa and the Danube, just as Glad used to do. Stephen sent a German army that defeated Ahtum, who was betrayed by his advisor, Cenadin [51 p.60]. King Stephen did not only fight Ahtum, but also Gyula and Kean [187 p.374], whose duchies were not subject to the Catholic influence of Strigonium. The Tisa was to remain a fee-charging border long after the defeat of Ahtum [187 p.376].

In 1050, the Persian geographer Ghardizi, in his work *The Jewel of History*, refers to the Romanians, noting that between a few Turks ("Hungarians") and Russins, there was a large population different from the others, being Christian and originating from the Roman Empire. According to the orientalist Aurel Decei, the Magyars settled between the Danube and the Tisa in a swampy place [216 p.877].

The painted chronicle of Vienna, *Chronicon Pictum Vindobonese*, unequivocally states that the Romanians were the descendants of those Romans who stayed in Pannonia (*Vlachis qui ipsorum Romanorum coloni existere ac pastores remanetibus sponte in Pannonia*, "Romanians who were Roman colonists as shepherds remained in Pannonia") [145 p792].

As a matter of fact, in a history published in 1860 at Budapest, Dr. Mihály Horváth (1809-1873) explains that the Magyars would let the old owners of those territories be, only asking for taxes; this was a model of nominal submission, which was practiced by all migratory Turkish-Tatar peoples, who, since they were numerically inferior, would struggle to enforce their rule directly. This historian, appreciated by scholar Ioan Slavici exactly for being the only Hungarian historian to have proved discerning, writes of the Magyar clans that had arrived in Pannonia that:

> *they were only able to graze their livestock in those places which their historians claimed they had conquered* [160 p.764].

This is a meaningful observation and of great help in rightfully placing the majority race that once interacted with the nomad tribes of the old Hungarians, whose number could not have been greater than a few thousand warriors. In fact, the time of the founding is also known in history as the time of robbery (in Hungarian: *rablo kalandok korszaka*) [160 p.764]. Ioan Slavici, who had been educated in Magyar schools, made a similar critical observation:

> *There is no Magyar historian who can produce data about the claim that Magyars allegedly reigned over these peoples: these peoples lived by the side of the Magyars, yet not with or under the Magyars. Moreover, one could in fact prove that even later they were relatively autonomous and had their own rights* [160 p.677].

This has been well-documented since at least the time of Ladislaus I, also known as Saint Ladislas (1077-1093), who, while addressing the monks of Monte Casino:

> *...introduced himself as head of the Hungarian tribes (Ungarorum), not as ruler of the country and, separately, as a king by the grace of the Lord* [89 p.9].

This is what Ioan Slavici wrote, referring to the rules laid down during the time of Ştefan/Vajk by the Germans:

They were made [our note: the rules] *only for the Magyar people, while the non-Magyar peoples lived by the Magyars, but not with them.* [...] *Both Romanians and Slovaks could not be part of the Magyar counties since they were not part of the Magyar ranks. Both Romanians and Slovaks led an autonomous life in their duchies, counties, and territories, even in later centuries* [160 p.739].

The Magyar tribes mattered little to Pannonia, since, as noted by Ioan Slavici, territorial divisions only had meaning for agrarian and sedentary peoples, whereas the Magyar tribes would move from one territory to another to graze their livestock [160 p.730]. This is how things happened south of the Danube as well where another Turanian clan lorded over the majority Dacian-Roman and Slavic populations. The names of these people in Byzantine and Latin chronicles are, generally, the names of small but dominant military formations, not of the dominated sedentary populations. In a similar manner, south of the Danube, after the arrival of the migratory Volgarians, the Latin chronicles mention *regnum Bulgacorum*, that is, the Kingdom of the Volgars. Only the masters mattered.

Later, after the Schism, another mistake was made when Orthodox populations, whether Romanian or Slavic, were simply described as "Greeks", meaning that they were under the religious jurisdiction of Constantinople. Before the migration of the Slavs south of the Danube, whenever there was mention of the population that lived here, the term *vulgari* was used; a term that, in its turn, created confusion. The inhabitants of Moesia had long been Roman citizens (by the Edict of Caracalla issued in 212), but they were lower citizens, that is *vulgarus*. Thus, in many subsequent compilations of the 9th century, *vulgarus* was mistaken for Bulgarus—notions that express completely different realities. As a matter of fact, Tsar Simeon I the Great (893-927) waged war against Constantinople (914-927) so that the empire would recognize his title of Emperor of all Romans: *basileus tôn Rhomaion*!

The first documents issued by the Chancellery of Vajk were in Greek and attested to Byzantine religious anteriority in Pannonia [219 p.299] and, implicitly, the Dacian-Roman and Slavic base of the province. After his marriage to Giselle of Bavaria, German monks started to arrive who used Latin and were under the jurisdiction of Rome.

Petru, Mândru, Costea, Sandrin, Nicolai de Pop, and Nicolai from Vizău brought to court a deed of donation from King Stephen (997-1038) to their ancestors, Negrilă and Radu, from the cnezate of Vizău (Maramureș County) [187 vol. I p.369].

The continuity of the Romanians in the Tisa Plain is also attested to by early administrative documents of Catholic royalty in Pannonia, as is the deed of donation of King Geisa from 1075 to the Benedictines of Strigonium who were given the "Rotunda" pond by the Tisa [103 p.37]. At the time, there were a lot of Romanian villages in Pannonia, since all of them were governed by *judices* according to the *ius valachicum* [104 p.139]. There is also mention of the names of serfs in Pannonia on the lands of the abbeys of Tihany, Bakony, and Panonhalma: Ciot, Micu, Nuc, Râu, Urda, Vreasc, Turba [103 p.23, 74 p.55] or Mutu, and Micu—all of them are Romanian in origin. Names such as Maniu, Bărbat, Barbu, Mutu, and Florea, etc., of Latin origin, were used by Romanians in the middle Danube basin without appearing in the Greek or Latin calendar [49 p.216]. But what about Sânmedru or Sânziene [151]? Where did the Romanians get those names unless they inherited them through many generations from the Dacian-Romans?

King Coloman (1095-1114) acknowledged to some Romanians—Voinea, Dinu, Vulcan, and Micu of Crasna County—that they were the owners of their lands and had certain rights. The original document was lost, but there is a copy of it made in 1227 including the signature of King Coloman [187 p.369].

Important treasures, which can be dated to 1088-1143 by the Byzantine coins they contained, from Streza (Făgăraș, Brasov County) and Amnaș (Sibiu County), also containing objects of art, indicate the high degree of culture and civilisation of those from whom, in 1204, land was taken for the Cistercian monastery of Cârța [194 p.44].

In 1137, there is mention of a cnez from Pannonia in the Catholic documents of the time [161 p.57]. Also, in the same region inhabited by *pastores Romanorum*, known as Vlachs, in Zala County, there is mention of a cnez Petru in 1157 [197 vol. III p.18].

The German bishop Otto of Freising passed through Pannonia in the year 1147, accompanying some crusaders, on which occasion he was able to identify the newcomers, the Magors:

> *they have ugly looks, staring eyes, small stature* [64 p.28], *savage in custom and language, one might easily mistake them for monsters* [26 p.25].

In other words, the Magors were easily noticeable by their looks, which were very distinct from the Europeans.

After defeating the Cumaeans (1147) and Hungarians (1167), and regaining control of Croatia and Dalmatia, Andronicos Comnen, the general of Emperor Manuel Comnen, plotted against his emperor. After being discovered, Andronicos fled, intending to take refuge in the Slavic Voivodeship of Galicia, but he was apprehended at the border of Galicia by the Romanians of Maramureş [161 p.48].

This is also the time of *the Nibelungenlied*, where, at the wedding of Atilla and Krimhilda, there were guests such as Duke Romun from the country of the Romanians who arrived with seven hundred people (*Der Herzoge Râmunc uzer Vlachenlant, mit siben hundert mannen kam er für si gerandt*) [187 vol. II p.368; 150 p.585].

In his book *On the Life of Christ and of all the Popes*, Bartolomeo Platina (1421-1481) wrote *Valachos olim Romanos, ulteriorem Danubii ripam incolentes et vulgaros vicinos*, "the Vlachs, who were once Romans, live across the Danube and are neighbours of the *vulgaros*" (the Dacian-Romans south of the Danube in 1197) [51 p.52].

At some point after the year 1200, the *castrum* Medieşul Aurit (Satu Mare County) was taken *de manibus Valachorum* (from the hands of the Romanians) and the inhabitants of the *castrum* and of the villages around it were forced to convert to Catholicism [103 p.44]. This *castrum* had 50 villages of schismatics in its vicinity, as mentioned in a letter by Ecaterina (Simeon's widow) to Pope Gregory XI (1370-1377) [104 p.163].

In 1204, Pope Innocent III (1198-1216) reproached the Catholic king of Pannonia, Henricus (1196-1204), because there was only one Roman monastery, but many Greek monasteries in the kingdom [109 p.15]. The pope also wrote to Emperor Ioniţă Asan: *Valachi quae a Romanis etiam carnem et sanguinem descendisse dicitur* [74 p.79]. The year 1204 was a turning point for the Orthodox and Catholic populations being the year when the armies of the Fourth Crusade robbed Constantinople, crushing icons and throwing the relics of saints away. The Byzantine chronicler Nicetas Choniates tells us that:

> *The Moslims didn't rape our wives ... they didn't push our people into abject poverty, they did not despoil them and parade them naked on the street, they did not starve them to death or burn them with fire ... But this is how these Christian people treated us, who make the sign of the cross in the name of the Lord and have the same religion as we do* [57 vol. III p.226].

In 1204, Pope Innocent III wrote to a bishop of his at Oradea (BH), telling him to visit the "Greek" (meaning schismatic) monasteries around, which had fallen into disrepair due to the negligence of the bishop of the diocese and to make them into a bishopric directly answering to Rome. On 16.05.1204, Pope Innocent III wrote that in the country of the sons of cnez Bâle, there was a bishopric that was not under the jurisdiction of any metropolitanate that needed to be brought under Catholic influence [137 p.83]. Between 1204 and 1205, the Cistercian monastery at Cârța (Sibiu County) was given land *exemptam de Blaccis* (taken from the Romanians) in Olt County between the mountains and the rivers Cârța, Arpaș, and Olt [28 p75].

In a letter dated 7.10.1207, addressed to the Byzantine clerics of northeastern Europe, Pope Innocent III urged them to accept the supremacy of Rome and keep the unity of the church, stating that, for having disregarded their duties to Rome, the Greeks *were left to be robbed and deprecated* [137 p.74]. This was a justification of the acts that had taken place at Constantinople in 1204! This view, according to which those who followed the Byzantine Rite could be considered heretics and could be robbed and despoiled, was to chip away at the trust that the Romanians in the basin of the Danube placed in the Catholic elite.

The fact that the Romanians are local to the region can also be seen from the names of localities in documents of the 10th-19th centuries. A document from 1214 writes about *a farm called Macra, that is, Apa* (water) [103 p.36]. According to a papal document from 1216, quoted by Msgr. Aloisie L. Tăut in the journal *Orientalia Christiana periodica*, there were Romanians who followed the Byzantine Rite from Balaton (Balta) and Somogy to the east, including Csepel Island (currently in Hungary) [82 p.8]. This was confirmed later by Franciscan Guillaume de Rubrouck who mentioned that some Bashkirs lived near Pest among the Romanians [136 p.24].

In 1219, the king granted territories near Vinț (Alba County) to the clergy in Strigonium, and their repossession was to be the task of a voivode, Iancu Vodă [87 p.46].

Pope Honorius III (1216-1227) wrote a letter in 1221 to the Bishop of Strigonium in which he informed the bishop that he was aware of the change that had taken place at Vișegrad (currently in Hungary), where king Andrew II had replaced the "Greek" monks who had long lived there with Catholic ones [109 p.15].

A diploma issued in 1222 by King Andrew II exempted German (Teutonic) knights from paying a fee while passing through *Terram Blacorum* [144 p.136]. In "the Golden Charter of the Transylvanian Saxons" (*Diploma Andreanum*), issued in 1224 by King Andrew II of Hungary, among the privileges offered to guests there is also mention of the *silva Blacorum et Bissenorum* (the forest of the Romanians and the Pechenegs). The term *bissenorum* is commonly translated in contemporary historiography as "of the Pechenegs". The presence of the Pechenegs in this case seems to be documented [28], yet we have to remember that the *bisseni* (*bessi, bessoi, bassaroi*) were in fact Thracian-Dacian groups and the Catholic sources that dated from about the same time (unlike those of modern historians), may, in certain cases, refer to remote local (Dacian) communities that might have appeared different to the majority of Dacian-Romans to a stranger's eye.

There is a document dating from 1231 that notes how Gallus, son of Wydh de Bord (a colonist from Flanders), consented, before the Catholic chapter, to return an estate bought in the village of Buia (Sibiu County). This was because the true owner, a Romanian, had been able to prove, using numerous witnesses, that this estate, close to Făgăraș County, had been in the possession of his ancestors since time out of mind, ever since the land of the Romanians had been the country of the Volgars [187 p.378]. This would mean that over the period 1160-1180, the village of Buia in Olt County (or Făgăraș) had been owned by the ruling Basarabs. This is confirmed by Hașdeu in *A Critical History of Romanians* in the chapter *The epoch when Făgăraș was held by the Wallachians*—the village of Buia was not initially part of Olt County, but was added by the Basarabs [80 p.22].

In 1234, the next ruler of the Pannonian kingdom, King Béla IV, was asked to swear to the legatus of the Vatican, Bishop Iacob Perestin, that he would eradicate all false Christians from the territory of his kingdom and bring the orthodox population under the guidance of the Catholic Church [104 p.97]. Pope Gregorius IX wrote to Béla IV about the Bishopric of the Cumaeans, asking him to fund the bishop in the Curvature Carpathians from his tax receipts using the fees taken for sheep from the Vlachs [104 p.109; 148 vol. I p.70]. He was referring to the Romanians living in the Curvature Carpathians, as clarified by a papal bull dating from 14.11.1234; Romanians had their own bishops who answered to Byzantium [137 p.51].

In 1237, the Dominican monk Ricardus in the *Great Hungaria* memoir, in which he described a visit to the Tatars, referred to Pannonia as the plain of the Romans, *tunc vero dicebatur pascua Romanorum*, on the arrival of the nomads in the 10th century [91 p.366].

A Romanian voivode was attested to have owned Prisaca and Spini near Caransebeș (Caraș-Severin County) before the great Tatar invasion [194 p.428]. A Cistercian monk who had crossed Pannonia in the year 1240, wrote a chronicle in rhyme that has been preserved in the Cistercian Monastery of Sticna (Slovenia). It is called the *Chronicon rhythmicum Sitticense* and in it the monk explains that where the Hungarians now ruled one would find the *Romanorum Pascua* (the pastures of the Romans) [3 p.33].

From the founding of the Bishopric of Strigonium up to the Tatar invasion of 1241, 170-180 monasteries of the Western Rite were founded in the new Catholic kingdom (11 of which still have their founding documents), with the purpose of bringing the locals onto a righteous path. At the time, there were as many as 600 Byzantine Rite monasteries in the territory [137 p.78]. It is difficult to calculate a ratio, in the sense that one cannot infer that 22 % of that population might have been Catholic by 1241, because many of these new Catholic churches were on exclusively Byzantine territory, as is the case for the monasteries of Cârța or Bălgrad, which had been erected in the middle of religious schisms to serve as outposts for Catholicization. This means that the figure of 22 % catholic monasteries transferred upon the population is groundless.

In 1303, the physician Fazel-Ullah-Rasid wrote the following using the archives of the Mongolian sultan of Persia:

> *During the spring of the year 1240* [our note: 1241] *the Mongolian princes crossed the mountains of Galicia and entered the country of the Bulgars and Hungarians. The horde that went to the right after traversing the country of Aluta* [our note: Olt], *was met by Bazaram-bam* [our note: Duke Basarab] *with an army, who was defeated. Cadan and Buri descended upon the Saxons and defeated them in three battles. Bugek went from the country of the Saxons across the mountains and descended on the Kara-Ulaghi (black Vlachs) defeating the Ulaghi populations.*

Referring to the same events, the chronicle *Annales Polonorum vetustiones*, written immediately after this invasion, reads:

> *After having enslaved the Bessarabians (Romanians), the Litvins and other populations, they also took the city...* [61 p.7].

The monk Rogerius actually witnessed the Tatar invasion in Transylvania. In *que Frata dicitur in vulgaris* (called Frata by locals), he conversed with villagers in Vulgar Latin. Rogerius also mentions the cnezate of Bihor. The Tatars, who were now the new masters, appointed new cnezes who would pass justice in local disputes and collect food, clothing, and weapons from the locals for their benefit [144 p.11].

In 1242, according to an order issued by the Tatar commander Cadan who had lain waste to Transylvania the year before, he encountered no Magyars in Transylvania, only Romanians, Saxons, and Szeklers [187 vol. I p.420].

Pope Innocent IV (1243-1254) answered a letter from King Béla IV on 4.08.1247 granting the right of ownership of the whole County of Severin to the Knights Hospitaller (the Knights of St. John), plus "the duchies of Ioan and Farcaş up to the River Olt, but not the cnezates of Voivodes Litovoi and Seneslau, that *are to be fully owned by Romanians, as they have been so far*" [51 p.64]. In the diploma issued in 1247 and given to the Knights Hospitaller, there is mention of the Romanian voivodeship on the land of the counties of Severin and Hațeg, which are noted as being inhabited by Romanians and belonging to the County of Severin [104 p.170].

Halfway through the 13th century, Toma (1200-1267), the Archdeacon of Spalato, writes the following about Pannonia: *Hec regio dicitur antiquitus fuisse pascua romanorum* (this region is said to have been the pasturage of the Romans in ancient times) [103 p.22].

Around 1253-1255, the Franciscan Guilleaume de Rubrouck (1220-1293), emissary of King Louis IX of France at the Court of the Great Khan, had the chance to meet not just the Khan himself, but also the Romanian envoys sent to him [194 p.423].

In 1260, under the command of Béla IV, the Romanians fought the Bohemians at the Battle of Kressenbrunn (Austria). The King of Bohemia, Ottokar II Přemysl (1253-1278), sent a report to the pope on his victory over Béla IV, whose army included Cumaeans, Magyars, Romanians, Bissenians, and Greeks [211 p.26; 26 p.31].

A *Wayvoda Olacorum* is mentioned as being in Cluj in 1370 [230 p.38].

In 1271, Voivode Ioan of Beiuș went to the head of Oradea to solve a dispute with his relatives [103 p.38].

In 1272, Archbishop Bruno of Olmutz (Czech Republic) explained that the kingdom situated by the middle Danube was in danger of renouncing the Christian faith for three reasons: a) the pre-eminence of the Cumaeans at the top of the hierarchy; b) the large number of schismatics (the three daughters of the king were themselves married to schismatics); and c) the greed of the new landowners who did not allow clergymen to thrive unless they met certain financial arrangements—there were, for example, clerics who had to steal in order to survive [174 p.61].

A document from 1274 sought to elevate several Romanians to the ranks of the local gentry, Petru, Paul, Micu, Ioan, and Niculae, *iobagio castri*, who had been guarding the borders [187 vol. I p.380].

The Tuscan chronicler Thoma Tuscus notes that the king of Bohemia, Ottokar II asked for the help of the Ruthenians in 1276 in the conflict with Rudolf de Habsburg, but they could not get involved because they were themselves at war with the Romanians [194 p.423].

After killing Count Alard from Ocna Sibiului, who had revolted together with the Saxons against the taxes levied by the Catholic bishop of Alba Iulia, on 21.02.1277, his son, Gan, set fire to the cathedral in Alba and killed 2,000 people in Alba Iulia. To help the bishoprics, the *serves* from the surroundings were removed from the jurisdiction of the voivode and placed under the jurisdiction of the bishop [216 p.398]. It is worth mentioning this when we speak of the army of the voivode or of the Catholic kingdom, the troops made available by the bishop of Alba were formed by the *serves* from the county, that is, by Romanians.

Secular power was in the hands of the pagans under King Ladislau the Cuman, while religious power, which had been foundational to the kingdom, was in disarray. In response, the pope intervened to reestablish the Catholic order. In 1279, the Council of the province in Buda decided the following concerning the schismatic Romanians:

They are not allowed to worship God, build up chapels of other holy houses and neither are the worshipers allowed to participate in such divine cult or to enter such chapels. If need be, against these priests brachial power shall be applied [107 p.15]. … *The schismatics are also not allowed to fill public offices in the new kingdom. There were also punishments for "Christians", that is, for the newly converted ones, if they are still in the services of the schismatics, or if they received sacraments from schismatic priests. Also, it was decided that the Jews, Saracens, and other non-baptized people should wear distinctive signs on their chests* [137 p.277].

The stone churches in Tara Hategului and most of the churches in Tara Zarandului were built before the council held in 1279. Where the community of Byzantine Rite was forced to convert to Catholicism, naturally, the church followed. Others made of stone were not built until the 19th century, apart from in some exceptional cases. Many Romanian wooden churches, schismatic in the papal point of view, were burnt down and bombarded in 1762.

In June 1288, Voivode Roland of Borşa, besides engaging in military confrontations with King Ladislau the Cuman, also convened a general assembly of noblemen from Transylvania, as *regnum Hungariae* and *regnum Transylvanum* were still different.

A document dated 11.03.1291 by King Andrei III mentions:

We, Andrei, by God's grace King of Hungary, let everybody entitled to know that holding us a diet (assembly) with all noblemen, Saxons, Szeklers, and Olachs (Romanian that is) from the lands of Transylvania in Alba Iulia [137 p.316].

The Hungarians are missing here because, in fact, there were none in Transylvania. There would be, later on, out of religious and social constraints, the families of Cândea, Drag, Ban, Chinezu, Bornemiza [93 vol. 1 p.5], Mailat, Petrovai, Bolya, Mihaly [5 p.11], Kemeny [6 vol. 3], Bekes [26 p.67], and others. According to recent research, during the reign of Andrei II (1205-1235), in the middle basin of the Danube there were 26 "aristocratic" clans. About two thirds of these 26 clans were of Asian descent (Magyars, Cumaeans, Tatars, and Turks), whereas the rest were German, French, Italian, and Spanish brought over by the Catholic establishment in the Kingdom of Pannonia.

Fig. 2.16. Wooden churches. Romanians were not allowed to build stone churches.

No matter how we read this royal text, *universis nobilus Saxonibus, Syculis et Olachis*, whether the noblemen were Saxons, Szeklers, and Romanians, or also included some noblemen considered Hungarian, there was no Hungarian population. The fact is that there was no Hungarian population in Transylvania in 1291, and nor was there in 1355 or 1602. After the Peace of Westphalia, there was mass Magyarization of the subject population, but in the documents available to us, references to schismatics or Greeks refer to Romanians, Serbs, or Ruthenians.

An act of Andrei III from 1293, under which "60 households of Romanians" were gifted to the lord in Alba Iulia, was confirmed in 1313 by Carol Robert of Anjou [137 p.192]. Only the local Romanians, *Blachi ac pastorem Romanorum*, in the newly created Catholic kingdom were paying the fiftieth share of their sheep (*quinquagesima*). The Germans and the Slavs in Pannonia did not pay *the fiftieth share of their sheep* [104 p.108]: this levy was specific to the Romanians. The Catholic kingdom had singled out its Romanian subjects in the early processes of conversion to Catholicism and Magyarization. We note that feudal obligations towards the king and local lords, including: *dijme* (levy), *cens* (tax), *cincizecimea* (the fiftieth), *daturi* (gifts), *slujbele* (*robota*, work without pay), and *nona* (the ninth); these obligations were diverse and arbitrary, mobile in time and geography [148].

Țara Maramureșului, covering about 10,000 km², well delimited geographically and having been recognised as a discrete geographical unit for a few centuries, had, at the end of the 13th Century, 100 Romanian villages led by a voivode [194 p.426].

The Orthodox Church in Crișcior (Hunedoara County) has preserved an icon bearing the inscription: *15 July 1295, the painting was completed...* [104 p.101].

Also from the 13th Century, we have mentions of Wallachian *castrensis* (military camps) in the County of Borsod (today in Hungary). In 1409, Romanians still populated the town of Mezo-Kferesztes (Borsod County) and it is noted that: *Universi Valachi in poss. Valachi Keresztes nuncupata* (the Wallachian community in possession of the village; so called Wallachian Keresztes) [104 p.131].

From ancient times, Romanians inhabited the territory of the current County of Abauj-Torna, organized in cnezates and a voivodeship, as attested in 1302. We find the names Vajda, Kis-Kinyis, and Nagy-Kinyis, beside names of localities including Vila, Ola, Gard, Karacson, Cupa, Saca, Szekpatak (Valea Seacă), Foncsal, and Toka, as well as people, such as Bogdan, Wajda, and Woyda, etc. [104 p.127].

In the Bruckenthal Library in Sibiu, there is a document dated to 1300, which notes that the noblemen and the Saxons had an important trial to judge and elected Boeriu of Scorei (Sibiu County) as arbiter, according to Iosif Sterca Șuluțiu [220 nr.5/1877].

The vast majority of the inhabitants of the approximately 150 citadels in Pannonia, Croatia, Slovakia, and Transylvania were Germans, organized autonomously in closed communities [136 p.25]. In terms of citadels, we may mention Eisenburg, Ofen (Buda), Pest, Gran (Strigoniu), Weissburg, Plintenburg (Vișegrad), Odenburg (Sopron), Erlau (Eger), Raab, Pressburg, Zips, Kaschau (Kosice), Schäsbrich (Sighișoara), Klausenburg (Cluj), Kronstadt (Brașov), and Hermanstadt (Sibiu), among others. Here, we should also mention the towns set up by the Germans, as it is a fact that the locals, Romanians and Slavs, as well as German settlers in the towns of Pannonia formed the basis of the new royal power created by the Catholics and its structure: the army and the clergy was formed by aliens from the Ritteri and Chevalierii, who brought with them their serfs and soldiers (Knappe, Landknecht) [160 p.698]. Here is how Ioan Slavici describes the era from St. Stefan onwards:

Led by the Germans and clergy around him and supported by the German troops in Hungary, Stefan began his reign as the first king with absolute power. The Magyar, who were a free people by nature, started an energetic resistance and the history of the Magyars since then has been nothing but a continuous fight between the king and the Magyar clans, except for the Cuman period [160 p.678].

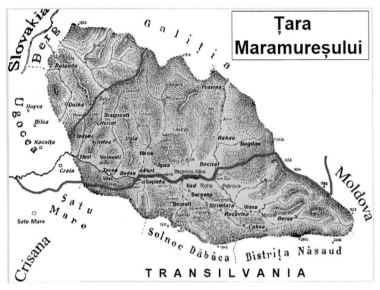

Fig. 2.17. The Voivodeship of Maramureş.

The new kingdom then developing had its economic base in the Slavic peoples around Nitra (Slovakia today) who were miners and craftsmen. It should also be noted that the Hungarian historians are silent about the Slavic traits of Pannonia [64 p47].

The Romanians from the counties of Berg and Ung, where centuries before there had been a captain, a "ducă" (duke), were still defending the border in the 12th-13th centuries and received donations from the Angevin kings. The Romanians were organized by valley and cnezate; several cnezates formed a district run by a voivode freely elected by the villagers. The voivode was lord and judge, responsible for the gathering of the *stronga*, a levy, usually on Pentecost. The gatherers, called *strongatores* in contemporary documents, were the cnezes of the villages. The levy, *stronga*, was the twentieth part of the sheep count and was recorded *vigesima ovium, census Valachorum* or *vigesima ovium, stronga dicta* [102 p.122].

As early as 1300, we find increasing mention of local serfs [104 p.248] and their villages in the Curvature Carpathians who were Romanian; the Szeklers, a military cast, were the only freemen and lived alongside and off the Romanians.

In a trial regarding a piece of land in 1306, the Romanian Ladislau Borșa claimed that his rights were *ab antiqua* and although he had no documents, as this would have been impossible, he won the case [158 p.11].

Although the last Arpadian kings acted as the armed force of Catholic development in the middle Danube, the pagan period of Ladislau the Cuman must have raised serious questions in the Vatican. The Franco-Italian king, Carol Robert de Anjou, arriving in 1300 and with his rule starting in 1308, represents the materialization of such doubts regarding the Ugro-Turano-Cuman superstructure, freshly converted to Catholicism. Catholic pressure on the Orthodox Romanians in the middle Danube basin became more intense under the Angevin kings. A letter threatening the Transylvanian voivode Ladislau Kan with excommunication (in 1307, he held "the holy crown", the so-called "Byzantine-Catholic" crown of Ștefan/Vajk) highlights that Tisa was the western border of the voivodeship at the time. This letter by a man of the cloth, Fra Gentile, who came to anoint Carol of Anjou as king, is dated Bratislava, 25 December 1309 [216 p.400; 158 p.89].

In 1310 the cncz Baciu of Banat complained about some people having moved from his land [104 p.170]. Also in September 1310, the judge of the voivode's court was expecting Ladislau Kan *to come from Hungary*, that is, from beyond Tisa, where the voivode had concluded an agreement with the delegates of Robert de Anjou [158 p.90].

A Tuscan document from 1314, in the *Apostolica Vaticana Library*, which refers to the province of Hungary, notes that the province was inhabited by Romanians and Wallachians who were in the majority, having their own structures and also being heretics [139 p.137].

In 1317, the Romanians were called as witnesses in a matter concerning the border of the Bârgău Mountains [104 p.233].

In 1326, the documents mention the Romanian cnezes from Pojon (Bratislava today) as having their own serfs [89 p.135].

In a diploma of 1326, Carol Robert de Anjou confirms the land of Stanislau, son of Stan [137 p.139], while in another from 1335, he mentions Voivode Bogdan, and in yet another from 1337, he mentions cnez Bârcan [104 p.171].

On 1.02.1327, Pope Ioan XXII (1316-1334) wrote to the Dominican prior of the Kingdom of Pannonia, asking him to start "a crusade" against all the people of Transylvania, Bosnians and Slavs, and destroy the "heretics" [137 p.286]. The people of Transylvania were entirely schismatic and were to be the targets of this crusade. At that date in

Transylvania, there were also Germans and Catholic Szeklers in insignificant numbers compared to the Romanians. For instance, in Chioar District (Maramureş County), of more a quarter of million people in 65 villages, only a few Romanians had converted to Catholicism and had possibly been Magyarized (in the sense that at the time the Catholics were considered Hungarians). Also at that time, in the domain of Baia Mare, of 14 villages, only two were Catholic. It is worth noting that in the valley of Crişul Negru, the villages were exclusively schismatic, while in Bihor County between 1332 and 1337, 36 % of the villages included Catholic parishes. We cannot accurately deduce the proportion of schismatic Romanians versus Catholic Romanians, but two centuries later, non-Catholic Romanians accounted for 84 % of the total population [6 vol. II p.37].

Referring to a royal concession to the chapter in Alba-Iulia, in 1331 the records of the chapter regarding the gathering of the Romanian *fiftieth* note:

> *...from all our cnezes, ... the said cnez owe us, each year, 9 marks and a quarter of good silver ...* [148 vol. I p.70].

A mark was 280 gr. of silver.

In Banat, between 1332 and 1337, converted Romanians were found in 10 % of localities, whereas the rest were schismatic. Banat was called Cisalpine Wallachia by officials, given the large numbers of Romanians living there (*gens grandis Olachorum*) [6 vol. II p.38]. Banat, which was also known as Little Wallachia, was one of the most powerful Romanian autonomous territories.

Significant numbers of Romanians are also mentioned in a letter from Pope Ioan XXII, who, in 1328, instructed that Catholic men of cloth *in Pannonia* manifest great leniency when taking the levies from the Romanians so that they would not return to the old rites [104 p.115]. This document is important exactly because although it is addressed, as is normal, to the masters, it refers to the people, the same people who filled the treasury through the payment of a "tenth" (a levy).

In 1341, a document speaks about the land of magister Nicolae, which was split amongst his Romanian successors: *sui succesores olacos* [187 p.378].

In 1342, cnez Toma was sentenced to a fine of one mark as he had not caught the thief of a horse in the County of Caraş—the cnezes also had the duty of ensuring the police of the cnezate [187 p.389].

When the noblemen assembled in Turda in May 1342, they complained about the foreign noblemen, imposed by Ludovic de Anjou, who called the former to trial and even oversaw the administration of justice [138 p.267].

A document of 31.05.1342, issued by the Chapter of Agria (today Eger, Hungary), informed the king that a disagreement between the Voivode of Transylvania and the sons of a former palatine in respect of the Chalan property had been investigated. To look into this matter, the voivode brought 120 noblemen as witnesses, while the sons of the former palatine brought almost 3,000 witnesses—Hungarians, Cumans, and Romanians—of whom 300 were noblemen [137 p.210]. Who could the more than 420 noblemen acting as witnesses be, as in the whole of the kingdom there were only 26 clans of noblemen including the voivodes, the judges, and the cnezes of the Romanians. Only the cnezes, masters of villages, could turn up in such numbers. As for the 3,000 Hungarian, Cuman, and Romanian witnesses, this could mean confession: Catholic, pagan, and Orthodox. At this time around 1300, what mattered was the confession of a person, rather than their ethnicity, as was made clear by the Catholics in Agria.

In the Catholic kingdom, above the locals—*blachi* and Slavs—there were Germans, Armenians, Cumans, Greeks, Poles, and Bohemians, all rigorously recorded in the Latin chronicles of the Catholic monks; there is no chronicle of that time that mentions the Romanian as emigrants and this is precisely because they were *ab origine*.

In an act of 1344, King Ludovic of Anjou sought to reconcile the differences between the *bishop and the Saxon and Szekler noblemen*, between the Church and the overlords, on the matter of levies [148 vol. I p.39]. Again, the Hungarians are not mentioned, although the Catholic and Catholicized noblemen would become Hungarians in time.

In 1345, Pope Clemente VI (1342-1353) (who "launched" the practice of indulgences) wrote to Luis of Anjou that a number of Romanians from Hungary, Transylvania, Wallachia, Moldova, and Sirmia (*Olachi romani commorantes in partibus Ungariaem, Transilvanis, Ultralpinis et Sirmiis*) had embraced the Catholic faith and that others beside were ready to convert. Encouraged by this, the pope wrote several letters encouraging the Romanian voivodes to convert to Catholicism from the Byzantine Rite. He wrote to Voivode Alexandru Basarab: *In Hungary, Transylvania, Wallachia and Sirmia there are the Wallachians-Romanians* [137 p.260; 144 p.106]. The pope sent letters not only to the Wallachian prince Alexandru Basarab from Wallachia (Ţara Românească), but also to the voivodes Nicolae of Remetea, Vlad of Bivin, Stanislau of Siparch, Ambrosius of Zopus, and Nicolae Voivode of Auginas, whose voivodeships were in Banat, Tisa Plain, and Maramures [137 p.260].

On 13.04.1346 at the Convent of Leleş (today Iasov, Slovakia), the Romanian Mic, son of Stanislau, son of Bârsan, and his brothers Neag and Radu, requested that the letters of donation by King Carol Robert, and backed by Louis of Anjou, be rewritten to give him ownership of the Strâmtura estate.

On 17.07.1349, the Catholic Bishop Dumitru of Oradea gave Voivode Petru, son of Stanislau, of the village of Vintere (Bihor County), permission to retain a Romanian priest, that is, a Greek-Oriental priest [137 p.183].

A royal act of 1.04.1350 mentions the Romanian villages of Herinceni and Lipceni in Maramureş, formerly belonging to the loyal cnezes Nicolae, Valentin, Luca, and Sărăcin, sons of Voivode Crăciun of Bilca [137 p.133].

On 15.07.1352, King Louis of de Anjou obtained from Pope Clement VI, by three acts issued in Avignon, the *dijma* (the Catholic tithe) collected from the kingdom, as well as the patrimony obtained by the holy pontiff from the conversion of "schismatics". The reason invoked by Luis was the high cost of *putting down the blows, dealings, and offences by the Tatars, schismatics, and other unfaithful* [137 p.289].

In November 1352, the Count of Banat confirmed to Iuga and Bogdan that a stretch of land in the Valley of Mâtnic was theirs *in all the liberty that the cnezes have in their free villages* [138 p.209].

A diploma of Louis of Anjou, dated 14.05.1353, speaks about a domain of Ştefan and Ion, Romanians, sons of Iuga, and loyal to the king [137 p.140].

A document of 26.05.1355 specifies the consistency of the General Assembly of noblemen, Szekler, Saxons, Romanians, and others [...] inhabitants of the said parts of Transylvania, held in Turda on 20 May [137 p.322]. As in 1242 and 1291, the Hungarians are nowhere mentioned. They should be mentioned from that date forward either as "foreign" royals endowed with the lands of the Romanians, or Romanian noblemen who had converted to Catholicism!

In 1356, Transylvania appeared in the eyes of papal power as completely "heretical" [136 p.42] and a crusade *contra omnes Transilvanos* was planned [137 p.308].

In 1358, the knight Nicolae Lachk erected Catholic churches in three villages around Arad *in the middle of the stubborn Romanians* [138 p.392].

In 1360, King Louis of Anjou donated to loyal Dragoş the Romanian villages of Slatina, Brebu, Copaci, Deseşti, Hărniceşti, and Sugatag of

Maramureş, with all the royal levies (the fiftieth) [148 vol. I p.71].

In 1363, King Louis of Anjou intervened in a property dispute between the loyal Romanian Count Vladislav, son of Muşat of Almaş, and the cnezes Stroe and Zaicu [60 p.590; 148 vol. I p.120]. Also in 1363, there was a trial on the delimitation of land in the city of Iladia (Banat) and it was there that Romanian cnezes came into the story as belonging to the citadel: *Kenezy olahorum ad ipsum castrum pertinentes* [103 p.28].

In 1364, Queen Elisabeth, the widow of Carol Robert of Anjou, issued a diploma demanding that the administrative bodies in Berg County (northwest of Satu Mare) should observe the old rights and privileges of the Romanians: they were entitled to freely elect their voivode, who was to decide on all matters according to old Wallachian law [103 p.55; 123 p.386].

The Byzantine emperor Ioan V (1341-1391), when going to a meeting with Louis of Anjou, went through Căvăran (Caraş-Severin County), where he was fed by the Romanian cnezes, who were militarily organized and led, in effect, almost autonomous territories, their land bearing the name of *Valahia Citerior* (i.e., "nearer Romania") [89 p.193].

In 1366, under pressure from Catholic proselytisers, Louis of Anjou made what amounted to an order on the organisation of the Romanians:

...so that in the entire county of Caransebeş (Banat) none other should be able to hold and keep land under noble or cnez title except for the true Catholics who follow the faith and confesses onto the Roman Church [134 p.89].

It is about this period that historian Ioan-Aurel Pop believes that Catholic proselytism supported by the armed forces compromised the possibility of attracting Romanians to Rome, including those living in the two Romanian states of Wallachia and Moldova. This inter-positioning of the Catholic kingdom between the Vatican and the Romanians placed the serfs forever under the net of the Byzantine religion [134 p.89].

An "act of peace" between the Romanians in the town of Sânpetru and the Saxons in the Rodna area of 1557 refers to an authentic document dated 10.06.1366, which mentions that the former had inherited the territory more than a millennium before; a territory which they had defended, both themselves and their forefathers with their own blood [104 p.233; 97 p.66].

In 1366, Louis of Anjou, donated the village of Aciuţa to the Romanian Şorban of Aciuţa and his sons for having been baptized as Catholics. He obligated that, besides service to the king, they should also pay the tithe (*dijma*, the tenth part of the income obtained from the tenancy) of pigs and the gift (*datul*) of sheep [148 vol. I p.69].

In an act issued by Louis of Anjou dated to 1368, there is mention of Bâlc, *voyvoda Olacorum*. The same Bâlc, under a decree of 1383 by Queen Mary of Anjou (1382-1385), held the title of count [161 p.58].

In 1371, the cnezes of the four districts belonging to the citadel of Deva asked King Louis of Anjou (1342-1382) for the right to judge their peasants according to *justa legem valachorum*.

A document of 1372 from Banat includes a list of the counties, towns, villages, and noblemen and cnezes of Banat who had sent people to dig defensive trenches for the Orşova citadel; there were 68 positions [137 p.137]. Vlaicu Vodă (1364-1377), the Prince of Wallachia, donated Şercaia (Făgăraş) to a relative [149 p.18].

A bull of Gregory XI (1370-1378) from 1374 mentions that certain parts of the numerous Romanian people (*certa pars multitudinis nacionis vlahorum*) had converted to Catholicism and that many of the people called Wallachians would be ready to follow suit if they had their own diocesan church, as they did not understand what was being preached [5 p.74].

The overwhelming number of the Romanians in Banat is also mentioned in the written order of Louis of Anjou of 1375, which is intended for the information of the inhabitants of Banat, *militibus, nobilus, clientibus et Walachibus, et aliis familis...* (to soldiers, nobles, clients and Wallachians, and other families...) [103 p.29]. In other words, under the stratum of agents of power—military, noblemen, and other clients—there was the Romanian people. Nothing had changed since a century before when the monk Simon of Chiza, confessor at the court of Ladislau the Cuman, critically noted the laziness of the foreign noblemen who had infiltrated the court (*de nobilis advenis*) and of the courtiers [97 p.90].

In the eight counties of Banat (Sebeş, Lugoj, Caraşova, Berzava, Mihald, Almaş, Iladia, and Comiat), which was Romanian, the privileges of the noblemen (of the cnezes) had certain legal aspects: *even before the year 1376*, they applied the old, approved law of the Romanian Counties (*juxta antiquam et aprobatum legem districtuum valahicalium universorum*) according to a diploma of Ladislaus of Habsburg, the Posthumus (1440-1457) [216 p.872].

In 1376, the cnez Ladislau Lehăcescu of Mehadia (Caraş-Severin County) ran away in Wallachia, to Vlaicu Vodă. In response, Louis of Anjou confiscated the cnezate and gave it to another Romanian called Raicu.

In 1377, King Louis of Anjou again gave to the City of Cluj the village of Feleac (Cluj County) together with the fiftieth share of sheep [148 vol. I p.71].

Antonius Bonfinius in *Rerum Ungaricorum decades quatuor cum dimidia* (Basel, 1568), referring to that time when serious efforts towards Catholicization were made, that is, the time of Louis of Anjou, praised the growth of the Catholic faith in the kingdom, which had increased so much *that more than one third of the population had been conquered by the saintly customs* [136 p.38]. But who could those be on whom the Catholic faith had been imposed other than schismatic locals? The Germans were already Catholic. Considering that all the cities had been German since their foundation, then the new Catholics could only have been the Romanians who followed the Byzantine Rite. This is confirmed by Franciscan reports of 1380, which note that 400,000 *schismatics had been rebaptized in the Roman Rite* [136 p.41].

On 13.01.1383, the judges of Sibiu, Cisnadie, together with some other judges, concluded an agreement with the surrounding Romanians [138 p.298; 28 p.259]. Also in 1383, the sons of Voivode Stanislau received the cnezate of two villages in the County of Berg (today split between Ukraine and Hungary) with an obligation of giving the king only half of the fiftieth part of the sheep [148 vol. I p.71].

In 1387, in the County of Ugocea Romanians and their villages, Criva, Cernatu, Turț, Bătărci, and Tarna, etc., are mentioned [103 p.53].

In 1391, Voivode Baliță of Maramureș left for Constantinople with his brother Dragoș to request Patriarch Antonie that the St. Archangel Mihai Monastery in Peri (Maramureș County) be placed under the direct authority of the patriarchy. According to the document of 13 August, the Patriarch of Constantinople also entrusted Abbot Pahomie with the churches in the lands of Ugocea, Berg, Sătmar, and Sălaj, up to the land of Bihor [103 p.50]. Also in 1391, Mircea cel Bătrân (Mircea the Elder), the prince of the Romanian Principality, gave the villages Scorei (Sibiu County) to the boyars Stanciu and Călin [149 p.18].

The trial of 1398 between of the branch of the Basarabs in Râul Alb and that in Râușor (Hunedoara County), that is, between the cnezes Dragotă and Ioan of Râul Alb, and the cnezes Ianusca, Basarab, and Costea of Râușor (*famosi viri*) shows that the cnezes owed the king one silver mark (233 gr.) per year of cnezate [187 p.389]. This quantity of silver was owed as a sign or recognition of the king *in signum domini*. Consequently, the king reigned over a territory in the way common to the Middle Ages—demanding taxes from subjects.

A trial in Ţara Haţegului took place in the time of Voivode Stibor who was tried by 12 Romanian jurors according to *ius valahicum* [50 p.176]. The trial is important not only because it illustrates the activity of the Catholic royalty, showing that the old *ius valahicum* was in place, as well as the fact that it was not the Voivode of Transylvania who judged the cnezes, but the university of Romanian cnezes according to *lex antiqua*, and also because it presents us with a glimpse of the process of feudalization in Transylvania. In the beginning, the ruling royalty was content with only a *cens* as a sign of recognition. Over time, however, a lot of intermediaries endowed with land appeared, feudal nobles who gathered the levies both for the king and, especially, for them, as the Turks did later on using the Greeks as intermediaries.

In 1408, after a lengthy trial between the daughters and the son of Voivode Petru and the chapter in Alba about the land at Oarda (Alba County), the parties concluded a convention [148 vol. I p.78].

Also in 1408, there was a significant rebellion by some cnezes, Ladislau, Mihai, and Dan, in the region of Timiş against King Sigismund of Luxembourg (1387-1437). The cnezes occupied a castle and it was only with difficulty that the king managed calm their agitated spirits [187 p.388].

In 1410, the congregation in Tara Beiuş (Bihor County), consisting of the Romanian cnezes, gathered to put the dispute between Bogdan and Merideu on the one hand and Moga and Şerban on the other hand to trial [187 p.396].

In a document dated 2.02.1412, in the assembly of the noblemen from the counties of Sablociu and Berg, Petru, son of Sandrin, demanded the sons of Ioan of Dolha, Stanislau, and Petre, to pay ... [104 p.163].

The lists of levies of 1427 for the County of Gyor (today Hungary) also include the locality of Olah-pataka (Valley of the Romanians), located on the River Saiu (Sajo) [104 p.126].

In 1428, Sigismund of Luxembourg reiterated the provisions of his father-in-law Louis of Anjou:

There shall be deposed of their entire fortune all noblemen and cnezes that harbour Orthodox priests, who lead to heresy. The property of the Romanian priests shall be seized and they shall be deported from the country. Marriage between Orthodox people and those following the law of Rome is forbidden until such time as the Orthodox are converted by a Latin priest. The noblemen, cnezes, and peasants shall lose their land if they do not baptize under Catholic law [107 p.15].

In 1434, the *Universi nobiles et kenesii, populique et iobagiones* of Dobra (Hunedoara County) "asked the Voivode of Transylvania ..." In the same year, Sigismund, in a letter from Basel, pledged the village of Popi and half of the customs of Mureş to *Ioan Valahul* (Iancu of Hunedoara) in exchange for 1,200 golden florins, which Sigismund had borrowed from Iancu de Hunedoara. In another letter dated 2.06.1435, from Trnavia (Slovakia), Sigismund further pledged the city and county of Comiat with all the villages, cnezes, and levies pertaining to it for another 300 golden florins [216 p.869]. Comiat County, as can be seen from the presence of the cnezes, is one of the eight Romanian counties in Banat.

In an agreement between rioters and noblemen in 1437, the Romanian peasants signed under the title of the "community of the Hungarians and Romanians in this part of Transylvania" (*universitas regnicolorum Hungarorum et Valachorum huius partis Transylvaniae*) [137 p.60]. Here, we may ask why not just sign "Valachorum" only, given that the number of Magyarized Romanians at the time would have been negligeable. This was because, as David Prodan notes, in the first part of the rebellion, even the few rioting noblemen were on the side of the rebels. These noblemen considered themselves to be Hungarian—at the time, a "Hungarian" identity was synonymous with being a nobleman—and according to this formulation, they were also represented in the agreement. However, in the convention of 6 July 1437 between the rioters and the noblemen, the peasants are referred to as *regnicolae*, i.e., the same as the noblemen. According to Professor Gavril Muntean (1856), a small group of Hungarian noblemen appeared following their acceptance of the Catholic confession and their separation from the people [127 vol. I p.747]. Finally, why would the *noblemen, the Saxons and Szeklers associate in* 1438, in *Unio trium Nationum*, if the Romanians where not in overwhelming numbers?

On 7.02.1439, Albert of Habsburg, King of Bohemia, Hungary (1437-1439), and Emperor of Germany, gave to Mihai and Vasile of Cerna *walahorum nostrorum*, being authority over Cerna and other land in Mehadia (Caraş-Severin county), which they had already had up to that point. The land was given again (*de novo et ex novo*), forever (*inperpetuum*) under the title of a new donation (*nove nostre donationis titulo*) [201 p.116].

In 1439, Dean Ioan Katakalon of Adrianopol, in a poem addressed to Emperor Ioan Paleolog V wrote:

> *It was not the Scit, the Mis, the Tribal* [the last two names given to Romanians South of the Danube], *not the Pannonians and not the strong people of the Wallachians who had pushed back the unfaithful Turks, but*

the tears and the many prayers [145 p.688].

One year later, in 1440, the King of Poland and Hungary, Vladislav Iagello, "gave" the nobleman Coposu of Vad, *walachus noster ut dicitur nobilis de Wad*, the land held by the latter from the time of his ancestors [201 p.117].

In 1442, the Bishop of Oradea, in his double capacity as both clerical and feudal lord of the domain, demanded that the cnezes of Beius appoint *12 cnezes jurors* so that together with the voivode they would listen to and judge matters laid before them concerning the province [148 vol. I p125].

In 1451, Iancu of Hunedoara (also known as John Hunyadi) gave the noblemen Ambrozie and Mihail stretches of land *like the face of the Romanian cnezates* [187 vol. 1 p.387], while on 15.11.1453 in Prague, King Ladislau of Habsburg, the Posthumous (1453-1457), recognised the service given by *our faithful Romanians, Ştefan and Simion for our kingdom, the so-called kingdom of Hungary*, confirming the land of Săcel and parts of the lands of Sânpetru and Recea (Hunedoara County) [134 p.64]. Once more, in the royal act itself, it is implicitly admitted that the Catholic kingdom on the Danube had an unsubstantiated name—Hungary—with the great majority of the people being schismatic and only the elite being Catholic. Also from this act, as well as from hundreds of other levies by the Catholic kings, we note the following inversion: the "real" noblemen were the ones who came around at court, the recent "incomers" endowed with land, and not the real judges, cnezes, boyars, dukes, and voivodes who had been there since the old days and had ruled in an undisturbed manner! In addition to the issue of incomers, the low nobility of the kingdom was formed by Romanian cnezes and voivodes who embraced Catholicism.

On 6.02.1456, Iancu de Hunedoara, at the insistence of the fanatical monk Ioan Capistrano, ordered the expulsion of all the Romanian priests in the villages of his domains who had been ordained by an Orthodox vicar. In only three months, this intolerant Papist monk converted 11,000 Romanian "schismatics" [104 p.99].

In 1456, the inhabitants of Wallachian "Craina" in the Iliuşa valley (Berg County) appealed to Elisabeta Szilagyi (the wife of Iancu de Hunedoara) asking that Berg officials respect their old privileges. Elisabeth ordered that, in future, the inhabitants of Craina should be required to give fewer sheep, the number changing from 12 to 6, and that the tithe should be collected not only in money, but also in kind [103 p.56].

In 1457, the nobles and cnezes, as well as the other Romanians from the eight Romanian districts of Banat (Lugoj, Caransebeş, Mehadia,

Almăj, Izvoarele Caraşului, Bârzava, Iladia, and Comiat) gathered to defend their old rights. On 29.08.1457, the King of Bohemia and Hungary, Ladislaus the Posthumous, confirmed the privileges of all the Romanian nobles, cnezes, and other Romanians (*consideratis fidelitatibus et fidelium serviciorum meritis eorundem universorum nobilum et keniziorum ac ceterorum walachorum*) of Banat as thanks for defending the fords of the Danube against Turkish incursions [187 p.382; 135 p.113]. Further on in the diploma, the King decrees:

> *not to donate to anyone any village or any estate located in any of the eight districts, but only in exceptional cases, and only to those, to whom the Romanian nobles will recognize merits for their faithful service* [216 p.871]

In the *Hymn to the Danube*, written by the humanist Aeneas Silvius Piccolomini, the future Pope Pius II (1458-1464), homage is paid to the great European river, which is fed by the whirlpools of the Inn, witnesses the splendours of Vienna, and flows down into the plains of Pannonia, dividing the Romanians in two [51 p.75].

The Maramureş *comes*, Mihai de Perestin, conferred (24.07.1462) part of his estates at Voineşti and Bărdari on to Ambroziu de Dolha and Mihai Mare de Rosalia—estates that belonged to Sandrin Bud of Voineşti.

In a diploma of Matthias Corvinus from 1475, we find recognition that the inhabitants of the valley of the Someş belonged to the *districtus valachorum*, which had always been free [6 vol. I p.738].

In 1476, during his battles with the Turks, necessity forced Matthias Corvinus (1458-1490) to allow freedom of worship for the Eastern churches in the domains of Stephen the Great in Transylvania. Matthias Corvinus, ironically named *Valachorum regulus*, convinced Pope Sixtus IV to forbid the Franciscans of Banat to offend the Eastern Rite under the pretext of being badly baptized [134 p.94]. The letter of Sixtus IV (29.01.1476) to the bishops of the Kingdom of Hungary and the Banat area towards Serbia attests to this temporary change of heart from the Vatican [51 p.87].

Fig. 2.18. Romanian peasant.

In 1479, Matthias Corvinus exempted the Romanian priesthood of Maramureș from taxes [104 p.146]. However, this policy did not last long and two years later he resumed his "anti-schismatic" policy and obliged all the Romanians of the Alba Iulia chapter to pay the usual yearly *dijma* (tithe) to the Catholic Church!

It did not matter to Matthias Corvinus that the 1437 rebellion in Transylvania was due to the actions of the Catholic bishop of Alba Iulia who imposed a Catholic tax on the Romanians, in addition to the sheep tithe and the obligation to defend the borders! Nothing had changed from the religious policy of Innocent III who considered the Byzantines heretics and "unjust possessors", only good for "pillage and plunder" [134 p.93]. Also in 1479, the nobleman I. Garai sold three castles with 90 Romanian villages in Banat to N. Banffy [104 p.183].

In 1485, the Romanian Simion Bococi of Uglea (Maramureș County) was secretary to Matthia Corvinus, as well as a cardinal and Bishop of Strigonium and in 1511 he was one of the candidates for the apostolic throne in Rome [5 p.11]. In this same year, a letter from the Germans and the Saxons to Matthias Corvinus is recorded complaining that the tyranny of the Voivode of Transylvania (Stefan Báthory) had resulted in a lot of peasants (Romanians) fleeing with their families to Moldova and Wallachia, leaving the noble domains without sufficient labour [161 p.30].

In 1493, Ioan Corvinus, Iancu of Hunedoara's brother of the same name, received Voivode Ladislau of Stanfalva (Berg County) at the fortress of Muncaciu with some diplomas and local lords who disputed his claim saying that in their land the voivode was elected [103 p.56].

In 1495, there was a voivodeship (*officium woywodatus volachorum*) covering the Jula estate and, later on, the estate of Șiria (Arad County); the voivodeship of Ștefan Moga had 48 villages [148 vol. I p.197; vol. II p.86].

Around the year 1500 in the districts of Banat, concerning judicial disputes there is talk of *Jure Volachie requiente* (according to the law), while in 1503 documents speak of *Juxta ritum volachie* (according to the customs of the Romanians) [104 p.184].

In 1504, the scholar Marcantonio Coccio published a history, *Enneades sive rapsodiae historiarum*, which reads [142 p.217]:

> *Wallachians are of Italic descent; their country was once inhabited by Dacians; now it is inhabited by Germans, Szeklers and Wallachians.*

The Code of Laws called the *Tripartitum*, published after the suppression of the peasant's uprising of 1514, notes that the plebs were made up of several nations, including Hungarians, Cumaeans, and Philistines [148 vol.

I p.174]. Who were these Hungarian plebeians (serfs)? Were they not the sedentary and Catholicized natives of Pannonia, i.e., alienated from the mass of Romanians who retained the Eastern Rite and who thought they were "Hungarians" since they belonged to a kingdom called Hungaria? Genetic research gives us an unequivocal answer. According to the *Tripartitum*, the social categories are reduced to nobles and non-nobles with a number of consequences; for example, among the category of nobles are included all the nobles of a session and even the paupers, if they have proof of their "nobility". We thus find in the documents of lords and nobles, with the meaning of magnates, great landowners alongside paupers with titles of nobility.

The German humanist Johann Boemus published a work in 1520 devoted to the customs and laws of the native peoples of the region, which was widely read in the 16th-17th centuries. Referring to Dacia, it says *Nunc Teutones, Siculi et Valachi tenent*, i.e., "now held by Germans, Szeklers and Romanians" [3 p.76]. Naturally, the Hungarians are missing because they were not yet there.

Analysing the texts from Măhăceni (Turda) around 1583, B.P. Hașdeu, referring to immigration after the Battle of Mohács (1526), noted that the Romanians Mircea, Mirea, Stancă, Cordoș, Pocol, Șușman, Raț, Părduț, Bărbos, Popa, and Hegeduș did not know where they came from, but that the people of Măhăceni displayed strong rhotacism in speech [81 p.34]. This is characteristic of the Romanians and becomes gradually more accentuated the further west one goes, reaching its peak among the Istro-Romanians (Pola penisula, Croatia). I believe Hașdeu to be mistaken when he does not make the connection to Mohach on the Danube with the argument that the locality of Muhaci, inhabited by the Szeklers, was mentioned as being in Transylvania in 1291 [81 p.37], but how many of the names Sărata, Glâmboca, Racovița, Mohu, Buda, Bedeu, Bucur, or Viștea do we not find in that area stretching from Bug to the middle Danube? Hasdeu is wrong in giving credit to a toponymic similarity and not to positive, tangible facts. The people here were not Transylvanian because the Transylvanian army did not reach Mohács, these immigrants were slightly different from their new neighbours, the Turdens, and their pronounced rhotacism goes beyond Transylvanian usage and "locates" them, in origin, much further west.

Peter Perembski, the Polish secretary of Elisabeth Jagelo, widow of John Zapolea (1526-1540), Voivode of Transylvania, wrote in 1542 that:

Peter Rares, the prince of Moldavia, with his army entered Transylvania, without encountering any obstacles ... this country being inhabited by Romanians, who, because of the identity of their language, easily joined the Moldovans [94 p.17].

An official report made by Habsburg commissioners on the state of the Maramureş salt mine in 1547 states:

> *...since most of the inhabitants of the County of Maramureş are Romanians, and since they are similar to the Moldovans in language, religion and customs, there is a danger that this county, little by little, sneaking in with the Moldovans, will, in time, on some occasion, alienate itself from the kingdom* [225 p.97].

Around 1550, Bishop Antonius Verancius wrote that the Wallachians originated from the Romans, calling themselves Romanians, *Valachi, qui se Romanos nominant* [3 p.87]; that their language had innumerable words with the same meaning as in Latin; and if you were to ask them something in Latin, they would reply: *do you know Romanian?* [137 p.22].

The Romanian humanist Nicolae Olahus (1493-1568), primate of the Catholic Church and regent of what remained of the Kingdom of Hungaria, now in the possession of the Habsburgs, was also very precise in his statement that the smallest part of the former kingdom was inhabited by Hungarian speakers, *Minima Hungariae portio est, que Hungaros, sive populum Hungarico, solum idiomate utentem, habet* [96 p.4]. In his work *Hungariae*, he wrote:

> *The Vlachs in their language call themselves Romanians, i.e., Romans, and reckon that they speak Romanian, i.e., the language of the Romans. Their language is purer and has a greater affinity with the Italian language, but the language they use, especially the people from Bihor, in church, is augmented with Slavic vocabulary, because of the religion which, having received it, if I am not mistaken, from the Slavic peoples who worship according to the Greek Rite and dogma, they preserve with the greatest obstinacy.*

A dispute in 1557 over land in the village of Romos (Orăştie, Hunedoara County) between Romanians and Saxons was settled in the second instance in favour of the Romanians, applying the principle of *equal burdens, equal benefits*. This reasoning was supported by the Romanians, being a modern legal principle that would later be reinvoked by Bishop Inochentie Micu [134 p.59].

On 16 July 1566, the widow of Voivode Stefan Mailat, Ana Nadasdy, together with 12 boyars, held court in Olt County [26 p.66]. This same year, almost all the villages belonging to the Ardud (Satu Mare County) domain, 59, were Romanian and most of them were organized under voivodeships and cnezates [5 p.79]. A few villages were in the process of being Magyarized—the inhabitants still had Romanian names such as Wayda, Jude, and Kraynik—but they paid the *ferton*, a tax specific to Germanic fairs and villages [148 vol. II p.261-328]. The Calvinist Synod of Dobrâtin (today Hungary) also dealt with the organization of the Romanian Reformed Church in those parts [103 p.71].

In 1569, at the Diet of Pojon (Bratislava), the Romano-German emperor Maximilian II (1564-76) demanded that the Ruthenians and Romanians no longer be exempt from the tithe (*dijma*, the Romanians in the northern parts of Slovakia, then under the Habsburgs) [148 vol. I p273].

Several Calvinist-Romanian manuscripts are known, dating from 1570, 1601, and 1642, of Grigory Sandor, and from 1697 of Ioan Viski from Lutița. These manuscripts were motivated by pressure from Calvinist princes for the Calvinization of the Romanians [216 p.298].

The Transylvanian Diet took half-yearly measures against fleeing serfs, but the Diet of 1581 demanded that runaway serfs should no longer be ennobled by the prince [148 vol. I p.443]. In other words, the number of nobles kept increasing, including serfs who redeemed themselves.

Adolf Armbruster brought back into circulation a document of the parish priest Grigore Vlad from 1655, in which it appears that the church of Turdaș at Coasta, which had remained with the Romanians from the time of the Dacians, in the year 1582 was under the rule of Bishop Alexă Turdaș [3 p.179].

We not only had the old voivodes, but new voivodes also. According to the *Tripartitum*, in 1593, in the domain of Satu Mare, Petru Șandru settled three villages, in one of them he had about 50 houses, for which merit he was named voivode of the village that also bore his name; this was not a unique case [148 vol. I p.488]. This custom and institution was well ingrained in the community and accepted by the new feudal lords and their proceedings.

From a 1595 record of Kecskemét (Hungary), we learn that there were many rich herds of fat oxen belonging to the Romanians around [103 p.68].

In 1599, the chronicler Istvan Samoskozy, seeing the entry of Michael the Brave's army into Transylvania, wrote that the Romanians (the serfs) arose from the confidence that they had a lord of their own kind, and that the *Valachorum natio inhabiting each of the villages and hamlets of Transylvania* rose up to prey on the lords.

In 1600, in the district of Beiuș out of 64 villages 61 were Romanian [148 vol. II p.828]. The other three were mixed with Hungarians, like

Beiuș.

For the whole of Transylvania, we have the 1602 report of the Catholic Bishop of Alba-Iulia, D. Napragy, to Rudolf II, which confirmed that the Hungarians were feudal, foreigners in the Voivodeship of Transylvania, few in number and exploiters, and the Romanians were their subjects [160 p.131].

Calvinist pressure in Transylvania experienced a lull with the Counter-Reformation of the Bathory family. Here is how the Saxon chronicler expressed himself concerning Cardinal Bathory, killed by the Szeklers:

> ...it was decreed to change the religion and all the evangelical or Orthodox priests, who would not return to the papist vomit, to hang them [97 p.102].

Prince Gavriil Bathory (1608-1613), who was also killed by his own soldiers, struck at the Saxons as if *they had set their sights on destroying you completely*, wrote George Barițiu, who translated the Saxon chroniclers of the *Chronicon Fuchsino-Lupino-Oltardinum* [97 p.103].

In the 15th and 16th centuries, the Romanian communities of Transylvania, who emigrated due to their unbearable serfdom, and later also due to Calvinization, preserved their *jus valachicum* in Moravia and Poland [23 p.112].

In 1622, the Habsburg King Ferdinand II (1619-1637) asked the administrative bodies of Croatia and Slavonia to respect the rights and privileges of the Romanians in these provinces. In 1630, Ferdinand issued a statute according to which the Romanians between the Sava and Drava rivers were divided into three captaincies headed by a captain elected by the cnezes on St. George's Day [103 p.66]. From a Vatican document published by the magazine Astra, we learn that south of Balta, between the Drava and Sava, there was a numerous and purely Romanian population, which, being under the Turkish yoke, went to the Emperor of the Holy Roman Empire in 1631 to intercede for the sending of a head of the Eastern Church for the instruction of its priests [191]. The Vatican responded in 1641 by sending the missionary Raphael to convert the Vlachs to Catholicism [103 p.67].

The Romanians of the counties of Bihor, Haidu, Sablociu, Ugocea, Berg, and Sătmar, by passing under the jurisdiction of the United Greek Bishopric of Muncaciu (Ukraine) in 1634, completely separated themselves from the mass of Romanians in Transylvania. The new "Ruthenian" episcopate sent only foreign priests who did not know Romanian to the Romanian villages [103 p.107]. In the 17th century, the chronicler Miron Costin, in a letter to the king of Poland, mentions that the most beautiful and correct Romanian dialect was spoken in Sătmar (our note: Maramureş), where, despite the emigration of Dragoş, the Romanians who remained there under his brother, the Voivode Bâlc, were as numerous as if no one had left the country [59 p.54].

The protocols of Dobrâţin, Seghedin, Tokaj, and Kecikemet (today Hungary), drawn up in the 17th century, often raised the issue of the Romanians in these areas [103 p.69].

The Saxon Protopope Andrei Gunesch (1663-1690), describing the Calvinist tyranny in the *Chronicon Fuchsino-Lupino-Oltardinum*, gives the example of the Orthodox Metropolitan Sava Brancovici (1656-1683), who was beaten to death in prison [97 p.104]. If even the Romanian Metropolitan was not exempt from *usque ad bene placitum principum ac regnicolarum*, then, along with the gallows that terrified Hildebrand [20 p.31], these liquidations were the concrete expression of the most pestilential feudal state in Europe. The Turks pushed the Hungarian feudalists towards Calvinism to separate them in religious terms from the Austrians, generating an interesting historical phenomenon that can be described as the Calvinistic Turkism of the Hungarians. The intense Calvinist propaganda made to the Romanians of the Tisa Plain led to their early denationalisation, especially in the counties of Bihor, Haidu, and Sablociu [103 p.71], and not just in the Tisa Plain!

In 1684, the Romanian Reformed community of Deva asked Princess Ana Bornemiza to allow them to take Mihai Eperjesi, who knew Romanian, as their pastor [6 vol. I p.709].

With the arrival of the emperors, Catholic pressure on the Romanians of the Tisa Plain intensified, as well as on the Reformed. The British historian R.W. Seton-Watson writes:

The reign of Leopold I (1657-1703), at once the least able and most bigoted of the Habsburg rulers, is disfigured by more than one ferocious persecution of the Protestants [179 p.32].

The Ruthenian Bishop Joseph of Camillis promoted the idea of the ecclesiastical union of the Orthodox with the Catholics in Berg, Ugocea, Sătmar, Maramureş, and Transylvania [67]. He preached Catholicism among the Romanians of the northwest, who, having come under the United Ruthenian Bishopric of Muncaciu, were also located among the Ruthenians [103 p.72]; something to bear in mind.

The imperial acts of confessional union of the Orthodox Romanians with the Catholics (1697, 1701) in Transylvania were of a contractual nature, namely, "we will unite with Rome in the garb of our Eastern Rite if you recognize our national rights". However, the imperial Austrians did not have the strength and character to hold to the signed contract. Not only did they show no character, but much more, they replaced character with mockery: they seized Bishop Inochentius in Vienna because he suggested that they should not only keep their word, but that the Romanians carried most of the public burdens—the taxes and wars of the kingdom—and therefore should be recognised as such and not just tolerated at the pleasure of the feudal lords. Bishop Inochentie Micu balanced for a second time (1742) the number of fellow countrymen with the number of profiteers, so that "He who feels the benefit must also feel the burden" (*Qui sentit commodum sentire debet et onus*).

Two late estimates from 1896 of the population of the Principality of Transylvania for 1700 (Benedek) and of Hungary and Transylvania for 1720 (Acsady), are pure fantasies, with no documentary or scientific basis, as the peerless historian David Prodan has demonstrated. These estimates were devised to support the political thesis of Romanian immigration to Transylvania and Hungary [150 p.27]. The two succeeded in doing the opposite by confirming with figures what we know from positive facts about the emigration of Romanians from Transylvania. From now on, we have in relation to the Romanian principalities the expression *Tota Transilvania ad nos venit* "All of Transylvania comes to us" [150 p.60]. Acsady's statistical fantasy, though laborious, has no basis, not even as much as Benedek's facile work, which supposes that in 1700 in Transylvania there were 250,000 Romanians, 100,000 Saxons, and 150,000 Hungarians. From among these figures, the number of Saxons alone (all free people without serfs and without nobles) can be justified: at the beginning of the 17th century, an evaluation found there to be 68,160, and at the conscription of 1761-62 there were 120,160. For the Romanians, Benedek uses a Jesuit report from 1701, but deliberately misquotes it to give 250,000 Romanians! However, the Jesuits wrote *ut 200 hominum millia fuerint, qui Unionem amplexi sunt*, i.e., 200,000 Romanians only who had

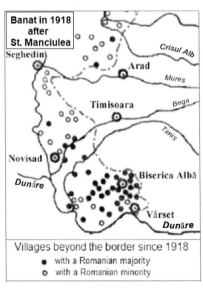

Fig. 2.19. Romanian villages beyond the frontier in Banat.

joined the Union [150 p.29]. Benedek adds another 50,000 to the Romanian figure to try and make it more believable! But where do the 150,000 Hungarians come from, since systematic Magyarization would only begin half a century later?

After the liberation of Banat from the Turks in 1718 (the Peace of Podul Lung (Passarowitz)), the Austrians found in the province only Romanians and Serbs from south of the Danube (these immigrant Serbs appeared after 1690, fleeing from the Turks, under the protection of Louis of Baden) [182 p.154]. Other nations were not then found in Banat. Even in 1767, according to a work by Franz Griselini (1717-1783) published in Vienna in 1780, there were no Hungarians nor Magyarized people! Later, Johann Jakob Ehrler presented the new governor of Banat with a piece describing Banat from its origins to the present day, in which the population by nationality in 1774 was as follows: Romanians 220,000, Serbs and Aromanians ("Greeks") 100,000, Germans 53,000, and Bulgarians and Hungarians 2,400 [56 p.30]. True, Banat was then directly administered by Vienna until 1778, when it was placed under the administration of Buda, then primarily a German town! The Serbs, newly arrived to north of the Danube because of Turkish oppression, knew how to make themselves useful to their new masters in Vienna. The Serbs became security agents for Vienna at the expense of the Romanians, even though they shared the same confession. With the dissolution of the Orthodox Metropolitanate, the church affairs of Transylvania and Bukovina were entrusted to the Serbian Metropolitanate of Carlowitz. This is how a contemporary, George Bariţiu, described the behaviour of the Serbs in 1860:

> In Banat, the Serbian superior clergy was making so much of its despotism exercised over the Romanian priesthood and communities that it seemed to one that if someone had poured millions into the purses of the Serbian bishops, they would not have worked with a better result to repel and turn the Romanians away from themselves [6 vol. II p.134].

The imperial principle *divide et impera* was respected by "little Austria", which had come to encompass dozens of peoples. This was the starting point for the reaction of the secular intelligentsia of Banat through the Mocioni brothers and Gojdu because, as Bariţiu explains, the priesthood was too much in its thrall.

When the Austrians asked in 1726 why the Romanians had fled Transylvania, the serfs of Recea (Brasov County) replied:

We are ruined and impoverished also because of our excessive work, for although in winter our lord leaves us one or two days a week to work on our own, but in summer not a single day, except on Sunday; but as soon as spring comes, he keeps us from Monday morning to Saturday evening, until mid-winter. When we have a feast, our work is even harder, for then we are manned by all the good men and women of the house. On top of that, although we are day in and day out in the job, our wives at home are constantly spinning, in winter hemp and in summer wool. Because of this hard work we do not get to work at all on our own, so that we remain without seed [150 p.103].

Formulating a mirror image to the "dark" Phanariot regime across the Carpathians, the days of "clacă" (collective work) owed to the landlords were 27, 24, 12, or 6 a year! The exception was the small peasant "republics" of Vrancea and Câmpulung Moldovenesc, where there was no clacă [150 p.126-139]. The enlightened monk Gh. Şincai (1754-1816), who had taken two doctorates at the Vatican, confessed:

...the fools [our note: the Romanian serfs] *had reached so much in my time, that they sold themselves like beasts without a place, not with the place they were barking together; apart from the services, which they did for the earthly lords, from Monday to Saturday evening, all week long, all year round, on Sundays because nothing else could be worked, the earthly lords, their serfs sent them by cart ...* [165].

At the trial of Count Alexandru Károlyi over a forest in the village of Mădăraş (Satu Mare County) in 1732, two Romanian nobles appeared as witnesses: Ilie Sabău (86 years old) and Ioan Pop (50 years old) from the village of Pişcari [201 p. 260].

Empress Maria Theresa wrote to the Archbishop of Muncaciu (Ukraine) on 28 March 1748 about Transylvania as "in our Romanian principality" *in dicto principatu nostro valahico*. In a memoir on the conversion of Orthodox Romanians to Greek Catholicism, dated 1750, it is stated that Transylvania was almost entirely Romanian: *Transilvania fere integro valahica est* [5 p.79].

In 1751, at the Feudal Diet of Transylvania, it was heard that:

...it is a law of nature that the serf should be a serf and any change made in this ordinance would weaken the foundation of this law and would undermine the rights of the feudal lords [10 p.46].

The historian Bujor Dulgău, in a passage on the extent and resistance of the Romanian nobles in Satu Mare County, describes a trial between the nobles Mihai Pop, Ursu Mogoş, and Ioan Dragoş, and Count Teleki regarding the regime of the *Codrul* "forest". During this trial, more than 40 witnesses, all Romanian nobles, were heard on 13 December 1751 in Mireşu Mare (Maramureş County). Over the course of 1761, another 15 Romanian nobles testified before the court of Şomcuta Mare (Maramureş County) in another trial [201 p.261]. We have given some examples, referring to the small Romanian nobility, the so-called "nobility of a session", which was not denationalised, was subjected to the same "vexations", injustices, spoliations, or physical elimination as the common serfs according to the goodwill of income, of foreigners, as Bishop Napragy said. This small nobility remained sympathetic to the people perhaps precisely because it was treated as we have described, but it was no less true that it remained even partially aware of its value and was an important factor in the Romanian renaissance. There were villages in the 19th century where the "nobles" and their descendants numbered 50-60 members! The historian Ládislau Gyémánt in [79] counted no less than 12,500 Romanian noble families involved in the process of national emancipation.

However, we can estimate the number of Romanians in 1761-62 when the Teresian conscription was violently enforced by General Adolf Buccow giving an exact count of 120,160 Saxons. After this conscription, we had 672,995 Romanians. According to the Astra Dictionary, in 1762, there were 128,000 Orthodox families and 25,000 United [197 vol. III p.491]. If we consider the index of 4.6 members of a Romanian family compared to the Transylvanian average of 4.5 [150 p.36], then these 153,000 Romanian families would mean 703,800 souls. The minor difference (703,000-672,995) can be explained by Buccow's way of working, with sword and cannon against the Orthodox [10 p.59].

In 1763, the Hungarian writer Adam Kollár pointed out that the Hungarian language was spoken only in a very small part of the country [5 p.72], as in the time of Nikolaus Olahus two centuries earlier.

The Catholic Seminary of Oradea published a Calendarium in 1765 listing the Greek Rite villages in the diocese, which were inhabited by Romanians and where the liturgical language

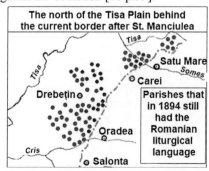

Fig.2.20. Romanian parishes in 1894.

was Romanian, while in other localities, with a mixed population, "Ruthenian" was mentioned in addition to Romanian. Some of these villages stretched as far as the Tisa: Poceiu, Acsad, Hosszupali, Abram, Vasad, Leta, Vertes, and Nadantelek (Hungary). The villages in eastern Haidu County and southern Sablociu County were at that time almost all Romanian and used the Romanian liturgical language [103 p.88].

Raicevici, the author of a booklet on the Romanian countries, wrote that in 1782, 13,000 families fled the Habsburg Empire (Banat, Crișana, Maramureș, and Transylvania) paying taxes of 140,000 piastres (one piastre was 19-24 gr. Ag) [161 p.31]. The court in Vienna was concerned (1783) that more than 11,000 families had crossed into the Romanian principalities. 11,000 families meant a lot to the Austrian tax authorities, who had just brought 60,000 Swabian settlers to Banat. Among these 11,000 families who fled across the mountains in 1782 were Romanians from eight communes in Arad. In the County of Arad, of 166 communes 137 were purely Romanian, 23 had a Romanian majority, and the remaining six were German, Serbian, and Hungarian [94 p.25].

In a letter by Emperor Joseph II (26.04.1784) to the Chancellor of the Hungarian Court, speaking about the Hungarian language, he writes that it is used only to a small extent in Hungary and its provinces, the greater part of the inhabitants using "the Illyrian language with its dialects, as well as the Wallachian language".

The historian Fr. Sulzer, referring to Transylvania in 1787, speaks of 8,000 families fleeing over the mountains [161 p.31]. Also, at the time of Joseph II (1780-1790), the villages of the counties of Sablociu and Hajdu (today Hungary) up to Dobrâtin were almost all Romanian and used the Romanian liturgical language [103 p.115]. On the death of Joseph II, all the royal provisions intended to make life easier for the serfs, i.e., the Romanians, were annulled under pressure from the feudal lords. Joseph II's brother, Emperor Leopold II (1790-1792), the former Duke of Tuscany, simply turned the clock back a century: he reinvented feudalism and reintroduced slavery [179 p.36-37].

In 1799, in the four classes of the Latin Gymnasium of Tg. Mureș, where Magyarization was already advanced, there were 86 pupils of whom 23 % were Romanians, 15 % Armenians, 25 % Szeklers, 2 % Germans, 2 % Hungarian barons, and 33 % Roman Catholics, with their nationality not mentioned. Among these Roman Catholics, it is difficult to determine the ethnicity of the pupils, since most of them were enrolled with Hungarian spelling and most were probably "new Hungarians". If we make an approximation, the fragile Greek-Catholic priesthood just set up after the pastorate of Inochentie Micu still suggests a quarter of the pupils (as extracted from the archives by the historian Vasile Lechințan). In 1762, the Orthodox were five times more numerous than the Greek Catholics, but being only tolerated *ad bene placitum* ... they were not admitted to the schools. We have the Saxons from the so-called Szekler seats who became Calvinists or remained Catholics, in time becoming Hungarians. We can make a simple calculation: if a fifth of the Romanians (Greek Catholics) gave 23 % of the Gymnasium students, then all the others, in 1799, were negligible. Therefore, what was denationalised by *cuius regio, eius religio* was still insignificant and from then on the systematic process of Magyarization began.

According to the data from 1822 for the Diocese of Muncaciu, Romanians formed the majority of the population: in 138 villages there were only Romanians, in 72 the population was mixed, while in 82 there were only Ruthenians [103 p.114], but we now know that some of these Ruthenians were Romanians.

The official data of the Austrian census of 1830 for Transylvania partially corrected by confession gives: 1,229,000 Romanians (Orthodox and Greek-Catholic), 237,000 Saxons, without Swabians, and 195,000 Hungarians [93 vol. 3 p. 58]! Among these 195,000 Hungarians were many tens of thousands of Magyarized Romanians, Swabians, Slovaks, Serbians, Czechs, Croats, and Poles.

In 1846 in Galicia (part of the Habsburg Empire), a thousand Polish nobles were slaughtered and 500 mansions were razed to the ground by Ruthenian serfs [45 p.30]. The situation was similar to that in Transylvania with foreign feudal lords ruling over the autochthonous population, with the great difference being that the Romanians were only tolerated—they were mobile things, *rer viventum*! The serf revolt in Galicia frightened Kossuth and led him to abolish serfdom. This action was taken not against the nobles, but on the contrary to save the nobility, i.e., the domination of a very small minority over the majority. This is how Kossuth expressed himself to Baron Wesselényi:

If the nobility falls under the sword of this bloody holiday [our note: the revolution]*, then this will also be the death of the Hungarian Constitution and the Hungarian nation... Under no circumstances should we let the government* [our note: from Vienna] *take the initiative so that it can legislate against the nobility. [...] The nobility can do no less* [our note: renunciation of the benefits of maintaining serfdom]*, otherwise it will perish. But it is not obliged to do more* [150 p.65].

The Saxon scholar Joseph Benigni (1782-1849), a long-time editor of the *Siebenbürger Boten* newspaper in Sibiu, who was brutally murdered by the Hungarians on the day Bem's troops entered Sibiu, estimated that in the 1830s there were 1,351,989 Romanians in Transylvania compared to 500,000 foreigners [33 p.13]. Therefore, if we take the year 1835 as a reference year, then after 15 years, with an increase of 0.756 %/year, we reach a population of 2,073,737, which is exactly what the census of 31.X.1850 found [15 p.37]. If Begnini's reference year had been 1838, with an annual population growth rate of 0.945 %, we arrive at the same population in 1850. The growth rates considered are in the range of the growth rate in Transylvania between 1850 and 1910 [15 p.37]. However, Benigni's figures are close to those of Ignaz Lenk [93 vol. 3 p.58].

On 26.05.1848, after the outbreak of the so-called Hungarian revolution and three days before the proclamation of the union of Transylvania and Hungary by the feudal Diet in Cluj, the Hungarian gazette *Marczius Tizenötodlike (15 March)* wrote:

> *In Transylvania two powers have to decide on the Union: the Diet and the Romanian people. The Diet represents only a few hundred people. The Romanian people means the whole of Transylvania* [194 vol. VI, tom.1, p.303].

Fig. 2.21. Anton von Schmerling: Minister of the Interior 1860-1865.

Captain Carl Klein wrote a history of the 2nd National Infantry Regiment, covering the jurisdiction "of the Romanians of the entire national military district of Rodna". In this history, he specified the population of this district at that time in 1848 as: 97 % Romanians, 2 % Germans, 0.25 % Slavs, and the rest Hungarians and Szeklers [120 p.55].

In 1849, the *Military Journal of the Scientific Military Committee of Petersburg* presented statistical data on the Austrian Empire, treating Transylvania separately. It is written that:

> *In Hungary the Magyars, or rather Hungarians ... their number hardly exceeds one third of the population* [45 p.136].

Obviously, the proportion of Hungarians in the Tisa Plain and Transylvania was less than a third!

In 1850 in *Uebersicht der Bevölkerung in der Woiwodschaft Serbien und in Temeser Banat*, the Banat region (Vojvodina without Bacica) is described as having the following demographic composition: Romanians and Aromanians 465,630, Serbs 229,020, Germans 212,080, Hungarians 54,975, Bulgarians 23,900, Jews 5,050, and Slovaks 508 [45 p.227].

In 1862, during the liberal period (1861-1865) of the Minister of the Interior Anton von Schmerling, the electoral lists for the principality's diet were prepared after the census had been completed and according to liberal principles mixed with old feudal privileges [153 p.61]. 40,692 voters were registered in the eight counties, which had been feudal domains until then, of which 28,946 were Romanians, 9,613 Magyarized and 3,567 Saxons. Of the "nobles" only 3,567 met the census requirement.

The counties, the land of the nobles of yesteryear, became in 1863 what they were and were in fact: Romanian land. Out of 38 deputies elected here 35 will be Romanians [153 p.65-67].

In 1880, in the villages of Csenger, Amacz, Szatmarzsadany, Nagycolcs, Reszege, Mezöterem, Vezend, and Vasad (today part of Hungary) in Sătmar County, all Greek Catholics had Romanian as their mother tongue; in other villages there were also Greek Catholics who were registered with a Hungarian mother tongue [31].

Since everyone knows that the Hungarian statistics were falsified, we must ask how many Romanians were left in so-called Hungary at the end of the 19th century. This issue was resolved by Prime Minister (1895-1899) Desideriu Bánffy in a conversation with the Romanian Minister of Public Instruction (1891-1898) Take Ionescu in Budapest (1896). The Romanian minister asked him why he created an intolerable situation for the Romanians and why he did not protect schools and churches from persecution and violence, as was done with the Saxons? To which Prime Minister Bánffy replied that this would never happen because the Saxons numbered only 230,000 and were 1,000 km from Germany, while the Romanians numbered 3.5 million and were near Romania [91 p.296].

Therefore, there were 3.5 million Romanians, and not 2.93 million as the authors of the Astra Dictionary deduced from the Hungarian data for 1900 [197 vol. III p.802]. Volume III appeared under Hungarian censorship in 1904 in Sibiu. The authors, much better informed and knowledgeable about the Hungarian spirit, were very scrupulous and used only official data, otherwise they would have been imprisoned. Officially, there were 2.77 million Romanians, but also 2.89 million Orthodox and

United Romanians [197 vol. III p.1161]. Among these figures of 2.89, 2.93, and 3.5 million Romanians in Hungary in 1900, the most factually accurate must be that declared by Prime Minister Banffy who had no reason to artificially "inflate" the number of Romanians. Later, the reader will be presented with an explanation of these statistical differences. The population of the whole of "Hungary" amounted to 16 million in 1900, and that of the part east of the Tisa River plus Maramureş to 6.37 million according to their data. The statistics—of 6.37 million east of the Tisa, 3.5 million were Romanians, while more than 1.5 million were others (Germans, Slovaks, Ruthenians, and Jews)—justified the violent process of Magyarization in the eyes of the Prime Minister of Budapest. Take Ionescu's request to protect some of the Romanians' own institutions from persecution and violence was both small and humble. He asked him directly if any Romanian could be elected by the electorate, to which Prime Minister Banffy replied *Not one, unless I want it* [85 p.104]. The answer shows this autocrat's certainty and contempt based on the presumed power of the monarchy, which he basically despised. In §9.2, we precisely analyse the disputed electoral law, which did not even formally ensure the equality of the Romanian majority and the dominant minority.

Even in 1908 in Seghedin beyond the Tisa, there were still a lot of non-Magyarized Romanians [127 vol. VI p.801], as well as many Slovaks dislocated/dispersed from their country by Magyarization. In Seghedin alone there were almost 10 Magyarization institutes, processing more than 4,000 non-Hungarian children every year [163 p.236].

A heavy blow was dealt to the Romanians by the establishment of the Greek Catholic Diocese of Haidu in 1912 by Pope Pius X. At that time, 20,000 Romanian faithful protested in Alba Iulia and submitted a memorial to Metropolitan V. Mihaly of Blaj to be sent to the Pope [103 p.111]. It was in vain as the Metropolitan of Blaj, in an atmosphere of hatred and chauvinism, did not dare act. On 1.07.1912, the Papal bull *Cristi fidelis graeci* was published and the Ministry of Religious Affairs in Budapest required the Metropolitanate of Blaj to carry out the division within six months. By a simple administrative act, 300,000 Romanian Greek Catholics were removed from the ranks of the Romanian nation in the Tisa Plain! Additionally, in 1912, the spirit of Hungarian chauvinism, drunk with the success of dealing with the Greek Catholics of the Tisa Plain, drove the establishment of a Hungarian Orthodox bishopric to solve the Romanian problem completely and definitively. This establishment was never completed as war came!

Summary

Up to this point, we have discussed the settlement of the Romans in the middle Danube basin, the Romanisation of the Dacians, and the continuity of the new Dacian-Roman synthesis from antiquity up to today. The first wave of sedentary people, the Germans, appeared in Transylvania with the First Crusade and it is not by chance that Adolf Armbruster, who knew all the Saxon scriptures, wrote that the Germans met in Transylvania an ancient and autochthonous population of Romanians [65 p.5]. As argued by Thomas Nägler, the very conservative Saxon dialect did not take over Slavic words except for those existing in Romanian [111 p.109], and therefore, the later arrival of the southern Romanians is an impossibility in this respect as well. We have seen that, in 1242, the Tatar innkeeper Cadan, referring to Transylvania, addressed "Saxons, Romanians, and Szeklers". We know that, in 1291 or 1355, the estates of the Voivodeship of Transylvania meant Romanians, Saxons, and Szeklers—Hungarians were missing. We know that in 1520 the humanist Johann Boemus did not mention Hungarians among the inhabitants of Transylvania either. We also recognise that there was an intense, fanatical Catholicism up to the Reformation, especially under Louis of Anjou (1342-1382).

The diet of 26 February 1543 is more precise: the nobles were required to offer support to the tune of 500 horsemen and the Saxons 500 riflemen [148 vol. I p.397]; but then a rifleman was worth more than a mounted horseman. Now, if we assimilate all the nobles, including the Saxon and Romanian nobles, with "Hungarians", it follows that there were, at that time, in all of Transylvania about 200-300 families of "Hungarian" nobles. By way of comparison, 20 years later the Olt (Făgăraș) country alone gave 200 horsemen for the partial raising of an army; but for a general muster, the Romanians had to raise their heads [148 vol. I p.404], as the serfs did. It is understood that if the petty Romanian nobles in an area of 2,400 km² (Făgăraș County) gave about the same number of horsemen as the nobles on a territory that was 50 times larger, then the number of nobles was insignificant. But the rule had become that the nobles should send soldiers and not go to war themselves.

In 1599, *Valachorum natio* was found in each of the villages and hamlets of Transylvania, wrote the humanist Istvan Samoskozy. In 1602, the "nobles", meaning great landlords, were the only foreigners in Transylvania—they were alien (*advenis*) [160 p.131]. Apart from those who became Catholic and then, in the shadow of the courts of the nobles, were Calvinized, until the arrival of the Austrians and the beginning of violent Magyarization, there were not many already Magyarized in Transylvania, and, in any case, far fewer than the Saxons, who were a nation. The "Hungarians", i.e., Hungarian speakers, were almost non-existent in Transylvania up to a certain point, and were only able to increase after the Peace of Westphalia (1648) when it was decreed that the religion of the people living in a feudal fief would be the religion of their feudal lord.

The result was religious resettlement throughout Transylvania, with whole villages that belonged to Calvinized noblemen being Calvinized, while those belonging to Catholic noblemen were Catholicized, with some being Magyarized. This process, the effect of the principle *cujus regio, ejus religio*, is still to be properly researched. It was only from then on, that the number of Hungarians began to increase and then exceed the number of Saxons. It was not until the 17th century that "Hungarian" serfs began to appear in Transylvania in any significant numbers. In Pannonia and the foothills of the northern Tatra, the peasants had long since lost their ethnic identity as Catholics. The partly Catholicized, partly Lutheranized Slovaks (they still had the memory of their Hussite precedent), also had an uphill struggle for ethnic survival; Lutheranism also gave them greater protection than Catholicism.

With the Peace of Westphalia in 1648, the destructive process of Magyarization began and the Romanian villages passed under Reformed, Unitarian, and Catholic priests according to the religion of the feudal lords they belonged to. After so much Catholicization, Calvinization, and Magyarization, the ethnic picture of Central Europe by 1785 showed that Magyarization had achieved 29 % of the total [Annex C]; of the rest, the majority were non-Hungarian (Romanians, Germans Slovaks, Serbians, and Ruthenians). This was the moment when the aristocracy launched the "modern" Magyarization campaign through savage cultural, administrative, and economic policies. To convince them, the stick, the fist, and the bullet were all used, and when "history" allowed it, colonisation, expulsion, and genocide. In Pannonia, the Tisa Plain and Transylvania we find the Romanians mentioned by St. Augustine; the Romanians referred to by the writer Prosper Mérimée (1802-1870) who described Romania as not being on the map, but whose language was spoken in "Hungary, Transylvania, Bessarabia and elsewhere" [88 p.102].

Over time, the "schismatic" natives west of the Tisa were Catholicized and then Calvinized; east of the Tisa, they were partly Catholicized and then Calvinized. Later, under the Habsburgs, they were Greek Catholicized and thus Magyarized; Magyarization in Transylvania gained momentum with the first genocide of 1848-49, as we will see in §7.

An analysis of the censuses from 1788 to 1900 by Ştefan Manciulea shows that 2,800,000 speakers of another language from the eastern part of the Habsburg monarchy were denationalised by the Hungarians [103 p.124].

Romanian teachers from Jula (today, Gyula in Hungary) were sent west of the Danube to be counted and not left at home, among the Romanian population in the Tisa Plain! In the 1970s, Professor Oltean, from Jula, discovered, during a census south of Balta (Balaton) Lake, several settlements of non-Magyarized Romanians in a meadow forest. The astonishment was so great that the teacher wondered how to register them? How could he record that he had discovered poor Romanians south of Balta in the 1970s!

2.6 Institutional Continuity

Among the "popular Romans", after the Roman Empire the Dacian-Romans had rulers and judges who governed counties, seats, courts, with rulers, holding assemblies in which they divided justice by judging according to laws [our note: in Romanian, the above words written in italics are all of Latin origin].

First, there were judges and courts, cnezes (*kines* from Sanskrit or German, not Slavic) and cnezates, and later voivodes (from Slavic) and voivodeships. In the Tisa Plain, Pannonia, and Transylvania we find seats, cnezates, banates, captaincies, and voivodeships versus the later *comites* (counties or shires introduced by the German elite into the Catholic kingdom after 1040, during its construction). The Hungarian tribes did not matter in Pannonia, for as Ioan Slavici observed, territorial division is meaningless to nomads—nomads graze their horses wherever they find grass [160 p.730].

How important must the Romanians have been, if not just the Szeklers, being very, very few in number, but even the Germans who came from the Holy Roman Empire, being the continuation of the Carolingian Empire, in Transylvania adopted the local Dacian-Roman system of courts and its organization into seats? In addition to judges and cnezes, in the villages, court seats, craines and cnezates, voivodes and voivodeships, countries and over countries, we had the Voivodeship of Transylvania and the Voivodeship of Maramureș.

If the warrior elite, the Szeklers, brought to aid the Romanians in the defence of the Curvature Carpathians, came without their own traditions and adopted the organisational system of seats using *Jus valahicum*, then for the Germans, who came later from the Holy Roman Empire, to adopt the same system seems surprising. But if we note Nicolae Iorga's and Horst Klusch's suggestions about the arrival of individual groups of

Germans in Transylvania at least half a century earlier, it is not so surprising.

2.7 Continuity Through Toponymy

The Carpathian Mountains, from the Danube to Maramures, only have Romanian names [187 vol. 1 p.266]. We have already seen that all the water courses have Dacian names, preserved by the Romans: Balta, Danube, Tisa, Mara, Someş, Crişuri, Timiş (Tibis), Zerna (Dierna) Ampoi, Mureş, Strei, Olt, Bârsa, Cibin, and so on. The toponyms Sărmaş (Sarmis), Mehadia (Ad Mediam), Severin (Severus), Pata (vicus), and Aries, etc., being Dacian or Roman, remain unchanged [187 vol. 1 p.235]. Rupea and Vulcan, Sântana, Sânpetru, Sântioana, Sânicoară, Sânmedru, and Sângiorz, are all Latin, with their old phonetics. All the migrants who came to the Carpathian Basin took them over.

Everywhere in the later counties of Somogy, Tolna, Alba (Feher), Vas, Zala, and Veszprém in Pannonia, toponyms are mentioned in monastic documents, immediately after the foundation of the Diocese of Strigonium, and are all of Romanian origin. Toponymic analysis shows that the villages of Pannonia, west of the Danube, were Romanian, thus we find the villages of Petra, Seaca, Rotunda, Părău, and Secu on the territories of the mentioned counties and of the abbeys of Tihany, Bakony, and Panonhalma, for which we have documents [103 p.23, p.74]. In a document of King Andrew I from 1055 founding the monastery of Tihany, the village of Petra (Stone) around Balta is mentioned [144 p.136]. From the years 1055 and 1093 we have ecclesiastical documents referring to a "magna villa keneaza" [54 p.43].

The organization of the Romanians north of Balta into cnezates is confirmed by toponyms like Kenes, Keneza, Knasni, Knagnin, and Voloszanka. In 1086, we find "villa Ocol", in 1109 a "villa Kensa" appears, and by 1234 a "villa Roman", "villa Costan", and "Baltafalva", as well as Keczel, Kechel, and Romantelke can all be found [104 p.133].

A 1206 decree mentions *Fântâna Mielului* and the *Podul mâinii* estate [87 p.45], and the *Măgureni* estate in the Reghin area is mentioned in a royal act of 1228, an estate adjoining the villages of *Lueriu* and *Budac*, the *Secu* valley, and *Piscu* mountain [87 p.48].

In 1238, the Saxons of Cricău, Romos, and Grabendorf were strengthened by certain privileges, and the villages of Bucerdea and Oieşdea, the river Ţelna, and the mountains of *Aciuţa, Suhodol, Geamănul,* and *Păstoreni* are all mentioned; they all have Romanian names [87 p.50].

A place, "Prat de Traian", so called from Roman antiquity, is mentioned by Martin Opitz (*wie die Walachen sagen*), the father of modern German poetry, in his poem Von Ruhe des Gemütes, written around 1622/23 in Transylvania. The Jesuit Franciscus Fasching from Cluj is also precise in 1725 when he writes: *the Romanians keep the memory of Trajan* in Trajan's Field, at Turda, or *Prat de Traian*. This missing link between certain Romanian linguists of the 20th century and the Saxon chroniclers was made by Professor Ioan Taloş of Cologne University [169 p263]. Adolf Armbuster made a similar connection between Romanian historians and Saxon chroniclers almost 60 years ago. *Pratum*, with the meaning of meadow, plain, has been preserved in all the Neo-Latin languages, as we can see in Transylvania. Below, we present the conclusion of Professor Ioan Taloş:

> *The toponym Prat de Traian or Campul lui Traian becomes, together with the toponyms Poarta Romanilor, Drumul lui Traian, Valul lui Traian, etc., a solid linguistic and folkloric argument for the continuity of the Romanians in Transylvania, as strong as archaeological or historical evidence, but having, in addition, the advantage that it includes the duration and life factor of a historical fact. It also confirms B.P. Hasdeu who said that, in our country, the tradition of the Roman emperor was not taught at school but was alive throughout time* [169 p.268].

Field marshal Ignaz Lenk von Treuenfeld, in his four volumes *Siebenbürgens geographisch, topographisch, statistisch ... Lexikon* published in Vienna in 1839, presents us with a treasure trove of tens of thousands of Romanian toponyms. For example, the waters of the *Criş Repede* springs on the mountain of *Vârfu-Poieni* flow for four hours along the border of Transylvania and Hungary, above the *Micului*, flow for another two hours through the *Drăgan Valley*, and gather four streams in the *Germinu*, *Boiasa*, and *Bologa valleys* (with the *Huedin*, *Călăţii*, and *Secuiului valleys* and, on the left bank, the *Caprei* and *Luncii valleys*) [93 vol. III p.31]. Examples can be given by the thousand. All the efforts made to give a Hungarian aspect to these lands through changes to the toponymy have failed. Alain Ruzé and Iorgu Iordan also observe:

> *Of the 80 toponyms in the domain of a single village, almost 90 % were still Romanian at the beginning of the 20th century, although at that time the village in question, today Petreşti, bore the Hungarian name of Petrid.*

The linguist Iorgu Iordan refers to the whole of Transylvania, the Tisa Plain, and Maramureş, while the French historian Alain Ruzé refers to "the allophonic stratum installed as the dominant minority" as having imposed

some microtoponyms in areas where Roman macrotoponyms were
preserved [157 p.66].

Siebenbürgens

geographisch=, topographisch=, statistisch=,
hydrographisch= und orographisches

LEXIKON,

*Fig. 2.22. Transylvania's geographical, topographical, statistical,
hydrographic, and orographic lexicon by Ignaz Lenk von Treuenfeld.*

2.8 Self-consciousness

As the first exegete of Romanian self-consciousness, the Saxon Adolf
Armbruster (1941-2001) has documented how the Latinity of the
Romanians came from the Romanians themselves, who did not forget for a
moment their august descent. Here is some of the evidence of the
collective consciousness of the Dacian-Romanians, concisely listed. The
transmission of the myth of Emperor Trajan (Trojan) to the Slavs who
came to the Balkans over four centuries could only be done by the Dacian-
Romans, who considered themselves descendants of the Roman soldiers
and farmers brought by the emperor [171 p.236].

At the time of Emperor Mauritius (582-602), probably in 601, General
Peter, after defeating the Slavs north of the Danube, remarked that "the
inhabitants of the Danube cities considered themselves Romans and their
territory of Romania" [86 p.35].

Additionally, Constantine VII Porphyrogenitus (913-959) called the
Vulgarians Romans (Ρω άνοι) because he said that they called each other
so [3 p.21].

The Persian geographer Gardizi, in his treatise *The Ornament of
Histories*, written sometime around 1050, records that there was a large
population lying between the Turks (our note: Hungarians) and Russians
with its origins in the Roman Empire. This information cannot come from
the West and probably not from the Byzantines, who considered
themselves Greeks, so Gardizi may have got this information from a
traveller passing through Dacia who saw the Romanians and talked to
them.

A document from the time of King Bela III (1172-1196) mentions Count Narad "who fought against ... Bulgarorum et Rumenorum" [139 p.138]. The Latin chancellery of the Catholic kingdom at that time did not use the names Valah (from the Germans), that of Voloh (Slavic intermediate), nor other later variants, but rather used the name the Romanians attributed to themselves.

On 27 November 1202, Ioniță the Handsome (Caloian) (1196-1207), in a letter to Pope Innocent III, wrote "thanks be to God, who has brought back to us the memory of our blood and homeland from which we descend" [3 p.29]. Basil, Metropolitan of Tarnovo, also wrote to the pope on the same occasion noting that the emperor (Ioniță) and the people were descended from Roman blood. Innocent III replies: "be like the Romans, as you are after your lineage and as your people claim to be descended from Roman blood". On 25 February 1204, Innocent III returned to this origin in a letter to Ioniță: *The Bulgars and the Romanians are descended from Roman blood* [3 p.29]. Innocent III, too, mixes up the notions of common people, of *vulgus*, with the names of the nomadic Turanian nomads who, four centuries earlier, had struck fear into Byzantium. Confusion reigned as with all the Latin monks before and after him, but only the autochthonous population, Dacian-Romans, the *vulgarorum*, could invoke Roman blood. The Turanians (Volgars), who had come from the banks of the Volga, the rulers, were gradually replaced by the autochthons, the Dacian-Romans (the vulgars), and the Slavs. These Slavs had, in turn, arrived two centuries before the Volgars. The historian Armbruster noted that in all the correspondence between Ioniță and Innocent III, it is the "Romanian consciousness" and "its 'noble' origin" that both Ioniță and his people refer to [3 p.30].

A judgement between the Romanians of the commune of Sânpetru and the Saxons of a village named Noul in the area of Rodna (Bistrița-Năsăd County) in 1557 concerning the nearby forest refers to an authentic act of 10.06.1366, which mentions that the Romanians said it was theirs from ancient times, that they have had the territory *for over a thousand years and that they have defended it many times with their blood, both themselves and their ancestors*. The judicial mayor and the German jurors of Bistrița decided that the boundaries in question "should remain unchanged", as they had been strengthened by their dukes "at the coming of the Huns (*ingressu Hunnorum*), and if the German colonia thought it could not live without the mountain forest, then it should move its village" [104 p.233; 158 p.99].

In a privilege granted by Vlaicu Voda to the Athonite monastery of Cutlumuz in 1396, "our Romanians" appears three times in opposition to the Greeks [66 p.85].

Archbishop John of Sultanyeh (Persia), who passed through the countries inhabited by the Romanians, from the Balkans to Brasov, observed *that the Romanians consider themselves of Roman origin* [3 p.46].

Around 1452-53, the humanist Biondo Flavio in an appeal to the crowned heads of Europe for common Christian action, wrote that the Romanians *prove by speech their Roman origin as a thing of quintessence* [171 p.18].

Nicholas of Modrusa, who travelled in Central and Eastern Europe and met Prince Vlad Tepes in 1463 at the court of Matthew Corvinus wrote in his work *De bellis Gothorum*:

> *The Romanians argue as an argument of their origin the fact that although they all use the language of the Moessians, which is Illyrian, yet they speak from their cradle a popular language, which is Latin, the use of which they have never left behind* [139 p.65].

The humanist Enea Piccolomini (Pius II) wrote in 1473 that the Romanians proved their origin by the popular Latin language they speak, which they had never abandoned [171 p.18].

Francesco della Valle, secretary to the adventurer Aloisie Gritti, passed through Dacia (Transylvania) and had the opportunity to speak directly with some Romanians. He claimed in 1534 that their language was little different from Italian. In Târgovişte, Francesco della Valle learned from Romanian monks that they *conservano il nome de Romani* [3 p.78].

In the act of ennoblement of Nicolae Olahus, signed by Emperor Ferdinand I (1503-1564), brother of Charles V, dated 23 Nov. 1548, it is written that the Wallachians are the descendants of the Romans sent to Dacia and for this reason they are now called Romans in their own language [3 p.85].

Deacon Coresi wrote the work *Christian Question* (1559, Braşov) in Romanian so that all Romanian Christians could understand it [3 p.95].

The Florentine Giovanandrea Gromo, who was captain of the guard of John Sigismund Zapolea (made prince of Transylvania by the Ottomans) from 1564 to 1565, and therefore directly acquainted with the Transylvanian people, writes that the Roman character of the Romanians is proved by their language, which is *similar to the ancient Roman one* [3 p.108].

The Frenchman Pierre Lescalopier, who travelled through Transylvania and Muntenia in 1574, wrote that these two countries claimed to be the successors of the Romans and said that they speak Romanian, i.e., the language of the Romans [139 p.111].

***

There are localities, such as Cuciulata in Tara Oltului (Brașov County), where habitation seems to have existed uninterrupted for 4,000 years. A miniature chariot from Cuciulata discovered in 1958, is in an excellent state of preservation and dates to the Bronze Age, 4,500-3,500 years ago. Also here we find the ruins of a Dacian fortress from the 1st century B.C. Cuciulata is documented on 16 July 1372 in a record from the time of Vlaicu Voda, Lord of the Romanian Principality, and we find evidence in all the towns of Tara Oltului up to today, as the writer Miron Scorobete from Cluj has observed. There are many, many such localities in the middle basin of the Danube, but let us see why it is so important to remember these arguments of continuity; it is not because of today's "plebs", who are ever more in a hurry and ever more ignorant, but because political leaders, some ignorant, others simply fearful (Fr. Mitterand [150]), are more and more subjugated to narrow and momentary interests, whether of individuals or groups. Superficiality and a lack of principles are also ravaging part of the scientific world today; in particular, in our so-called scientific world there is still the scourge of not calling a spade a spade, and of not calling a genocide what indeed it is lest people get upset.

It should also be remembered that Dacia was heavily Romanised and that most of the settlers, the veterans, were farmers who clung to the patch of land they received that sustained their livelihood. When imperial authority left Dacia, only the higher officials and active military retired. In addition to the veteran farmers, the craftsmen and merchants remained because it suited them. This fact of the stability of sedentary people is demonstrated by the preservation of customs, language formation, linguistic peculiarities, toponymy, the reception of Christianity in Latin form, political continuity (jude, cnez, voivode, seat, cnezate, country, and voivodeship), and a collective self-consciousness beyond that which written documents and mathematical evidence can confirm.

Fig. 2.23. Young people from Țara Oltului in 1900.

As Iorga so profoundly considered, we are not lacking in documents for what other documents are stronger than the people, than their consciousness, their language, their customs, and their linguistic particularities, which are planted here and only here?,

Nowadays, there are "Hungarians" and Calvinists (Petrindu Sălaj County), who still come to the Orthodox Rite priest for religious assistance at certain moments of hardship because "the Orthodox service is stronger". Or perhaps because of how diffuse the cultural memory of their ancestors is even today.

CHAPTER 3

THE ARMY

3.1 The Army of the Kingdom and Voivodeship

In *The Alexiad*, Anna Komnene (1083-1153) wrote about events during the reign of her father, Emperor Alexios I Komnenos (1081-1118). One of these events was the crossing of the Danube by an army made up of Scythians (Cumaeans), Sauromatians, and Dacians (Romanians from north of the Danube) led by a general named Tzeglu [212 p.95]. There was another group of Dacians led by a chieftain called Solomon in addition to those led by Tzeglu along the lower Danube, wrote Anna Komnene, who was contemporary to these events [86 p.45]. King Coloman/Căliman (1095-1116), contemporaraneous with Alexios I Komnenos, reigned over the catholic kingdom in Pannonia, but a king could not be downgraded to a chieftain, i.e., to the head of a company. The essential point is that Solomon had come with an army of Dacian-Romans along the Danube and joined the group led by Tzeglu in attacking the Byzantine Empire. Some modern translators translate the word *Dacians* (Δακικον) as *Hungarians*, because they came along the Danube from Pannonia. On what other grounds they justify this, we do not know; it is probably because they had no knowledge of the demographics of the middle Danube basin. In 1096, during the First Crusade, the Byzantine emperor, surprised by the "Celtic" invaders that were plaguing his empire, thought that the westerners wanted his throne and so his armies were stationed on the borders, facing the Cumaeans and Dacians [212 p.117]. These two pieces of information, as written by Anna Komnene, need to be read together, specifying that the Cumaeans refers to the warrior elite, while the Dacians were Romanians.

In 1167, the Romanians, aware of their Roman descent as noted by Ioan Kynnamos, stood with the empire against the catholic kingdom [135 p.84].

In 1204, King Henricus (1196-1204) exempted *Ioan the Roman from villa Riuetel* (Răşinar-Sibiu County) and his heretics from all taxes for the rendering of military services [126 p.36].

In origin, serfs were free peasants on the king's lands and around the cities. In exchange for their freedom, they had to do military service. In the registry of the city of Oradea, between 1208 and 1235, serfs of the king or of the free cities are mentioned—free people, who only had to complete their military service. The serfs considered themselves to be the *oldest, the truest, the most natural* (*a prima origine, antiqui, primi veri, naturales*) [148 vol. I p.157]. The same registry also contains a note about Petru, the head of the serfs in the city of Borsod (Hungary), who wanted to force them to guard the prisons. To this command the serfs answered that they did not have to do anything apart from go to battle and that they could not be forced to render other services than those already established [187 vol. I p.388].

The Romanians in the area of Sibiu were mentioned as having their own independent military organizations: in 1210, Earl Ioachim of Sibiu, leading an army of Saxons, Romanians, Szeklers, and Pechenegs, went to the aid of Czar Borilă Asan to crush a Cuman rebellion in Vidin at the behest of King Andrei II [94 p.43]. It appears that there were hardly any Hungarians among the combatants!

In his chronicle, the Minorite Paulus of Venice (†1334) writes that the defence of the eastern passes of Transylvania was *an old habit of the Romanians* in those parts; in 1231, the passes were closed [104 p.248]. This habit continued even after the Szeklers (*Siculi*) were brought in. This fact is confirmed by a later document of the German emperor Sigismund of Luxembourg (1388-1437), which states that the Romanians, whether cnezes or peasants, would in the future have to defend the borders and raid Moldavia, *as their habit has been so far* [201 p.170].

In 1260, the cnezes Crețu, Cupisa, and Racu of Sirmium, were given titles of nobility for having defended Béla IV from the Tatar invasion [187 vol. I p.388].

At the Battle of Kressenbrunn in 1260, Béla IV attacked Bohemians with a large army of Cumaeans, Szeklers, and Romanians, as well as *Islamic, Schismatic, and Greek men.*

In 1268, Voivode Nicolae of Transylvania bestowed titles of nobility on the Romanians Mihai and Niculai Goștian for valour in battle against the Bulgarians [187 vol. I p.380].

In 1275, more serfs from Făgăraș County were raised to the ranks of the nobility for military services rendered, while in 1287 Dionisos, a serf from Castle Ung (Ukraine), was given a title of nobility for his bravery in the fight against the Cumaeans [187 vol. I p.398].

In 1285, the Tatar invasion was stopped in southern Transylvania by the *Siculi, Olahi et Saxones* (Szeklers, Wallachians, and Saxons) [158 p.20]. No Hungarians were present among the combatants!

In 1291, fighting against Duke Albert of Habsburg, the army of the Kingdom of Hungary definitely included Romanians in its ranks [137 p.86].

Documents of the Royal Chancellery dating to 1303 mention Voivode Nicolae of Maramureș, who was in an on-and-off relationship of friendship with the royal house [104 p.140].

A document of Carol Robert of Anjou from 1326 attests to the donation of the estate at Strâmtura to cnez Stanislau, son of Stan, for having distinguished himself in battle [187 vol. I p.388].

The army of Carol Robert that fought against Basarab (1330) was mainly made up of Romanian cnezes from Banat, Hațeg, Zarand, the Tisa Plain, and Maramureș. For the bravery they showed in battle, Carpat, Stan, Neagu, Vlaicu, and Vlad were all granted titles, estates, and villages by the River Timiș [104 p. 171].

In 1333, Carol Robert elevated Marcu, vice-castellan of Unguraș (Cluj County), as well as Toma, his brother, the sons of Nicolae, the son of Bartheleu ... from their state of servitude (defenders) of the city of Fagach (which is at present in Hungary) making them free servants and noblemen of the kingdom for the important services they rendered during the Battle of Posada against Basarab [137 p.257].

In 1335, another Toma, the castellan of the city of Chokalw (Hungary), had his rights reaffirmed for his memorable deeds in 1330 [137 p.258]. From another document, dating to 1358 and issued by Carol Robert, cnez Socol was granted two estates for valour in battle [187 vol. I p.388].

For Dragoș's part in the war to punish Voivode Bogdan, founder of Moldavia, in 1359, King Louis of Anjou granted him hereditary rights over the properties of the disloyal Bogdan and recognized a title of nobility for his offspring.

In 1360, Louis of Anjou granted the property Rona de Sus (Maramureș County) to Stan, son of Petru, for services rendered to the crown. In 1362, the same king granted Vlad, son of Mușat, the village of Zlaști in the County of Hunedoara for military services rendered to the crown and loyalty to the king [104 p.196].

In 1365, Dragomir was killed at the Battle of Diu (Vidin Bulgaria), while his brother was killed in Poland fighting against the Lithuanians [104 p.141]. In 1369, the Romanians complained to King Louis of Anjou that, although they had defended the cities while the king was busy with the war against Voivode Vlaicu and paid all the expenses of the army, they had been robbed by the army on their return [104 p.175].

In 1371, a document mentioning the village of Cărămida (*vero olachos Caramada*) notes the obligation of the Romanians from Banat to maintain the fortifications and *castrum* in the area [104 p.172]. In 1371, Sigismund of Luxembourg recognized the right of cnez Dobre to own the family estate in Leşnic (Hunedoara County) on condition that he should continue to provide military support to the city of Deva.

In 1371-1372, 60 Romanian cnezes from Banat were forced to provide 300 workers to complete work on the fortifications of the city of Orşova [104 p.173].

On 19.06.1376, King Louis of Anjou made a gift of the estate of Bolvaşniţa to *our Romanians Surian, Dumitru, Toma, Bogdan, and Blasiu, sons of Voicu* for *their worth and valour in many of our expeditions and especially fighting against the Serbians and Bulgarians* [137 p.145].

In a letter of King Louis of Anjou to the Voivode of Transylvania, from 1377, it transpires that the villages in Alba-Iulia were inhabited by Romanians and governed by cnezes and mayors according to the old norms of Romanian law, which were applied in all counties. The cnezes decided how the troops of riders were put together, selecting men from their schismatic Romanian villages, which together formed the *banderium* of the catholic bishop.

In 1378, King Louis of Anjou gave Mihai, Ion, and Niculae, the sons of Timan, *de genere Olacali*, an estate for valour in battle [187 vol. I p.378].

During the reign of Sigismund of Luxembourg, the Holy Roman Emperor and King of Hungary and Croatia (1387-1437), the Turks conquered Adrianopolis and threatened the territories north of the Danube. The emperor, who was at the time living in Germany, left the defence of the city to the noblemen and the Catholic bishops who would use bands of locals. Against this background, the military role of the Romanians from Banat, Haţeg, and Hunedoara can be seen as significant and this importance grew exponentially under Iancu of Hunedoara. Soldiers that distinguished themselves in battle against the Turks were "rewarded" by the recognition of old rights and by titles of nobility bestowed in the German and Catholic fashion.

A document of reconciliation between the Romanians and Saxons from 1383 mentions the duty of Romanians to *defend the mountains from Tălmaciu to Săceni* [187 vol. I p.400].

In 1387, Emperor Sigismund granted Ion Românul the estates of Iza and Apşa (Maramureş) for military valour. In 1397, Sigismund made a gift of the estate at Pogăciuni to Ladislau the Romanian from Caransebeş (Caraş-Severin County) as a reward for military services rendered [104 p.176].

In 1415, King Sigismund reconfirmed that the Romanians from Feleac were exempted from taxes for their services in defending the road to Cluj. They were also exempt from the sheep tax dating to the time of Louis of Anjou [104 p.223]. In another document dating to 1420, he acknowledged the great military services rendered in the Battle of Severin against the Turks by cnez Bogdan, son of Nicolae, son of Măgoiu [187 vol. I p.388]. Sigismund, who had been both a German king and emperor since 1433, in a document dating to 1427 refers to the Romanians from the counties of Deva and Hunedoara, who were organized as military troops and had the duty to build

Fig. 3.1. Iancu of Hunedoara (1407-1456).

fortifications and strongholds and raid beyond enemy lines. He calls these duties *an old and commendable custom* of the Romanians [50 p.170].

Rinaldo degli Albizzi (1370-1442), a Florentine diplomat in the kingdom of Hungary, writing about the peoples in the east of Europe who lived in "Slavonia", mentions the Romanians who "have a language almost like Latin" (*habent quasi Romanam linguam*) [142 p.203].

In 1428, Sigismund held a council with Romanian noblemen and cnezes from Mehadia and confirmed ownership of the estates of Ruginoasa, Toplița, and Leorgis as a reward for the sacrifice of the Romanian noblemen Mihai and Roman of Măcicașu in fighting the Turks by the Danube [104 p.177].

In the 15ᵗʰ century, we find Romanians everywhere where that the danger was greatest in Central Europe. This is confirmed by Sigismund himself in a military document from 1429, which mentions that the Romanians of Hungary were obliged to take up arms whenever the need arose. Furthermore, in 1433 the diet of the Catholic kingdom decided, faced with the Turkish peril, that Banat should be defended by Romanians, Serbians, and Cumaeans [104 p.184], with all of them abiding by Romanian law (*valachi, ruteni,* and *sclavi fidem valachorum tenentes rustici*) [5 p.75; 6 vol. II p.36]. Why did the Ruthenians and the Serbians have to observe Romanian law and why is there no mention of

Hungarians? This is because the latter were not there, while the number of the former was insignificant in comparison to the *gens grandis Olachorum*. Emperor Sigismund of Luxembourg sought to strengthen the army with territorial troops recruited from among the serfs and the free cities, as well as the Cumans and Romanians from Hungary who had military obligations imposed on them [148 vol. I p.149-150]. As some historians have noted, these people lived in Pannonia by the side of the Magyar clans. For a serf, doing military service was not just a duty, but also a right that pertained to *the status of a free man* (arms bearer), elevating one up the social hierarchy. *Even now* (in 1437, serfs) *covet the status of the old serfs of the king, who only had military duties* [148 vol. I p.153].

In 1439, the brothers Iancu and Ion of Hunedoara successfully took over the defence of the cities of Severin, Orşova, and Mehadia in Banat [5 p.74]. The defence was undertaken by Romanians and led by Romanians, as there were no other people in those parts.

In 1442, King Wladyslaw I Jagiello (1440-1444) gave the Romanians Ştefan and Mihai of Crăciuneşti the villages and estates of Crăciuneşti, Bocicău, and Lunca (Maramureş County) for military services rendered to the crown [104 p.145]. In the same year, he also gave the cnezes Nicolae and Mihai of Banat three areas in the counties of Berzeasca, Ohaba, and Toplicean for military services rendered [104 p.179]. In the longest campaign, which was led by Iancu of Hunedoara and started in 1443, the purpose of which was to occupy Adrianopolis and chase the Turks out of Europe, most of the "crusaders" were Romanians under Iancu from Transylvania and under Vlad the Impaler from Wallachia. The Romanian army occupied Sofia, but did not manage to cross the Balkans to Adrianopolis due to the onset of winter [34 p.32].

In 1444, the same king gave Voivode Chindriş of Sălaş another estate, Crivadia, for valour in fighting the Turks.

In 1446, Iancu of Hunedoara gave the Duchy of Cinciş to the nobleman Dan and his brothers for extraordinary valour in battle against the Turks. For the outstanding military merit of the nobleman Murgu, he conferred the ownership of Nădăştie on him. The next year, the nobleman Ioan, son of Cândea of Râu de Mori, received the city of Sântă Maria and the County of Toteşti for military merit [104 p.201]. All these estates were in Hunedoara County.

In 1447, Iancu of Hunedoara made a gift of the Duchy of Cuhea (MM) to Simion of Cuhea and his brother for extraordinary valour in battle against the Turks [104 p.145].

In 1449, Iancu of Hunedoara conferred the Duchy of Băieşti on Nicula, son of Ungur of Băieşti in Haţeg country, for his service and for the sacrifices made by his father during the long campaign (1443-1444) in the Balkans [201 p.122].

In 1450, *Nicolai Woywoda Wlachorum* received the village of Tăuţi (Cluj County) on condition that he continued to fulfil his military duties. In 1451, another donation was made by Iancu of Hunedoara to the brothers Dan, Suscă, and Gostoian, sons of Mihai of Săcel. They received the Duchy of Săcel for fighting the Turks [104 p.145].

During the summer of 1456, Mehmed II descended upon Belgrade with the intention of taking the city, believed at the time to be the key to conquering Europe. Iancu guessed the plans of the Ottomans and managed to gather more than 25,000 volunteers from Banat, Zarand, Transylvania, Crişana, and Maramureş. By the time the battle started, Iancu's camp had grown, reaching approximately 40,000 volunteers and mercenaries. The garrisons of the Southern Carpathians had also left for the city of Belgrade, while the southern flank of the Christians was left to be defended by Vlad the Impaler. Most of these soldiers were commoners: *agricolae, fossatores, et arattores fere inermes* (farmers, diggers, and ploughmen without arms) [34 p.55]. On July 4, Mehmed arrived at the walls of Belgrade. On July 22, Iancu occupied the Turkish camp, capturing all their cannons. Seized with panic, the Turks fled during the night of July 22/23. A royal letter from the archives of the city of Bistriţa, written at the time, invited the Voivode of Transylvania to force the Saxons to lead their contingent by the side of the contingent of Romanians from Rodna Valley.

The treatise *Cosmographia*, written during the pontificate of Pius II (Enea Piccolomini, 1458-1463), states that Transylvania was inhabited by Saxons, Szeklers, and Romanians [142 p.205].

In 1462, Matthias Corvinus gave the estate of Subcetate together with the stone tower and the border of Hateg (Hunedoara County) to the Romanian nobleman Ioan Chende for outstanding military service rendered to his father. In the same year, Matthias gave the nobleman Ioan of Ilia the counties Cicmău and Techerău as a symbol of gratitude for his valour shown in many military expeditions [104 p.202]. The Romanian nobleman Ioan of Nădăştie, from Tara Haţegului, son of that Ioan Ungur who had distinguished himself in the Crusade of Varna (1443-1444) fought by Iancu of Hunedoara, provides an example of such a military career. The younger Ioan Ungur took part in Matthias Corvinus's campaigns in Bosnia (1463-1464) and in many battles that Matthias fought against Christian princes, including: Moldavia (1467), Bohemia (1468-

1472), Poland (1472-1474), and the war against Austria from 1477 on [201 p.168].

In 1475, Sebastiano Baduario, the Venetian ambassador to the court of Matthias Corvinus, wrote the following about the Romanians from Transylvania: *They are praised above all others for their bravery against the Turks and have always fought by the side of his father* (Iancu of Hunedoara) *and by his majesty's side* [219 p.493].

Pavel Chinezu, a Romanian of humble origin from Banat, distinguished himself through bravery and military talent and was made county head of Timișoara and captain of the kingdom's army (1478). At the time, King Matthias Corvinus was fighting against his Christian neighbours. The Venetians also made peace with the Ottomans, albeit after 10 years of inconclusive fighting. Pavel Chinezu asked King Matthias to allow him to stop fighting Christians and dispatch him to the Ottoman frontline by the Danube. This is how he became county head of Timișoara and captain of the armies of Banat [201 p.152]. In 1479, Pavel Chinezu was summoned by the Voivode of Transylvania to help on the battlefield at Câmpul Pâinii. 10,000 of the 40,000 Turks that were estimated to have been on that plain had a narrow escape, fleeing the battle. Alongside Pavel Chinezu during his military campaigns were a multitude of cnezes or royal servants, all Romanian, mentioned by Ioan Hațegan in his chronicle *Banatul la 1478* [201]. Most of the people mentioned in this work were from Maramureș, Hațeg, and Banat, and this is why Ioan Hațegan was correct in noticing that there was *a Romanian party* at the court of Matthias Corvinus.

A Florentine document from 1479, recently brought to the attention of the public, provides information with respect to the men in the armies of Matthias Corvinus against the Turks: 38,000 were from Wallachia, 32,000 from Moldavia, 28,000 from Transylvania, and 14,000 from "Hungaria" [199 p.18]. Since the smaller part of "Hungaria" was made up of speakers of Hungarian, out of this 14,000, one can appreciate, from what has been already presented here, that the bulk would have been men from Banat, Crișana, and Maramureș, with the rest represented by Germans and Slovaks registered as Hungarians. The same conclusion, i.e., that only 3 % of the kingdom's army was Hungarian, has been reached by the reputed historian Ștefan Meteș [107 p.473].

In 1481, Matthias Corvinus confirmed and reaffirmed cnez Teodor as owner of his old estate for the loyal service he gave to the father of Matthias, Iancu of Hunedoara, facing great peril at Câmpia Mierlei in 1448 [187 vol. I p.388].

In 1494, King Wladyslaw II Jagiello, the Pole (1490-1516), exempted the Romanian noblemen of Hațeg from paying the tax of 200 sheep to the crown for military services rendered by defending the kingdom against the Turks [104 p.113].

Fig. 3.2. A Romanian knight.

In 1514, King Wladyslaw II Jagiello armed the peasants in order to start a crusade against the Turks. However, the peasants were more inclined to use these weapons to fight against the noblemen who had robbed them of their freedom. The rebels were joined by the Romanian gentry. A Szekely fighter (who might have been Szeklerized) by the name of Dosza climbed the ranks to lead these "crusaders" and the rebellion spread across Pannonia and Transylvania. The Slovak Ioan Zapolea, leading Romanian troops from the Banate of Severin, managed to put down the rebellion [87 p.115].

A triumphalist political historiography tells us that in 1526, at Mohács, the King of Bohemia and Hungaria perished together with *the choicest members of the Magyar nobility.* The Hungarian Pal Engel explains this as [62 p.385]:

> *...the choicest members: 2 archbishops, 5 bishops and some 20 barons.*

Among these was Filip More of Ciula (Hațeg) and Ioan Dragfy, great-grandson of Dragoș-Vodă [87 p.125], with his army of men from Maramureș. Other Romanians took part in that battle, such as those from Mohács on the Danube, who settled near Turda after the end of the battle and founded the village of Măhăceni [81].

Between 1564 and 1565, the Florentine G. Gromo was captain of the royal guards of the Prince of Transylvania. He wrote a study about the autonomy of Transylvania, which he dedicated to Cosimo de Medici. In this study he explains that not even the prince could stay in Sibiu for longer than three days and that his retinue was limited and the army stationed outside the walls of the city [5 p.11; 3 p.107].

In 1599, the Romanian nobleman Daniel of Zlaşti abandoned his position in the army of the Voivode of Transylvania and joined that of Michael the Brave [138 p.245].

In Olt country, *rusticus Valachus*, a part of the army had to be recruited at their own expense—they had to supply 200 riders and in the event of "a general call to arms, they were supposed to answer unanimously" [150 p.93].

During the time of Prince Mihai Apafi (1661-1690), who had been installed on the throne by Ali Pasha, the voivode's guard, consisting of 1,000 men, was made up of Romanians, Serbians, and Germans. [6 vol. I p.105]. A document from 1664 by Anna Bornemisza commands the Romanians Sandru, Candrea, Stanciu, and Stoica to continue their military service to the city of Făgăraş [187 vol. I p.400].

Referring to a victory in the year 1705 of poorly armed Romanians (having only pitchforks and axes) over the imperial armies, the Saxon Marc Fronius writes that the Romanians were to be feared because they might aspire to rule Transylvania [3 p.206]. Even after almost a century of Habsburg rule in Transylvania, the regular army and the border army of the empire having already been established, the "army" of the feudal lords was still formed of serfs, i.e., Romanians.

George Bariţiu noticed that while internal fighting between the magnates of Germany had by then ended, in Transylvania it lasted until the reign of Joseph II [6 vol. I p.471]. One such case was the conflict between two magnates, Nicolae Wesselenyi of Jibou and his neighbour, Count Ioan Haller of Gârbou (Cluj County). The mercurial, violent, vengeful, and irresponsible nature of Wesselenyi was well known to all. In October 1781, not being able to put up with the beatings of this magnate any longer, two serfs fled and took refuge on the estates of Count Haller. Wesselenyi demanded that Haller send his serfs back right away. Haller responded by sending him only one of the serfs who had already been proved to be Wesselenyi's, i.e., his property. Consequently, Wesselenyi decided that all the arms-bearing serfs on his estate should gather. On October 16 1781, Wesselenyi led 540 armed men (with rifles, scythes, iron forks, and bats) and headed to Gârbou where he attacked Haller, leaving behind many dead and wounded. He was condemned, but would not submit to sentence. Some years later in 1785, he was apprehended by imperial troops [6 vol. I p.472]. If this is how things were with the army of feudal lords at the end of the 18th century, it stands to reason that the army of the former kingdom relied on the serfs gathered together by feudal lords and bishops, as previously discussed.

***

After all, who else but the cnezes and the voivodes together with the locals could have made up the bulk of the army in the Catholic kingdom? Who else could have supplied soldiers for the Voivodeship of Transylvania? Who did the Magyar clans serve? For that matter, who did the Hungarian speakers serve? How did they do it? We can examine the fighting between the Catholic kings and the Magyar clans, the massacre of the first wave of crusaders made up of the poor (1096), and the battle at Câmpia Mierlei (1389) when the German Sigismund of Luxembourg, King of Croatia and Hungary, fought the internal factions to consolidate his grip on the throne, but would not take part in armed confrontation with the Ottomans alongside the rest of the Christians. The Voivode of Transylvania, the Slovak Zapolea, did not take part in the Battle of Mohács (1526), bowing to Sultan Suleiman. Then, in 1599, at Şelimbăr, Andrew Báthory, a Catholic cardinal, confronted Michael the Brave because he had made a deal with the Turks. When Pannonia was freed from Turkish rule (1683-1699), "the Hungarians" of Chieftain Tököly fought shoulder to shoulder with Turks and Tatars against the liberators, the Austrians. Again, in 1848/49, as well as in 1866 the Hungarians joined the enemies of the liberators! Even after 1940, they were allied with Hitler, whom they also ridiculed, using him for their racist-chauvinistic purposes as they pleased. The "pure" army of Hungarian speakers did not fight by the side of the Germans, but rather against civilians in Transylvania, against the unborn children of Valeria Gurzău and Tavi Isăilă's wife, against the five-year-old Rodica Petrea, against children, women, and peasants from Ip and from Trăznea, and against the Jews from Sărmaş, as we will discover in §11.3.

3.2 On their Own

In 1849, an army of peasant lancers wrote an astonishing page of history (the revolution of 1848 is dealt with in chapter 7). They were led by Avram Iancu and his tribunes, seeking both freedom and survival. Alexander von Lüders, a German general of the Czarist imperial army admitted to a French diplomat in Bucharest that:

Without the Romanians of Transylvania, conducted by Iancu, the Russians wouldn't have been able to stand against Bem [105 p.159].

Fig. 3.3. Avram Iancu (1824-1872).

20,000 men from Bem's army were immobilized by the Romanians. The Magyars made their cause into the cause of a caste, as noted by Karl Marx [105 p.159]. With respect to this moment, both Magyar and Magyarizing historiography as well as Romanian historiography note that in March 1849 the "revolutionary" Hungarian army led by a Polish general managed to "occupy" the whole of Transylvania. Not exactly all of Transylvania, for neither Alba Iulia, nor the Apuseni Mountains were actually *occupied*. Yes, the verb is correct because this is what it is all about—the occupation of a territory which, in its essence, has always been foreign to the feudal occupier. The term *occupation* was taken by Romanian and Hungarian historiographers directly from Kossuth, who wrote from Dobrâțin, on 6.01.1849, to general Bem:

> If we win the occupation [Besitz in the original], *which is so important, of Transylvania*, for as long as we own Transylvania, we will have the back of *Dobrâțin and of the area of* Tisa *secured*, then we have no way of doubting, even after 10 lost battles, the final victory of our cause [53 vol. III p.255].

Nor was it "revolutionary", if we understand properly what a revolution is. The extermination of a defenceless civilian population by gangs of soldiers and civilians of those feudal lords, shielded by the army, by units of the army that behaved with excessive cruelty, can hardly pass for a revolution. From the very beginning, they used the gallows and impalement, killing women and children, and burning villages and churches.

Iancu's first military act, at the behest of General Püchner on 18.10.1848, was to rescue a unit of dragoons from the regiment of Eugene of Savoy that was surrounded by rebels in the area of Hunedoara. He pulled this off by using a surprise attack [12 p.139]. Captain Karl Grätze, who knew him well, reports:

> *He distinguished himself through just, impeccable behaviour, as he treated the armed enemy differently from the unarmed enemy* [12 p.61].

In May-June 1849, having occupied the plain, "the Hungarians" attacked the Apuseni Mountains from all directions: Kemeny from Brad, the Ruthenian Vasvari from Huedin, Egloffstein and Papai from Turda, Iuhasz from Teius, and Kovacs from Săcărâmb (Hunedoara County). Faced with the lancers of Avram Iancu, their valour melted away. Here are two Hungarian accounts of the fighting in the mountains when Bem "occupied" Transylvania. Major Hatvani, who led the campaign against Avram Iancu, in his report to Commissioner Szentivanyi, after the campaign of 15-20 May 1849, wrote:

> *I declare only that my officers turned tail and fled right from the thick of battle and when we arrived here at Brad, only I and three other officers were left from the entire officer corps.*

He, however, failed to report that the last order he had given on the battlefield was: *Each man save himself.* Lieutenant-Colonel Inczedi, who was in Brad to support Hatvani, wrote:

> *The lack of morale is at its utmost state; the soldiers would flee at the sound of the first gunshot, and you cannot image more formidable fear amongst an army* [52 p.192].

The determined lawyer, Axente Sever, hurried to where the danger loomed largest, from Geoagiu, Alba-Iulia, Teiuş, and Aiud to Brad and Zlatna. On 17.05.1849, when the Hungarians had almost conquered the field, Axente broke the blockade of Bem (officers Stein and Kemeny) and entered Alba Iulia with an 800-strong army [6 vol. II p.497]. From the north, the women of Motz came to their aid with stones and bats. On 6.07.1849, "the Hungarians", that is, the Vienna legion (young men from Vienna who wanted Austria to become part of the German Reich) led by the Ruthenian Paul Vasvári, attacked Motz from the north. At Fântânele, the Motz women led by Pelaghia Roşu, chased them away. Avram Iancu was not only an outstanding strategist, but also a man of impeccable morals.

The elementary goal of the people—the liberation of the peasants from feudal bondage—was achieved by "counter-revolutionaries", if we were to accept the infelicitous logic (see the exceptional *Older Notes Regarding our 1948 Revolution* by David Prodan [150, Annex D]) of Hungarian historiography! The poet Octavian Goga stated in his speech on the 100th anniversary of Iancu's birth that *the war fought by the Romanians in Transylvania against the feudal occupant was the first campaign of the war for independence.*

3.3 In the Army of the Empire

In 1687, the arrival of the imperial armies in Transylvania meant the imposition of the "iron yoke": 260 florins per gate in 1688 compared to the Turkish "wooden yoke" of 36 florins per gate in 1680 [150 p.119], combined with the greediness of the tax collectors and executors [6 vol. I p.152]. A *gate* meant 10 families who had to pay tax to the Ottoman sovereign and then to the Habsburg sovereign in addition to the taxes and labour due to the local feudal lords. Under the Leopoldian Diploma of 4.12.1691, Transylvania was required to raise tax from 50,000 imperials, as required during peace times, to 400,000 Renanian florins (a Renanian florin was about 3.2 gr. Au, whereas an imperial was 4 florins and 30 creițari (a Transylvanian coin) and a florin was 60 creițari). The maintenance, supply, and billeting of the army, during both peace and war, was supported by the Romaian bondsmen and free Saxon peasants, in the most demanding way possible.

Maria Theresa (1740-1780) needed new recruits for her war against Prussia. She addressed the Diet of Pressburg (Bratislava) in 1741, calling for support from the Hungarian magnates. In response, these magnates drew their swords and theatrically shouted: *Vitam et sanguinem pro rege nostro Maria Theresia*! Then, they left for home and sent the empress Romanian regiments [190 p.13].

In 1744, when Empress Maria Theresa requested a new recruitment drive, "the noblemen" refused and, after lengthy argument, the Diet of Sibiu voted to send a regiment of 1,000 horse-riders comprising: 48 Saxons, 112 Szeklers, and the rest being Romanians [6 vol. I p.376].

The border regiments were set up by Maria Theresa in 1763 in the Romanian districts of Năsăud, Orlat, and Caransebeș, and in the so-called Szekler districts of Turda-Ciuc and Trei Scaune ("Three Seats"), but these regiments were primarily comprised of Romanian soldiers, as we shall see. The expenses incurred by military equipping and maintenance were borne by the population of the respective districts, that is, the Romanians! The Romanian battalions of regiments were termed *phalanx valahica prima*, *secunda*, and *tertia*, which was an indirect form of recognition for the heroism manifested by the Transylvanian border regiments. These names were maintained in the orders of the day of the Austrian army until 1852.

In the last war between Maria Theresa and Frederic II of Prussia over the Bavarian succession (1778-1779), the imperial officers acknowledged how bravely the Romanian regiments fought [190 p.12]. Captain Carl Klein described the Romanian border soldiers as follows:

They have fought all wars with courage, boldness, resistance, cold blood and bravery, beautiful qualities recognized by the great army leaders of the 19th century: Emperor Napoleon and Archduke Carol [120 p.52].

Archduke Carol confronted Napoleon in Aspern and Essling in 1809 with notable success.

On 8.06.1790, during the Austrian-Russian-Turkish war, the Austrian troops, including the 2nd Romanian Border Regiment, besieged the city of Giurgiu. Three Austrian battalions of a line regiment were surrounded by the Turks and were facing total annihilation.

In that decisive moment, the two border-guard battalions formed a square, on whose right and left sides were their sharpshooters as well as 160 Romanian volunteer horse-riders; thus, they advanced slowly, spreading death and destruction among the Turks [...] they broke through their ranks with unstoppable momentum and reached their surrounded comrades [120 p.87].

In the opinion of Captain Carl Klein, this is where one of the most outstanding feats of valour of the Regiment of Năsăud took place. At the famous Battle of Arcole, from the 15th to the 17th November 1796, the French army, led by a young general called Bonaparte, defeated the Austrians. Bonaparte sought to surround the enemy by crossing the Alpone River. But there was one obstacle standing in the way of a great victory: the *phalanx valahica secunda*. 396 Romanians lost their lives, but Bonaparte could not cross the bridge. Two more French attacks were rebuffed by the Romanians. More than that, the Romanians from Năsăud took 350 French prisoners. It was not Bonaparte, but a cold and calculating general who solved the problem of the Romanian defence at the Bridge of Arcole. He ordered General Guyenau to come from Ronco to Arcole with the reserve brigade and occupy the left bank of the river. By the time the reserve brigade arrived, the bridge had been cleared and the city of Arcole evacuated. The Austrian general withdrew the Romanian battalion while regrouping his army so as to to hold out against the French, who were whittling away the Austrian forces. The first step taken by the Austrian general, which proved to be decisive, was to place the bulk of his forces in Arcole. Bonaparte himself, in a document addressed to the Directorate of the Republic, explained that it was the resistance of this battalion that prevented him from surrounding and crushing the Austrian army. Bonaparte failed to encircle the main forces of the Austrians at Arcole, but by adapting his tactics he managed to separate General

Wurmser from General Alvinzi. Finally, Wurmser capitulated and Alvinzi was defeated after five days of fighting.

In 1848, in Transylvania, apart from the three exclusively Romanian regiments of border guards, there were also the imperial regiments of Bianchi (partially Romanian), Siskovich (exclusively Romanian), and Carol Ferdinand (mostly Romanian). The Carol Ferdinand Regiment from Cluj, led by General Kahlbrun and Colonel Fiedler, was made up of Romanian troops [217 p.231]. The three Szekler regiments were also made up of Romanians: *By 1849, the men of Măhăceni (Cluj County) served as horse-riding border guards in the Szekely regiment* [81 p.35]. Other Romanian regiments were found in other parts of the empire, for example, the infantry regiments Spleny and Orosz, as well as the cavalry regiment Toscana [100 p.119].

1866 was a disastrous year for the Habsburg Empire whose image was severely damaged. The defeats in Bohemia (Königgraetz-Sadova-Czech Republic) by Prussia are hard to explain and the betrayal of certain regiments stirred by Hungarian conspirators cannot fully justify them. In the midst of this general disaster, one of the few heroic pages in the history of Austria was written by the Romanian regiments at Trautenau (27.06.1866) where General Gablenz defeated the Prussian II Army Corps. Another such page was written at Olmütz (Czech Republic) and at Biskupitz, on 14.07.1866, when two companies of Regiment 64 Orăştie made a Prussian Cuirassier regiment flee [131 p.120]. The last "Austrian" heroic page of history was written by the Romanian David Urs, commander of the fortified Isle of Lissa (today Vis isle, Croatia), against naval attack from the Adriatic. With 1,800 men at his disposal, he made a laughing stock of the fleet of Italy led by Admiral Persano [6 vol. III p.408]. Meanwhile, other people, such as General Georg Klapka who was a German from Timişoara and a "Hungarian revolutionary", in 1848 were seeking to stir up trouble among Slovaks and Poles in the Habsburg Empire in the name of "revolutionary Hungary", encouraging them to rebel against Austria [131 p.116]. Those who profited from this disastrous era of Austria were not heroes, but traitors [6 vol. III, p.413]. After 1866, by law, the "noblemen" of Transylvania exempted themselves of military service to the monarchy!

In 1907, the Hungarians petitioned the emperor to allow the Hungarian language to replace the regimental language for the regiments from Hungary. The emperor declined, which was an exceptional decision for the generally inadequate Franz Joseph I. The imperial answer is worth paying attention to: the number of those who spoke Hungarian was too small and so this measure would have been unpopular and would have created discontent [132 p.62]. This meant that, at that time in Hungary, too few people spoke Hungarian to force a change in regimental language despite Magyarization! As a reaction to this imperial refusal, the famous law of "total Magyarization" was developed and implemented through schools for those who held *their heads high* in international congresses like Apponyi. In spite of all this, the pressure of chauvinism and the culture of hatred was so great that, in 1914, even the enrolled Saxons spoke Hungarian, and the Romanians fighting on the frontline were beaten, whipped, and bullied for not understanding the Hungarian spoken by officers who believed themselves to be "Magyar" [172].

On 5.02.1907, Deputy A. Vaida-Voevod said in the Parliament of Budapest:

Of 47 regiments, 14-17 have a Hungarian majority and at least 30 are regiments with a non-Hungarian majority ... If we take stock of this situation [...] we reach the conclusion that only the regiments 68 Solnoc, 46 Seghedin, and 38 Kecskemét are exclusively Hungarian, which means only 3 regiments in total, whereas all the others are not. Quite the opposite, in fact ... I cannot help but notice that there would be even more completely non-Hungarian regiments if the Jews in the regiments weren't considered Hungarian [166 p.240].

In 1909, there was only one regiment where Romanian was spoken; all the rest had been formally "Magyarized". However, the command language remained German [112 p.31].

In 1914, Austria-Hungary fired its cannons for the first time over Belgrade during the Great War. Consequently, more than 80,000 young Romanian men took refuge in the Kingdom of Romania. Additionally, more than 1,734 were arrested and their assets seized. In the autumn of 1914, there were half a million Romanians from Transylvania in the K&K army [141 p.311]. Thus we have half a million men from Transylvania; but how many were from Banat, Crișana, Sătmar, Maramureș, and *Țara de sus* (Buchenland, as the Austrians called it)? How many of the Romanians from Transylvania passed as Magyar? Tens of thousands of young Romanians from Transylvania were in America in the midst of the Great War. When President Woodrow Wilson addressed the American nation and made an appeal to build an army of volunteers, in just the first few months more than 17,000 people from Transylvania and Bucovina tried to sign up [132 p.122]. They could not enrol, however, because American law did not allow it, as they were citizens of an enemy state. Through the efforts of Ioan Podea from Youngstown, those men from Transylvania who had gained American citizenship organized themselves into an

American company of Romanian nationality (Heavy Weapons Company 112). This does not include the 17,000 volunteers, who were subjects of Franz Joseph I and had crossed the border to Canada for the same purpose of fighting for Romanian unity and against the feudal regime.

In 1915, more than 55 priests were sentenced to death by hanging. According to the journal *Pester Lloyd*, by the end of 1916 there were more than 2,500 Romanians in Hungarian prisons, among them lawyers, school teachers, and priests [163 p.328].

According to the "Hungarian Census" of 1910, which is full of misinformation, only 6.27 % of the population was Romanian speaking; however, Romanian speakers accounted for more than 33 % of the army! They would have accounted for more if so many had not been forced to emigrate to America and Romania. Being 6.27 % of the population, but 33 % of the army, would thousands of emancipated young men have refused to die for a state that denied the minimum rights of recognition of their existence? This provides yet another piece of indirect evidence of the chauvinism in Budapest. Given the estimate of 33 % of the entire K&K army being Romanian, let us see if we can actually verify this percentage, at least indirectly. According to the Astra Dictionary of 1898, the peacetime numbers of the empire's army were 19,793 officers, 273,503 men, and 52,515 horses [197 vol. I p.327]. This gives a total of 292,296 men. In 1908, there were concerns in the empire about the incorporation of Bosnia and Herzegovina. Although it did not pose a serious military problem, still the guerrilla war claimed many Romanian lives. Let us assume, therefore, that, in 1910, the total number for the K&K army in peacetime reached 300,000. According to Liviu Maior [100 p.110], quoting Deak Istvan (*Beyond nationalism. A social and political History of the Habsburg Officer Corps, 1848-1918*), the Romanian force amounted to 103,814, that is, more than one third.

During wartime, considering the devious ways of the culture of hatred, the proportion of Romanians must have been a lot greater. In 1910, the professional officer corps was: 78.7 % German; 9.3 % "Hungarian"; 4.8 % Czech; and 0.9 % Romanians. The reserve officers were: 60.2 % German; 23.7 % "Hungarian"; 9.7 % Czech; and 0.6 % Romanian [205 p.356]. We do not know what the largest contingent of the K&K army consisted of, but we do know the Romanians accounted for at least one third of it.

The enlisting of Romanians as cannon fodder continued throughout the war! According to more recent evaluations, for WWI in Transylvania and Banat alone about 500,000 Romanians were recruited by the K&K army [131 p.199; 141 p.311]. We also do not know how many Romanians were registered in the military as ethnic Hungarians! Based on the documents

*Fig. 3.4. Volunteer officers from Transylvania and Bucovina are welcomed
by General Prezan in Iasi.*

that we do have, as biased as they may be, the expendable component of
the K&K army was predominantly Romanian. What about the Romanians
from Banat, Bucovina, Crişana, Sătmar, and Maramureş? The problem of
the ethnic makeup of the K&K army remains to be thoroughly researched
and studied. The work by Teodor V. Păcăţian (*The Sacrifices of the
Romanians of Transylvania, Banat. Crişana, Sătmar and Maramureş in
the War from 1914 to 1918*) must be continued [100 p.126]. In terms of
Romanians victimized by the K&K army, we have at least the data left by
Octavian Tăslăuanu regarding Territorial Regiment 23 Sibiu (three
battalions: in Sibiu, Deva, and Făgăraş) and 11 Company from 3 Battalion
Făgăraş, which he led in the disastrous campaign in Galicia from
September to November 1914: only 4.85 % of 3,500 people in the
regiment survived, while of the 267 people of 11 Company, only six
survived, i.e., 2.24 % [172 p.243]. At the same time, the so-called
Hungarian companies in Pannonia did not see any action, remaining
behind the frontlines. The quality of command in the K&K army was
beyond description [172] and can be summed up with three words:
stupidity, *bureaucracy*, and *chauvinism*. One should not mistake the
territorial regiments (reserves aged over 30) for the line regiments, which
were regular army, permanent, and commanded by career officers, i.e.,
Territorial Regiment 23 Sibiu was different to Infantry Regiment 31 Sibiu,
etc.

Ethnic Romanian regiments were brought mainly to the Serbian and
Galician fronts (the campaigns of 1914 and 1915), and then to the Italian

front, avoiding the Russian front as much as possible, where there were many Romanians from Bessarabia and Transnistria, and, later on, the Romanian front. Given the numerous changes of sides of the Romanian soldiers in Galicia in 1914 [172], the newly formed regiments of 1915, from Banat, Crişana, Maramureş, Bucovina, and Transylvania, were sent directly to the southern fronts.

In the autumn of 1918, the K&K army disintegrated for ethnic and social reasons. When the Bolshevik revolutions and the revolutions for the liberation of minorities in the empire took place, some Romanian troops were on the Italian front, others were in Vienna (Regiment 64 Orăştie), Bohemia (Regiment 2 Braşov), and Prague (Regiment 51 Cluj), while still others were at the French front.

20,000 troops, soldiers, and officers were stationed in Prague. The exit from the monarchy, proclaimed by the Czechs, on 28.10.1918, was protected by the Romanian regiments in Prague. Captain Alexandru Simeon not only refused the orders of his superiors to block the Czechs, but the Romanian troops under his command disarmed the loyalist units commanded by generals Kastranek and Stütsche. They offered weapons and ammunition to the Czech detachments. They also maintained contact with General Ioan Boeriu (1859-1949) and Lieutenant Iuliu Maniu, who controlled, militarily and politically, Vienna, Prague, and Budapest [100 p.140]. In Salzburg, Colonel Fleşeriu arranged the welcoming of the Romanian regiments, arriving in compact and orderly groups from the front lines, and directed them to Vienna and Budapest. In Regiment 64 Orăştie, formerly on the Italian front, the German commander handed over command to Captain Octavian Loichiţa. The priests of the regiments held services on 3.11.1918 to *unbind* the soldiers from the oath they had taken to the emperor. The officers and soldiers were sworn to "the Romanian nation" and King Ferdinand of Romania [100 p.141].

Fig. 3.5. Marshal of the K&K, Ioan Boeriu, master over Vienna, Prague, and Budapest.

Regiment 64 Orăștie, headquartered in the Franz Ferdinand Barracks, was, at the time, in charge of public order and safety in Vienna. In Vienna and Neustadt, there were 40,000 Romanian soldiers and officers, according to some sources, and 50,000 according to other sources.

At the express request of the imperial war minister, Rudolf Stäger-Steiner, who was confronted with general insubordination, the Romanian units chased away a Bolshevik rally, guarded the armaments and food stores, and re-established public order in Vienna. In recognition, Carol I, before abdicating, granted Ioan Boieriu the rank of Marshall! As an instance of historical irony, the Romanian regiments, ideologically intact, very orderly, conservative, and hostile to anarchy given their rural spirit, re-established order in the imperial capital, which had fallen prey to chaos, robbery, and Bolshevism; the same capital city which had refused to grant equal citizenship status to the Romanians in Transylvania!

Romanian sailors in the ports of the Adriatic Sea supported the formation of the Serbian-Croat-Slovenian state. In a declaration given on 13.11.1918, the Romanian Sailors on the Istria Peninsula pledged allegiance to the Romanian National Council in Arad, as the former imperial authorities had disappeared.

Regiment 50 Alba-Iulia, occupied the barracks of the royalist officers in Budapest and supported the secessionist forces and the creation of an independent Hungarian State. After re-establishing order in Vienna, Salzburg, Prague, and Budapest, the Romanian troops came home and formed the national guards to ensure the security of the Transylvanian people, which had been severely challenged by the criminal gangs of the former feudal "landlords".

A year later, Hungary, detached from the imploding empire, was Bolshevized and attacked Czechoslovakia and Romania. The Romanian army, now including many Transylvanians, crossed the Tisa, occupied Budapest, and obtained a capitulation on August 1, 1919. Everywhere they were received as liberators from the terror of the "red bands".

When the Romanian army was preparing to leave Hungary, the Hungarian prefect of Szablociu interceded with the Romanian army headquarters to prolong their stay in Hungary and to protect the population from the red armies; a month later, the Romanian army received a similar request, but this time it was motivated by the population's fear of the reaction of the white guards [71 p.134].

CHAPTER 4

TRANSYLVANIA:
A COUNTRY ISOLATED OR PROTECTED?

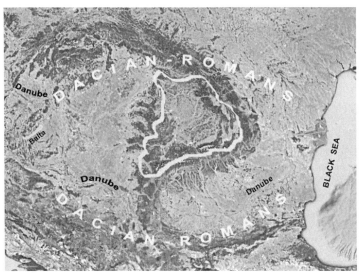

Fig. 4.1. Transylvania: the centre of the Dacian-Romans.

Of the provinces that witnessed Romanian ethnogenesis, Transylvania and Maramureș were the best protected from the whirl of migrating peoples in the 4th to the 10th centuries. Transylvania had been the nucleus of the Dacian state and the centre of the Roman province of *Dacia Felix*. This was noted by the diplomat Nicolae Titulescu and, long before him, by Mihai Eminescu:

> *The mountains separate the Romanians into parts, although these mountains, which preserved their nationality in the Middle Ages, constitute today an enduring barrier in the way of their unification, there arose intellectual contact between the various provinces in which these people lived. Most curious and most important of all is the unity of their language,*

and of their legal, religious, and family customs [59 p.37].

A similar historical conclusion was arrived at by David Prodan:

> *The precariousness of the past meant that the mountains represented stability, whereas the plains saw change and instability. Not the mountains, but the plains and steppes are the classic locus for nomadic life. Given the economic potential of the soil, the density of the highlanders was undoubtedly high in those years. The census of 1785 ordered by Joseph II shows the following figures: Bucium: 2,761 inhabitants; Ponor: 2,705; Abrud village: 2,621; Bistra: 2,838; Lupşa: 2,688; Râmeţi: 2,433; Câmpeni: 5,456; Râu Mic (Vidra): 4,376; Râu Mare: 8,308* [our note: all in these places are located in the mountains]. *These figures compete with those for the most populated villages in the field, to say nothing of the figures for the town populations. Thus, the same census gives for Alba-Iulia: 4,777 inhabitants; Mediaş: 4,484; Orăştie: 3,190; Sighişoara: 5,481; Târgu Mureş: 5,196; Bistriţa: 4,566. The mountains provide a haven for natural growth, as well as a shelter from danger* [150 p.157].

In this intra-Carpathian space, the seats of judges have been preserved since ancient times and the cnezates were formed. The cnezates, dukedoms, and "countries" with judges, chairs of judges, cnezes, and voivodes were formed, as elsewhere in the foundational area of the Romanian people—from the Adriatic to the Black Sea and along the banks of the Danube. We have "countries" or "lands" (Ţări) everywhere, including: Almaş, Haţeg, Severin, Banat, Zarand, Beiuş, Codru, Lăpuş, Oaş, Maramureş, Bârsa, and Olt, etc. Just on the western side, from Maramureş to Severin, we have about 20 "countries" [194 vol. III p.425].

According to historian Gheorghe Brătianu, it is in this intra-Carpathian space that both Ţara Muntenească (the country of Wallachia) and Ţara Moldovenească (the country of Moldova) emerged, as proven by historical tradition. However, the "popular Romanians" filled the entire space around the axis of the middle and lower Danube, inhabited by aborigines rather than those who migrated there starting in the 4th century right up until the final wave of nomads arrived. No less protected was the forest belt outside the Carpathian Arch, that is, east of Siret, south of the Gaetic Piemonts, and west of the mountains of Banat and the country of Crişuri, not to mention Maramureş, which was also surrounded by mountains. To this we should add the Carpathian forest belt, with plain and oak forests, which occupied, except for the meadows by the rivers, almost the entirety of Dacian-Roman territory. The Romanist Ernst Gamillscheg, studying the frequency and localization of Romanian words of Latin origin, found the heartland of the Romanian people to stretch as far as the Apuseni

Mountains and Crişana [68 p.43]. Hence, a single conclusion arises, also drawn by Nicolae Titulescu: in their early period of existence, the Romanian people were protected by the mountains. On the one hand, the mountains protected the intra-Carpathian Romanians, while on the other, they weakened them, as they failed to develop enough state and military organization, considering the aggression that was to come.

The aggression of the nomads noted here was not, *per se*, insignificant in itself, but pales rather in comparison to the terrible religious aggression that followed. The Carpathians with its forest belt ensured the protection of the entire Trans and Cisalpine area. It was from this intra-Carpathian space, after early Catholic conversion, that some Romanians crossed the Carpathians and formed villages of "ungureni" (Hungarians) and "săcuieni" (Szeklers), which lasted for centuries.

The serfs with their wives and children were pledged and sold to and by feudal landlords after 1514; this was also the case for the clergy. The serfs and their families, houses, and animals were used as guarantees by their feudal landlords for monetary loans, or for settling other personal needs. For instance: the Alba Chapter (the gathering of the Catholic monks) *donated two serfs for eternity* to a feudal landlord in the year 1554 [148 vol. I p.470]. In 1589, Barbara B. sold to Lazăr F. for 24 florins 3 houses of serfs (families, houses, and lands), received as a wedding gift [148 vol. I p.472].

The diet of 1522 dealt with the serfs who had moved from the lands of the great magnates after the riot of 1514 and asked the king to persuade the foreign princes to return such runaway serfs, *as otherwise the lands of the border would become deserted* [148 vol. I p.430]. The Transylvanian Diet of April 1593 at Alba-Iulia noted that the serfs were gathering in large groups and were committing a crime by going to the Romanian countries without paying tax [148 vol. I p.445]. The serfs, that is, Romanians, were not just fleeing to the Romanian countries, and so the Alba Iulia Diet of November 1599 decided that those serfs who ran to the free Szeklers, supposedly for freedom's sake, but actually because of the tax burden, should be hanged [148 vol. I p.446]. Therefore, they would not stay free for long, as Mihai Cserei bitterly observed, because the freedom of the Szeklers would soon be suppressed in response.

In 1662, the Transylvanian prince Mihai Apafi wrote to the Saxons in Bistriţa that the poor, i.e., the Romanians, were running to Moldova because of hunger and he asked them to guard the roads and even the paths well, because if they all went, who was going to pay tax to the sultan? [68 p.55].

As such, due to the feudal dues, which were a heavy burden, and since they were entirely at the disposal of feudal landlords up to their lives, and, later on, due to forced Magyarization, Romanians *emigrated* to their brothers in the extra-Carpathian spaces of the east and south, or, by the beginning of the 20th century, to America.

There are no known mass emigrations from south of the Danube, apart from the Serbs, who ran away from their homeland north of Danube in response to Turkish oppression. However, fictitious emigrations have appeared in the historiography of some researchers of historic "rights". Still, if the mountains protected the Romanians, did they not also separate them? The answer is no, as Lucian Blaga along with many others have stated referring to the lack of Romanian dialects among the Romanians north of the Danube!

Were the mountains somehow at least an economic barrier? Let us examine the exports and imports of Transylvania in florins with the various Romanian countries and with Hungary in the years 1837 and 1838 [150 p.160].

		The Romanian Countries	Hungary and the Austrian Provinces
1837	Exp.	2,947,169	64,569
	Imp.	3,186,835	285.199
1838	Exp.	2,995,891	89,144
	Imp.	4,157,055	172,408

The overwhelming differences are clear and need no comment.

CHAPTER 5

THE GENETIC STRUCTURE OF THE POPULATIONS OF THE DANUBE BASIN

5.1 The Genetic Makeup of the European Population

In the wake of establishing considerably improved methods of extracting/restoring DNA from fossilized bones, we can objectively rewrite history starting with the origin of man [117]. These new methods of extracting/restoring DNA from the bones of bodies that lived many hundreds of thousands of years ago allow us to estimate that the DNA of today's European population (with slight variations) is comprised of ~1.5 % Neanderthal, ~0.8 % Denisovan, and ~97.7 % *Homo sapiens*. The presence of the Denisovans was only discovered about 10-15 years ago. Accurate knowledge about the genetic makeup of the European population enables us to rectify the widespread confusion that still lingers in European historiography to this day. For example, the Turkic-Uralic-Mongolian migratory peoples left almost no genetic traces in Europe, but were completely assimilated.

Neanderthals were hunter gatherers and their presence in Europe has been dated to as early as 700,000 years ago. As such, there must have been some kind of symbiosis with the Denisovans that is traceable in our genes, but not yet in our historiography. *Homo sapiens* came along in a succession of three waves over several millennia. Given the wide gap between these waves, subsequent migrants would have found an established local population where the previous wave had been assimilated. During the Palaeolithic, ~50,000 years ago, the Neanderthals saw a first wave of *Homo sapiens* hunter gatherers coming in from the Near East—a population somewhat more adaptable than the "hosts" and perhaps more fertile [117]. This migration occurred gradually, one valley at a time. Those *Homo sapiens* who remained in the Near East, in the region called the Fertile Crescent (Syria, Iraq, Lebanon, and Israel), began to grow plants and domesticate animals. Consequently, the population grew, driving further migration, with one branch heading towards the

Indus valley and the other towards Europe. This second wave of *Homo sapiens*, consisting of Neolithic farmers, entered Europe along the Danube valley some 10,000-8,000 years ago (8,000-6,000 B.C.). These newcomers started the great European Neolithic civilisations of Vinca, Turdaş, Hamangia, and Boian-Gumelnița etc., as well as the amazing Cucuteni (all found in present-day Romania). ~ 6,000 years ago (4,000 BC) a third wave of *Homo sapiens* came from east of the Dniester River—the Yamnaya population, Indo-Europeans from the northern shore of the *Pontus Euxinus* (Black Sea). These Indo-Europeans were shepherds and had domesticated the horse. As such, their migration was much faster than that of their predecessors. These Indo-Europeans—Bronze Age Thracians, Celts, Germans, and Slavs—imposed their ruling warrior elites on exisiting populations. The Indo-Europeans left traces in the newly formed languages that were common to the Thracians, Celts, Germans, and Slavs. There is perhaps only one cultural curiosity in today's mosaic of European nations: the Basques—a people who, although genetically identical to all the other Europeans, continue to speak a language with Neolithic roots from before the Indo-European Celts arrived. The Inuit are probably the only genetic exception in this picture.

The Romanian physicians Petru Râmneanţu and Petru David attempted to scientifically establish the ethnic origins of the population in southeastern Transylvania based on blood. In 1935 they published the results of their research in the work *Research into the ethnic origin of the population in south-east Transylvania based on serological traces in blood* in the journal *Buletinul eugenic şi biopolitic* (The Eugenic and Biopolitical Journal). After 10,600 serological tests on the Szeklers, the research found that their blood index was overwhelmingly identical to that of the Romanian inhabitants and significantly different from the blood index of the actual Turano-Turkic-Mongols. The distribution frequency of the AB0 blood groups, rich in antigen A (European Thracian) and poor in antigen B (Asian), was the same as that of the Romanians! With such clear scientific determination, the logical conclusion could not be more obvious! A handful of defenders of unidentified origin, the Szeklers, sent to keep travellers safe against the Cumaean-Mongol invasions, could not have changed the ethnicity of the intra-Carpathian population. In his book, Milton G. Lehrer observes:

> *Here is an appendix of history, which the Hungarians could not have foreseen when they began their ill-fated endeavour of transforming a thoroughly Romanian territory into a purely Hungarian land* [91 p .172].

Today, paleogenetics and comparative DNA analysis validate the above-mentioned studies and contribute new data to the study of history. Moreover, the anthropological features of the Romanian population and that of the Romanians assimilated in Hungarian communities are completely different from the Hungarian ones [5 p.86].

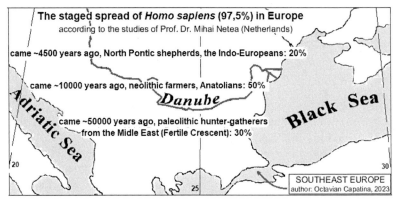

Fig. 5.1. The Danube valley corridor in the migrations of Homo sapiens.

After the Turks were expelled from the plains of the Danube, Austrian statistics reveal that in 1725, 19 % of the inhabitants were Hungarian speakers in Buda and Pest, and in the fictitious kingdom, 62 years later this was 29 %. This means 19 % were Hungarian speakers in 1725 and 29 % in 1787. But how many of these were assimilated citizens and how many native Magyars? Today, genetics can resolve this dilemma. Two studies issued by the *Institute of Genetics* of the *Hungarian Academy* have shed some light. For the benefit of the public, we provide in the following text some definitions borrowed from Corneliu Tarba (Professor of Cell Biology, University of Cluj-Napoca; PhD Cornell University, USA):

Genetic polymorphism in a population involves the possible existence of several types/sequences of nucleotides in a specific area of a DNA strand. Certain genetic characteristics, which are passed on maternally, can be studied in sequences of mitochondrial DNA (mtDNA), since mitochondria are inherited exclusively from the mother. Paternal kinship can be studied from the DNA in the Y-chromosome, which is passed on from father to son. The term haplogroup generally refers to a genealogical group that has the same origin, most likely in a common ancestor.

5.2 A Genetic Analysis of the Maternal Lineage in Hungarian-speaking Populations

The article *Comparison of maternal lineage and biogeographic measurements of ancient and modern Hungarian populations* [223] analyses the maternal lineage of today's Hungarian-speaking populations. Below, we briefly present its conclusions.

In order to study the continuity in maternal lineage between ancient and modern Hungarian populations, polymorphisms in the HVSI and protein coding regions of mitochondrial DNA sequences of 27 ancient samples (10th-11th centuries), 101 modern Hungarian, and 76 modern Hungarian-speaking Szekler samples from Transylvania were analysed. The data were compared with sequences derived from 57 European and Asian populations, including Finno-Ugric populations, and statistical analyses were performed to investigate their genetic relationships. Only 2 of 27 ancient Hungarian samples are unambiguously Asian: the rest belong to one of the western Eurasian haplogroups, but some Asian affinities, and the genetic effect of populations who came into contact with ancient Hungarians during their migrations are seen. Strong differences appear when the ancient Hungarian samples are analysed according to apparent social status, as judged by grave goods. Commoners show a predominance of mtDNA haplotypes and haplogroups (H, R, T), common in west Eurasia, while high-status individuals, presumably conquering Hungarians, show a more heterogeneous haplogroup distribution, with haplogroups (N1a, X) which are present at very low frequencies in modern worldwide populations and are absent in recent Hungarian and Szekler populations. Modern Hungarian-speaking populations seem to be specifically European. Our findings demonstrate that significant genetic differences exist between the ancient and recent Hungarian-speaking populations, and no genetic continuity is seen [223].

The results of this mtDNA study indicate that only 2 out of 27 old samples were of Asian origin (Cuman, Pecheneg, Turkish, Avar, and Hungarian).

5.3 Y-chromosome Analysis of Hungarian-speaking Populations

The 2008 study *Y-chromosome analysis of ancient Hungarian and two modern Hungarian-speaking populations from the Carpathian Basin* [224] written by a team from the *Institute of Genetics* in Seghedin of the *Hungarian Academy* confirms Râmneanţu and David's studies. The population we see today is, in fact, the result of the assimilation of a pre-existing population into the Hungarian-speaking community.

The Hungarian-speaking population linguistically belongs to the Finno-Ugric branch of the Uralic family. The Tat C allele is a marker found/distributed in all Finno-Ugric speaking populations except for Hungarians [224]. The researchers of the Hungarian Academy in Szeged asked whether the ancestral Hungarians who settled in Pannonia and the Szeklers who settled a few centuries later in the Carpathian Bend had this polymorphism or not. Below we present the final two sentences of the abstract of the paper:

> *The two modern Hungarian-speaking populations, based on 22 Y-chromosomal binary markers, share similar components described for other Europeans, except for the presence of the haplogroup P*(xM173) in Szekler samples, which may reflect a Central Asian connection, and a high frequency of haplogroup J in both Szeklers and Hungarians. MDS* [our note: multidimensional scaling] *analysis based on haplogroup frequency values, confirms that modern Hungarian and Szekler populations are genetically closely related, and similar to populations from Central Europe and the Balkans.*

Prof. Corneliu Tarba made the following comment on this abstract of the paper *Y-chromosome analysis of ancient Hungarian and two modern Hungarian-speaking populations from the Carpathian Basin*:

> *We should not forget that this analysis belongs to Hungarian authors. Therefore, despite the appearance of scientific objectivity, and since their data treatment lacks a solid statistical basis, I have certain reservations. If for the so-called Szeklers, a population of probably several hundred thousand, a sample of almost 100 individuals is somewhat adequate, for the 9 million Hungarians an adequate sample would have to be at least 1,000 individuals, and at least 27 samples should have been used for the ancient populations, as was done in the mtDNA study. This begs the question: How come only 4 samples were chosen, out of which, miraculously, 2 revealed Asian features? Anyway, according to these Hungarian authors themselves, they are only speakers of Hungarian. The statement about the close relationship between Hungarians and the Szeklers based on the close frequency inside the haplogroup (actually, the J haplogroups, because there are more than one) is a bit far-fetched. I think that the conclusions of the paper are presented more objectively, although both texts omit to mention the presence and the related genetic characteristics of the Romanians.*

The conclusions of the authors of the study *Y-chromosome analysis of ancient Hungarian and two modern Hungarian-speaking populations from* *the Carpathian Basin* [224] offer a more precise analysis than the abstract. The Hungarian researchers found: 1) that the Tat C allele, which is widespread in Uralic-speaking populations, was present in the ancient Hungarian population when it came to Pannonia; and 2) that there was an absence of the Tat C allele in recent Hungarian-speaking populations, except for one male subject from the Szekler group. They explain this contrast by the use of political-historical arguments. Thus, they believe that despite the relative linguistic stability, the lack of the Tat C allele can be attributed to the mixing of the old Hungarians, a dominant elite, and numerous post-Magyar people. The language of the warriors was accepted by the larger pre-existing population (mostly Slavs and Avars). However, although the researchers found, in line with previous studies, that Hungarian-speaking populations are closely related genetically to their geographic neighbours, they contradict this in the conclusions they have drawn. To sum up, the argument goes that when the Hungarians came to Pannonia at the beginning of the 10th century, they found Slavs and Avars, although today's Hungarian speakers are closely related to the Balkan populations (they do not tell us which ones) and Czechs and Slovaks! There is one exception—the haplogroup P*(xM173) found in one individual of the 97 surveyed, which is almost absent in continental Europe. However, they admit that *there is an increased frequency of haplogroup J.* This *may* reflect contributions from Anatolian and southern Balkan groups (which ones—Greeks, Bulgarian, Albanians—they do not tell us) to the Hungarian and Szekler gene pools. But, in true Hungarian political spirit, the authors continue in the same vein, suggesting that *the historical data* and the analyses of the maternal filiations of the Magyar nomads support the idea *that the previous migrations of the Hungarians* could also have contributed to the presence of haplogroup J in the Carpathian Basin [224]. We might say it is astonishing that genetics researchers would take up such political fantasies. How could this happen? The warriors of the Magyar tribes crossed the Danube coming from north of the Black Sea in the year 895 where they fought with the Volgarians of Tsar Simeon in the Balkans. The Hungarian warriors returned home that same season. The Volgarians were not shaken after this incursion and the following year (896), together with the Pechenegs, they destroyed the Magyars at the mouth of the Dnieper. However, according to this paper, the Hungarians in this *previous migration* did not leave the Balkans empty-handed, but with haplogroup J—just as the Red Army entered Romania in September 1944 and when it left, in October, every soldier had countless watches on their wrists. Prof. Corneliu Tarba further notes that the authors follow a certain pre-defined historical route:

Sure, this last statement in the conclusion of the study in question could be partially true, but why do these authors systematically avoid mentioning that the most likely source of this haplogroup J2 could very well be assimilated Romanians? They are not mentioned among the important neighbouring groups and are probably treated as being part of other Balkan populations. The authors do not indicate which of the two J haplogroups is being addressed here, but the reference to "Anatolian and South Balkan contributions" suggests that it is haplogroup J2. It frequently occurs in the Romanian population (even more so than in some populations south of the Danube, e.g., Serbs, Croats, and Bulgarians) and its incidence is at least twice as high as in today's Hungarian population. This is obviously the most reliable source of so-called "Hungarian genetic characteristics" as it is, most likely, part of the "Thracian-Dacian genetic print of the Romanians". This is not a simple assumption, but is supported by the research of a number of foreign geneticists who noted that certain isolated populations of Vlachs (speakers of a Romance language) in Macedonia and northern Greece show a very high frequency of haplogroup J2 (25 %), which is only slightly lower than the frequency found in the places supposed to be the of origin of this haplogroup.

The two studies issued by the Institute of Genetics of the Hungarian Academy close the circle of knowledge on the matter of the ethnicity of the inhabitants of Transylvania, the Tisa Plain, and Pannonia. When the nomads arrived in Pannonia, there were perhaps 10,000 warriors at most, out of the 20,000 who inhabited the Ural region (according to the Persian author Ghardizi) at the beginning of the 10th century. The whole nomadic group with their animals were able to spend the first winter in Pannonia on an island in the Danube (Csepel) sometime after 904 [1 p.81]. As such, in the year 1000, we must recognise that this was a small warrior population in a sea of Dacian-Romanians, Slavs, and Germans. Two centuries later, there were 16-17 Hungarian-Cuman clans; today, less than 1 % are of Asian descent, including not only old Hungarians, but all the other Asian migrants [223, 224]. Furthermore, the Turano-Turkish nomads left no traces in the genetics of Europeans, except for the Volga river basin (Russia) where no genetic determination has been made [117].

Science, in this case genetics, is not militant and the truth does not lead to long-term harm. However, the truth can shock comfortable consciences contorted by the culture of hate and tampering with scientific results is a problem, as shown in the conclusions drawn from the studies above. L.L. Cavalli-Sforza, professor of genetics at Stanford University, in relation to those who today identify as Hungarian, said:

One can hardly find traces of Hungarian genes in the contemporary population [64 p.53].

Another paleogenetic study done in 2012 by Georgeta Cardoş and Alexander Rodewald at the Institute of Human Biology and Anthropology of the University of Hamburg established that there is a clear genetic relationship between the current population of Romania and the population that inhabited this territory 2,500-5,000 years ago. Other genetic studies have highlighted the I2a2 haplogroup, testifying to the continuity of the Thracian population in southeastern Europe [40 p.169]. Genetics certifies what we knew from other positive research in history, archaeology, toponymy, linguistics, and pre-Christian traditions, i.e., that the continuity of the native populations in these lands is a fact and that, implicitly, a part of these populations 'became' Hungarian. The lack of Asian genes in today's Hungarian-speaking population has been revealed and historians need to have the courage to tell the truth. In a seminal work, *La conscience* [130 p.78] (part of the collection *Le developpement de la conscience nationale en Europe orientale*), Janos Perenyi, looking at the independently formulated Latin chronicles of Anonymous and of Simon of Chiza, notes the encrypted idea that the nobles were the descendants of the nomadic conquerors (Magors-Magyars), while the peasants were the natives. Moreover, in the very first sentence of the genuinely original part of the *Chronicle of the Hungarians* written by Simon of Chiza, e.g., the *Appendix*, he clarifies the number of foreign nobles, courtiers, *castrensis* serfs, libertines, and slaves in the kingdom. About the nobles he wrote:

> Since the real Hungary has no more tribes or clans than the 108, let us see where the settling families [our note: here in Pannonia] come from: Italy, Germany or other parts [145 p.647].

The conclusion that can be drawn from these genetic studies is that today's Hungarian speakers have no genetic connection to the Magyar nomads who arrived at the beginning of the 10th century, as the Hungarian scholar Tibor Jóo (1901-1945) recognised long ago.

As such, we cannot talk about different races sufficiently well in Europe as in the middle Danube basin.

CHAPTER 6

HATRED AND INTOLERANCE IN AND THROUGH CULTURE

6.1 Hungarian Classical Literature

Among the Hungarian speakers of the middle Danube basin, only a very tiny percentage were Ugro-Turano-Turco-Mongolian; the rest were comprised of ethnic Romanians, Slovaks, Germans, Serbs, Croatian, Czechs, and Swabians, etc., who were Magyarized. Thus we ask, what makes these denationalised people Hungarians? The answer is culture, as we will see in the research of the Hungarian philologist, the Danube-Swabian Dr. Johann Weidlein (1905-1994) [182]. The work of the Romanian writer Ioan Slavici (1848-1925) is of great help in this regard [160]. All the quotes below without references are from [182].

Fig. 6.1. Johann Weidlein on Hungarian culture.

István Horvát, historian and university professor at Pest (1784-1846), claimed that Adam and Eve spoke Hungarian in paradise and that Hercules and Homer were also obviously Hungarian. In other words, this is the only culture in the world that managed to nationalize God! God is not transcendent, he is not above everything, (their) God is Hungarian! Freedom, just like bread, is also Hungarian! In what follows we have included just a few examples from this unique culture, extracted from the work of the aforementioned doctor of Hungarian philology [182]:

The poet Pálóczi Horváth Ádám (1769-1820):

Curse the Germans/ Lord, beat/ The cursed dog/ The garbage of our country.

The novelist Dugonics Andras (1740-1818):

If the few descendants of the Pannonians [our note: blachi ac pastores romanorum] *show themselves to be submissive, do not believe these sly ones with their rude and repulsive words* [our note: the Germans] *until they have been integrated with Hungarian blood.*

In *Joseph II*, Mitrofanow N. wrote:

Boil, my blood, boil, when the German dogs... Take your revenge hundredfold on the Germans, crush the damned Germans.

The dramatist Katona József (1791-1830) transformed a legend of Queen Gertrud of Meran and a historical drama by Grillparzer into an ultra-nationalist tragedy, through which he incited Hungarian spirits against the Germans. He was a forerunner of the anti-German Hungarian cultural direction. In addition, the mentor of Magyarism Széchenyi István (1791-1860) fixed the direction:

All my enterprises are expanding, but they are directed against the Germans. I hate from the depths of my soul any development that is not Hungarian. Magyarization is the most sacred task of every Hungarian.

This is despite writing that the Hungarian peasant was *a horse thief, unpolished, wild, ignorant, and swore all the time* in *Diary*, IV [p.61]. To make matters worse, in *People from the East* Széchenyi describes the Germans as the *blight of Hungarians*, as if the Hungarians were the majority in the middle Danube basin and the Teutonic minorities would Germanize them! The same Count Széchenyi complimented the Bavarians in the following manner:

To be a Bavarian and to appear spiritual is in itself a contradiction.

Ľudovít Košut (1802-1894), a Slovak from Zips (his mother, Karolina Weberova, came from a Lutheran family), wrote:

Our cities are mostly German, the industry of the homeland is German; German trade... I will no longer tolerate any Saxons in the territory of the Hungarian crown, but will drive them out of the country ... to compensate for the endless thieving, plundering and war expenses.

We find ourselves in financial straits... Make the Saxons pay big anyway. They are to pay two million. Half of this amount as tribute... If they resist, have them executed.

Kossuth does not care for details, logic, or demography:

A hundred languages cannot be spoken in a country, there must be only one, in Hungary it is Hungarian, because freedom is Hungarian too.

Johann Weidlein explicitly clarified that:

Kossuth's most promising troops were made up of jurists, young parliamentarians, and students, who had already terrorized Bratislava during the Diet of 1832-36, and now (b. 1848) they were haunting Pest and Magyarizing aggressively, even resorting to violence against the German inhabitants.

On April 8, 1848, a delegation of Serbs asked Budapest to ensure they would be able to continue using their language. Kossuth's answer was brief: *This will be decided through war* [182 p.66]. On October 10, 1848, L. Kossuth, along with Count Mihai Esterházy, gave an ultimatum to the Romanian people. It began rather mildly, blaming the Austrians, but ended differently:

Then it would have been better not to have been born at all... But even so, the Hungarians and the Szeklers will be ordered get their weapons and let the storm sweep away all the dissatisfied filth... So that the Hungarian and Szekler people rise up, all of them, and wipe from the face of the earth every traitor and rebel... Take note... do not bring punishment upon yourselves [128 vol. 1 p.441-444].

Indeed, after this *Ultimatum* the first genocide in modern Europe followed: well over 50,000 Romanians were executed in 1848/49 in Transylvania. Among those executed on Kossuth's order was the humanist, Lutheran pastor, and pedagogue Stefan Ludwig Roth, as well as the lawyers Ioan Buteanu and Petru Dobra for the reason that they opposed Magyarization in Transylvania and its union with Hungary.

The poet and literary critic József Bajza (1804-1858), also a Magyarized Slovak, opined:

I mean that as long as we do not exterminate the German language in our conversations, as long as there will be Hungarians who speak German with such pleasure, if they do not feel that by using this language, they are committing a crime against the nation... I am not worried about the Slovak

and Wallachian peoples, whom we rule...
Let's close our ranks, let's be proud to be Hungarians, members of the one
people of God, and probably in the world...

The Slovak Bajza was not worried about the *Slovak and Wallachian*
peoples because the Hungarians ruled them, but about the Germans who
had settled in our cities! Although the reality is exactly the other way
around: the Germans built all the cities in the Danube basin and were then
Magyarized in an oppressive manner.

The son of Ştefan Petrovici and Maria Hruz, Alexandru né Petrovici
(1823-†Siberia), known by his Magyarized name Petőfi, like any
assimilated individual felt obliged to permanently prove his Magyarhood.
The strongest proof consists of his continued vilification of the non-
Hungarian majority, particularly the Germans. Here is some evidence from
his literary work:

Pious neighbour, German... And let the lightning not kill you/ Let the
Hungarians be entrusted with this work!

What are these Germans talking about!/ If only they would get
thunderstruck without delay!/ These Swabians demand from us/ To pay
their debts./ Pay your debts yourself,/ Until your tongues are hanging out,
like dogs,/ Even if you were to croak,/ Cursed swindlers...

The German came to us as a guest,/ But soon he acquired the right of
lord,/ And how basely he did everything,/ How many evil deeds he was
able to commit...

... you, German, your days are numbered!.../ Should the German, the
Slovak, rule the country?.../ Only the Hungarian has the right to be master
here...

From the Carpathians to the Lower Danube/ A roar of fury, a wild
storm!.../ Croats, Germans, Serbs and Romanians,/ Why are you all
rushing to the Hungarian land?/ The sword that spared you from the Turks
and Tatars/ Flashes in the hand of the Hungarian.../ There will be no
peace until the last drop of blood/ Will flow from your cursed hearts/ Rise
up, Hungarians, against this horde,.../ We once fought with the lions,/ Now
shall this cesspool of lice devour us?

Now God is not sufficient,/ For he is not harsh enough,/ I pray you, hell, on
New Year's morning:/ Plant in our hearts all your wrath,/ Let us know no
mercy until these bastards/ are wiped off the face of the earth.

In the poem "Lehel" from the edition *Petőfi: Complete Works* (Budapest, 1953), the leader of the tribes, Lehel, gives advice to the young prince Zultán to scold the whole world, but especially the Germans and to show so much love to the Germans as to drag them into hell. Farkas Gyula (1894-1958), in his 1943 book *"Hungarian Vormärz: Petőfi's Era"*, wrote that Alexandru Petrovici was born in the Slovak town of Kiskörös in the Tisa Plain and for a while called himself Kunfi, being ashamed of being a Lutheran. Even Goethe did not escape Petőfi's hatred for the Germans claimimg that *he had a heart of stone and posterity would topple him from his pedestal as a false idol.* Johann Weidlein [182 p.87] mentions that some contemporaries spoke of the vileness of his creation and thought, to which Petőfi replied:

> *Before the judgment seat of my conscience... I have always written and will always write only as I felt and as I feel.*

A comparison of Petőfi's "patriotic" lyrics with those written during the German War of Liberation (1809-1815), reveals stark differences, noted Johann Weidlein. The difference is found in the expression of a lack of self-control and generosity, an inability to look at the adversaries in any other way than scornfully, and through the primitive lust to kill and injustice specific to those who are parochial. According to Márton Horváth (Schiller) (1906-1987), Petőfi's poems represent the contribution of Hitler's ally to his downfall—after Soviet troops occupied fascist Hungary, the translated anti-German poems were allegedly handed to Soviet soldiers to instil hatred against the Germans in them with.

Among the apostles of hatred, Petőfi, one of the most dangerous agitators in history, deserves the greatest attention. The seed he spread in an artificial people, without its own ethnic substance, a people that was easily instigated, bore fruit in the bad deeds committed, which, in the end, proved to be horrible [182 p.92].

Arany János (1817-1882) brilliantly continued Petőfi's insults, slandering all that was German, wholly unrestrained:

> *I swept out the Germans,/ These three hundred years old pieces of trash.*

In his *Ars poetica*, Arany writes that the streets of Budapest are dominated by *German speech, which is filthy!* In 1946, the academic Kondor Imre drew attention to the symbolic significance of Arany's choice of words:

> *Have you ever thought about the symbolic significance of the fact that Arany János, speaking here in Buda, put these 2 expressions side by side...?*

Because Sigismund of Luxembourg, German-Roman emperor and king of the Catholic kingdom in the middle Danube basin, was German, in his ballad *Rozgonyiné*, Arany makes him a coward who was afraid of the Turks. Arany forgot one essential element—those belonging to his "nation", Magyarized or ethnic Hungarians, made a pact with the Turks. Besides, Arany János was never hindered by historical truth, like other Hungarian intellectuals from both the past and the present.

In his poem *In pusta*, Tompa Mihály (1817-1868) writes:

> *And the beggarly trash of the peoples/ Rushes from the west,/ Settling where/ Milk and honey flow...*

The Germans were for him *impertinent and garrulous sparrows*.

The novelist Mór Jókai (1825-1904), a popular writer among the restless spirits of the Magyarized, publicly declared that *among the muses, only Clio is not sacred*. All the Hungarian writers disparaged her, as we have seen, but no one mistreated Clio as much as Jókai did. In a letter from him to his German editor, he speaks of the Hungarian tradition that the poet, not the politician, is the true leader, and continues:

> *The Germans were given everything: goods and blood, the only thing missing is national respect.*

Johann Weidlein wrote:

> *The goods and blood, which the Hungarians had given to the Germans, probably refer to Maria Theresa, to whom the Hungarian nobles had promised to give a helping hand for one year (1741).*

I have already mentioned this "helping hand" and exactly what it consisted of! He despised the Saxons, who were the least willing to be Magyarized. Jókai wrote in his poem *Poor Saxon*:

> *He has a separate homeland,/ For which his heart longs/ Here only the pot of meat holds him back/ Angling in troubled waters/ Then he rejoices when we mourn/ Our joy for him means mourning/ Poor Saxon.*

Among his characters, the German who is Magyarized is always a positive hero, while the German who does not accept Magyarization is presented as mean, cowardly, scheming, and selfish. In the novel *The White Woman of Leutschau*, the judge Fabrizius, who is on Rákóczi's side, is a noble character, while his deputy Alauda, who contributed to the city falling into the hands of the Emperor of Vienna, is a negative character. He denies his anti-German sentiment, despite the evidence present in the *Neue Freie Presse* of 1.05.1896:

> *There are many people who spread the news around the world that the Hungarian effort to establish a state* [our note: minority state] *would involve oppressing non-Hungarian nationalities* [our note: of the majority]. *These statements are as far from the truth as light is from darkness.*

Thaly Kálmán (1839-1909), a poet and politician, produced some songs that were claimed to be from the time of the Hungarian-Tatar-Turkish brotherhood. These were called *songs of the Curuts against the liberators of the Pannonian plain from the Turks*. A contemporary, the Szekler Cserei Mihály (1667-1756), wrote:

> *...all the robbers, murderers and scoundrels who, under the name of the Curuts, have tormented, tortured, killed and thrown into the fire so many honest people, noble or common...*

Szekfű Gyula (1883-1955), in *Hungarian History* IV, gives the matter the following perspective:

> *The Curuts had been educated by the Tatars, they could not be distinguished from them except that they did not drag people into slavery. But where could they drag them? But they seized every valuable thing, whether in sight or in hiding, they walked in great bands through the plains, turning everything in their path into ashes and heaps of stone* [p.293].

Petőfi wrote about the leader of these bandits, Rákóczi, a Northern Slav on his father's side and a Southern Slav on his mother's, who allied with the Turks and Tatars, and would have allied with the French and the Russians if they had taken him seriously:

> *Saint of our homeland, leader of freedom,/ Our bright star in the dark night!*

Here are some lines from these made-up songs of Thaly Kálmán:

> *Look what the German has done in our country:/ He has defiled our women and girls...*

> *I don't believe the word of the German zealot any more than the bark of the dog./ He came to lay waste not to help, to conquer our country.../*

Therefore, kill him and the Hungarian who keeps him company!/ Drink the wine so that when you hear the trumpets/ You can drink blood and make piles of German corpses!

Wretched German/ with crane's feet,/ with a snub nose;/ he runs from us, he's afraid of us,/ wretched nation!

You, Germans, and you racz, this is how you have to atone, this is how God punishes you, you beastly son of a whore, a truant and a robber, a terrible thief. You today, Germans, now you strut around! Racz You bastards, now of course, you'll leave...

Don't believe the Germans, Hungarian people,/ No matter what he wants to deceive you with.../ Jesus Christ would punish him...

Run, you Curuts, the Germans are coming,/ Behold what a learned worm...

Thaly Kálmán caused consternation in the Vienna Chamber of Deputies by associating Germans with worms:

The German is a learned worm. That he is learned, cannot be disputed, but neither that, at the same time, he is a worm, because he enjoys crawling.

This political fanatic engaged this sentiment in many places by these imaginary songs of the Curuts. Further on we find:

Innumerable weapons threaten us,/ For the German is among us/ And strikes with thirst.../Like an executioner,/ He knows no mercy for him whom he reaches,/...Because of him/ There's almost no bread left in the country.

God forbid that the Hungarian/ Be mocked and defiled by an enemy/ As repulsive as the German/ Do not allow that such a conceited people/ Rob them/ Of their eternal and glorious reputation.

The cult of these robbers was amplified by dozens of other "Hungarian" and Magyarized writers through the later spread of *Turanism*. The mechanism is described by Sassi Nagy Lajos (1867-1945):

It is necessary to feed this national feeling from above, so that it then permeates the entirety of society from below, in the form of an invincible force.

In these songs, everything is faked, Weidlein argues, except for the hatred expressed, which is genuine.

In the novels of Tolnay Lajos (1837-1902), the Germans are called *dung and garbage, wretched worms,* and *castaways of humanity.* In the novel *The Honourable Baroness* we find the following song:

> *Let it be as it was before!/ Both the German,/ As well as the Croatian and the Slovak/ Let them take off their hats to the Hungarian... The dear Czechs, the German philosophers and the Galician usurers had to leave Hungary.*

The linguist, novelist, and poet Gárdonyi Géza, whose real name was Ziegler (1863-1922), renounces his own people, thus proving his Magyarhood. In his short novel *You, Berkenye!*, the father of his heroine writes a book entitled *The Mirror of German Stupidity* from which we quote:

> *German wisdom is also characterized by the letters they use. The German writing and the German typed letters look as if they were designed by a lousy ophthalmologist who thought only of his profit. 99 out of a hundred Germans wear glasses... Is the German blind from patriotism or from stupidity?*

In his poem *On the Polish Border*, he talks about the cursed German who drives the Hungarians out of their country. The hero, Fr. Rákóczi, *God's most beautiful hero*, shouts to his fugitive compatriots:

> *We can only go back, back, I'm also going to the homeland/ Let the Germans go to hell from there!*

The Magyarized German Herczeg Ferenc (1863-1954), the son of Franz Herzog and Luisa Hoffmann, born in Banat, was the most acclaimed Hungarian writer of the Horthyst period, a member of the Hungarian Academy, and president of the Hungarian Revisionist League. In his pseudo-historical novel *Pagans*, he deals with the period of anarchy after the death of King Stephen, when a pagan uprising (1044-1046) threatened the young Catholic kingdom with disintegration. Herzog's sympathy goes to the sons of the Turanian Vazul, who *will bring back the old law* (i.e., pagan) *sweeping the foreign garbage* (i.e., Christian German) *from Hungary.* The hatred channelled by Herzog in this novel against the Germans is based on a radical mystification, deliberately forgetting that the founders of the young kingdom were Germans in all respects—

religious, administrative and military. Innumerable churches and monasteries are destroyed by the revolt of the pagans, but those who rob the holy treasures are the German knights:

> *Pushing against each other, with furious cawings, like those of ravens rushing to corpses, they seize the jewelled crucifixes, the goblets and fibulae. The precious scarves were torn in the struggle to get hold of them; but they threw away the heavy silver cups.*

The nuns take refuge with the pagans from the monasteries devastated by the Germans!

In the historical story *The Waning Moon*, the Hungarians and Turks are the main heroes. The peasants side with the Turks because the king of Vienna did not honour the Hungarian oligarchs! Through these ideas, they associate themselves with the false heroes of freedom—Bocskay, Thököly, Bethlen, Rákóczi, allies of the sultan, and the peasants—meaning the Hungarian people. Obviously, Herzog does not care for history, nor for demographic statistics either. In the short story *A Sword Affair*, three officers of the Austro-Hungarian army come in civilian clothes to Pollatschek's tavern and ask to hear the *Song of the German Pig*, which was sung in Hungary after the anthem *Lord, bless the Hungarian.*

All these proofs of Magyarhood mean nothing to the poet Ady Endre, who characterized Herzog as *confused and of limited imagination*. Ady Endre (1877-1919), being more racist than the racists before him and a culmination of them all, targets not only the non-Hungarians, but also the assimilated:

> *Here, in this antechamber of Europe with so many doors, where from east and west, from all sides, the garbage is swept in, absolutely nothing is safe. Stephen the Holy was our first, almost conscious, supplier of rubbish... That race of the first arrivals (the Germans) has proved for this poor country like an invasion of locusts. The first arrivals, by plundering and through association, are still a burden today.*

In the poem *The Hungarian sleeps* he reveals his true meaning:

> *...although I love all the nations, if the Romanians wake up the beast in me, I will attack them, hitting and cutting...* [177 p.81].

When the assimilationists Jeno Kremsner and Ferenc Herzog questioned Ady's origin, he erupted in rage:

For the meddlesome and the filthy,/ For the bastards and those greedy for jewels,/ For the half-dead, the foaming-at-the-mouth,/ For those who cheat the Hungarians and the fog-eaters,/ For the Hungarians hailing from Swabians/ Am I not Hungarian?

The racist novelist and ethnographer Kodolányi János (1899-1969) wrote:

The Swabian servant, whether her name is Resi or Lesi, is beyond stupid, dirty and lazy—everything about these Swabian women disgusts me.

An ideologist of the *new Hungarian reoccupation of the country*, in 1928 Szabó Dezső wrote:

It [the new literature] *grasped the hundreds of thousands of locusts of the destructive German lust, how they ... have deprived the Hungarian people of all their rights, robbed them of all possibility of living, forced them out of their land, but also out of their soul, and become so vehemently Hungarian that they can destroy Hungary.*

In 1933, the poet Babits Miklós exclaimed:

Is there a greater danger and a more ancient curse for Hungarians than the German?

The poet Hidas Antal (1899-1980) wrote:

For four hundred years you've been fighting the greedy German,/ But he still hasn't finished sucking your thick, good blood,/ Hungary.

And in 1933, the poet Illyés Gyula (1902-1983) offers the following wake-up call:

Transdanubia is in the most terrible peril... The German Sea is swelling, assaulting the Hungarian villages, and there is nothing that can stop it...

In 1938, he concluded that *in the past, the Hungarians were a nation only in so far as they were hostile to the Germans*, while in 1945 his historical merit was recognised by the nationalist Communist regime:

I was among the first who then—even before Hitler seized power—brought up the German danger in Transdanubia. Since then, I have repeatedly mentioned the expulsion of the Germans, sensing the roots of the matter.

In 1970, Illyés Gyula received the Herder Prize!

In 1946, the writer Szabó Pál (1893-1970) wrote:

...the front against the Germans has always been an obligation of the Hungarians and that the Hungarians sucked the hatred against the Germans with their mother's milk!

While the poet Horváth Béla (1908-1975) wrote:

So, tremble before me you stupid Swabians,/ In your faces I vomit the plague./ I hunt you dead or alive,/ Murderers, blood-drinking heathens!/... Drown the bastard, kill the evil worm,/ The smug fisherman, the fatuous executioner!

Fig. 6.2. Cover of Dordai Lorand's "Without Mercy".

Pesti József was jubilant, writing *the time is coming for us to jump to their throats* in the paper *The Year 1956 Reflected in my Poems*. Here, the cutting of the neck refers to Jews and Swabians [182 p.13, p.18].

Dordai Loránd (1908-1970), a Horthyst until 1945 and a Communist after, wrote under a pseudonym in 1939 in his work *Nincs Kegyelem* (*Without Mercy*):

I do not wait for revenge to come. I can't wait! I will suppress every Wallach in my way. There will be no mercy! I will set the Wallachian villages on fire at night. I will put the entire population to the sword, I will poison the wells and I will kill even babies in the cradle... I will suppress every Wallachian and then there will be only one race in Transylvania, the Hungarian, my nation, my blood!

To commemorate this illustrious representative of Hungarian culture, in the 1990s the Democratic Soviet of Hungarians in Romania (RMDSz) requested of the Dej City Hall, through an address, the right to emplace a memorial plaque. The request of the RMDSz was supported by Mircea Opriţă, the president of the Union of Writers of Cluj-Napoca!

At the end of his book *The Kingdom of Saint Stephen. The History of*

Mediaeval Hungary, 895-1526, the historian Engel Pál (1938-2001) summarizes as follows:

> *By no means did the Mohács generation disappear, but its ideology remained alive... Its xenophobia, bias, illusions and narcissism lived on, from the end of the 17ᵗʰ century, in the form of a virulent nationalism, causing serious disfigurements of conscience and society, serving as a model for ethnic hatred in the Carpathian basin* [62 p.387].

After examination of Johann Weidlein's careful and restrained review of Hungarian culture, the following sentence written by Fabchich József, the Catholic priest of the then entirely German town of Raab, in a letter to the singular poet Kazinczy Ferenc (1759-1831), should not surprise those who read it:

> *The Swabians, with whom we quarrelled, must be forcibly given Hungarian names. They must learn Hungarian or die.*

Ioan Slavici (1848-1925), at the request of the writer Iacob Negruzzi, researched and completed his work *Studies on Hungarians*, published in the *Latin Orient* of Brașov and *Literary Conversations* of Iași. These have been published recently in the series *Works of the Romanian Academy* (vol. VIII) [160]. Slavici treats the Hungarians with sympathy and observes their Asian specificity and how they resisted European influences, showing a "natural antipathy" towards Europeans. Slavici also discusses the untranslatable term *szilay*. For example, *szilay fergeteg* is "a furious storm", "extreme passions" would be *szilay szilayem*, and "a stormy peroration" would be *szilay beszéd*. *'Szilay', he will say, extremity in everything,* concludes Slavici, saying paradoxically, that the Hungarian is worthy of pity in his virtues and worthy of admiration in his vices! Furthermore, he suggests that we see in the Hungarian, *the most beautiful public and private virtues that change quickly and directly into the most wretched passions.* Hungarian nationalism is also extreme: it results in an aggressive appreciation for everything Hungarian alongside a blind contempt for everything foreign and non-Hungarian. The English historian C. Macartney (1895-1978) observed the same thing about the Hungarian: *Everything, with him runs to extremes* [91 p.391]. Voltaire, Rousseau, Hugo, Goethe, Schiller, Kant, and Schopenhauer are good, but:

> *...they couldn't be a Petöfy, a Vörösmarty or the other Hungarian Lucifers!*

Expanding on this, Slavici writes:

Hungarian nationalism manifests itself in two forms: in a concerned appreciation of everything Hungarian; and in a blind contempt for everything foreign and non-Hungarian. A contempt mixed with a deep compassion occupies every serious person seeing the blind divinization with which the Hungarian wants to give a sublime nimbus to everything Hungarian*. 'Magyar' for Hungarians is synonymous with 'perfect', everything Hungarian is better; and the worst, because he is Hungarian, becomes as good as possible, 'Magyar' will mean the ideal of man or the most perfect man. But let's take a few concrete forms, a few more general expressions of the Hungarian language, which we will clearly see the reflex of this divinizing nationalism: 'Magyar Isten' as the Hungarian God would say and he will understand: True God, 'Magyari vílaga' 'Hungarian world' 'happy world', 'Magyar élet' 'Hungarian life' 'happy life', 'Magyar jog' 'Hungarian law' 'good law', 'Magyar ijaszág' 'Hungarian justice' 'holy justice', 'Magyar szépzág' 'Hungarian freedom, true freedom', 'Magyar szát' 'Hungarian lunch' 'rich lunch', 'Magyar beszél' 'speak Hungarian' 'speak logically, well, beautifully', 'Amúgy magyarosan' 'also Hungarian' 'as is proper'.

Another facet of Hungarian chauvinism derived from an exaggerated self-appreciation is contempt for neighbouring peoples. In this sense, we continue to quote from Slavici:

The Hungarians do not hate anyone (except the German); they only despise. All the peoples living with them have one or more attributes they despise; they have for every nation a collection of mocking anecdotes; even the very simple names of the nations of Hungary are in the Hungarian language attributes and predicates of mockery. This is how it is said for instance: A német hunczut = the German is cursed, Az oláh naponsült = the Romanian is roasted in the sun, A rácz vad = the Serb is wild, A tot nem ember = the Slovak is not a man, A zidou búdös = the Jew stinks, Bugyogós sváb = big-bottomed Swabian, Medve = bear = Romanian, Piszkos = dirty = Slovak, Cseh (Bohemian) = human garbage, etc. Hence it follows, that the Hungarians, wanting to mock one another, attribute their names to some neighbouring nation. You bearish Olah! You wild Serb! You Slovakian! You Jew! And so on. This is where most fights come from. The result of this systematic debasement was that from the side of their neighbours they looked at themselves as better, but that from the side of their neighbours they were also looked at in the same manner. Romanians, Serbs and Slovaks were ashamed of their names until recent times; and as for the Germans, Jews, Russians and a large part of the Slovaks, even today there is no greater insult for them than to tell them that they are what they are. Because of this, Romanians claim to be called 'românok' instead of 'olâhok'. These people cannot be a danger to me and especially to society. They simply are, and I could say that after they perish their being will leave no trace. 'A magyar szalma tuz' (the Hungarian is

*like a straw fire) as a very typical popular proverb puts it, in them there is
nothing true, nothing permanent; in their whole being there is no intrinsic
power* [160 p.692].

The study by Slavici, who was a subject of the Austro-Hungarian Empire,
was also published in Brașov, despite the risks.

The Swabians who lived along the Danube (see fig. 11.6) were labeled
with attributes such as "smelly", "idiot", and "whore" (*budos, hulye,* and
kurva) [183 p.6]. Everything is extreme in those feeding on hate. On
25.03.1848, news of the revolution in Vienna and its reply from Pest
reached Tg. Mureș where Chancellor Samoil Poruțiu addressed his
Hungarian-speaking colleagues: *Brothers, why do you claim that they are
all only Hungarian? Let's say and swear by the God of the peoples!* These
words were rejected with terrible fury [116 p.43].

In the campaign diary of the officer Octavian Tăslăuanu (1876-1942)
from the 1914 campaign in Galicia, the shameless cowardice of the
Hungarians takes shape:

> *Until now I had not seen hussars operating. I was therefore curious about
> the bravery of the 'red devils', as they were called with Hungarian pride. I
> advise the captain to send them over to reconnoitre. To my delight he
> agrees. From the top of the bridge, they cross the water, spread over the
> field and step forward. We hear two gunshots, and the next moment brave
> hussars came galloping, eating the ground. I am the first to stop them:
> 'Well, what did you see?' - Their commander, a rank and file, reports to
> me in fright that the Russians fired at them from a distance of 80 paces.
> Me, 'what, are you lying? What did you see? Go back!' They were all
> trembling on their horses. This is how the hussars behaved, the notorious
> 'red devils', and now we understand why our reconnaissance service was
> null* [our note: Austro-Hungarian] [173 p.272].

But "fame" can also be obtained by lying and being brazen! On November
20, 1914, after a comical and deadly skirmish with the tsarist army, with
dozens of dead and hundreds of prisoners, the 11th Company of second
lieutenant Octavian Tăslăuanu did not give up its position. Szőllősy, a
cheeky officer who was not even in the vicinity, went to the commander
and said that the first Russians were made prisoners by him and so was
decorated [173 p.315].

Archdeacon Nicolae Vasiu (1895-1981) from Cluj, a man of integrity
who did not shy from judging the Orthodox and Greek-Catholic hierarchs
for their cowardly behaviour during the Horthyst period, speaking about
the hypocrisy of the Hungarians on the occasion of the arrival of the Red
Army in Cluj on 4.07.1945, offers the following summary: *Two-faced*

people are numerous in the world, but peoples similar to this type of people are few [177 p.366]. In other words, the same answer was given by the Viennese students in 1878 to the Hungarian students: *we cannot forget how blatantly the facts contrast with your words* [179 p.170].

6.2 Some Examples from the Hungarian Press

Ellenzék, no. 115, 1884:

> *I don't find any fault in the behaviour of the (Hungarian) youth, I don't even see debauchery... The youth did well to break the windows of the Romanians and prevent them from holding the feast and the banquet... the non-Hungarian youth must be given a Hungarian education. Their heart and soul must be transformed; patriotic thoughts must be instilled in their brain; Hungarian culture must be infiltrated in their blood, and in this sense the love for Hungarian culture must be spread* [190 p.131].

Pesti Napló, no. 209, 1888:

> *As far as we are concerned, we believe that the question of nationalities cannot be solved in a satisfactory way, except through the complete Magyarization of nationalities* [190 p.130].

Nemzet, 11.05.1890:

> *The loyal Hungarian nation, which for centuries has been exceedingly magnanimous towards other nationalities, has enunciated the equal entitlement of nationalities by law; but the nation never stated the equal entitlement of nationalities with the Hungarian nation* [190 p.128].

Kolozsvár, no. 36, 1891:

> *The Magyarization of the names of the townships has long been the persistence of those who deal with the spread of Magyarization... This is something worthy of praise, because it is more natural that the names of all cities and villages should be Hungarian* [190 p.130].

We recall the observation of the scholar B.P. Hasdeu that *the Hungarian custom of translating the Romanian nomenclature dates back to 1380* [80 p.84].

The Law of Asylums (law XV of 1891) refers to the law of orphanages, which established that Hungarian was the language to be used and taught in orphanages. In other words, in countries or provinces like Slovenia, Croatia, Slovakia, Banat, Crisana, Maramureș, and Transylvania, all institutionalized children should be Magyarized. Szathmár, February 28, 1891:

> *We expect people who live here to respect our language and to recognize it as sacred and lawful. Be they Slavic, German or Dacian-Romanian, they will never make merry at the Hungarian nation's wake... Let those who hate Hungarians leave our country. Those who do not respect Hungarians are all traitors! ... In Beiuș [Bihor County] and in other places, the Romanians, rabid and furious, are agitating against the orphanage law. All the beasts are thirsting for Hungarian blood, snarling, what an abomination to watch! We'll throw you out of our country, you ungrateful, cunning people. If you don't like our language—get out of here! We don't need traitors, to hell with you! The legions of ravens and the countless ancient trees on our snowy peaks have long waited to claim your carcasses.*

Egyetérts, July 29, 1891:

> *Another nest of Germanization in old Buda. The school inspectorate in the 2nd circle is fast asleep, if not deliberately closing its eyes to the action of another orphan institute in old Buda. Under no. 106 in Matroz Street there is the second German nest, which is kept by a so-called Mrs. Pitt, Frau von Pitt, who has been Germanizing in old Buda for 12 years* [190 p.131].

Magyar Hírlap, 13.10.1891:

> *This much is certain, that from this scandalous event, the most sacred duties are born to the Hungarian youth: the youth from the universities now have the duty to search, to report one by one and by name who are those young Romanians* [our note: who wrote *The Romanian Question in Transylvania and Hungary—Reply*] [190 p.132].

The Hungarian newspapers, which "cultivated" their public with such savagery and threatened the varied peoples of the country in this infamous way, have never been subject to press trials. In contrast, Romanian and Slovakian newspapers were brought to court even when the prosecutors were reading accusations against the Hungarians between the lines! Romanian newspapers and Romanian journalists were placed under incredible pressure. From 1884 to 1895, 47 political processes were brought against them; in the subsequent four years (1895-1898), another 96 political processes and abusive administrative measures were brought! Romanian personalities convicted before 1894 include: Eugen Brote, convicted 7 times; Ioan Slavici, 4 times; Vasile Lucaciu, 4 times; I. Russu Șirianu, 3 times; Aurel Mureșianu, 3 times; Septimiu Albini, 3 times; Aurel C.

Popovici, 2 times, and many, many others. Between 1884 and 1894, 107 publicists were sentenced to a total of 59 years and 10 days in prison and fined 11,840 florins. The Tribune (*Tribuna*) and People's Newspaper (*Foaia poporului*) from Sibiu alone were dragged into 29 lawsuits and ordered to pay fines of over 56,918 crowns [112 p.40].

As Seton-Watson wrote:

> *Persecution has been carried so far that it is almost impossible to find a Romanian newspaperman who writes for a political newspaper, and who has never been in jail, charged with a political crime* [91 p. 288].

6.3 Hungarian Historiography

From István Horvát to Paul Lendvai

We do not allocate space here for the junk and aberrations from Hungarian historical culture, written by academics like István Horvát, who saw even Hesiod's titans as Hungarians! However, we must observe their continuity. In March 1943, Hitler's allies, through the university professor Janos Chalnoky at a conference about the cultural superiority of the Turanians, claimed that the Hungarians introduced the "Constitution" to Europe [91 p.390, p.205].

We are referring to the high point of Hungarian historians, Balint Hóman. The American Milton Lehrer wondered (91 p.221):

> *And when a historian like Bálint Hóman says about the desolating expeditions of the first Hungarians that they were sporting enterprises [Sportartige Unternehmungen], what can we expect from improvised historians in the service of chauvinism?! And if they vanquished countries and to kill—as it appears from the annals of Fulda—20,000 people a day, means for the Hungarians to make sport, what must it mean for these missionaries of civilisation in the Central European region to be truly cruel?* [91 p.409].

Bálint Hóman (1885-1951), more of a historian than many other propagandists of chauvinism and hatred, was nevertheless a racist, a fascist, and a minister in Horthyst governments. Another historian, Gyula Szekfű, of similar stature to Bálint Hóman, distinguished himself in 1913 when he had the courage to publish archival documents that were somewhat unflattering of Rákóczi II, considered a national hero (see references to the Curuts). He had a rather tortuous, but edifying career in Hungarian culture: in 1918 Béla Kun's communist government offered him a university chair;

in the interwar period in the work *Three Generations* he blamed the decline of mediaeval Hungary on the nobility and the Jews, becoming the ideologue of middle-class anti-Semitism; after 1946, he also had a prodigious political career, and wrote among other things that Stalin, *a hermit*, was *the object of the greatest respect and love.*

Today, according to the Humanitas Publishing House's note on the work *The Hungarians*, Hungarian historiography is crowned by a leading political journalist in Europe, Paul Lendvai [92]. This "masterpiece", which claims to be modern and free from prejudice, is from one end to the other a consolidation of Hungarian xenophobia and chauvinism. The first procedure is simple: he tells us that the character or the event is controversial, even very controversial in Hungarian culture, even in European culture, then he resorts to substantiating the position of the character not based on documents, but with anecdotes and subsequent echoes from Hungarian literature! Another method is omission. Thus, the "glorified" deeds of a small detachment are explained by whole pages of text without any historical relevance, but many significant historical moments are not even worthy of a sentence. If we have a sentence about the robberies and murders in the west being definitively stopped by Otto the Great and another sentence about the robberies being stopped in the north by Ottokar II of Bohemia, about the expansion of the Catholic kingdom in the south being stopped by Basarab, not one word is mentioned.

Half-truths work wonders if skilfully handled, for example, in April 1740 Prussia crushed the Austrian army near Breslau and the Habsburg possessions in the north were threatened. Empress Maria Theresa (1740-1780) needed new recruits and addressed the Diet of Pressburg (Bratislava), the Hungarian magnates, on 11.09.1741. The magnates, theatrically drawing their swords from their sheaths, shouted *Vitam et sanguinem pro rege nostro Maria Theresia!* The magnates went home and sent the regiments from Transylvania to the empress. So, this historian from the third millennium seems to forget that the "Austrian" regiments 31, 33 and 37 sent by the Hungarian magnates to shed their blood *pro nostro rege* were actually Romanian [190 p.13]. How could it be otherwise since, in 1787, the Hungarians did not even constitute 29.9 % of the population, even in Pannonia? [29 p.34]. In the last conflict between Maria Theresa and Frederic II of Prussia for the succession in Bavaria (1778-1779), *the Romanians from Transylvania behaved with the greatest bravery*, writes Raicevici in *Osservazioni intorna la Valachia e la Moldavia*, which was printed in Naples in 1788 [190 p.12]. Rather, Lendvai is charm itself when he talks about the Hungarian national conception of warfare, inherited from the "hero" Thököly who fought alongside the Turks and Tatars against the Austrians, who were liberating Pannonia from the Turks. This conception was something with which Thököly's successor, in Turkish exile, would no longer agree: *(The enemy) to be attacked with ferocity and savagery; if he runs, you can follow him, if not, then quickly retreat.* Although this is exactly what the Curuts did, according to the national conception, even when led by Fr. Rákóczy, the son. Szekfű himself confirmed this in *Hungarian History* [vol. IV p.293]:

> *But as soon as they saw a band of armed and experienced men, they did not even wait for the first fire, but ran away over the hills and through the valleys.*

Lieutenant Octavian C. Tăslăuanul similarly experienced this "national" concept on the Galician front in 1914: the 23rd Romanian Territorial Regiment was cut in half by its losses, while the 5th Hungarian Territorial Regiment Seghedin had not even come under fire, since it had been consistently held back in reserve [172 p.83, 182, 186].

Another procedure frequently used by Lendvai is the logical fracture! When Lendvai refers to Hungary, he always refers to the maximum extent of territory that ever fell in relation to the Catholic kingdom, regardless of whether certain parts were at times Turkish vassals, Habsburg countries, Romanian countries, or equal legal subjects in the Habsburg monarchy! The Turkish desolation affected only the Hungarians, not the other inhabitants! Does this mean that all the natives had been Magyarized by the 17 Hungarian clans by 1526? That was not the case as even the Catholic primate and regent of Habsburg Hungary, Nicolae Olahus, tells us. The emperors Maria Theresa and Joseph II tell us the same thing, and the documents of the Vatican clarify things for us! Lendvai, however, does not deal with documents and goes further in stating that, while the Turks only "nullified" the Hungarians, the Slovaks and Romanians occupied the Turkish territories in the middle Danube basin changing the demographic ratios in Hungary! Where did the Slovaks come from in Lower Hungary? If they came from "Upper Hungary", i.e., from Slovakia in the Pashalik of Buda, they did not change the demographic relations in Lendvainian Hungary! Logically then, if they changed the demographic ratios in "Hungary", the Slovaks came from outside "Hungary". The author does not tell us where this mysterious homeland of the Slovak invaders could be. The Romanians, yes, could have infiltrated from Wallachia, but historical data show us the opposite process [107]. Because of the blind oppression to which they were subjected by the authors of the *Tripartitum*, hundreds of thousands of Romanians from Transylvania took refuge in Moldova and Wallachia, founding villages of "Hungarians" and "Szeklers" that remain easily identifiable to this day [107].

The contemporary display of this phantasmagorical maximalist conception that exceeds even the most absurd feudal conceptions is downright absurd. If Lendvai were a Turk, or rather an agent of Turkish nationalism, and operated with the same unit of measure, he would have demanded Greater Turkey to extend to the walls of Vienna; what does it matter that there have been wars lost and peace treaties! If Lendvai were English it would justify the occupation of half of France by the kingdom of William the Conqueror! Flanders should also be a subject of Spain! For Lendvai, published in Germany and commended in Austria, it is not relevant that in the mediaeval Banat up to the final colonisation of the 1880s, there were no Hungarians, but Romanians who lent their armies to the Catholic kings in all the wars and defended Christendom on their own. Furthermore, upon liberation from the Turks, the first Austrian censuses did not find Hungarians there either. Lendvai repeatedly and staunchly asserts that Banat was stolen from the Hungarians at Trianon. Croats should not have a state of their own and neither should Slovaks: Croatia was stolen from the Hungarians! Slovakia was stolen from the Hungarians!

Lendvai's *The Hungarians* is intended for the modern, superficial, and hasty commons, uneducated and greedy for anecdotes; a populace that can accumulate untruth on top of untruth without ever noticing it. The French, English, American, or German reader will be left with those impressions suggested by the author. The reader will be left with the idea that Hungary defended the west from the Turks for 300 years! The Turks appeared on the southern border of the Catholic kingdom in 1439, 10 years before the Romanians, Iancu and Ioan Corvin, sons of Voicu son of Șerban, successfully organized the defence of the Danube fortresses of Severin, Orșova, and Mehadia in the Severin Banat. Iancu of Hunedoara, after crushing Mehmed II in Belgrade, died of the plague. In 1456, Mehmed fled at night with the remnants of his army! Iancu's chieftains were the princes Simion de Cuhea, Gheorghe Mareș, Mihai Tatu, Dan Suscă from Maramureș, and Bogdan from Zalău, as well as many princes from Banat, Hațeg, Hunedoara, Zarand, and Crișana. This was a local and popular "crusade", with *farmers, diggers, and ploughmen, without arms*, as noted by a participating monk [34 p.55]. It was not a crusade organized by the papacy and also many Germans, even students from Vienna, jumped in to help in Belgrade in 1456. The Turks headed towards Wallachia and Moldova, where Mehmed II was seriously hindered by Vlad the Impaler in 1462—the Turkish garrisons considered themselves lucky to once again set foot in Asia—and by Stephen the Great in 1475 in Vaslui.

For 24 years, the Catholic kingdom defended the west with Iancu de Hunedoara and, from 1457 to 1469, with Paul Chinezu at the helm, primarily fighting with Romanian troops. Afterwards, Matthias Corvinus was rightfully accused by Engel Pal of making a pact with the Turks [62 p.327]. The mission was a heavy burden for the Romanians (Ioan Vodă and Mihai Viteazul, the Brave) and then a responsibility placed on the Habsburgs. Thus, for 24 years, not three centuries, and fought by Romanians with Romanian leaders! King Matthias Corvinus (1458-1490), the son of Iancu de Hunedoara, only skirmished with the Turks: in Bosnia in 1463 with some success and in 1464 with great losses [62 p.322]. In 1476, Matthias wrote to Sultan Mehmed II about *peace and good friendship* [62 p.328].

Let us look again at the *athleta Christi* to which our narrator refers based on hearsay. In 1238, John Asan II, emperor of the South Danube Vlachs and Bulgarians, attacked the Latin Empire of Constantinople from the west while the Greeks of Nicaea attacked it from the east! So that this outpost of Catholicism, the creation of the Fourth Crusade, might not perish, Pope Gregory IX urged King Bela IV to go to Constantinople:

> So that through you the Catholic faith may be spread, the freedom of the Church preserved, and the Christian religion defended, to this end you may go to battle **velud fortis athleta Christi**, in order to merit the crown promised to those who take up arms for the faith and their place in the kingdom of heaven.

Here we find the exhortation: "go forth like an athlete of Christ to defend the faith". That is all and nothing more? No, after an amazing victory at Podul Înalt in 1475 against an army of 120,000 men, Pope Sixtus IV conferred the title *athleta Christi* on Stephen the Great! Or to Iancu de Hunedoara after his magnificent victory at Belgrade in 1456! There is a difference! After the establishment of the Turkish-Phanariot regimes in the Romanian countries, the anti-Ottoman struggle fell to the Habsburgs, who expelled the Turks from the middle Danube basin at the end of the 17th century. The Turks were supported by Hungarians and Tatars.

Lord Rothermere in the service of xenophobia

Lendvai has an entire soap opera dedicated to Lord Rothermere, who was promised the Byzantine Catholic crown of Hungary by the secret services. He is not sure how much Rothermere knew or did not know from the part written for him by the Hungarian secret services. In the interwar period, the racist and fascist state and its secret services bought Rothermere, who engaged in a campaign to review the Romanian-Hungarian border. This fact led G.B. Shaw to take a categorical stance. In this campaign, Rothermere laid on the line his entire media empire in the Anglo-Saxon world. To fuel Rothermere's campaign, the Hungarian intelligence services sent, among others, an agent to Bucharest, who obtained the approval of the Romanian Minister of Justice (notable for his lack of intelligence) to inspect Romanian prisons with Hungarian-speaking inmates. The agent successfully carried out his mission and, in 1945, he was sent again into Romanian territory to engage in diversionary actions to benefit Hungary at the subsequent peace conferences. He was arrested by accident, with his actual activity not being a matter of suspicion. He entered the Romanian concentration camp system and here alongside Romanian intellectuals he gradually changed his feelings cultivated by the culture of hatred. He confessed to the physician Șerban Milcoveanu, with whom he shared a cell at one point, as follows: with the approval of the Minister of Justice (Valer Pop), he went to the cells of Hungarian prisoners, i.e., those Magyarized, and recorded those positions or fragments of positions that suited him; he only recorded the answer, the question being later completed by Budapest before sending the wax plates to Rothermere. Thus fuelled, Rothermere effectively carried out the pro-fascist, revisionist campaign. Secret British documents, made public in 2005, show that Rothermere wrote to Hitler to congratulate him on the annexation of Czechoslovakia (1938) and to encourage him to invade Romania.

The other side of 1956

In general, what is known about the 1956 uprising in Budapest is what the Russian and Hungarian intelligence services wished to be known. In June 1956, the Soviet ideologist, Mihail Suslov, sent the following message to the Hungarian communist leaders: "there are too many Jews in the leadership of the Hungarian communist state". On October 23, students in Budapest started a nationalist demonstration. In front of the parliament in Budapest, they shouted not only the old slogan *Hungary belongs to the Hungarians!* but also the xenophobic slogan *we want a new government, without Jews and Swabians!* (see *Der Aufstand in Ungarn und das ungarlandisches Judentum*, Weidlein, J. p.17). Here we find what their problem was and it was not Bolshevism, if Bolshevism did not prevent them from hating everything that was not Hungarian. It stands to reason, then, that the Hungarian emigration of 1956, partly directed by the Russian and Hungarian secret services, would have accommodated its Western hosts, who wanted to hear about an anticommunist revolution. As such, all those Hungarians who fled presented a convenient and profitable image, one that was different to reality, in which their xenophobic and antisemitic feelings were substituted by anticommunist slogans. What did those Swabians expelled from communist Hungary in 1946 feel in relation to the commemoration of the 1956 uprising and the leader Imre Nagy, asks the Danube Swabian Franz Wesner in the *Frankfurter Allgemeine Zeitung* (no 269/17.11.1990). We may recall the words that the NKVD-ist Imre Nagy spoke in parliament:

> *The Swabians are a reactionary pillar, thanks to their expulsion—of this we are sure—democracy has strengthened considerably among the people.*

In 1956, many young Romanians also went to prison for expressing their political creed. At the Sighet Memorial, in the long list of students imprisoned in 1956, only one Hungarian name appears, but considering the programme of Magyarization practiced without interruption for centuries, the Hungarian name does not necessarily mean that the bearer was Hungarian. The new communists, being former Horthysts, also denounced their Romanian colleagues, who stood in solidarity with the anticommunist side of the uprising in Budapest. Anyway, the Hungarian intellectuals in Transylvania, such as the writer Andras Sütő, defended the purity of the Stalinist line against the "deviationism" seen in Budapest.

The intoxication of German public opinion

The publicist Lendvai, for the modern, hasty, and ignorant man, is credible and his words are intoxicating for the German world. Lendvai presents a reversal of the facts, of history—a rewriting of it for his German readers. In this model, the Russians are the mortal enemy of the Hungarians. As we have seen in relation to the Russians, in 1945, the Red Army was taught to hate the Germans through Petőfi's poems! What more could be added about such hypocrisy?

The political journalist Lendvai seems to have had access to only one source of information: István Horvát and his followers. He does not seem to have read any other alternative source, be it Byzantine, Papal, Slovak, Romanian, German, or South Slavic! He does not seem to have understood, for example, that under feudalism, collecting taxes from subjects does not mean that the payers were of the same ethnicity and religion as their feudal lord. It is not his fables that are so worrying, but their racist and chauvinistic brazenness, after the destruction of the 20th century. It has been translated into German and Romanian without critical apparatus, holding the hundreds of thousands of victims of chauvinism, racism, and hatred in contempt.

The historiography of the Magyarized, beginning with the academic who claimed that Adam and Eve spoke Hungarian and ending, in the 21st century, with the support of the same feudal aberrations amplified by racist, chauvinistic connotations does not seem to have made much progress. The multi-award winning European historian today is more objectionable than István Horvát in 1800!

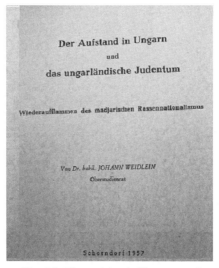

Fig. 6.3. The uprising in Hungary and Hungarian Jewry.

CHAPTER 7

THE FIRST GENOCIDE IN MODERN EUROPE

The Hungarian *sui generis* "racial" phenomenon has several important aspects: simple Magyarization; savage Magyarization; colonisation; expulsion; and, finally, genocide. All this was preceded by the religious turmoil of the early Middle Ages directed by the Vatican, i.e., schismatics could be subject to pillage and plunder (*dati fuerint in direptionem et praedam*). In 1848/49 the first genocide in the history of modern Europe took place with well over 50,000 Romanians and Saxons being executed in Transylvania alone, in the most barbaric way imaginable, by fellow Europeans.

Fig. 7.1. Simion Bărnuţiu (1808-1864).

The essence of the Hungarian movement in Transylvania in 1848 is captured by the words of T.V. Păcăţian:

> *They did not care about 'equality, freedom and brotherhood'. On the contrary, they remained very cold on hearing these words, because they knew that the moment they would be turned into deeds, their supremacy would be over, and the role they played in the public life of Transylvania would be reduced to ashes. That is why the movement of the Hungarians in Transylvania was started from the first moment in this direction* [127 vol. I p.237].

7.1 A Few Points

Genocide is the partial or total extermination of a civilian population belonging to an ethnic group.

Simion Bărnuțiu (1808-1864) was a philosopher, professor of law, and connoisseur of the writings of important philosophers from Kant and Krug to Fichte and Hegel. He was also the mastermind of a revolutionary and national programme for Romanian action and Romanian destiny. His ideas were based on the principle that *the right of personal existence, the right of personal freedom*, and *the right of equality of persons* are natural, otherwise individual rights derive from natural law, and natural law is inherent in human beings. Bărnuțiu founded his revolutionary programme in Transylvania on these ideas.

Avram Iancu (1824-1872) was a jurist, well-known personality, and capable strategist and commander. He took up arms and did not surrender the land of the Mots (Tara Motilor), immobilizing, as the tsarist general Alexander von Lüders recognized, half of the "Hungarian" forces [105 p.81].

The Saxon leaders, during the events of 1848/49, followed an oscillating course—sometimes they sided with the idea of German unity (Frankfurt); sometimes they called themselves loyalists (Vienna); and sometimes they were opportunist (Pest). After Kossuth asked Bem to destroy Sibiu (the centre of Saxon resistance), the latter refused, contenting himself with its occupation, and the Saxons fell in with the Hungarians and wrote to thank Kossuth for having been spared "Austrian despotism" [6 vol. II p.24]. Very worthy, however, are the positions of some of the learned Saxons from Sibiu, such as Joseph Benigni and Franz von Reichenstein as described in the *Sibiu Defence Committee of 31 December 1848* [6 vol. II p.413].

Joseph Bem was a Polish artillery officer from Galicia, which was contested by the Poles themselves [116 p.162]. He saw in the defeat of Austria a chance for the rebirth of Poland, then divided between Prussia, Austria, and Russia. He first joined the revolution in Vienna (14-28 October 1848). After the Viennese surrender, he came to Budapest to continue the fight against Austria. On 1.12.1848, he received command of "Hungarian" troops with a mission to occupy Transylvania. Here in Transylvania, he was regarded critically as nothing more than an odious mercenary in the service of criminals, a dubious and slippery character (he had also turned to Islam) [116 p.157].

Carol Urban was a principled and energetic Polish officer who took command of Romanian Border Regiment II. Immediately after taking command, on 13.09.1848, he convened the delegates of the townships and the battalions of the "military border", asking them for their views. They responded that: 1) the separation of Hungary from the empire was treason; 2) they did not want to be Magyarized any longer because the Hungarian ministry engaged in tyranny over non-Magyar peoples; and 3) that this tyranny of language was the reason why the Serbs and Croats had risen up to fight to defend themselves. Having this popular basis, Urban remained firm in his attitude, siding with the people of Năsăud and the Habsburg emperor.

Axente Sever (1821-1906) was a jurist and an extremely determined and true leader. He led his legion into the hardest battles.

George Barițiu (1812-1893) was a theologian and teacher. A clear-headed man, he participated in the revolution and was both a publicist and historian of Transylvania, and especially of the 1848 revolution.

Andrei Saguna (1809-1873), Bishop of Sibiu, was a diplomat who tried to obtain what he could for the Romanians and their religion, which were merely tolerated in their own land.

Artemiu Publiu Alexi (1847-1896) was a naturalist, having undertaken university studies in Vienna and doctoral studies in Graz. He obtained the list of victims convicted by martial courts in 1848/49 from the Ioanneum Library in Graz, to which we will refer later [114].

Carl Klein was an officer, originally from the Upper Country of Moldovia, taken by bribery by the Habsburgs from the Turks, who were only suzerains in Moldavia. C. Klein joined the 2nd Romanian Border Regiment in Năsăud of his own free will, horrified by the looting and assassinations carried out by the Hungarians in the summer of 1848. He wrote a valuable history of this regiment [120].

Gal Laszlo and **Boczko Daniel** came from Hungary. They were appointed by Kossuth and carried out, among other things, slaughter and robbery in the County of Arad as a means of repressing the Romanians who had refused to recruit Hungarians and dared to ask for the raising of the royal flag in Hălmagiu (Arad County) [114 p.64].

General Eugen Beothy came from Hungary as Kossuth's commissioner extraordinaire in December 1848. He was an angry old man, bristling with thirst for Romanian blood [6 vol. II p.403], he set up blood tribunals, militias, and civilian manhunting squads. His troops were given the mission to prey on, kill, ravage, and set fire to the Romanians—a kind of precursor to the Turkish Ba'athists [6 vol. II p.507]. Beothy also said in relation to the Serbs that *we must wipe out the whole race* [179 p.94].

Ladislau Csányi, also from Hungary, replaced Beothy (22.03.1849) and continued the campaign of hunting civilians. He placed militias and civilian manhunting teams at Bem's disposal.

Emeric Miko was an official under whose auspices the Szeklers of Lutița went out to commit arson and murder [6 vol. II p.377]. He informed the Hungarian minister that Sibiu had declared itself independent and obeyed only Vienna, calling for vigorous measures against the people of Sibiu. He also called for the intervention of Russian troops against the Hungarian "revolution" [6 vol. II p.451].

Ferdinand I, emperor from 1835 to 1848, sanctioned the union of Transylvania with Hungary on 10.06.1848 with the promise of Hungarian help against Prussia. Prussia's goal was the subordination of Austria within the German Empire! On 14.11.1848, Ferdinand appointed Emeric Miko president of the Transylvanian government.

Generals Anton von Püchner, **Wardener**, and **Pfersman**, **Colonel Augusti**, and **Captain Ivanovich** were all imperial officers who were incapable, indecisive, cowardly, selfish and double-dealing, both with the emperor and the "revolutionary" feudalists. After occupying Budapest, **General Windischgratz** whored himself out to the Hungarian barons, who were playing both sides [6 vol. II p.449]. How would these imperial officers have been otherwise, if the emperor, a man of straw, understood so little about what was happening in the empire?

Insurgents/rebels/mutineers/revolutionaries are all names that define the "Hungarian" armies of extermination, looting, and plunder in Transylvania and the Tisa Plain.

The Hungarian troops were also troops from Transylvania, the Tisa Plain, and Maramureș (Romanians, Slovaks, Ruthenians, and Germans, etc.) recruited by the Hungarian "revolutionaries", and volunteer corps from German countries and Polish and Italian areas, who were seeking to defeat of Austria.

Hussars were cavalry soldiers. The name comes from the Serbian and means "plundering soldier" [62 p.329].

Lancers were Romanian peasants who enlisted out of a sense of duty in the legions (*Landsturm*) of the prefects. They were self-equipped with lance, bread, and bacon from home.

The Szekler regiments had some Szeklers, but were mostly made up of Romanians. In 1879, Father Colceriu, from Măhăceni, wrote to Haşdeu stating that until 1849 the Măhăceni (Cluj County) served as mounted guards in those Szeklers regiments [81 p.35]. The Romanian Lieutenant Crainicu led a wing of the Szekler hussars (*ein Flügel Szekler Hussaren*) made up of Romanians in Hălmagiu against the Romanians [12 p.59].

7.2 Genocide

The "revolution" was not supposed to change anything, because *any democracy impinges on nationality* and the nobility had long been aware of this. This is because the nobility was, in fact, Hungarian, the rest being Romanians and Saxons, with an insignificant number of Magyarized Romanians, Slovaks, Swabs, and Saxons. The great problem of the nobility was the transformation of the Western spiritual currents, which could not be stopped. According to J. Weidlein, this meant that, while preserving democratic forms, the great mass of the population of the country was still excluded from making decisions [182 p.54]. As Count Stefan Szechenyi declared on October 5, 1844, in his speech to the Diet of Bratislava, the Hungarians, then, were represented by the nobility and any rights granted to the people were seen to impinge on Magyarhood. As a result, he hated any development that was not Hungarian from the bottom of his heart [182 p.54]. Kossuth tried to radically implement Szechenyi's imperative of Magyarization as the holiest task of every Hungarian. In the newspaper *Pesti Hirlap*, Kossuth wrote: *let's hurry, let's hurry to Magyarize the Croats, the Romanians, the Saxons, otherwise we will perish* [166 p.97]. On March 15, 1848, Kossuth declared in the diet that *Hungary owes its existence only to the nobility* (105 p.147). The demagogue asked to whom Hungary belonged; he replied that it belonged to the Hungarians—this was his solution to the question of the non-Hungarian-speaking majority [182 p.54]. Therefore, the "revolution" did not surprise them—they knew what they had to do to maintain their domination over the majority. The "revolution", as far as it can be called one, was not actually a war of liberation from Austria; in reality, in addition to the abolition of feudal servitude, it was an attempt by the non-

Hungarian majority to free itself from the Hungarian stranglehold. Kossuth's troops responded with terror, looting, and the extermination of Romanians, Slovaks, Saxons, Serbs, and Croats. On 10.03.1848 in Lipto (Slovakia), the Slovaks demanded equal representation and a Parliament (Reichstag) of all the peoples. At the congress of 15.05.1848 in Carlowitz (Serbia), the Serbs also demanded freedom of national life. Transylvania, however, was not Hungary, and the Romanians, in particular, vastly outnumbered the "Hungarians"! Therefore, it was necessary to immediately render the mass of Romanians leaderless. In this way, the systematic liquidation of teachers and priests began. An inventory of the formations that acted in Transylvania to exterminate the Romanians has been identified by the historian Gelu Neamțu [115 p.124]:

1) Until the Mihalț massacre (2.06.1848), repression was carried out by imperial troops made up of Szeklers and Polish volunteers.
2) After the Third National Assembly in Blaj (9.1848), invading troops from Hungary acted.
3) The particularly bloody indigenous "Hungarian" civil guards.
4) The bloodiest turned out to be the "blood tribunals", which executed people on the spot or within a matter of days. Sometimes the "judges" would draw their swords and cut down the "accused" during the "investigation".
5) Volunteers concentrated in bands of fanatics who hunted the Romanians.
6) Mobile bands of volunteers composed of poor townspeople and small landowners who robbed cattle, sheep, piglets, geese, turkeys, ducks, and chickens, etc.
7) Bands of "Szekler" deserters who looted Romanian villages in the Szekler regions.
8) The repressive actions of the county officials who had small military formations under their command and used them to terrorize Romanian villages.
9) Special troops made up of criminals released from prison who terrorized the civilian population.
10) The nobles who had previously fled and returned to take a ferocious revenge upon the serfs once the military-political circumstances allowed.

The beginning: the "revolution" of the feudalists

After 20.03.1848, in the midst of the turmoil, when the first information about the revolution in Vienna arrived in Cluj, the feudal authorities accepted the "revolution", but without the freedom of the press, because the Romanian and Saxon press undermined them, and without the freedom of the person, because Romanian youth were holding meetings! Consequently, many young Romanians were arrested and executed after April 3 [217 p.237]. On April 25, the feudal authorities of Transylvania declared a *state of siege*, when there was no threat to the feudal state of affairs, which they were guarding! On the night of 26/27 April, the arrests of Romanians began: Florian Micaş, a lawyer, then young Ioan Dărăbanţ, Ştefan Molnar, Ioan Petrovici, Nicolae Şuluţiu, and Ieremia Verza from Cluj [115 p.24].

Before any warlike action was taken, the feudal lords, supported by the authorities, erected two gallows and a stake in every village in Transylvania; these 4,800 gallows and 2,400 stakes were later supplemented by another thousand [114 p.27]. Their role was to maintain the old feudal order through terror. The poet Vasile Alecsandri, passing through Transylvania, noted that the towns and villages *were illustrated with numerous gallows and stakes* [116 p.183]. Something similar occurred in 1656. Konrad Jakob Hildebrand, when crossing Transylvania, was horrified by the terrible sight of Romanians impaled at the entrances to all the villages [20 p.31]. "Preventive" gallows were not just erected in Transylvania, but also in Slovakia in that period [64 p.183].

The peasants began to withhold their labour from the feudal lords. Immediately after the Blaj Assembly of May 15, a wave of executions was unleashed against the participants and the serfs who refused to perform their "statutory labour". As it was a "revolution", the Hungarian civilians armed themselves, forming national guards called *honved* at the request of the feudal authorities and "correcting" the Romanians! Captain Carl Klein observed the beginning of the so-called Hungarian "revolution", of the national guards, and of the *honveds*, which consisted of: desecrating churches; looting and burning villages; raping women and girls; and catching and shooting Romanian intellectuals and supporters of Romanian intellectuals [120 p.154]. The particularly brutal military executions of Romanians by the imperial army made up of Szekler and Polish contingents. In Transylvania, the imperial army was then still in the service of the feudalists.

On 27.05.1848 in Abrud, after the guards were armed by the Transylvanian authorities, only the good nature of the priest Simion Balint prevented a massacre by assuring the Romanians that all the guards' vicious behaviour would be forwarded to the central authorities who would take action [6 vol. II p.221]. The Kozma Pal Commission of 14.06-20.07.1848, sent by the feudal authorities of Cluj, investigated almost 300 witnesses in the land of the Mots, noted the opinion of the local Hungarians: first that the Romanian priests should be hanged, followed by the common Romanians [113 p.27]. Indeed, the priests were targeted according to the principle of killing the shepherd and scattering the flock, but the peasants were not spared either. Kozma's renegade commission established that the massacres were not carried out by Hungarian guards, but by Romanians, who had fought each other with knives.

The ensuing genocide was foreshadowed by the assassinations of Jucuri, Vaida Cămăraş [120 p.467], Sâncrai, Mihalţ, and Luna. At Mihalţ (Alba County), an orchard where there had once been a Romanian church, but which had since been occupied by the feudal lords, was claimed by the township as grazing land. Indeed, the Romanians grazed their cattle on that land. On 30.05.1848, the feudal landowner obtained a favourable sentence and carried out a *military execution on the township*, on the peasants of Mihalţ, who still opposed the dispossession of their land [6 vol. II p.221]. On 2.06.1848, 12 peasants were shot by the army, led by a civilian, the official Nicolae Banffy, in Mihalţ, while nine others were wounded. Another 11 peasants were ordered to pay compensation! There were then thousands of violent occupations of serf estates by feudal lords and thousands of trials in courts of law that gave sentences in favour of the potentates of the day [6 vol. II p.222]. In other words, there was no talk of abolishing feudal obligations, liquidating feudal arbitrariness, or installing the rule of law. George Bariţiu notes that this is how the "union" began: with the Mihalţ bloodbath! Faced with such excess, in the spring-summer of 1848, the vicar of Sibiu observed that the legal-administrative representatives ruled the Romanians with the stick, the dungeon, and the gallows [113 p.28]. To give another example, on 20.07.1848 in Caila (Bistriţa-Năsăud County), the noble judge came with the imperial army to arrest the priest Ioan Sigmirean. As he was not at home the judge rushed in and hit the old priest Simion Sigmirean, the father of the wanted man. The discussion between the judge and the priest is enlightening as to how the Hungarian "revolution" started in Transylvania: the judge assured the old priest that the emperor gave him the soldiers *to mock you, despite not being guilty* [113 p.28].

The notary of Copşa Mare informed the *Saxon University* that the landowner Benkő from Sântioana (Mureş County) burned his serfs, who refused to perform statutory labour [116 p.16]. At Luna (Cluj County) in September 1848, we find another kind of massacre, but one that would be multiplied thousands of times: 32 young Romanians were shot by the feudal-revolutionary authorities for refusing to be "conscripted" into the "revolutionary" army. The Romanians refused conscription on the grounds that the conscription law was not sanctioned by the emperor, as was indeed the case.

Unite or Die

From the beginning, the representatives of feudal Cluj, who went to Pest on 23.04.1848, declared to the government that they were determined *to make the union happen through the means of blood* [44]. Starting with thousands of pre-emptive killings in the villages, it was a short step up to massacres without any motivation. Before any revolutionary movement had begun, George Apor, son of Baron Lazar Apor, had already hanged 26 Romanians in September 1848, just for the sheer pleasure of it, as he himself confessed; that is to say, two weeks before the Romanians began to try to disarm the Hungarian civil guards according to the order given to them by General Püchner [6 vol. II p.303].

On 23.10.1848 in Aciuța (Arad County), the Hungarians set fire to 86 houses, barns, and stables. All of them were reduced to ash. The people were left with great shortages and cattle from across the area were either driven over the Tisa to Hungary or killed. In addition, dozens of Romanians were either cut down or shot in Aciuța alone [114 p.180].

From the autumn of 1848 to the summer of 1849, teams were organized to hunt Romanians. This does not mean that in the summer of 1848 the "Hungarians" did not murder people, burn whole villages, and demolish and burn Romanian churches, but only that these "civilizing" actions intensified. Hungarian guards hanged or cut up Romanians and even Germans all over the land. In November 1848, the guards killed priests from Arad and Bihor, then, descending into Banat, they left the task to robbers (*Rozsa Sândor's gang*), who entered the German township of Lagerdorf (Straja, Serbia), which they plundered, mercilessly killing the inhabitants—men, women, old people, and infants. In the township of Iecia (Timiș County), the guards also killed prisoners of war [6 vol. II p.303]. On 8.11.1848, a troop that came to Zarand from Hungary slaughtered 700 Romanians in the village of Bătrâna (Hunedoara County) in the Apuseni Mountains [114 p.44]. In the report of Major Gál Lászlo of 17.11.1848 on his campaign of repression in Zarand, he boasts that in the Battle of Poieni *all those captured were killed* and that 1,187 Romanians died in the slaughter of Târnava-Vața (Hunedoara County) [114 p.71]. After this expedition of killing and looting, on his return to Arad, Major Gal hanged the priests Sinisie Grozav from Aciuța and Pavel Farcaș from

Pleșcuta (Arad County) for having spread Avram Iancu's proclamations [3 p.22].

After the insurgent army was dispersed following the Battle of Dej (Cluj County) in November 1848, the 3rd Battalion of the 2nd Border Regiment pursued the insurgents as far as Somcuta (Maramureș County), without being able to catch them. Everywhere the horde passed, they left behind corpses and smoking ruins—only 32 Romanians were found on the gallows [6 vol II. p.385].

During the action of collecting weapons from civilians, as ordered by General Püchner, Avram Iancu, entering the burnt and ravaged Upper Vinț (Alba County) in November 1848, made an ominous discovery—a large number of Romanians asphyxiated in lime pits [12 p.144].

The veteran border guard Ștefan Echim from Șieuț (Bistrița-Năsăud County), on guard duty in the spring of 1849, opened fire on a carriage with rebel officers. A bullet lightly grazed Iosif Bem, who did not stop and went further into the rebel camp. It did not take much for the civilians, old men, women, and children of Șieut, Monor (Bistrița-Năsăud County) and the surrounding area, to immediately find themselves in the grip of a cruel and savage repression. In each village through which they passed, they shot and slaughtered between 30 and 50 wretched souls, but also plundered 1,600 oxen, cows, horses, and sheep, which they took home [120 p.137].

Hundreds of hunting parties—gangs of civilians—killed thousands of Romanians and even Saxons: they entered people's homes and murdered everyone in their path—men, women, old people, and children. Entire families were exterminated. They chased fugitives through the fields and forests. Hunting teams led by Iosif Jeney from Târgu-Mureș and Ludovic Szabo from Turda became infamous. Each boasted of having executed several hundred Romanians, naturally, without trial. On 17 March 1849, the team led by Iosif Jeney murdered 600 Romanians [196 p.34]. The Hungarian press proudly recorded the successes of these hunters [52 p.125]. At Uioara (Ocna Mureș-Alba County), 400 Romanians were seized in the salt mine sheds; they were taken out one by one and shot, then thrown into the Mureș [6 vol. II p.482].

On 22.02.1849, Baron Fureszi hunted six men and a woman in Chirileu (Mureș County); on March 15 in Berghieș Forest, 11 Romanians were hunted; in Hodac (Mureș County) and its surroundings, seven men and a woman were chased down; and in Ibănești (MS: Mureș County), seven men were killed. Another example from the excerpt published by Artemiu Publiu Alexi highlights that even the "judges" of the blood courts during interrogation *cleaved with sabres* the Romanians brought before them by the hunting teams [114 p.288].

The records of the death register of the Greek-Catholic church in Cluj reveal that 28 Romanians were executed by the blood courts. From the list extracted by A.P. Alexi in Frata village (Cluj County) alone, we can see that 25 Romanian men were killed [114 p.287]. One man, by the name of Bocskai, assassinated and also ordered the assassination of 27 men in Gambuț (Alba County) and 17 in Ciuci (Sântana de Mureș: Mureș county) [6 vol. II p.486]. In Boiu Mare (Maramureș County), they pulled out the priest's hair and beard after beating him. The priest's wife, who had given birth two days before, was hacked and torn to pieces along with her child. Count Haller, fleeing towards Odorhei in November 1848, set fire to all the villages he passed through; then, in Teleac (Harghita county) he hanged 12 Romanians, tying up others and throwing them alive into a fire [114 p.21]. On 19.02.1849 in Prodănești (Sălaj County), five men and an infant were killed before the village was set on fire. A 10-year-old girl was thrown into the fire before her father's eyes, who was then also burned; others died of torture [114 p.281].

The priests who urged the faithful *not to support the Magyar rebels*, as two priests from Iosași (Arad County), Dan Ioan (47 years old) and Dan Iosif (28 years old), did, were hanged [114 p.144]. Receiving or being accused of having received a letter from Transylvania in the Hungarian parts (Tisa Plain) was treated as seriously as having committed murder and there was always some Hungarian official available to file a complaint. To give just two examples: the priest Simion Groza from Gurahonț (Arad County) and the former mayor of Satul Rău (Arad County), Bărbuță Onu, were hanged for such accusations [114 p.139-144].

A rich category of assassinations is that of the so-called "preventive" ones. Three peasants from Merișor (Satu Mare County), Nutiu Pop and Flore and Petru Roman, who had been suspected of intending to flee to the mountains to Avram Iancu, were tortured on a rack. They were taken to a hill where there were 12 hangmen and another 20 Romanians from Remetea (Maramureș County) were brought there to be executed. Before the execution, they were made to dig their own graves after which they were hanged two at a time on the gallows. For this mass execution, a crowd of people was forcibly gathered to dance during the execution [114 p.22].

The guilt of daring to dream constituted another category of murder. Ioan Oprea, from Ștei, Bihor County, was hanged because he dared to dream about the establishment of a Romanian kingdom [33 p.22], while Adam Goleș admitted before the blood court that he believed that a special Romanian kingdom was to be established for the Romanians. Nicolae

Petrovici admitted that he and his Romanian relatives, tired of Hungarian rule, considered a Romanian kingdom to be welcome [33 p.22].

Hundreds of villages were completely destroyed and burned to the ground, in addition to Reghin and a hundred other nearby villages [116 p.125]. Let us also not forget the 71 churches burned to the ground, another 12 partially burned, and 715 looted [114 p.60].

After the capitulation of the "assassin-revolutionaries", or "rebels" as Vienna and the non-Hungarian majority regarded them, on 13.08.1849, retreating beyond the Tisa the Hungarian troops continued their campaign of robbery and assassination. For example, in the deanery of Buteni in the County of Arad, seven villagers from Bârsa signed a certificate describing how on August 18, 1849 retreating Hungarian rebels engaged in looting and those who opposed the looting were shot on the spot [114 p.138]. Furthermore, in the deanery of Buteni, five days after this capitulation, we have a list of 15 assassinations undertaken by the retreating Hungarian troops. A 48-year-old Roman Catholic German, Lambert N., who managed a mill, did not escape either. After they shot him, they also set fire to the mill [114 p.136]. And so on and so forth.

7.3 "Revolution" or Murder and Robbery?

On October 26, 1848, the official Voros Antal reported to the Hungarian Defence Committee that, according to information received, the Austrian commander Berger from the citadel of Arad incited the Romanians on the Mureş River to rebel, authorizing them to disarm the nobles [114 p.64]. And yes, the Romanians from Arad and Zarand refused to be recruited into Kossuth's army. This is how Major Gal Laszlo's repressive raid began, first in Arad County—in Şiria, Covăsinţi, Galşa, and Musca, etc. Major Gal's campaign of repression continued in Zarand after October 1848, once the pacification of Arad had been achieved. In the mountains, in Hălmagiu and the villages around it, there was not a house left that had not been plundered by the Hungarian rebels; they also sought to extort money from poor Romanians, as well as taking clothes and other goods. The poor Romanians, frozen with terror, remained silent in the hope that they would not be killed [114 p.33]. The commander of the imperial border guards, Lieutenant Clima, together with some Romanians, hid in a stable in Hălmagiu thinking that they would escape; but Gal's gangs set fire to the stable, claiming that there were Kossuthan hussars inside whom the Romanians had set on fire [114 p.187]. Everywhere in Transylvania, robbery went hand in hand with murder. Here is a typical example. On 24.10.1848, the band of Hungarian rebels led by Gal was greeted by 11 villagers, men and women, with a white flag at the entrance to Hălmăgel (Arad County). The Hungarian rioters surrounded the peaceful delegation of the village, tore down the flag and mocked it. The first eight they killed with their swords, the next two they threw alive into the flames of a burning house, and the final villager was wrapped in sackcloth and then thrown into the fire. The "revolutionary" action did not stop there—they set fire to the whole village (including the church) and shot the villagers and threw them into the burning houses. All of this took place after rounding up all the cattle and sending it to Hungary [114 p.33].

Civilian and *ad hoc* hunting teams roamed Romanian villages killing and looting. Even the bloody commissioner Csány, who came from Hungary, admitted that what motivated them to organize was a lust for robbery [52 p.124].

The "Szekler army" began requisitioning and pillaging Romanian and Saxon villages. The first devastated township was Archita (Mureş County) near Sighisoara, which was inhabited by Saxons and Romanians. The robberies and murders of the rebels continued without interruption until December 16, that is, in just seven weeks, more than 100 Romanian and Saxon townships were burned and devastated, according to report no. 5166 of 16.12.1848 by General Püchner and addressed to Prince Windischgrätz [6 vol. II p.325].

On 1.11.1848, Lieutenant Colonel Carol Urban retreated with 300 veteran border guards and 2,000 volunteer lancers from Reghin (Mureş County). His goal was to save the city, which was no longer a battleground with the "Szekler" rebels, hoping that it would be spared from the destruction of war. This hope was deluded. The insurgent army, consisting of 16,000 soldiers (four brigades of 4,000 each) [6 vol. II p.326], entered Reghin and demanded 50,000 florins as a protection fee from the civilian inhabitants in order not to loot and burn the city. As soon as the citizens of Reghin, the Saxons, promised to pay 50,000 florins, the rebels increased their demands. As the Saxons could not raise the increased sum, the rebel leader, the chieftain Berzenczey, ordered the looting and burning of Reghin. The orgy of robbery lasted three days, in which time the rebels committed acts of barbarism that, as Captain Carl Klein states, *even the Bedouins of the desert would not have surpassed* [120 p.194]. For three days they looted and burned Reghin! Carol Urban did not know about this "army" of robbers raised against the Romanians and Saxons. He had just come from Vienna and was not aware of the latest developments in the area. Moreover, a number of officers of the Năsăud battalion, the Germans Dorschner and Betzman and the Czech Czerniko, abandoned the emperor's flag and joined the rebels [6 vol. II p.327]. The numerically imposing (16,000 combatants), but pitiful marauding "armada" melted away, not in battles, but in plunder. They looted so much in and around Reghin that hundreds of freight cars, themselves belonging to the plundered citizens, loaded with everything they found in the houses, plus herds of animals, returned directly to the "soldiers' houses under the plunderers' whip" [6 vol. II p.330]. After the looting and burning of Reghin and the departure of Colonel Carol Urban to Bucovina, the so-called revolutionaries devastated and then burned the residence of the 2nd Romanian Border Regiment (from the 17th Regiment of the Austrian army) in Năsăud with all the schools there, all of Năsăud, and several surrounding townships [6 vol. II p.409].

In the fall of 1848, in Chioar district, Baron Huszár Zsigmond burned 27 Romanian villages:

> ...throwing several women, girls and children into the flames, after raping them, had staked them to the ground while still alive by pushing stakes through their chests or through their bellies [114 p.20-21].

Women also participated in the robberies! On 28.10.1848 in Hălmagiu, the women who accompanied the band from Hungary, stripped the Romanians of their clothes and not being able to divide them amongst themselves, fought until they were separated and forced to load the loot on the carts and get on the carts as well to head back to Hungary [114 p.187]. These robberies are difficult for an uninitiated person to understand; at the time, poverty in the steppe (Pannonia) was so stark that even the clothes of the Mots seemed like wealth the inhabitants could not have hoped to gain in a lifetime.

On 13.03.1849 in Zdrapati (Hunedoara County), Csutak, who had been sent by Bem to defeat the Zarand prefect Ioan Buteanu, made his debut in the campaign with small "achievements"—the deaths of 13 men and 19 women, some being split open and others being burned in a fire [6 vol. II p.492]. At the end of May 1849, Farkaş Kemeny resumed the "fight" in Zarand to gain control of the Apuseni Mountains. His gangs, the territorial militias, set fire to many houses, kidnapped horned cattle, and killed eight women and children. The parish priest Simion Groza with his lancers put them to rout and returned the stolen cattle to their owners [6 vol. II p.524].

The terror, murders, and robberies intensified after the defeat and expulsion of the imperial army in March 1849. Thousands of Hungarians began to strip the Romanian villages of all possessions, on the grounds that the possessions of the Romanians had been stolen before the reign of Ladislau Csányi [6 vol. II p.480]. In the hall of records of the Sibiu Orthodox Consistory, there are thousands of examples, some of which are cited by the historian Gelu Neamțu in *Documents for the Future* [114] regarding the first genocide in Transylvania. The examples presented below reveal the character of this war of the Magyarized:

> *Sofia Miheț: 32 years old, on May 29, 1849. She was killed while carrying her baby in her arms, nothing remained of them. Doichița Lazăr: She was 32 years of age and had her daughter in her arms, they shot them both, leaving 3 poor children behind. ... Șara Suci: 31 years of age, on March 29, 1849. They killed her in the garden of the house as well as her 2 children and they were thrown in the fire. Ana Macra: 32 years old, on March 29, 1849. They threw her in the flames of the fire, and only ashes were left of her. Catuța Feier: 4 years old on March 29, 1849, died after being thrown into the fire ... [114 p.24].*

The commanding general of Transylvania, General Pùchner, from Sibiu (in both the military and civil sense), after initially defending the feudal order against the Romanian serfs, when confronted with the evidence, publically disapproved of the barbarism of the Hungarians in proclamation no. 4557 [114 p.38].

7.4 Comparison: The Issue of Reciprocity

Let us examine Gal Laszlo's campaign and the thousands of murders, including the 1,887 lives lost in the villages of Batrâna and Târnava (Hunedoara County) alone, particularly how the assassinations were carried out and how Axente disarmed the Hungarians in 120 villages, which had cost the lives of six people of Hungarian speakers [6 vol. II p.369]. The Hungarian feudal lords had raised gallows and spikes and had killed several thousand to instil fear in the hearts of the Romanians, who believed that serfdom had been erased with the proclamation of the *revolutions*. When looking at the victims of the genocide, we must not count soldiers killed in combat. Prisoner rebel soldiers were spared, while prisoner Romanian soldiers were sadistically slaughtered.

We have given numerous examples of how the Magyarized rebels behaved, let us now see how the Romanians behaved. The retired major Kornisch (a Romanian name in German spelling), pretending to be Hungarian, gathered 300 volunteers armed with rifles in addition to several hundred men from the territorial army from Dej (Cluj County). According to Carl Klein, who was present to witness the events, this band tried to instil fear in the Romanians by looting/attacking the villages [120 p.188]. But they were not satisfied with the robberies and murders in the vicinity of Dej, a wholly Romanian region, and headed up the Someșul

Mare River to Beclean (Bistrița-Năsăud County), which was equally populated by Romanians. On 28.10.1848, the veterans of the retired lieutenant Grigore Mihăilaș appeared—several hundred of them, mostly armed with spears—and the insurgents lost some of their previous boldness, as displayed during the robbery and murder of civilians, laying down their weapons and surrendering! They were escorted to Năsăud, the centre of the 2nd Romanian Border Regiment, where the troop was released and each soldier was sent to his home by Lieutenant Colonel Reininger. Major Kornisch was handed over to Lieutenant Colonel Carol Urban in Reghin. He released him on condition that he would no longer fight against the imperial troops [120 p.189]. On 29.10.1848 at Beica (Mureș County), Carol Urban repelled a Szekler battalion of 140 horsemen and a detachment of volunteers, but he also captured 320 "Szekler" prisoners in addition to weapons. Prisoners fit for battle were escorted to imperial-held Galicia [120 p.192].

The 1st Battalion of the 2nd Romanian Border Regiment went to the Serbo-Croatian front at the request of Budapest and with the foolish complicity of General Anton Püchner, the commanding general of Transylvania. The battalion, which refused to commit criminal acts towards non-Hungarian nationalities and assume the role of an instrument of extermination as contrived by "revolutionary" Budapest, arrived in mid-February 1849 at a barracks in Budapest, where they were sequestered. The battalion did not receive any bread for five days and 30 of them sickened and died without being given medical assistance [120 p.192]. This battalion of the 2nd Regiment, which resisted Hungarian pressure to kill/loot the Serbs and Croats, did not betray Austria and was rewarded by the emperor with a gold medal bearing the inscription *For constancy in sworn loyalty in the year 1848* [120 p.231].

Another interesting example is noted below, its relevance residing in the fact that it shows again, if needed, the civilized and orderly treatment of our people, but also reveals just how "Magyar" the Hungarians were. On the night of February 5, 1849, at Muresenii Bârgăului (Bistrița-Năsăud County), a company led by the officers Storch, Pantelimon Domide, and Grigore Bota captured 11 officers, 1 doctor, 44 hussars, 600 infantrymen, 60 horses, 2 wagons with ammunition, 2 cannons, and the flag. During the fighting, a rebel was wounded. The 11 captured officers were: Felix Kofler, Heinrich Hoffmann, Johann Bayerle, Johann Krischan (Ioan Crișan), Albert Redl, Oskar Claner, Georg Mezzey, Josef Ritter, Karl Liebits, August Raneker, Nicolaus Baros, and Ferdinand Petrovich [120 p.208]. That is, nine Germans, one Romanian and one Serbian.

A detachment of insurgents led by Colonel Teleki, consisting of 230 infantry and 130 cavalry, advanced towards Monor and assassinated 23 Romanians, including some who were bedridden. The horde did not stop and vanquished the villages of Ruși Mountains and Morăreni (Bistrița-Năsăud County) belonging to the border guard company from Monor, where 42 invalids were shot and the inhabitants had their animals confiscated. After this, the insurgent detachment attacked townships in the counties of Cluj, Turda, Inner Solnoc, Middle Solnoc, and Dăbâca, in the seat of Mureș and the district of Chioar, where unimaginable atrocities were committed [120 p.216-217].

Another problem that Hungarian historiography raises is that of reciprocity, i.e., that the Magyarized committed atrocities, but the Romanians did the same! Here is an example of such reciprocity described by an eyewitness, the archpriest Iosif Bașa, who saw the scenes with his own eyes while hiding in the forest, just above the place where the hangmen were. On 4.11.1848, a band that had come from Hungary to Halmagiu (Arad County) hanged five priests before shooting the sixth, alongside other Romanian peasants. Then the band set fire to the surrounding villages, shooting the fleeing peasants. After these glorious deeds, they left for Baia de Criș (Hunedoara County) and in the village of Bătrâna they slaughtered 700 Romanians (8.11.1848). On 10.11.1848 in Baia de Criș, on the occasion of the retreat to Hungary, they hanged seven Romanians and two Germans before setting fire to the villages of Lunca and Căstău. When the Romanians came from Abrud and Zlatna (Alba County) on 14.11.1848, they took down the nine people who had been hanged and buried them. They hanged six Hungarians speakers in revenge because that was what they could find. The description of these events was given by Archpriest Iosif Bașa in a letter to Bishop A. Șaguna, which can be found in the archives of the Consistory of Sibiu [114 p.44].

On the one hand, we have hundreds of Romanian villages burned and completely destroyed and other villages partially destroyed, as well as the Saxon towns of Reghin, Feldioara (Brașov County), Hărman, Sânpetru, Archita, Hoghilag, Slimnic, Șura Mare, and Sebeș, as noted by the *Siebenburger Bote* newspaper on 12.02.1849. On the other, we have Aiud and Zlatna (Alba County) burned by the Romanians. Let us take a closer look at how the burning of Zlatna and Aiud took place. The Hungarian civil guards from Aiud reduced the villages of Cascovia and Măgina (Alba County) to ashes, after which the Romanians took revenge by burning down Aiud. At Zlatna, the leaders of the Romanian defenders of the land of the Mots showed up for peace negotiations with Kossuth's proxy and agreed to lay down their arms (May 6/7, 1849), but they were shot and hanged. The revenge of the surviving Romanians was commensurate with the enemy's actions, but the women, children, and elderly Hungarian speakers were sheltered and protected in the house of the Romanian priest Sterca-Şuluţiu.

Beyond the looting and burning of Reghin, let us see how Lieutenant Colonel Carol Urban proceeded after victory at Dej (Cluj County). On 24.11.1848, the rebel leaders Katona Mikloş and Teleki Sandor fled with their concubines, leaving their sick and wounded in the hands of the 2nd Border Battalion. In Dej, the rebel women also fired on the border battalion led by Carol Urban. The horde of 14,000 rebels dispersed, killing civilians and setting fire to villages. In Şomcuta alone, 32 Romanians were found hanging after they had left. On the other hand, the Romanian battalion took care of sick and wounded rebels [6 vol. II p.385].

On 28.10.1848 in Iernut (Mureş County), 23 Romanian soldiers who had been taken prisoner were hanged [116 p.45]. On 12.02.1849, the Romanians led by Cernoevici captured 500 insurgents in Deva who they escorted to Timişoara, handing them over, according to the law, to the imperial garrison.

On the one hand, we have thousands of Romanian civilians killed in the campaign of repression in Zarand, while on the other, we have six Hungarian speakers killed in the campaign to disarm the killers in 120 villages on the plains by Prefect Axente Sever. We have an army of murderers and arsonists in Dej and Beclean—Kornisch's army—while on the other, the commanders of the 2nd Romanian Border Regiment let the "army" go home based on an oath given by the murderers that they would no longer unjustifiably kill and commit arson! On the one hand, the area saw robbery, arson, and assassinations not seen in Europe for hundreds of years, on the other, the perpetrators of these robberies and assassinations were sent to Galicia or Timişoara to be taken back by their superiors. On the one side, they did not merely kill the wounded in the hospitals, but also the invalids left in the villages abandoned by the healthy residents for fear of repression, while on the other, the wounded left on the battlefield were taken in and cared for by the 2nd Romanian Border Regiment. On the one hand, they did not merely kill mothers, but also babies. Moreover, there are known cases when the rebels defended themselves by putting Romanian women and children in front of them [6 vol. II p.520]. The young Florian Lăscudean from Cucerdea (Mureş County) was cut down with a sword, when the blockade of Bem was broken, entering Alba Iulia (he died after three days). Breaking the blockade was reason enough for the rebels to kill his family: children, sisters, and parents [116 p.113].

7.5 Contemporary Accounts of the Nature of the War

On 10.10.1848, Kossuth gave a speech to the Diet of Pest, declaring that, although he felt sorry for the Romanians, he would *slaughter them terribly* [115 p.87]. On the same day, together with Esterhazi, he signed an ultimatum addressed to the Romanians:

> *Then it would have been better not to have been born at all ... But even so, the Hungarians and the Szeklers will be commanded to rise up and for the storm to sweep away every dissatisfied piece of garbage... So that the Hungarian and Szekler people rise up, all of them, and to erase from the face of the earth every traitor and rebel ...* [127 p.441].

The threats, it goes without saying, materialized in the field in the form of assassinations, each more savage than the last. In November 1848, the Hungarian feudal lords addressed the Saxon leaders with a call for reconciliation and that together, Hungarian and Saxon, *united should wipe the Romanians from the face of the earth* [114 p.39]. Lajos Kossuth, the agitator who became the governor of the country, sent Ioan Dragoș, the deputy from Bihor, to propose terms for an armistice to the Mots. In order to get them to lay down their arms and achieve a truce, he wrote of brotherhood, love, goodwill, and olive branches. Kossuth's long letter is dated April 26, 1849/Dobrâtin. Ioan Dragoș arrived in Abrud a week later and the meetings with Iancu and his prefects took place May 4-6. Major Hatvani, aware of Dragoș' "mission", occupied Abrud on May 6, while Dragoș was negotiating with Iancu, Buteanu, Dobra, and other Romanian leaders, thus trapping them! They arrested the Romanian leaders who had been lured into a lull of "pacification", including Buteanu, Dobra, and Boeriu, as well as other Romanian leaders, and then the band broke into people's houses, killing, defiling, and robbing [52 p.174]. Three days later, the women and children of the Hungarian speakers from Abrud were sheltered and protected in the houses of the priest Sterca-Șuluțiu; these were the same Hungarians who days before had killed women, children, and old people because they were "Wallachian" [220 no. 7/1 April 1877]. Iancu miraculously escaped the trap. We also have the direct confirmation of the perversion of the renegade Slovak through the report of the "commander of the free troops and the army", of the lawyer Major Imre Hatvani, dated 05/07/1849, to the president-governor Kossuth, who told him that he acted according to instructions received [52 p.172]. But what stronger evidence of deception is there than the simultaneous start of "pacification" with the assault on Abrud led by the lawyer Hatvani? Taking into account the few days necessary for the information to get from

Dobrâtin to Abrud, taking a detour through Arad, we have further confirmation of the lack of honour from May 11, 1849, in Kosuth's letter to Hatvani. Kossuth specified that *under the pretext of the armistice they should by all means continue the military invasion* [53 vol. II p.112]. The original text and its translation can be found in the *Newspaper of the Transylvania Association* [no. 2/1877, Braşov January 15, 1877]. Perversity and lack of honour were present from top to bottom in order to achieve a singular goal—the extermination of the Romanians, as summarized in the expression *unite or die* (*unió vagy hálál*). After Iosif Bem, disgusted by the mass executions perpetrated on Romanians, had given the second proclamation/threat/amnesty in March 1849, but Kossuth immediately dismissed that amnesty. As a result, every officer, every Hungarian claimed the right to take the lives of Romanians [6 vol. II p.481]. It still needs to be investigated whether this amnesty-dismissal was not a tactic in itself!

Iosif Bem, a Pole, and, according to Bălcescu, a false man [116 p.152] with a weak character, was disturbed by the number of atrocities committed by the Hungarians (by the time he had returned from Banat to Sibiu, a further 4,000 unarmed Romanian civilians had been killed; according to George Bariţiu's amendment, this figure was 6,000) and on 14.06.1849, he once again asked Kossuth in writing to stop the activity of the blood courts [6 vol. II p.482]. Bem's approach was different, namely to take the clergy, women, and children hostage [116 p164].

On 16.01.1849, Lieutenant Colonel Czecz (nephew of the Romanian priest Ţeţu from Săsciori, Făgăraş) wrote from Turda to the General Commissioner for Transylvania, Ödön Beöthy, that in order to be rid of the Romanians, all the villages must be burned and all the Romanians killed [53 vol III p.275].

Bethlen Janos Jr., the commissioner of the seat of Mureş, showed that the practices of the "Hungarian" army, in defence of the feudal lords, resulted in ethnic cleansing [116 p.45].

Colonel Baron Farcaş Kemeny, after receiving another 4,000 men and 18 cannons, wrote a letter at Abrud on June 12, 1849, addressed *To Iancu and his Wallachian gang*, threatening him and revealing that the "revolutionaries" planned to exterminate every last Romanian [114 p.39], including *babies in the cradle* [52 p.214].

On 21.06.1849, Colonel Josif Simonffy sent a letter from Vascau where he was stationed with his unit. In the letter addressed to Iancu, he asked him to accept Kossuth's offer, otherwise *eradication and depopulation by fire and iron* awaited him [115 p .97].

On June 24, 1849, when they thought they were on high ground,

Captain Gabány, from Kemeny's army, wrote from Dărăbanț (Alba County), *let's exterminate without mercy* the rebellious Romanians [114 p.40].

Paul Vasvari was the son of a Ruthenian priest from Nir (Tisa Plain) and had been Magyarized through his schooling. He wrote to Kossuth that they must deceive the good-natured Romanians with words and proclamations and *exterminate those who do not convert* (*e faj kiirtattott*) [52 p.224].

Captain Carl Klein, a participant in the terrible events of 1848-49, concluded that the leaders of the Croats, Serbs, Romanians, and Slovaks would become the tools of oppression and destruction of their own nations. Thus, the Croats and Serbs from Banat, as well as the Transylvanian Romanians took up arms to fight for the Habsburg dynasty, seeking to secure their education and their national identity [120 p.157].

George Barițiu observed that, at a time when few believed that Kossuth and his gang were determined to wage a war of extermination, the lawyer Ioan Buteanu, prefect of Zarand, knew only too well the arrogance and the fanaticism of the Hungarians [6 vol. II p.368]. From the very beginning, the watchword of the Transylvanian insurgents was extermination. Barițiu supports this perspective with the following argument: extermination was clearly the goal considering that the Hungarians had made the decision to kill unarmed people, untried, without having been accused of any capital crime, through the blood courts and in a matter of hours; this was in addition to the killings committed in houses, yards, fields, and on the roads, given that all the Romanians had been disarmed, with the exception of those living in the Apuseni Mountains [6 vol. II p.481]. George Barițiu, involved as he was in the events of his time, called this war one of extermination as well as a civil war, since, as we have already noted, a good part of those that fought for Hungary was Romanian, especially Romanians from Maramureș, the Tisa Plain, and Banat, as well as some from Transylvania. It was a conflict in which most battles saw Romanian fight Romanian; given that one officer commanded dozens or even hundreds of soldiers this was a serious enough reason for Romanians to be kept in total ignorance, in the dark—they could end up being used in any "affair", even in the sordid one of their own annihilation.

From a cultural perspective, freed from the context of the battles in Transylvania, about which he probably did not even know that much (an objective history has never been published in Hungary), Johann Weidlein bluntly stated that the Hungarian liberation struggle of 1848-49 should be called the fight for the freedom of nations against Hungarian oppression [182 p.66].

7.6 More than 53,000 Romanians and Saxons Murdered

The census of 1850 shows that approximately 50,000 people were missing compared to the year before these events [141 p.213]. With an absolute increase in the population of Transylvania of about 15,000 per year between 1848 and 1850, we should have seen an increase of about 40,000 people. In other words, 90,000 people were missing. The historian Ioan Bolovan established a figure of 92,000 [189 p.377] in more accurate terms, of which 52-55,000 were due to genocide. The rest were due to disease, lack of shelter and food (hundreds of villages burned, with mobile wealth taken to Hungary), and emigration to Romania. Even this approximation of 52,000-55,000 victims is not definitive; it still needs to be rethought and reanalysed on the basis of a number of documents from 1848/49. The historian Gelu Neamțu was the first to undertake this task. The notoriety of the figure of 40,000 Romanians killed comes from both Barițiu [189 p.376] and Andrei Saguna. But the bishop already had this figure in October 1848, sourced from a document written by the Roman Catholic canon Ráduly published in the *Südslavische Zeitung* on 30.12.1849 and republished both in Bucovina on 6.01.1850 [114 p. 46] and in a fascicle *Die Romänen der oesterreichissen Monarchie* in Vienna, also in 1850 [219 p.939]. This figure of 40,000 must be considered incomplete if only because the Romanians who remained alive were so terrorised that only a few dared to expose the atrocities of their past and present masters. Moreover, the fact remains that many testimonies have not been published even up to today and those that have been published have not yet been brought together in one archive. Tens of thousands of Romanians, including hundreds of priests, were sent to the afterlife, being hanged, put to the sword, shot, and burned; often entire families perished. Such losses would not have been reported. The figure of 40,000 victims is also the result of an incomplete calculation: if the statistics note the absence of 55,000 citizens in Transylvania, then the pseudo-historiographers, and not only them but also the Romanian intellectuals trained by the Communist Party of Romania, claimed that there would have been 4,858 victims (4,449 Romanians, 252 Saxons, 165 Hungarians, and 72 others) [114 p.47]. Yes, 4,858 victims from some of the *blood court records* published and those were incomplete in themselves! The list of 4,858 victims in the document of Canon Ráduly is reproduced in full by Gelu Neamțu in [114]. What about the rest of the 50,000? We must seek the truth and not give in to "appeasing" political temptations, which will give rise to new crimes that are the same as the old ones, as was shown in 1848-49, 1914-19, 1940-45, and 1989, that is to say, throughout history. If

40,000 victims in Transylvania come from an incomplete computation (as described at the time by Romanian intellectuals), can we make a better approximation and come closer to the reality of the number of genocide victims in Transylvania? What arguments do we have?

1) 92,000 inhabitants missing in 1850 in Transylvania, of which 55,000 followed the genocide.

2) The figure of 40,000 Romanian casualties results from a fatally incomplete and partial account. The data on the assassinations led by the "revolutionary" nobility and the murders by the "revolutionary" army in 1848/49 were gathered from the notes of Romanian priests; however, some of the priests who were supposed to gather evidence were themselves assassinated and others, because of the unrelenting terror, did not dare compile accurate data. The priests who were assassinated, but known by name, were actually few in number, such as Ioan Pop, father of the philologist and historian Augustin Trebonius Ilarian who became president of the Romanian Academy. However, most of those murdered remained unknown. The official Count Francisc Haller boasted to G. Barițiu in June 1861 that he had shot three Romanian priests in October 1848, not just one as had previously been believed [6 vol. II p.303]. And there were hundreds of such cases. Other priests who were lucky enough not to meet "revolutionary" feudalists did not have the courage to communicate the data requested by the archpriests because of the violent and unrelenting terror that followed even after the defeat of the rebels by the tsarist army; an army that restructured, though only partially, the feudal order. There were hundreds of villages in which there were no priests, no churches, and no parishioners left; the killings here were never added to the final count. There are communities that shifted under the shadow of this terror to the Hungarian cults, such as the Romanians of Sângeorgiu de Pădure (Mureș County) who "reformed" overnight. Beyond Transylvania, we do not have estimates, but we know what happened in Banat, the Tisa Plain, and Maramureș. For example, the Hungarian troops stationed in Moisei started to burn down Borșa (Maramureș County) and there would have been no people left, and no market, if the mayor had not intervened, as the Jews of Moisei wrote to the Austrian authorities [6 vol. II p.781].

3) In 1870, Artemiu Publiu Alexi published "a list of names of those deceased" from an official work of the time, found at the *Ioanneum* library in Graz. This work is important because it provides some details about the

victims of martial law during the 10 months of terror of the
"revolutionary" feudal lords. Out of 4,834 (plus 24 from Dej) victims, 252
were Saxon, 72 other nationalities, 165 with Hungarian names, and the
rest Romanian [114 p.47]. Let it be clear, 165 unarmed men with
Hungarian names were convicted by the martial courts! However, what
this means is that 3.4 % of the victims were so-called Hungarians,
Magyarized, or had Hungarian names. But we should not consider the
Romanian, Slovak, and German victims of the rebel camp to be
Hungarian. Even the several thousand serfs hanged and impaled in the
spring of 1848 by the feudal lords do not appear in the list from the
Ioanneum. They are not the 1,887 victims from Batrâna and Vața (October
1848), for the commission of these mass murders the assassins did not
need any court, not even a martial tribunal! In the list published by
Artemiu Alexi we find in Saxon Reghin a civilian victim (Adamu Kirila,
shot in April 1849) [114 p.253]. We have described, briefly it is true, the
genocide committed in Reghin over November 1-3, 1848, and have also
mentioned the 17 wounded at the hospital in Reghin killed by the
marauding rebels! In the list extracted by Alexi in Șomcuta (Maramureș
County) there are six men who were killed by the blood court at the hands
of Katona Mikloș [114 p.281]. Moreover, we already know that Lieutenant
Colonel Carol Urban, after the Battle of Dej, following the looting "army"
towards Baia Mare, took down another 32 murdered Romanians and
buried them in Șomcuta. In the correspondence between Artemiu Publiu
Alexi and George Barițiu, we see Alexi insisting in every letter that all
Romanians must write and testify about the terrible years of 1848-49.
Alexi was aware that information about the genocide was incomplete. An
example appears in his letter sent from Graz in July 1870 to George
Barițiu [114 p.245].

4) Let us not forget how the slaughter of the Romanians began in the
spring of 1848 at Luna, where 32 young Romanians were murdered
precisely because they refused to be conscripted into the army of the
feudal "revolutionaries". While, in particular, in Transylvania, Zarand,
Bihor, and mountainous Arad, Romanians were slaughtered because they
refused to betray their sworn allegiance to the emperor, in Banat, the Tisa
Plain, and Maramureș many Romanians and Swabians were recruited
without any problem by the "revolutionaries"! And the Romanians were
not just recruited by the rebels there, but also in Transylvania. Lieutenant
Mihăilaș in a letter to the command of the Năsăud Regiment from Sadova
(Bucovina) dated 14.04.1849 wrote that in the Someș Mare valley there
were rebel troops made up of Romanian farmers and boys recruited by the

rebels from among the civilians of the province [120 p.135]. We know that recruitment was achieved through terror and resulted in many victims.

5) According to the Hungarian historian Kővári, the army taken over by the Polish general Josef Bem at Ciucea numbered 12,535 men (without the militias, the gangs of robbers, and the guard regiments of the Szekler areas) including 3,000 of the national guard from Bihor, in which the Romanian soldiers were so numerous that the Greek Catholic bishop of Oradea Mare (Vasile Erdeli) had to give them two Romanian chaplains, especially as there were also many Romanians in the Hungarian line battalions. [6 vol. II p.403]. That is to say, 7,481 Romanians out of a total of 12,535, with Slovaks and Ruthenians, as well as Polish, Italian, and German volunteers from the Germanic countries. A researcher from Budapest, Mr. Bona, put forward a figure of 25,000 Romanians in Bem's army [116 p.161]. Having taken control of the Transylvanian plain by 22.03.1849, the rebels recruited Romanians, Saxons:

Soon after, Bem set about forming battalions. He formed thirteen [battalions] out of the Szeklers. They then recruited as many boys as they could get from the Romanians and Saxons as could not escape, either in the Apuseni Mountains or in Romania and Bucovina. In a few weeks, Bem had formed an army of recruits numbering 30,000 from this country alone [6 vol. II p.476].

The German legion was made up of several companies, the 6th, called the *Totenkopf*, fought alongside Hatvany at Corna (Alba County) in the Apuseni Mountains against the brave tribune Vlăduț's soldiers from Bucium [6 vol. II p.520]. At the Battle of Dej in November 1848, 12,000 men, including 600 Viennese pan-Germanist students, fought against Lt. Col. Urban [6 vol. II p.384]. The pan-Germanists fought against the House of Habsburg because they believed that Austria should be part of the German Empire. There was also an Italian legion [32 p.415] and a Polish legion commanded by Zarzicky [6 vol. II p.565]. In other words, among the many "Hungarian" soldiers who died in the war, there were those of many other nations who were clearly not Hungarian, but rather Romanian, Saxon, and Magyarized people, in addition to foreigners (Poles, Italians, Austrians, and Germans). Finally, there were not just Romanian troops, but also Romanian officers in the so-called Hungarian "revolutionary" army, such as Ioan Crișan, Alexie Foro, and Colonel Czecz who was in command of the insurgent army in Ciucea for a few days until General Bem took over. Not to mention the Saxon and Slovak officers who were the most numerous in the "revolutionary" army. We have already mentioned the officers Dorschner, Betzman, Czerniko, Felix Kofler, Heinrich Hoffmann, Johann Bayerle, Albert Redl, Oskar Claner, Georg Mezzey, Josef Ritter, Karl Liebits, August Raneker, Nicolaus Baros, and Ferdinand Petrovich who left the 2nd Battalion of the 2nd Romanian Border Regiment to join the rebels! And so on and so forth.

6) The proportion of military victims, i.e., regular war casualties, is tiny compared to civilian casualties. For example, the battle for Mariselu lasted six hours until the "Hungarians" had lost 13 men and retreated; the Mots lost six men [52 p.131]. On February 20, a troop of 200 soldiers led by Carol Zudor attacked the Mots on the Arieş River at Valea Poienii and were repulsed. On February 27, the reinforced troop returned to attack Baia de Arieş (Cluj County), but Balint with his tribesmen repelled them again; the rebels lost 15 men in the skirmish. On 20.11.1848, a Szekler battalion together with 100 cavalrymen headed towards the Sântioana area, met the Năsăud Border Guards of Lieutenant Colonel Carol Urban and were forced to run, 36 of them being taken prisoner. Six Romanians were seriously wounded, while among the Szeklers we find one dead and 10 seriously wounded [52 p.190]. Everywhere the number of soldiers killed in battle was small.

Research on the genocide must continue

A start must be made with the publication of all the documents from the Romanian, Slovak, Serbian, and Hungarian archives. At least in Romania, many archival documents regarding the events of 1848/49 have not been published. The recent publication of two original valuable manuscripts found in the archives is a good start: Captain Carl Klein's *History of the Second Romanian Regiment* [120] and *Der Guerillas Krieg* [12].

Further investigation is required to uncover the truth, the number, and the fate of the Saxon and Romanian soldiers imprisoned by the rebels and subsequently killed. The number of Romanian and German victims in the rebel armies from Banat, the Tisa Plain, and Maramureş remains to be investigated as well.

Among the casualties in the regular "Hungarian" army we have a logical basis, both in the structure of the Hungarian army, which reflected the demographics of the time, accentuated by the recruitment policy, and in the difference in the treatment of prisoners and wounded between the imperial armies and the insurgents and their gangs. Ioan Slavici, who was very well informed from the point of view of Budapest, and who was also extremely thorough, wrote:

In Hungary [our note: in the broader sense], *there were 4.5 million Hungarians before the revolution—apart from the elements represented in smaller numbers, still 5 million Slavs, 1.3 million Germans and 2.7 million Romanians* [160 p.760].

Slavici was working with official data and not amending them after receiving a confession! That is, in 1848 Hungarian speakers were a third of the total. From Partenie Gruescu's report we know how the Romanians were recruited into Bem's army in the spring of 1849 and *the worst crimes against humanity were committed* [116 p.160]. These crimes were not recorded either.

Andrei Saguna, who received reports from his archpriests throughout Transylvania, was horrified by the scale of the slaughter unleashed by the "Hungarians" and at the meeting of the *Pacification Committee (the defence of the country)* in Sibiu he declared:

> *But I am convinced, gentlemen, that if this country remains under the power of the insurgents and at their will, out of one million two hundred thousand Romanians, 200,000 will remain, and out of 200,000 Saxons, twenty thousand* [6 vol. II p.401].

That is, only those Romanians who "settled in" or served the feudal order would be allowed to remain alive! That is why he, together with the Saxons, pleaded for the intervention of Russian troops in order to prevent the genocide that had started with such hatred directed against the Romanians and the Saxons, without knowing that Emperor Ferdinand I had secretly asked Tsar Nicholas I to intervene long before. In the Pacification Committee of December 31, 1848 in Sibiu, after Joseph Benigni's report, the Saxon Franz von Reichenstein drew the following conclusion:

> *If ... it is not able to defend Transylvania ... then Austria no longer deserves to reign in this country* [6 vol. II p.413].

At the end of January 1849, several Hungarian feudal lords, among them Count Emeric Miko, asked Tsar Nicholas I to take a stand and intervene against the "revolution" [6 vol. II p. 451].

Should we thus call it a Hungarian revolution? "We should not!" according to what the greatest historian of Transylvania wrote with "mathematical" precision in his famous *Older Notes on Our 1848 Revolution* [Annex C]. After the proclamation of democratic rights in Vienna on March 13, 1848, could it be called a Hungarian revolution considering the annulment in Transylvania of the freedom of the press and the freedom of assemblies with the maintenance of the "noble hierarchy"? Or described so given the expulsion of the Jews from Cluj after the riots of March 21, 1848 [217 p.227]? Or considering the (preventive) execution of thousands of serfs, *viventum rer*, by hanging and impaling in March 1848 by the last feudal lords of Europe according to the principle of *usque ad bene placitum* be regarded as a revolution? Or given the execution of Romanian intellectual youths in Cluj as a preventive measure to hinder any future Romanian movement, in April 1848 [217 p.238]?

CHAPTER 8

DENATIONALISATION WITH BATS AND STICKS

The phenomenon of the Magyarization of the Romanians between the Tisa and the Carpathians took two main forms: the *Magyarization of groups* across large territories, including entire towns and villages, and the *Magyarization of families*. The phenomenon of Magyarization was not peculiar to Transylvania and the Tisa Plain, but spread throughout the whole of the area administered by the culture of hatred and chauvinism. Its consequences were just as devastating in Pannonia and Slovakia. J. Weidlein, the most knowledgeable of the connoisseurs of this culture of hate, points out:

> *Kossuth's most trusted troops were made up of jurists, young parliamentarians and students, who had already established a veritable terror in Bratislava at the 1832-36 Diet, now prowling through Pest and punching and beating the city's German inhabitants, including Szechenyi's partisans. Since Szechenyi considered the higher culture of this bourgeoisie to be the greatest enemy of the Magyarization efforts, they began to destroy the cultural establishments of the Germans. They targeted first of all the German theatre in Pest* [182 p.64].

The final result was the same as in the "Szekler areas" where those who spoke the mother tongue were beaten. As such, Germans in Pannonia no longer had the courage to speak German. In contrast, in Turkish Swabia, by 1900, about 85 % of the non-Magyarized Swabian population remained! Thus, something else was needed, apart from the bat!

8.1 Szeklerization and Magyarization

A handful of horsemen, Szeklers, were sent by the Catholic royalty, a *German-hailing* royalty, to the eastern edge of Transylvania with the obligation to help the Romanians guard the mountain passes to Moldova. The Szeklers—literally, "guardians" in Turkic—were, perhaps, not a specific ethnic group. In fact, the ethnic origin of the old Szeklers remains unknown to this day. In addition to the traditional guarding duties of the

Romanians and the Szeklers, the Romanians alone were responsible for guarding the Vlăhiţa and Breţcu cnezates [154].

An act issued by Sigismund of Luxembourg, published by Fejer in *Codex Dipl. Hungarorum* X, 6, 796-798 and quoted by Nicolae Densusianu states that the Romanians, lord and peasant alike, from the Curvature Carpathians are obliged according to custom *sicut hactenus sunt consueti* (as they have hitherto been accustomed) to defend the frontier and make incursions over the mountains into the lands of Moldavia, now and on into the future.

In his chronicle, the Minorite monk Paulus of Venice (†1334) wrote that the defence of the eastern passes of Transylvania was an old custom of the Romanians in these places [104 p.248]. This confirms, directly, the ethnic origin of the autochthonous population—nowhere in the historiographical record is there any mention of the colonisation of the Szeklers. That the number of Szeklers was insignificant is evident from the very fact that in 1211 the pope required the Teutonic Order, after the armistice with Saladin, to support the Latin Empire (of Constantinople), which was under attack by the Cumaeans and the Dacian-Romans of 'Milcovia'. Pope Innocent III sought, through this military order that depended directly on the Vatican, to address many key geopolitical issues. In 1225, as the goals of the pope and King Andrew II (1205-1235) came into conflict, the Teutonic knights set out for northeastern Europe, summoned by the Polish Duke Konrad of Mazovia to fight against the pagan Prussians [111 p.49].

The Szeklers, a handful of families, were militarily organized and received economic and legal privileges above the mass of natives. They elected a captain and a judge at their head and ruled according to *jus Olachalis* (Romanian Law), they retained their organization in seats, that is, they took everything from the Romanians. Later, in some documents *jus Olachalis* appears alongside *jus Olachalis* and *jus Siculicalis* (Szekler Law), but it is not certain whether the change in name would have resulted in a change in content. Legal judgments for the Szeklers were made in the seat, which had 12 members plus judges, just as in the case of the Romanians!

In 1228, the Dominican Bishop of Milcovia, Theodoric, appointed by Pope Gregory IX (1227-1241), i.e., Bishop of the Curvature Carpathians, addressed the Szeklers. His goal was not to insist on the creation of a new diocese of the Cumaeans, since:

> ...*in the same church the Szeklers, the Cumaeans and the Romanians can meet together ... just as they can hear the Apostle: there is no Greek or Jew, no barbarian or Scythian* [51 p.58].

A diploma of Béla IV from 1251 concerning the settlement of the Szeklers in the Curvature Carpathians speaks of "our peoples" in that area. In 1256, the tithes to be collected *ex parte Sicolorum et Valahorum* (from Szeklers and Romanians) were destined for the Bishopric of Strigonius [154 p.244]. In the first half of the 13th century, only garrison villages were found. After the retreat of the Tatars, however, castles were built and those living around them gained the rank of *jobagiones castrenses*, forming villages that received certain privileges and broad autonomy. King Ladislaus Cumanus (1272-1290) required the cnez Ursu to appear before him with the magistrum Dominic, as chiefs of all the Romanians of Vlăhița. They complained about the endless pillaging they had to endure from the Szeklers to the extent that the Romanians were no longer able to supply the fortress with the wood it needed to be fortified. The king, after listening to their complaint, took the township of Vlăhița under his protection and obliged the Romanians to provide the wood needed to fortify the fortress. In exchange, he granted them the following favours: to be exempt from any tithe; give only the dues owed to the Catholic church of Odorheiu (Harghita County); to be exempt from the so-called *dicatione tax*; and, in exchange, to pay their dues to their cnez. Additionally, no one should try to collect the tithe of oxen (*signatura bovum*) from them, according to local custom.

The toponyms in the Curvature Carpathians are of Romanian origin. Most mountain peaks bear Romanian names, such as Archita, Găluga, Cioara, Putna, Bucin, Saca, Piatra, Ciucașu, Jomșa, Bogdan, and Găinușa, etc., all of which can be found in the Harghita Massif located in the middle of the "Szekler-settled land". The names of the highest peaks in the Bodoc Mountains, where there is no trace of a Romanian element today, are also of Romanian origin, such as Ciomagu, Tițelu, Moara Mare, Vârful, Bordei, Gogan, and Vertej. Among the so-called Szeklers of today, from the Curvature Carpathians, from the slopes of the Harghita and Bodoc mountains, we find purely Romanian names, such as Feher Nyiko (Alba Mică), Părul, Sâncele, Găini, Foiu, Desag, Bogata, Bâscu, Ion, Dungu, Roman, Galata, Gemenii, Goran, Letea-Mare and Mică, Bădeni, and Rața [104 p.246]. Since then, over the centuries, the privileges of the "military", whether Szeklers or Szeklerized, have consistently grown, fed by increasingly unbearable discrimination against the natives. The unbalanced coexistence between the small "elite" of newcomers and the great majority of Romanians, deprived of their rights and reduced to poverty, was partly regulated by "denationalisation" and emigration. Many moved to Moldova; in 1767 alone, 24,000 families fled the area [106 p.25]. From the beginning of the 19th century, the struggle against the Romanians took on institutional forms. In addition to the *Hungarian churches* (a *notion* taken from the Hungarian speakers who, when referring to their churches, did not refer to them with a Christian attribute, but with a racial attribute), in the administration, state companies, schools, and the army Magyarization societies were established. Magyarization manuals and procedures were published and plans, maps and pathways for Magyarization were drawn up.

The Orthodox confession was merely a heresy, tolerated according to the goodwill of the prince and lord—*usque ad beneplacitum principum ac regnicolarum*, as written in the feudal constitution of the autonomous Principality of Transylvania. Whether even life was to be tolerated or not was at the whim of those in power! The German Konrad Jakob Hildebrand, accompanying three Swedish ambassadors through Transylvania on their way to Constantinople in 1656, was struck by the large number of Romanians, whom he regarded as descendants of the famous Roman soldiers; but these Wallachians endured such harsh treatment that they considered being hanged instead of impaled a favour. The terrible sight of the impaled Romanians at the entrance to all the villages he passed through in Transylvania shocked Hildebrand [20 p.31].

Because the Szeklers were not Hungarians, Magyarization did not bypass them either. In his book *Historia* (1852, Budapest) the Szekler writer Mihaly Cserei (1668-1756) is trenchant in his criticism:

> *Transylvania's misfortune has always been drawn from Hungary and from the Hungarians. That's how we lost the country and our freedom* [166 p.85].

A document from 1699 concerning the Romanians of Trei Scaune (Covasna County) records many Romanian craftsmen, including numerous millers, furriers, blacksmiths, bakers, rope makers, saddlers, and butchers. The study was made by Pál Judit, who observed the phenomenon of the mass Szeklerization of the Romanians, first in linguistic terms and then in religious ones [217 p.161]. According to a record for Inochentie Micu in 1733, there were 565 Romanian families in the seat of Odorhei out of a total of 5,867 [150 p.56], i.e., constituting approximately 10 %. After the 1857 census, only 3.53 % of the Romanian families were found to survive in Odorhei [206]. Here is a further and more recent example of the process of Magyarization through the church: around 1892, Boer Traian built a Roman Catholic church to attract Romanians to this confession, after his father Traian Boeru, a Greek Catholic priest, had switched back to the Orthodox Church in 1872; in 1874, the Romanian Orthodox community switched to Catholicism [154 p.156]. This change was necessary because the Vatican did not formally admit the direct conversion of Greek Catholics to Catholicism. Another typical example of Magyarization that is complementary to the one mentioned above: in 1860 in Lăzăreni, Tuşnad, and Cosmeni the majority was Romanian. Until 1910 the Romanians had their own priest, when an envoy of the government gathered the Romanians and gave them a "patriotic" speech, insulting them. Then he had a recording of the proceedings drawn up in which the Romanians asked to be transferred to the Roman Catholic Church. The Romanians scattered without signing, but that was no obstacle to the envoy of the government—the request was submitted to the Ministry of Religious Affairs, which approved it. As you can see, Rome's scruples no longer mattered

Fig. 8.1. Ethnic groups in Hungary by Pal Balogh.

in Budapest by 1910. This explains why, in the Greek Catholic Church's yearbook of 1911, out of the vast network of 179 parishes in the Curvature Carpathians, 162 were without priests [132 p.70].

In the Niraj Valley, Magyarization was so massive, intense, and even violent, especially at the end of the 19th century, that the Romanian language had completely disappeared by 1920 [154 p.84]. The pressure and terror exerted on the Romanians and Romanian-speakers was taken to extremes. As a "Szekler" from Sândominic told a journalist from Arad in 1862:

I am honestly not a Szekler, but if I speak Romanian I risk being beaten up [154 p.180].

Children's surnames were Magyarized and thenceforth spelt in Hungarian. For example, Gheorghe Sibianu from Aita Mare, who had two children, had to bring a document to his children's school renouncing his Orthodox confession, otherwise they would not have been accepted. Having no other alternative, the man's name was changed to Szebeni [112 p.14]. Such cases number the tens of thousands in Transylvania, the Tisa Plain, and Maramureş. Moreover, once patience had run dry, or as described by Samuel Decsi "Magyarization on the sly", Magyarization was done forcefully in the streets and with weapons, as happened in the German *oppidum* Ofen-Pest, where Hungarians reached 19 % of the total population, in 1725. Magyarization with a stick in the street is not a metaphor [182 p.64]!

In Bixad (Covasna County), according to Balogh Pál in *Ethnic Groups in Hungary* (Budapest, 1902), according to the 1890 census, the majority were Hungarians, 1-10 % were Germans, and there was a small minority of Slovaks; however, in terms of denomination he admits that 30-40 % were Orthodox [35 p.17]. In other words, a purely Romanian township in 1750, after a century of Magyarization, became, in the work of *male fide* Balogh Pal, more Hungarian than in reality. It became "purely Hungarian", although with 30-40 % Orthodox, many more Greek-Catholics, 1-10 % Germans, and a few percent Slovaks [35 p. 17]. This 1-10 % percent Germans says enough about the accuracy of the author's work! Ilieşi (Mureş County) was a purely Romanian township in 1850 and today it is purely Hungarian (i.e., 1972), except that the confessional majority is Greek-Catholic [177 p.41]. On this typically "Hungarian" basis, the same author establishes, according to the 1890 census, that in Transylvania (the country behind the Piatra Craiului Mountains) 652 localities had a Hungarian majority, 178 had a Saxon majority, in two the Slovaks were in the majority, and the Romanians in 1,785 [35 p.11]. In 1848, the number of Romanian villages was 2,400 [114 p.37]. Is it possible that in a matter of 52 years, from 1848 to 1890, the Romanians lost 615 villages, no longer holding the majority in some of them, while others were completely burnt down in 1848/49 and never rebuilt? The number of Romanian villages completely burned in 1848/49 was 230. In the case of others, which were only partially burned, the "culture" of hatred was clearly at work. However, in many cases, they were first Magyarized on paper. The proportion of the Hungarian villages that were Magyarized remains to be investigated. In 1848 in Sângeorgiu de Pădure (Mureş County), the Romanians were subjected to the atrocities we have mentioned and became victims of genocide. They were left without a priest and the church was destroyed. What followed was presented in the report of Archpriest Partenie Trombiţaş in Sângeorgiu de Pădure, a Romanian village (Orthodox and Greek-Catholic), in which the 100 Romanian Orthodox families were forced to switch to the Reformed religion. The Romanian Greek Catholics were not favoured either [114 p.22]. We do not know how many Greek Catholics there were at the time of the report of Archpriest Trombiţaş. *Today*, Archpriest Nicolae Vasiu has observed that in Sângeorgiul de Pădure, which was declared fully Hungarian by the Communists, there is still an Orthodox confessional minority amounting to 40 % of the population [177 p.41]. In the commune of Ciucsângeorgiu (Harghita County), the Romanians were recorded in the statistics of the time as follows: in 1750 there were 178; in 1871: 197; in

1910: 183; and in 1930 there were 231. Before 1940, there were 300 and two state schools that taught in Romanian and Hungarian. In September 1940, the teachers and the priest were expelled and since that time the Romanians were no longer educated in Romanian. The same happened in Ghelniţa, Lemnia, Lisnău, Căpeni, Mereşti, Crăciunel, Plăieşii de jos, Plăieşii de sus, Ocland, Vârghiş, Băţanii Mari, Aita Seacă, and Cernatul de jos. As I.I. Russu recalls:

> *Before 1866 the majority of the population of Cristur was Romanian, in 1900 Romanian was spoken, but after Apponyi's law, all those who spoke Romanian were blamed; the Romanian priest was expelled, the church destroyed, instead of Romanians, Germans, Armenians and Hungarian-speaking gypsies were settled there; the old Romanian families in Cristur, some are called Sztojka, and others like Fogarasi, Balint, Fodor, Simon, Balas, Fejer, Eleches or Demeter have Hungarian or Magyarized names [154 p.76].*

If we take a look at only these few examples, out of the hundreds available, we have at most 600 completely Magyarized villages, not 652, even considering Catholicized Romanians and Calvinized Romanians Hungarians. But there are hundreds of such cases. Certain corrections can be made on the basis of the Orthodox and Greek Catholic confessions, as in the case of Bixad, where the number of Orthodox, Greek-Catholics, and Lutherans constitute an overwhelming majority, while the Magyarized Catholics and Calvinists remain in the minority and are hard to identify. In the scientific world it is recognised that all Hungarian censuses were rigged in order to inflate the Hungarian share of the population: this was done methodologically, if you spoke Hungarian, you were automatically counted as Hungarian, in the field through intimidation, and finally when processing the data at the statistical office.

Then, where does the modified *învârtita* (Romanian folk dance in which the partners spin around), i.e., the *csárdás* (Hungarian folk dance in two distinct movements, a slow one and a second in which the movements become increasingly fast), come from in a nomadic people? Dancing in pairs can only be typical of a sedentary, agricultural people. The name *csárdás*, the so-called Hungarian national dance, is in fact a "modified *învârtita*". It appeared for the first time after 1850 at the initiative of Baron Bela Wenckheim [197 vol. II p58]. Ioan Slavici, who knew and understood these dances well, draws a clear distinction:

> *The Hungarians have one game in common: csárdás apart from this there are three other local dances. The csárdás consists of two parts: lassu-slow, and friss-fast. Lassu-slow is the Ardeleana (Romanian folk dance); friss-*

fast is a combination of the Romanian folk dances Bătuta, Pe picior, Crișana, Lugojana and Mărunțaua. [...] *The Romanian sings when he dances, but the Hungarian swears.* [...] *In such a way the Hungarians have changed the Romanian songs sung by them. Although lassu csárdás is the Romanian dance Ardeleana, the aria it is danced to is not Ardeleana, but the "doina"* [a Romanian folk song usually in the form of a lament: Merriam-Webster Dictionary]. *The aria of the Romanian doina is, however, the basis of Hungarian folk music. Friss csárdás is played according to the aria of the Romanian dances.* [...] *All these arias of the Hungarian, properly speaking, are often sung very badly, in inarticulate shrieks* [160 p.795].

Ion Slavici wrote about the Hungarian folk song *dal, dana*, saying that it is a genre of poetry with very few new (shrill, strident) elements, while the rest actually comes from the Romanian *Doina*. According to the harmonic nature of the *doina*, the misinterpretation of the Hungarian *dana* does not fit and the result is usually quite bad [160 p.793].

For example, in the *doina*:	In Hungarian, it becomes:
To a cloud I'd ride the moon	*Kossuth Lajos has announced,*
But for my darling's longing,	*That the regiment is weak,*
To a star I'd ride the moon	*If it's once again announced,*
But for my darling's yearning	*We all have away to sneak*

The writer Milan Kundera, drawing on his own culture, made his own observations without understanding things as deeply as Ion Slavici did. Speaking of Slovak music, Kundera noted its antiquity through its "veils", i.e., its succession of thin layers. The closest veil to the surface is a young, trivial, and noisy, seven-decade-old layer from the Czech lands. The second layer came from the period of the invasion of the Hungarian language into Slovakia and was brought by the Gypsy *tarafs*. The third wave is authentically Slovak and dates to the 17th and 18th centuries. But the 4th wave is much more beautiful, with much older tunes that go back to the 14th century when the Wallachians roamed the Tatra Mountains. The essential aspects are found beneath this layer, born of the ancient compositions of the pagan period and from the time of the Moravian Empire, but originating in antiquity in the Dionysian feasts [90 p.191].

In the Curvature Carpathians, the houses, style of woodworking, the sedentary lifestyle, agricultural work, carved wooden ornaments, costumes, fabric, pottery, songs, denominations, names, and Christening, wedding, and burial customs are all Romanian. How did steppe nomads come to the Curvature Carpathians with a woodworking tradition that is identical to that of the Romanian Cisalpine and Transalpine countries from

Maramureș, the land of the Mots, the Upper Country, Vrancea to Hobița (Gorj County), and Timoc (Bulgaria and Serbia)? Our typical country house would be the oldest European *Aryan house form*, both in terms of interior and exterior architecture, with the front porch and the disposition of the surrounding courtyard. This Aryan plan is characteristic of settled peoples, devoted to agriculture and not to nomadic life, to which *the Semitic house* corresponds, the plan of which emerged from the tents of nomadic tribes and has its rooms arranged around *an inner courtyard*, according to German scholars. The clothes of peasants and women were similar to those of the ancient Thracians and the national dances of the *hora*-type recall *the Chora* of ancient dramas [55 p.266]. How would pottery have come from nomadic peoples who drank water from horse-skin flasks and did not use fragile household implements? Where did the name of the feast of the birth of the Saviour *Karacioni* come from, if while passing through Kiev at the beginning of the 10th century, neither the Slavs, nor their chieftains had yet become Christians? Obviously from the Romanian *Crăciun*, i.e., Christmas. Where did the form of organization into seats and of the Germans into *Stuhle* come from, if not from the seats and judges of the Romanians in that corner of Dacia-Romania?

After the Peace of Westphalia in 1648, by applying the principle *cuius regio, eius religio*, Romanians were massively denationalised through religion. They 'left behind' their Romanian identity, but they took with them all their immaterial heritage (pagan and Christian beliefs, customs, carols, stories, chants, dances, embroideries, and wooden ornaments.

In 1871, Ioan Slavici wrote that among the characters of the "Hungarian" stories we find typical Romanian fairytale characters, such as mythical horses, "muma pădurii" (usually depicted as an ugly and evil old woman who wanders the woods luring children and killing people), dragons, fairies, Saint Friday (an old hag that punishes women who either work on Fridays or who are lazy), etc., or mysterious images typical of the Romanian people such as fights with giants. Moreover, the "Hungarian" often used Romanian syntax, [160 p.792].

*Fig. 8.2. The wooden house presented as Szekler
in the album published in 1891 [202].*

*Fig. 8.3. Romanian house from Harghita.
Ethnographic Museum in Cluj-Napoca.*

The exceptional man of culture, Ioan Slavici (1848-1925), who knew the "Hungarian" people like no other, could not gather new objective data, since it was not taken from the archives or revealed later by science (genetics); nor could he reach any conclusion other than the logical one that the Hungarians assimilated the local music, poetry, dance, and all other forms of folk culture from the Romanians! Now we know that the Romanians, when they became Magyarized, brought with them all their ancient cultural creations! At first in an extremely hostile environment, and then also put to the wall by the ecclesiastical, political, administrative, legal, school, and military apparatus, and finally as a result of the confessional division of the Romanians overseen by Vienna at the beginning of the 18th century, the Romanians of the Curvature Carpathians had only two possibilities: to be Magyarized or to take refuge in Moldova. Those who remained borrowed another language, but they could not borrow their blood! Even the German ethnographer Paul Hunsdorfer (1810-1891, Magyarized as Hunfalvy), admitted that the Szeklers were mixed with the natives [154 p.118]. The scholar Nicolae Iorga rightly concluded that:

> *The Carpathian Szeklers are mostly denationalised Romanians, as shown by their traditional habitat, the way their houses are built and the way the land is toiled* [154].

Recently, Judit Pal, a historian, acknowledged that the mass Szeklerization of Romanians took place in two stages: first in linguistic terms and then in religious ones [217 p.161]. The "Szekler" block is a recent invention, coming after 1848 [154 p.133]; nowadays the post-1848 "block", has been changed into the Szekler "land" in the minds of the ignorant.

8.2 The Magyarization of Orphans

Without offering any comment, we quote from an article by a Slovak priest published in 1876 on the subject of orphaned children and children from poor families taken by force to Pannonia:

> *The poor Slovak orphan children were taken to the towns in the Lowlands, which offered to take them in, where, like masterless calves* [gazdátlán tulkek], *they were given into the hands of those who needed servants without payment, and they received them as such. For it is a lie, if any one believes, that the orphans have come into good hands and according to Christian love, ... for anything that seems good, is done by calculations, and the orphans thus distributed among a few landlords have become slaves, who among their masters, for a piece of bread, as apprentices or as servants, in all and for all* [mindenesek] *are very obedient and reward them very much. They have become servants among strangers, over whom, after their distribution, no one has any control, and who—in spite of their inhuman behaviour towards them—cannot even complain, because they*

have no one ... [64 p.251].

This was not a special law and procedure for Slovaks, but for all minorities, be they Romanian, Ruthenian, Swabian, Serb, Croat, or Saxon! In 1891, another step was taken towards the Magyarization of children from poor families or orphans hailing from the non-Hungarian majority with the Kindergarten and Asylum Act (see §6.2):

> *By the Law of 1891 the State has deliberately assumed the attitude of the Sultans in earlier centuries. Just as the Christian rayah was regarded as a breeding-machine to supply janissaries, so today the non-Magyars of Hungary are breeding-machines whose children must be taught Magyar from their earliest age, in the hope that they may become renegades to the traditions of their ancestors* [179 p.222].

8.3 The Magyarization of the Cities

Magyarization in urban areas has been extensive. First, Romanians were forbidden to settle in the cities. For example, a Romanian from a nearby village could not even stay overnight in Sighisoara. The Romanians who entered the towns either Magyarized their names or accepted Magyarization. The Saxons were also Magyarized, even though the towns from the Pannonian plain to the Carpathians were built by them! In the town of Deva, situated in the centre of a purely Romanian region where Magyarization had not assimilated too many people in the countryside, nevertheless between 1880 and 1910, the ethnic structure evolved as [29 p.6]:

Hungarian speakers	+ 293.9 %
Romanians	+ 21.2 %
Germans	- 67.7 %

The same unnatural evolution can be observed throughout Transylvania where the percentage of Hungarians in the cities increased from 36.4 % in 1851 to 60.8 % in 1910, while that of Germans in the same period decreased from 29.8 % to 15.6 % and that of Romanians decreased from 30.1 % to 23 % [141 p.222], according to traditionally falsified Hungarian data. The statistical expression of the Magyarization of the urban area of Transylvania [15 p.32] between 1850 and 1910 [15 p.207] is:

	1850	1910
Romanians	30.1 %	23.0 %
Germans	29.8 %	15.6 %
Hungarian speakers	36.4 %	60.8 %

The Magyarization of the cities also encountered problems, for example, the city of Bistrita in 1910 had only 1002 "Hungarians", in addition to 5,887 Germans, 3,753 Romanians, and 1,316 Jews [203 vol. I p.785], while in the whole County of Bistrita-Nasaud there were a total of 1,924 Hungarians in addition to 25,825 Germans, 6,385 Jews, and 81,311 Romanians [204 vol. XII p.88]. On 9 August 1885, the government newspaper *Nemzet* triumphantly announced to its public that Magyarization had made great progress in the upper part (Slovakia) and gave the example of the town of Niytra which had become almost *purely* Hungarian [160 p.23].

The Magyarization of Budapest

When looking at the process of Magyarization, the best example is provided by the dynamics of the Magyarization of Budapest, once a thriving German *opidum*. The two entities Ofen and Pest, *magna et ditissima villa Teutonicorum* [185 p.40], were established and re-established by German merchants at the end of the first millennium, when trade with the East was developing rapidly and Catholicism was taking the initiative to Christianise people in the far northeastern territories.

	1725	1737	1750	1850	1880	1890	1900	1906
magyar	19·4	22·5	22·2	36·6	56·7	67·1	79·6	85·1
német	55·6	57·7	55·2	56·4	34·3	23·7	14·0	9·4
tót	2·2	5·6	6·5	5·0	6·1	5·6	3·4	2·6
egyéb	22·8	14·1	16·1	2·0	2·9	3·6	3·0	2·9

Note: nemet = German,   tot = Slovak,   egyeb = others

Here we present statistics on the Magyarization of Budapest from *Révay Nagy Lexikona* [Budapest, 1912, vol. IV]. The ultra-rapid Magyarization of the Germans, whose share of population fell from 57.7 % in 1737 to 9.4 % in 1906, was done with a stick, as Johann Weidlein has shown [182 p.64].

Following the aristocratic restoration of 1790, Pannonia became the graveyard of the overwhelming Romanian-German-Slovak majority, through the hatred of the minority towards otherness. It was also the hinterland of Budapest! Johann Weidlein:

The writer Szabo Dezso began his agitation against the German peasants in Hungary, especially against the German villages around Budapest, which stood like a thorn in his side and had to disappear. In 1831 Count

> *Szechenyi had called for a concentration of the Hungarian population and its institutions in the German towns of Buda and Pest; Szabo Dezso went much further, for in 1931, a hundred years later, he demanded: 'We must make the appearance of Budapest and its surroundings, through their whole atmosphere, through their institutions and through their whole appearance, the expression of the Hungarian psyche'* [182 p.170].

The non-Hungarian majority in Budapest was forbidden by the local council to erect gravestones bearing inscriptions in languages other than Hungarian [179 p.286]. After the German theatre in Pest had been burned to the ground, a representative delighted parliament with the following statement: *It is to God's help that we owe the burning of the German theatre* [179 p.291].

8.4 The Magyarization of Swabian Turkey

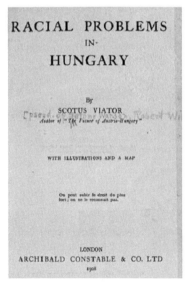

Fig. 8.4. One of three essential books for understanding the phenomenon.

Magyarization was imposed all over. Branau county (Baranya), or as the Swabians call it Swabian Turkey, has its centre at Funfkirchen (Pécs). At the beginning of the 18th century, after the liberation of Pannonia from the Turks by the Austrians, it was almost a *wasteland*. Austria colonised the area with Swabians brought from the Swabian countries of Baden and Wurtenberg and the area was predominantly German by the end of the 18th century. A century of Magyarization followed with no effort spared, yet, at the beginning of the 20th century, the Germans still constituted about 86 % of the population in Branau. However, there was now no German school and therefore a question mark about the future of the community [128 p.86]:

The situation of the German schools in Hungary before
1914 is the most eloquent illustration of the Magyar policy
of denationalization of the national minorities and it deserves special attention. No national minority was subjected to so brutal and adverse a school policy by the
Budapest government as the German one. That can be
seen from the following data:

County	No. of Magyars in 1910	No. of Germans in 1910	Elementary schools in 1914	
			Magyar	German
1 Baranya. . . .	19,659	112,297	400	–
2 Fejer	218,822	24,265	245	–
3 Moson	33,006	51,997	97	–
4 Sopron.	141,004	109,160	271	–
5 Tolna	189,521	74,376	239	–
6 Bars	62,022	17,366	221	–
7 Nyitra	100,324	27,937	438	–
8 Pozsony. . . .	131,662	21,032	222	3
9 Pressburg, City	31,706	32,700	24	–
10 Trencsen . . .	13,204	9,029	348	–
11 Turocz	5,560	10,993	48	–
12 Bacs-Bodrog.	267,714	178,950	261	20
13 Pest Pilis . .	906,294	83,496	659	–
14 Budapest the capital .	756,070	78,882	235	–
15 Saros	18,088	9,447	273	–
16 Szepes	18,658	38,434	182	19
17 Arad, without City of Arad .	78,130	34,330	145	–
18 Caras Severin	33,787	55,883	142	2
19 City of Timişoara. . .	47,518	120,683	145	20
20 Timiş	28,551	31,644	22	–
21 Torontal. . . .	128,405	165,779	220	12

In Somogy County, after 1848, the abolition of feudal rights was not by
virtue of new laws, but only conditional in the sense that former serfs
could not receive land from the feudal landed estate unless they knew
Hungarian [179 p.62].

8.5 Colonisation with Hungarian Speakers

On 15.11.1861, delegates led by Bishop Şuluţiu in a notice submitted to the
emperor, counted the lands owned by Romanians, Saxons, and
Hungarians. It showed that 4/5 of the former serfs of Transylvania were
Romanian [127 vol. II p.671-685]. To these must be added the *Jelers* who
were also Romanian. In this sea of Romanians there were also some
Saxons (10 %) and a few Magyarized inhabitants. This was the rural
picture of Transylvania then and thus a complementary solution to the
Magyarization of the natives was the colonisation of the Romanian blocks
with Hungarian speakers. According to the 1857 census, there were 172
houses and 879 inhabitants in Nimigea (Bistriţa-Năsăud County) [206

p.100]. In the village of Nimigea, as early as 1869, 25 Hungarian-speaking families had been settled, being allocated significant plots of land of 14.4 ha. each. With the settlement of these 25 families and in the context of the known feudal terror, rapid Magyarization was ensured.

In Luduş (Mureş County), which lies on the corridor of Magyarization destined to break Romanian unity, we find another typical case of ethnic purification: Magyarization mixed with colonisation. If we take the official data for Luduş, systematically falsified in 1857, we probably have a few Hungarian-speaking families; the data from 1910 reveal that the number of Romanians increased by only 12 %, while that of the Hungarian-speaking population by 4,768 %!

Luduş	1857	1880		1900		1910	
Romanians	1235	1024	-17.1%	1359	10.0%	1385	12.1%
Hungarian speakers	64	625	876.6%	1351	2010.9%	3116	4768.8%

Population growth in Transylvania between 1857 and 1910 was 33.8 % [15 p.77] and so in Luduş we have two simultaneous processes: a generalized Magyarization of the Romanians in all possible forms alongside colonisation and settlement with Hungarian speakers. In a report from that time, a Minister of Agriculture writes:

Through the colonisation effected by government, Ludus on the Mureş grew into a strong Hungarian stronghold [132 p.53].

CHAPTER 9

WILD DENATIONALISATION

Perhaps to the untrained reader, this attribution of denationalisation may seem excessive. It is excessive only to those who have not received a proper representation of the terrible phenomenon, not to those who have lived it; not to the authors of *The Rejoinder of the Romanian Academic Youth* [190], who, in 1892, under the relentless threat of the authorities, wrote of *The savagery of the gendarmerie, The fanaticism of the Hungarian press*, and *The brutalities of the Hungarian academic youth*. Nor to the Slovak Svetozar Hurban when he saw the actions of the

*Fig. 9.1. The Saxon scholar
Stephan Ludwig Roth (1796-1849).*

gendarmes at a parade, *animal brutality* [179 p.306-310], and the English historian C. Macartney (1895-1978) who recognised the *extremely violent Magyarization* [91 p.432]. In the 1899 edition of the Meyers Lexikon, the authors write that *from 1868 a brutal Magyarization began in Hungary* [5 p.17].

The adoption in 1842 by the Diet of the Grand Principality of Transylvania of the law on the introduction of Hungarian as an official language was not only an attack on the national identity of the Romanians, but also of the Saxons. The response of the Saxon humanist Stephan Ludwig Roth to the decision is enlightening:

> *The gentlemen in the Cluj Diet want to see an official language born and now they are happy that the baby has been delivered. There is no need to declare a language as the official language of the country because we have a language of the country. It is neither German, nor Hungarian, but Romanian. No matter how much we, the nations represented in the Diet, twist and turn, we cannot change anything. This is the reality* [141 p.174].

Between the genocide of 1848/49 and the establishment of the Dual Monarchy, under the liberal government (Anton von Schmerling, the Minister of the Interior), the Romanians were able to stand a little taller. Only a little because all the state jobs remained in the hands of the feudal lords. Moreover, as the jurist Schuller-Libloy, professor at the Academy of Laws in Sibiu, observed: *The aristocracy itself drew up the Patent of 1854* (which distributed *urbarium* land to the peasants), *absolutism* (the Alexander von Bach government) *did nothing but implement it* [153 p.225]. So, feudal relations were formally erased, but the aristocracy appropriated all the wealth that did not belong to them anyway (*alodium*, freehold land) and as for the state institutions, they remained in their hands.

George Barițiu wrote about the new conception in Hungarian society: of *spiritual destruction*, i.e., *alcohol, discord* between brothers (united and non-united), and *corruption* through the actions of renegades, after the failure of the extermination of the Romanians demanded by Kossuth on 10.10.1848. This technique of *spiritual extermination* wreaked widespread havoc [6 vol. 3 p.499].

The preparation of Dualism

All critical histories of Dualism begin with the defeats administered to Vienna by Prussia and reveal the role of Hungarian opportunism in the matter. No further notice is taken of the internal preparations made by the Hungarian aristocrats. On 17.02.1867, "the Straw Emperor" Franz Joseph, in a letter to the Andrassy committee, consented to a Hungarian government in the monarchy; a government that *would* deal with the *untying of the* union of Transylvania with Hungary *to satiation* [6 vol. III p.426]. Immediately, violent actions were organized: imperial coats of arms and flags were systematically destroyed; German and other inscriptions were defaced; and those who stood with the imperial government were beaten. These were called little disturbances of public order by Andrassy, which would cease with the signing of Dualism [6 vol. II p.428]. Such things continued, now no longer directed against the empire, but against the non-Hungarian majority. In Cluj, the young Hungarians shouted at their Romanian colleagues, *stupid and block-headed Wallachians, you will soon perish*. On 15.04.1867 in the township of Logigu (Bistrița-Năsăud County), a certain Geza Forro shot a child of Alecsandru Graur out of the blue. On 31.05.1867, two young gentlemen (Teleki and Banffy), from the Calvinist college in Aiud, bet with their colleagues that they would go to Blaj and would beat as many Romanian students as they could find there. In the end, this did not happen, as the Romanians were not intimidated [6 vol. III p.429]. George Bariţiu noticed that *the Slovaks had also suffered badly* and gives an example: the Hungarian officials of a Slovak town imprisoned six teachers, doctors, and priests according to their own desires. Broken windows and beating with clubs on the backs of Romanians, Slovaks, and Germans were mere trifles! The picture of Dualism presents, on the one hand, the betrayal of Austria's interests on the battlefields of 1865-1866, and on the other, the challenges from within undermining Vienna with a weak and spineless emperor facing a clever Magyarized Croat, Franjo Deak. Deak's approach to the relationship with Austria focused on the long term: first compromise, then strengthening Hungary, i.e., Magyarization of the Romanian-Serbian-Slovak-German majority, and once denationalisation was over separation from an enfeebled Austria. In Austria, the minorities were "daring to take steps" and were pursuing the federalization of the empire, a terrible thing for Hungarian chauvinism. Bishop Roman Ciorogaru, who lived through Dualism in his youth, summed it up as follows:

> *Hungarian diplomacy succeeded in enslaving Vienna to Hungarian imperialism ... with the assent of Emperor Francis Joseph* [38 p.35].

9.1 The Right to Petition

The mockery of the right to petition can be seen from the humiliating experience of the *Memorandum*. In 1892, a petition addressed to the emperor and supported in Vienna by 300 leading intellectuals, *in persona*, was sent unopened to the feudal government in Budapest. The emperor complied, like a lackey, with the Hungarian Prime Minister's request. The prosecutors demanded that the Romanians be punished with five years in prison for daring to send a petition to the monarch. The judges acted in accordance with the guidelines received from Budapest. Ion Raţiu, a lawyer who defended the memorandists in court after they were sued, remarked that Hungarian racial fanaticism was without parallel in Europe [163 p.215]. The petition asked for very little relief from the pressure of assimilation by respecting the law, discriminatory as it was. By the time of the *Memorandum* in 1892, more than 50,000 Romanians had died in Transylvania since 1848/49 for this emperor lacking in intelligence and driven soley by concern for etiquette! Romanians had also died by their thousands in 1866 for the wasted victories at Tratenau and Biskupitz! And how many others had died in wars for the monarchy before his reign? But out of this "imperial" mockery came a document of the highest value,

Replica (Rejoinder) [190], which circulated in civilized Europe and internationalized the problem of Hungarian chauvinism and racism. In newspapers, Hungarian intellectuals exulted in hatred. Below we present a quote from the Magyar Hirlap newspaper of 22.09.1894:

> *More's the pity that the salutary institution of 'impaling' has gone out of fashion. How radically the Wallachian question might now be settled, and what an uplifting sight to our hearts it would be, to see the heads of the renowned agitators in the sharp point of the spike of the national tricoloured flag* [25 p.113].

9.2 The Electoral Act and the Election Travesty

This new law from 1874, in fact the feudal law of 1848, was actually an exceptional measure taken by the minority against the non-Hungarian majority. According to this, one part of the deputies was elected, while the other part was appointed. Qualification for the right to vote was based on five elements: feudal privilege, official position, profession, property (amount of property tax), and location (depending on whether a region had a non-Magyar majority or not) [190 p.35]:

1) All those who had the quality of "noble" had the right to vote without any census, on the basis of their ancient rights (art 2).

2) In rural townships in Hungary, all those who owned at least eight *jugars* of land (one jugar was equal to 5,775 m^2) had the right to vote; in rural townships in Transylvania, only those who paid tax after a cadastral income of at least 84 florins (equivalent to 75 jugars), or those who had houses subject to taxation and paid a tax of at least 79 florins and 80 kreuzer (a coin initially made of silver and then of copper, unit of currency: 100 kreuzers = 1 Austro-Hungarian florin), had the right to vote.

3) The law left it up to the local officials, i.e., to zealous Hungarians, to decide whether a voter had the right to vote or not [179 p.168] and hence a whole series of unimaginable abuses resulted. There is much documentary evidence of the illegalities carried out locally against non-Hungarian citizens [179 p.494-497]. We can list the names of the entries in the election minutes in which certain citizens who met all the conditions of the law were deprived of the right to vote: a) electors who mispronounced the name of the candidate (according to the official's judgement); b) electors who were omitted from the election lists (the town hall omitted them, intentionally or not); c) electors who were entered with an incorrect age in

the election lists (by the error or intention of the town hall); and d) electors whose identity could not be established (by the official)! On this basis only, electors belonging to the Romanian and Slovak majority were rejected [179 p.497].

4) Electoral constituencies were established in Transylvania, Slovakia, and the Tisa Plain so that areas with non-Magyar majorities were sliced up and attached to other constituencies; this patchwork was intended to prevent the non-Magyar majority from having elected representatives. Additionally, voters of the non-Magyar majority were required to travel dozens of kilometres to polling stations. In 1884 in Cehu Silvaniei (Sălaj County), the candidate Gheorghe Pop de Băseşti, under the census conditions set out by the law, despite having about 900 voters still lost the election to the Hungarian candidate who had 140 voters. Pop de Băseşti's rural voters, about 600-700, came to Cehu Silvaniei, which was the polling centre, around 10 a.m. They were met by the army *with bayonets at the tip of their rifles* and were not allowed to enter the town. The Hungarian representative was subsequently declared the winner [190 p.38].

From the first regulations of the law, it appears that the "nobility", great and small or impoverished, had the right to vote unconditionally, while the Romanians were required to have a census value about nine times higher than the citizens of Pannonia in order to vote. On top of all this, the vote was not secret and the voter had to face the electoral commission of local officials on whom his life depended. The peasant was asked the name of the one he wanted to vote for and if he said the non-Magyarized name, the commission declared the vote invalid. For example, a voter might name the candidate Gyula Markocics, the official would answer that there was no candidate called Gyula, the peasant would then have to call his candidate's full name of Iuliu Marcovici Markovics Gyula so that the vote could be recorded [179 p.261].

All these obstacles contained in the law seemed insufficient to the Hungarian authorities, so they invented new "practical" obstacles: sometimes a bridge was broken so that voters could not reach the polling station; sometimes villages were declared under veterinary quarantine during the voting period; in 1875 in Panciova (today in Serbia), Romanians were kept for two days in the cold and blizzard conditions in the fields [179 p.255]; where the peasants had to overcome the listed obstacles, they also had to avoid the bullets of the gendarmes and the army, for example, in 1896, 32 voters were killed and more than 70 seriously wounded in the elections [179 p.255]. In elections in Slovak and Romanian districts, the deployment of thousands of soldiers and gendarmes in addition to the entire local police force was considered "normal". In Senteş (Hungary), 50 gendarmes and two infantry battalions were deployed to support the local police in the elections of January 1900 [179 p.256]. For the elections, the military units deployed in Hungary were insufficient and additional troops were brought in from Galicia and Styria [179 p.256]. Seton-Watson and Eugen Brote, contemporaries of those elections in Hungary, considered them to represent *a real civil war*.

Another phenomenon was official bribery—money from the budget that was given only to government candidates, on average 8-10 kroner per voter; this money did not have to be justified. If we take into account that the government man was also elected with 100 votes and that the constituencies had around 1,000 electors, then 9,000 crowns were not justified as a bribe either [179 p.265]. A *sui generis* scheme, an indisputable plot was afoot. The picture of election fraud is complete if we mention the last instrument: the "institution of declaring the winner of the election". This *institution* was in the hands of the government representative, a sort of governor in the county who had the power to decide everything. Thus, in the 1879 election of the deputy governor of Sibiu County, the renegade Saxon governor Wachter declared the renegade August Senor elected, even though he had received 27 votes out of the 150 votes cast. The election was confirmed by the government of Coloman Tisza and the parliament!

As a sign of protest, the *General Conference of Romanian Voters' Representatives* (Sibiu, 12-14.05.1881) decided to continue the policy of passivity—non-participation in the electoral competition [59 p.50]; the Romanians demanded an electoral law based on universal suffrage or at least the granting of electoral rights to any citizen paying taxes. In 1905, the Romanian leaders in Transylvania decided to become active and to participate in the elections. Between 1881 and 1905, only the inhabitants of Banat, Crişana, and Maramureş took part in the elections.

In Transylvania, the census requirements for electoral registration in urban localities were three to six times lower than for rural townships. The reason for this was that unlike the towns, which were already substantially Magyarized, in 1874 the rural townships were still Romanian. After the elections, there were 411 deputies for six million Hungarians and no deputies for 10 million non-Hungarians. Take Ionescu discussed this law with Desiderius Banffy in Budapest in 1896 (§ 2.5). This law is a testimony to the essence of the electoral process: the "union" sanctioned by the emperor in 1868 did not work as Hungary and Transylvania were different countries. In Transylvania, which was Romanian, the law had to be different.

Another paradox arose in that governments were building their majorities on the backs of a non-Hungarian majority. Paragraphs 70 and 71 of the electoral law stated that if half an hour after the announcement of the first vote for one of the candidates, a vote for another candidate was not announced, the election was finished, the vote ended, and the first candidate was proclaimed winner by the elected chairman of the electoral commission. How many times were Romanian voters forcibly kept from reaching the polling place until that half hour had expired [25 p.94]?

Fig. 9.2. REPLICA (Rejoinder): the answer of young Romanians to the young Hungarians.

The government could not get more than 67 deputies (from 182 constituencies) for its parliamentary majority from the Hungarian territory, [while] *179 government deputies (from 229 constituencies) came from the Romanian and Slavonic territory, where the discontent against government policy is so great* [25 p.95].

The elections were not just a travesty! In the village of Serpeuş (Arad County), a purely Romanian village, the praetor Csukai did not accept the candidacy of the Romanian candidate requested by the people and wanted to impose a subservient candidate. On 13 May 1903, the villagers protested and the gendarmes, on the orders of the praetor, killed four people, seriously injured 10, and lightly wounded 30 others [163 p.293]. On 24 April 1904 in Aleşd, the Romanians brought to a socialist meeting did not want to listen to the chauvinist speakers. The gendarmes and hussars fired on the Romanians, resulting in a massacre: 23 dead and dozens seriously wounded of whom seven more died later on. On April 17, 1906, in the village of Birchiş (Caraş-Severin County), gendarmes shot at voters who did not want the Hungarian candidate, resulting in one dead and one seriously wounded [163 p.299]. On April 27, 1906, in Amaţi (Satu Mare County), the Hungarians killed Gheorghe Conci, Ion Şuta, and Iosif Dragoş at night using axes because these three men were promoting the Romanian candidate. No gendarmes were sent to investigate and the Romanian peasants remained at the mercy of the Hungarian thugs. On

29.04.1906 in Corni (Sălaj County), the gendarmes shot several peasants because they wanted to go to Şomcuta for the elections. Similar situations occurred in Baia Mare and at Dobra (Hunedoara County) [163 p.300]. In Tinca (Bihor County) on 9 May 1907 on the occasion of the deputy elections, the gendarmes shot Gh. Mărcaş and arrested several others for disobedience to the authorities [163 p.306]. The 4th Battalion of the 24th Regiment was housed in the village of Pănade (Alba County). The lodging of the officers and soldiers was thus at the expense of the villagers: food, drink, cleaning, fodder, and carriages, etc. On 25.08.1907, drunken soldiers went on the rampage, killing and seriously injuring as many women and men as they could catch. The investigation established that, since they were attacked by the men of the village, *the soldiers had only defended themselves* [163 p.307]. In addition, the peasants were charged 800 kroner [127 vol. VIII p.689].

In 1910, the electoral law was tightened for the non-Hungarian majority. The Saxons remained unrepresented and being pressed by circumstances the seven elected Saxon deputies joined the Hungarian liberal party [190 p.41].

In the eastern part of the dualist empire, on average 6.1 % of the population was theoretically registered to vote, while in the provinces, things were different: in Pannonia 7-7.5 % of the population could vote; in Transylvania, the figure dropped to 3.2 %. Here, one deputy could represent 60,000 Romanians, while in the Curvature Carpathians, where Magyarization had reached 70-80 % of the total population, one deputy represented about 4,000 inhabitants [179. p.249].

9.3 A Travesty of Justice

Justice has never been independent, but always political. After 1848, Transylvania experienced four different systems of organization and justice: the feudal one until 1851; the "German" one, more operative and almost impartial, until 1861; the one restored by the nobility: feudal and Magyarizing until 1868; and an absolutely discretionary one after Dualism, for which the very term "justice" is inappropriate. The great invention of the Hungarians, that of the 'political nation', was that any legal action under the crooked Hungarian laws if it did not suit the 'political nation' was denounced to the Minister of the Interior, who had the authority to change any sentence, ruling, decision, or vote (to take the place of the deliberative bodies). There was no rule of law, no respect for votes, and no autonomy, just blackmail, fracturing the majority by pitting some against others. An example is that of the *Saxon University*, formerly the Saxon decision-making forum. By a decree of 14.07.1877, issued by the Coloman Tizsa government, the committee was empowered to manage the *Saxon community* and this to pay the Saxon committee a grant of 2,000 florins annually; in other words, goodbye autonomy. After the *University* protested, Tisza issued a new decree on 5.10.1877, obliging it to incorporate the content of the decree of 14.07.1877 into its statutes. When the *University* asked to debate the change of statute imposed by the government, the renegade Wachter in his capacity as government steward in the county retorted that if there were a single vote in favour, he would then inform the ministry that the *University* had changed its statute in the sense demanded by the government. And yes, two Romanians voted *for* and 16 Saxons *against*. Wachter announced to the government that the *University* had adopted the change of statute. Therefore, on 19.11.1877, the government of Tisza issued a new decree:

> *The fact that the changes in the statute indicated in my decrees were made not by the majority, but by the minority, in no way weakens the legality of these changes; since, by its unlawful action, the majority has voluntarily abdicated the execution of the privileges which the law confers on it, it has thereby, by its consent, conveyed to the minority the legal right of representation in the Assembly* [179 p.244].

Other examples are presented in the following. Under Ordinance 384 of 24.02.1885, the gendarmes of Câmpeni stormed Lupşa and Valea Lupşii (Alba County) to stop the "preparations" for the commemoration of the martyrdom of the heroes Horia, Cloşca, and Crişan; teachers were threatened that they would be shot *like dogs* if they left their houses on that day; and the priests were thrown out of the churches by the gendarmes [190 p.88]. In 1886, during a dispute between tenants from Bucium in Mogoş township at a country party, the gendarmes intervened and killed 15 Romanians. Nothing happened to the Hungarian murderers, as Count Széchenyi said: *the Hungarian must be forgiven even when he kills his own father* [182]! In the township of Rişculiţa (Hunedoara County), the inhabitants, who made their living making parts for looms, bought some plots of forest. In September 1890, the praetor and gendarmes showed up in the village telling them that the forest would be taken from them and annexed to the *erarium* (state financial administration) and if they resisted, they would expropriate the land by force. Because the villagers resisted, they were arrested by a company of soldiers; some were imprisoned for four months, while others were sequestered in the village by the soldiers. The captain of the company, after investigation, could not hold anything against the villagers and withdrew his soldiers releasing those kept confined without reason. In the lawsuit brought by the township for the recovery of the soldiers' maintenance expenses and the time lost in prison, the praetor ruled against the plaintiffs [190 p.85]. On 8 June 1897, Dr. N. Nilvan and V. Dragoș from Șomcuta Mare were fined 1,300 kroners each for singing the imperial hymn "Gotterhalte" in Romanian [163 p.285]. In the village of Corniareva (Caraș-Severin County) in October 1901, a crowd asking for clarification from the town hall about communal land was dispersed by gendarmes who shot dead three men and injured many others. Thirty peasants were condemned by the court for "disobedience to authority" [163 p.290]. On 4.09.1902 in Bichiș-Ciaba (Hungary), Victor Popovici, a priest, issued a baptismal certificate in Romanian; the town hall turned the Magyarized population against the priest. More than 600 raided the priest's family and destroyed his house; the gendarmes, amused by this, encouraged the savages [163 p.292]. On 13.10.1907 in Cristian (Brasov County), a drunken hussar was mocked by the village children. Other Hussars came to avenge him and seriously injured 25 Romanians, as *the Wallachians were not allowed to make fun of Hungarians*; "justice" was applied on the spot. On the same day, the court at Oradea sentenced three peasants from Tinca to two years and 11 months in prison for having "agitated against the Hungarian state", although 36 witnesses claimed the accused were innocent and the primary accused had not been in the village on that day [163 p.310].

The 24-year-old Francisc Pollakovici, who had returned home from America with different ideas about freedom, told several Slovaks at a meeting in Borbo on 6.10.1907 that *those belonging to the Slovak nationality* [should] *hold together as Slovaks*. For this he was arrested and sentenced to seven months in prison. The sentence read as follows:

> *...it is clear that Francisc Pollakovici's intention was to incite the Slovak inhabitants to hatred against the Magyars* [179 p.499].

Just the use of the word "emperor" instead of "king" in Hungary was enough to be subjected to justice, as happened to the deputy Fr. Veselovsky of Trnava (Slovakia) [179. p.320].

A massacre in Cernova, Lipto County (Slovakia), on 27.10.1907, resulted in 14 dead and 23 wounded. After the massacre, all the peasants were blamed because the Slovaks were agitating. The Cernova massacre enjoyed relative notoriety due to the fact that Czech and German MPs discussed it in the Vienna Parliament. In Budapest, the Slovak MP who sought to question the massacre was charged with murder!

The dehumanisation and complicity of the Catholic hierarchy in Hungary in the face of chauvinism and hatred must be highlighted. The

Vatican did not lift a finger to assist and the historian Seton-Watson included a whole chapter in his book to discuss this travesty of justice [179].

In June 1910, the peasant Stan Tudor Dobos, from Apateu (Hungary), a father of seven children, was sentenced to three months and 10 days in prison because he said that the Romanians had been in Transylvania since Emperor Trajan, 800 years before the Hungarians [163 p.318].

Laudatio criminis. Although the Hungarian penal code did not provide for the conviction of *laudatio criminis*, it was used for political purposes. *Laudatio criminis* also meant bringing a bouquet of flowers to an intellectual on his release from prison, having been imprisoned for writing two articles that opposed the Magyarization of the Slovak folk schools [179 p.328].

Coercive detention. People accused of inciting hatred against the *Hungarian nation* (never against the non-Magyar majority) or promoting *race hatred* (i.e., against the landowners) were thrown into prison months before any trial began. If the person happened to be acquitted, the detention was just a well-deserved "lesson" from the point of view of chauvinism, for "justice" must be an instrument of the executive, as justice ministers Bela Peczel and Alexander Erdely acknowledged. When the executive made excesses that went beyond current law, the law was immediately adapted [179 p.317-318]. In parliament, the MP Komjatti argued that the majority should be Magyarized *by iron and fire* [127 vol. VI p.793].

The reader understands that such examples can be given by the thousand. It should be noted, however, that the laws were of variable scope and elastic in application; their versatility made them sufficient to serve Magyarization. Count A. Apponyi, in an electoral assembly (1896), admitted:

> The laws are merely an instrument for concealing the arbitrary action of the government [179 p.274].

9.4 Denationalisation Through Schools

In 1766, Empress Maria Theresa asked the governor of Banat to "see to it" that a school was established in each township. "Taking care" meant that 100 Orthodox parishes were free to set up 100 confessional schools, also called *people's schools* or *Greek-unified national schools*. 108 years later, Ministerial Ordinance no. 3763 of 1874 decreed that all the people's schools in Banat would be communal, i.e., Hungarian schools! By ministerial ordinance, 100 schools of the Romanian community became Hungarian schools [190 p.63].

Immediately after Dualism was signed off, the pressure on non-Magyar schools intensified. In September 1894, the renegade professor Ludovic Lang noted the extent of this political manipulation based on official data: in 1869, out of 13,798 primary schools, 6,458 did not teach children in the Hungarian language, and only 5,818 schools were Hungarian (1,452 were mixed) [25 p.103]. In 1879, a law made the teaching of Hungarian compulsory in all non-Magyar primary schools. Obviously, this measure was preceded by all kinds of discriminatory measures against the non-Magyarized majority. School inspectors blackmailed teachers for generalizing Magyar rather than Romanian, Serbian, and Slovak [190 p.48]. The community-supported folk schools were no longer for the cultivation of the people, but tools of Magyarization [190 p.44-49]. In the gymnasiums, Magyarization was taken for granted. In the school year 1889/1890, out of 40,596 pupils in these secondary schools only 2,470 were Romanian. Of these 2,470 Romanians, only 1,013 were pupils in Romanian secondary schools, the rest were in Hungarian secondary schools. That is to say 6.5 million Hungarian speakers accounted for 91.7 % of pupils [190 p.49] and 3.5 million Romanians, according to Banffy, accounted for only 6.08 % of pupils! Out of 180 secondary schools, six were Romanian and 167 were Hungarian [190 p.49]. Budapest did not support a single non-Romanian secondary school. Moreover, the non-Magyar nations were not allowed to set up their own cultural institutes, even with their own money [190 p.50].

In 1881, the communal representatives of 84 communes in the old military borderland of Banat decided to establish, at their own expense, a higher gymnasium in the language of the inhabitants of Caransebeş. The communes erected a school building and endowed it with an annual income of 17,525 florins per year. In 1882, General Traian Doda, the former head of the topographical service of the imperial army, submitted a request for the establishment of the gymnasium requested by the Romanian townships [190 p.52]. The petitioners received no reply from the ministry.

In 1885, the Holy Orthodox Eparchial Synod of Arad decided to establish a gymnasium in Arad. According to Hungarian statistics, falsified three times over, 63.36 % of the county's population was Romanian! To support this gymnasium, the church authorities offered the government all possible guarantees including a suitable building and taxes based on a fortune of 800,000 florins. There were also other sources of revenue, including a public subscription from the Romanians. The

Minister of Education in Budapest *denied this right* [190 p.51]; as we have seen, the law bound the Hungarians in *their holy war*. There was not only the denial of private rights in Năsăud, Arad, and Caransebeş, but also the forcible Magyarization of the Romanian gymnasium in Beiuş [190 p.53-54].

This is how the "higher schools" in Transylvania, Banat, Crişana, and Maramureş looked in 1910 [100 p.240].

	High schools	Gymnasiums	Teachers	Students
Hungarian speakers	41	5	736	15,062
Germans	6	3	109	1,944
Romanians	4	2	66	1,652
Serbs	1	-	19	469

The table should be read with one observation: the Romanian language was becoming peripheral in "Romanian" schools. Or as we have already mentioned, in the German gymnasium in Timişoara, as early as 1856, all subjects were taught in Hungarian except for German literature. Ruthenians do not appear in the above table, but it is understood that they did not have gymnasiums and high schools.

The peak of Magyarization through schooling was reached under Count Albert Apponyi with the law passed in 1907. The historian R.W. Seton-Watson dedicated chapter XI of his book *Racial Problems in Hungary* to this monumental infamy [179], which cannot be avoided by anyone who studies the phenomenon of Magyarization. Apponyi's law buried the mother-tongue education of the non-Hungarian majority entirely, even if it was denominational education; the law provided that teachers in denominational schools maintained by non-Hungarian churches were officials of the state, answerable to the state, and accepted, controlled, and dismissed by the authorities; by the clause of compulsory patriotism, any teacher was at the disposal of the local authorities, who happened to be the most hardened chauvinists [179 p.225]. The outward, compulsory symbolism in schools encouraged a *hysterical form of patriotism* [179 p.231]. By this law, a real addition to the criminal code, teachers were spied on, pursued, denounced, blackmailed, and subjected to Hungarian racism [179 p.233].

On 29.01.1912, 16 Romanian students were expelled from the Catholic theological seminary (Hungarian, of course) in Oradea for daring to speak Romanian amongst themselves. On 15.03.1913, the Romanian students of the Catholic seminaries of Budapest and Ung were subjected to bitter humiliation because they had not been enthusiastic enough on the occasion of the celebration of the first genocide in modern Europe in 1848 [163 p.326].

About school policy results

The ministerial adviser Ferenc Halász, in his book *State Public Education* published in 1902, provided the following information on the results of this policy [41 p.178]: a) the Magyarization of the Romanians in the valley of the Crişu Repede River (Bihor County) with the help of the state schools was only a matter of time; b) the state school in Târnava Mare, opened in 1879, had so Magyarized the Romanian population that the population now spoke only Hungarian; and c) the children of the workers in the coal mines of Hunedoara (where 80 % of the population was Romanian), who attended the state schools, declared themselves to be Hungarians, from the first generation.

In 1911, the school inspector of the Hunedoara district boasted in an article that he had suppressed 125 Romanian schools, having replaced them in his four years of activity (1907-1911) with 80 Hungarian schools. The school inspector of Zemplin district (Slovakia) in 1911 reported that in the 127 primary schools maintained by Slovaks, only Hungarian was taught [41 p.179].

9.5 Denationalisation Through the Church

Magyarization through the church, which has been very effective since the beginning of the Catholicization of the middle Danube Basin, has always borne fruit. In the early days of Catholic kingship in Pannonia, the foundation of the country lay with the schismatic Wallachians and the Slavs. The Provincial Council of Buda (1279) called for the use of brute force against schismatics, Jews, Ismailites, and Saracens. The Romanians and Slavs, left without political and religious support, switched to the church of the new centre of power (the Germans in the market towns were Catholics). The Romanians, once converted to Catholicism, lost their ancestral language over time. Catholicization was carried out in Hungarian according to the principle of intolerance: *learn, leave, or die.*

An interesting cultural detail from the time of the Reformation in Transylvania is that the Saxons (at the Council of Brasov) supported the printing of a catechism in Romanian, published in 1560 without any interference in doctrine [81 p.94].

Around 1750, the Catholic Archbishop of Calocea (Hungary), a town then inhabited almost entirely by Serbs, introduced the method of *12 florins or 12 strokes of the stick* for native speakers [179 p.62].

In 1829 in Oedenburg (Sopron, Hungary), it was made a requirement that in all parishes where there was at least a single believer who knew some Hungarian, the service should be held only in Hungarian [179 p.62]. In 1907, in Covacica (Serbia) in Banat where there was a Slovak Lutheran colony, an attempt was made to introduce the divine service in Hungarian. The parishioners did not wish this and so "bayonets" were used and the priest was suspended by the superintendent and *whipped into shape*. Trials followed against the obstinate parishioners: 36 people received six years and eight months in prison, in addition to fines of 5,980 kroner [179 p.322].

It is worth noting the different destiny of the Slovaks among whom the elements of the Greek Rite were quickly lost under the Catholic influence of the Franks with only the Bishopric of Strigonius in their midst. The Hussite movement influenced them, trained them, and on the occasion of the Reformation a significant part of them became Lutherans. As such, we have Slovak Catholics and Slovak Lutherans, and there, as in Transylvania, the Lutherans put up more resistance to Magyarization. The Catholic Slovaks were easy victims of Magyarization. Somewhat paradoxically, under the Habsburgs, fanatical Catholics one and all, the Catholic Slovaks of Pannonia, Banat, and Satu Mare were Magyarized en masse. Rome, which considered itself the universal church, did not care for the Catholic peoples of the middle Danube basin, abandoning them to Hungarian chauvinism.

After the establishment of Dualism, all governments sought to have the seven Romanian episcopal seats (Sibiu, Arad, Caransebeș, Blaj, Gherla, Oradea, and Lugoj) occupied by malleable priests who would put themselves at the service of Magyarization. They interfered in the church and school affairs of the Romanians in all sorts of ways and directed them in the interests of Hungarian politics [25 p.99].

In the counties of Satu Mare and Bihor alone, there were 35,473 Hungarian Greek-Catholic Romanians, ten years before the establishment of the Hungarian Greek-Catholic Mitropoly by the papal bull *Cristi fideles graeci of 1912*. The concept of Hungarian Greek-Catholics constitutes a nonsense in itself! In Careii Mari (Satu Mare County) there were 2,900 "non-Romanian", i.e., Magyarized Greek-Catholics; in Baia Mare there were 27,98; in Hăndal (Maramureș County) 907; in Botiza (Satu Mare County) 709; in Macău (Cenad) and Nir-Abran (Sablociu) 1,703; in Nir-Aciad (Sablociu) 1,300; in Nir-Adon (Sablociu) 1,971; in Sanislău (Satu

Mare County) 863; in Satu Mare 3,800; in Tarna Mare (Satu Mare County) 500; and in Vetiș (Satu Mare County) 642 [5 p.29]. With the establishment of the Hungarian Greek-Catholic Diocese of Haidudorog under Pius X, more than 300,000 Romanians were Magyarized.

One interesting aspect to be considered on this occasion is the play, specifically that one acted by the Hungarians, which was performed for the benefit of the ignorant man sitting in the papal chair. Budapest justified its approach to the establishment of the Greek Catholic diocese by claiming that *300,000 Greek Catholic authentic Hungarians* were prey to the influence of the Wallachian and Ruthenian church and in danger of being Wallachianized or Ruthenianized [132 p.70]. Preparations were made in advance and it was written in a document submitted to the government that the priests of these "Hungarians" came from Wallachian and Ruthenian churches to corrupt the poor Hungarians [132 p.72]. In response, Romanian churches were forcibly evacuated by the police and kept under guard by the gendarmerie; hundreds of Romanians were brutalized and taken to court as disturbers of public order. Only after 1918 did some of the Romanians of Crișana and Maramureș return to the dioceses from which they had been forcibly torn [132 p.74].

9.6 Seizure of Assets

After 1858, the feudalists, having failed to completely dispossess the peasants of their land by applying the land law of 1847, due to the genocide of 1848/49 and given the new historical circumstances of the theoretical abolition of slavery, unleashed a new offensive over peasant lands on the grounds of "rights". This new mode of dispossessing the peasants was focused on the demarcation between the *urbarium* properties to be ceded to the peasants and the allodial lands [153 p167]. The landowners speculated that the properties, *urbarium* and allodial, were not registered. The boundaries of the allodial lands could thus be shifted this way or that, as the landowners desired. Another loophole was found in the imprecision of the Patent of 1854, drawn up by the feudal landowners, which allowed them to legalize older land seizures, thus turning many serfs into *Jeler* [153 p.212]. Trials of former serfs followed, listed in the documents drawn up by them as *Jeler*, and the trials were also judged by the landowners. Among the thousands of examples, we may only mention the bizarre situation of Brasov, where the Magister of Brasov judged more than 3,000 trials against former serfs of Brasov, all of whom were Romanian [153 p168].

The dispossession of the peasant from his wealth, though continuous and systematic in all times, reached a high degree of savagery under "Hungarian constitutionalism", i.e., Dualism. After the feudal relationship was abolished in 1854, the feudal landowners were compensated, leaving the question of ownership of forest and pasture to be resolved. The imperial patents issued could have solved this problem, but they were not applied in Transylvania. The feudal lords resorted to lawsuits with entire villages seized and sold at auction, as happened in Tofalău (Mureș County) when Baron Carol Apor, also president of the court at Mures, took possession of the village and evicted 300 souls [190 p. 84].

The 2nd Border Regiment from Năsăud, founded by Maria Theresa in 1762, was disbanded in 1852, after the guards had shed blood in over 133 battles for the monarchy. The training of non-commissioned officers and the equipping of the regiment with uniforms was done through two funds supplied by the 40 townships of the borderland. With the disbanding of the regiment, the state recognised the property rights of the border guards and of their descendants over these funds and over the mountains, forests, and pastures of the borderland. All these possessions were subsequently stolen from them by administrative trickery! In 1885, the government appointed Baron D. Banffy as *Government Commissioner of Funds* and as a result, the funds no longer reached the owners. There were still other estates in the borderland and so the government came back and appointed the same renegade Romanian commissioner over all the estates of the borderland townships. From this new position followed a "settled" lawsuit with a former owner, Kemény, compensated, and the townships paid the compensation again; thus, the mountains and the pastures of the borderland townships, which had fallen into the hands of the administrator Bánffy, passed into the actual possession of Banffy himself!

9.7 Denationalisation Through the Army

Either under their own cnezes, princes, and voivodes, as serfs of the high clergy who had to give the king a *banderium* in case of war, or as *castri serfs* the Romanians formed the backbone of the army of the Catholic kingdom. This was conventionally called the Hungarian army, but could hardly have been so, precisely because of how few Hungarians there were (in the 13th century, according to Simon of Chiza, there were 108 clans). In the last phase of denationalisation, the army was also caught up in the game, even though it was under Austrian command. The Austrians were not able to rein in the savagery of Magyarization, not even for the Swabians for whom they had direct responsibility, and much less for the

Fig. 9.3. How to Magyarize Surnames by Telkes Simon.

Slovak-Romanian-Saxon majority. As such, in the regiments of Banat, Maramureş, and Transylvania where the language of the regiments had been Romanian, Hungarian was introduced; the commands were and remained in German. In 1909, out of nine Romanian regiments only one retained the Romanian language as the primary means of communication. The war was an opportunity for racial purification that the apostles of hatred could not miss.

9.8 The Magyarization of Names

The denationalisation of personal names began systematically after 1867, but by then Magyarization had already been operating for a while. For example, Georgius Barabas, Georgius Hepes, Ladislaus Barabas, Szakats Vaszi, Ladislau Atyim, Elias Barabs, Hepes Gábor, Georgius Reszketo, Georg Fulep, Mate Vooya, Atyim Mihály, Demeter Barabas, Joannes Reszketo, Joannes Atyim, Joannes Barabas, Mihael Barabas, Máté Todor, Mihael Molnár, Béres Kosztin, Nyisztor Josi, and Pakulár Gligor were all Romanians from the Orthodox village of Murgeşti (Mureş County), and not Hungarians as their names might suggest [150 p.37]. Hundreds of thousands of Romanians had their names Magyarized, giving us new "Hungarians" like Radu, Răduţ, Crăciun, Bogdan, Dragoş, and Ciobanu, etc. We also have unknown Hungarian names from translations: Listeş, Astaloş, Covaci, Sabo, Molnar, and Cherecheş, etc. At the post office and the railways, the Magyarization of the name was a condition that could not be overcome, even when someone asked to work a simple porter's job. After 1896, all kinds of Hungarian societies and organisations were involved in the movement, with the *Emke* (The Transylvanian Hungarian Cultural Society) being the most significant. In addition, the Central Society of Budapest and the official bulletins of the ministries were put at the service of this cause. At the beginning of 1898, the Banffy government relaunched the campaign to Magyarize names. When the Saxon MP Oscar von Meltzl tabled a question on the subject in parliament, far from receiving a reply, he was subjected to abuse and insults by Magyarized MPs [179 p.187]. The ministers themselves ordered the heads of authorities to urge their subordinates to change their non-Magyar names [132 p.48]. In 1898, Simon Telkes published the guide *How to Magyarize Surnames*. The book mentions that the Magyarization of the name is an old custom, dating back to the time of King Matthias Corvinus [192 p.132].

9.9 The Magyarization of Toponyms

In 1897, the law on the Magyarization of place names was passed. The reasoning behind the law was *for easier differentiation of place names.* Article 4 states: *Each locality may have only one official name.* This official name was to have been Magyarized. Protests followed, including by scholars, against this act of historical vandalism [179 p.188]. A delegation of German women from Transylvania sought to meet Emperor Franz Josph to protest against this barbarity, but an audience was refused because the emperor would not receive delegates from "Hungary" without the approval of Budapest [179 p.189]. Thus, localities with an absolute Romanian majority were renamed, such as Magyar Silvaș with a population that was 93.6 % Romanian, along with Romanian Silivaș. According to the Statistical Office in Budapest, more than 70 localities in Transylvania in total had their toponyms changed with the addition of the particle "Magyar". We give some more examples [5 p.27]:

Magyarbogata - 88.5 % Romanian
Magyarborosbocsard - 99.2 % Romanian
Magyarfeleg - 99.2 % Romanian
Magyarkekes - 99.4 % Romanian
Magyarosag - 99.1 % Romanian
Magyarpeterd - 96.8 % Romanian
Magyarszentfal - 95.9 % Romanian
Magyaruzfalo - 92.2 % Romanian
Magyar-kekes - 99.4 % Romanian
Magyar-Flemish - 99.2 % Romanian

Sibiu, where in the Middle Ages the Catholic king could only enter without an army and stay for no more than three days [5 p.11], now had no Hungarians apart from Hungarian officials and soldiers; it was renamed

Nagyszeben.

9.10 Statistics: Another "Tool" of Denationalisation

Fig.9.4. Romanians in Hungary: The Secret Book of Budapest.

The tradition of census falsification was well known, not only to intellectuals, but also beyond the borders of the Habsburg Empire. The *Deutsche Allgemeine Zeitung* of 30.12.1934 reminded its readers that the former director of the Budapest Institute of Statistics had been officially congratulated for his statistical contribution to Magyarization [7 p.39]. In 1930, an album dedicated to the Central Institute of Statistics was published in Budapest in which the results of the Magyarization programme were highlighted: between 1720 and 1850, more than 500,000 Romanians, Germans, Serbs, and Slovaks were Magyarized; and between 1850 and 1910, another 1,500,000 were Magyarized [7 p.31]. With Dualism, the complex process of Magyarization had accelerated sixfold! The Slovak priest Rohacek from Nyíregyháza (Hungary), who had urged the Slovak population to resist the pressure of officials and declare their nationality, was charged and sentenced to five years in prison for the crime of incitement against the Hungarian state! A small part of the misrepresentations, on three levels of the official Hungarian statistics, can be corrected by taking into account the recorded confession, as we have already shown for the particular case of Bixad (Covasna County). If we make this small correction to the Hungarian census of 1900, when for the first time, officially, the Hungarians exceeded 50 % of the total population in the area administered by Budapest, then we actually have a figure of 49.68 % Hungarian [197 vol. III p.1161]. The conclusion of Balogh Pal's book on the 1890 census is that the Magyarization of the Romanians by imposing the Hungarian language did not produce the results expected by the government [35 p.10]. For this reason, the Minister of the Interior, Iuliu Andrássy, and the Minister of Religious Affairs and Education, Albert Apponyi, supported the drafting of a large treatise by Antal Huszár, neutrally entitled *Romanians in Hungary* [Budapest, 1907], with 25 copies printed and of a secret nature. Onisifor Ghibu wrote that it not only contained a huge amount of informative material, but also a systematic plan for Magyarization, i.e., the denationalisation of the Romanian majority through government measures [192 p.154]. The first part of the work, among other things, lists factors that fuelled Romanian resistance to Magyarization. This *nationalist, extremist* resistance was stated to be directed against the Hungarian Nation State! In the second part of the work, the author offered solutions to destroy the compact mass of Romanians. In the third part, he addressed the necessity of the Greek-Catholic Church being part of the Roman Catholic Church. In the fourth part he dealt with the need to abolish the autonomy of the Orthodox Church and repeal its organic regulations. Antal Huszár proposed that Romanian journalists should be sentenced to ordinary imprisonment and also that Romanian credit institutions must be abolished [192 p.161]. In terms of culture, Antal Huszár stated:

> *Romanian culture can in no way be included, because in Hungary there can only be Hungarian culture* [192 p.160].

9.11 Latest Censuses

1900 Census of greater and medium "Hungary"

Another method of chauvinism, which R.W. Seton-Watson also observed after his first visit to Hungary in 1906, was evasion and sophistry, when not resorting directly to the most uncouth infamy and deception [179 p. XI-XX]. According to the census, uncorrected as far as possible on the basis of religion, in 1900 the population on the other side of Leitha was 45.4 % Hungarian and 54.6 % non-Hungarian [179 p. 3].

Hungary (all Trans-Leithana)	1900	
Hungarian speakers (including Jews)	8.679.014	45.4 %
Non-Magyar speakers (German, Slovenian, Romanian, Serbian, Croatian, etc.)	10.443.326	54.6 %

The Hungarian sociologist O. Iaszi, himself Magyarized, presented the evolution of Magyarization according to "Hungarian" statistical data [Annex C].

Hungary w/o Croatia & Slavonia	1787	1869	1890	1900	1900*
Hungarian speakers	29.0%	44.4%	48.5%	51.5%	49.68%*
Non-Magyarized population	71.0%	55.6%	51.5%	48.6%	50.32%*

Author's partial correction based on confession

And then, strictly according to Hungarian data, falsified three times in succession, how many Hungarian speakers were there in Hungary in 1900, 45.4 % or 51.5%? Why the difference? In claiming what was not theirs, they also referred to Croatia, Rijeka, and Slavonia (today divided between Croatia, Austria, and Slovenia), on the territory of which there were few Hungarian speakers. When presenting the demographic structure of the region by nationality, they presented only "middle" Hungary (without Croatia, Rijeka, and Slavonia) where, with the falsifications included, the Hungarian-speaking share of the population was 51.5 % [179 p.3]. If we partially correct the falsified official figures on the basis of Greek-Catholic and Orthodox confession, then in Hungary, without Croatia, Rijeka, and Slavonia, 49.68 % were Hungarian speakers.

1900 Census east of the Tisa River

We refer here to the ethnic structure as it can be reconstructed from the official Hungarian census of 1900 in the territories east of the Tisa (Banat, Crișana, Maramureș, and Transylvania). Here are the falsified official data: 6,814,000 souls of which 2,779,000 were Romanian, 2,624,000 were Hungarian, and 754,000 were German [197 p.1161]. If we take confession into account, then, in 1900, in the whole of Hungary 379,397 Greek Catholics and Orthodox were not included amongst the Romanians, Serbs and Ruthenians [197 p.1156]. As all these were from eastern Hungary, i.e., in the territory we have defined above, they were registered as Hungarians. As such, we actually have 2,244,603 Hungarians, with the amendment, however, that among these Hungarians there are also Swabians from Satu Mare, Jews, and Catholicized and Calvinized Romanians and Ruthenians. The Jews were not few in number either—in 1900 they accounted for about 5 % of the population [64 p.229]. On the other hand, we have 2,895,650 Greek-Catholic and Orthodox Romanians [197 p.1161], with the note that in this number we do not have the Greek-Catholic Romanians from Sătmar, Ugocea, Maramureș, Bihor, and Sablociu, who were under the Ruthenian Diocese of Muncaciu. Thus, we can only partially reconstruct the ethnic structure in 1900 east of the Tisa.

1900	Official Hungarian data		Partial correction by denomination	
Romanians *	2.779.000	40.8%	2.895.650*	42.49%
Hungarian-speaking **	2.624.000	38,5%	2.244.603**	32.94%
Hungarian speakers***	2.354.000	34.5%	1.974.453***	28.9%

Notes: *Romanians without the Catholic and Calvinist Romanians; **Hungarian speakers with the Swabians, Jews, Romanians, Slovaks, Ruthenian Catholics, and Calvinists; and ***Hungarians with the Swabians, Romanians, Slovaks, Ruthenian Catholics, and Calvinists, but without Jews.

East of the Tisa with all of Tisa plain and Maramureș we have a share of 42.49 % Romanian and only 28.9 % Hungarian, as well as about as many Slovaks, Ruthenians, and Serbs still not Magyarized. The correction can be taken further, with some effort, to obtain a clearer picture of the ethnic makeup of the population in 1900, taking into account, by locality, the presence of Swabians, Jews, Romanian Greek-Catholics, and Ruthenians east of the Tisa, in Sablociu, Haidu, Ugocea, and Maramureș.

1910 Transylvanian Census

The 1910 census captures the peak of denationalisation. In Transylvania and the County of Sălaj [10 p.32], the linguistic structure after this census, erroneously called the ethnic structure, shows: 53.7 % Romanian speakers; 10.7 % German speakers; and 31.6 % Hungarian speakers [141 p.219]. We come closer to the ethnic structure in 1910 if we also consider the confessional structure established by the same Hungarian census: 58 % Romanians; 3.5 % Jews; and only 28.1 % Hungarian speakers. But in this percentage of 58 % Romanians, we do not have the Romanians who happened to have one of the confessions traditionally shared by Hungarians, Saxons, and Swabians. In that census, as in the other, the Catholic Saxons were counted as Hungarian speakers, as well as all the employees of state companies. Let us recall the example cited by I.I. Russu from the Curvature Carpathians when a community was switched from the Greek-Catholic to the Orthodox confession in order to then be switched to Catholicism [154 p.156]. Or the Calvinized Romanians of Deva that we mentioned. Or the Romanians of Sângeorgiu de Pădure, forcibly converted to the Reformed confession in 1848 [114 p.22]. According to the 1910 census, in the whole territory that united with Romania, the Romanians (Orthodox and Greek-Catholics) numbered

3,058,793, i.e., at least 228,692 Romanians and 184,508 Jews were missing, which only appear in the confessional data, i.e., at least 413,200 Romanians and Jews appear amongst the Hungarians. With this minimal correction, the Hungarians registered in 1910 accounted for 23.8 % [209].

Looking at the Austrian tax records and Hungarian censuses, not to establish the percentages of Hungarians, since the proportion can be determined genetically, but to show the bias and falsity of these data. As O. Iaszi acknowledged, Habsburg Hungary *had embarked on a vigorous campaign of national assimilation* [226].

9.12 Denationalisation in Administration

We have seen how the problem was posed in feudal Transylvania immediately after the Peace of 1648, which generalized the principle *cujus regio, ejus religio*, as described by Konrad Hildebrandt! We saw the terror in the thousands of hangings and impalements of the bodies of Romanian serfs in the spring of 1848. In the work of a "traveller", the poet Vasile Alecsandri, towns and villages were shown in images *illustrated with numerous hangings and impalements.*

Representation in local government, after the genocide of 1848/49 and the reforms that followed was divided between elected and appointed members; but the appointed or the "elected" belonged in one way or another to the landowners [179 p.242]. The value of the vote and its result has been clarified. Below, we present a clearer picture of administrative Magyarization in 1900 [132 p.78].

Urban	Hungarian speakers	Romanians
State Admin.	8124	135
Admin. of counties w/o cities	4130	137
City Admin.	4680	91
Judges, etc.	3715	86
Rural	**Hungarian speakers**	**Romanians**
Municipal notaries	4219	71
Public notary assistants	2349	188
Officials	2683	351

Romanians in the administration accounted for about 3 %. The reputed and impartial historian, R.W. Seton-Watson, who came to Hungary with the best of intentions stated in relation to the adminstration: *Nous sommes en pleine Asie* [179].

9.13 Denationalisation Through Mental Terror

It should be noted that this method no longer remained the purview of the Hungarian elite alone, but became a tool in the hands of every Magyarized person who wished to prove his Magyarhood. It was not only for a literary magazine like the *Scientific Collection* that Slovaks were considered a revolting dream and a despicable thing [179 p.60], but for the average Hungarian the same was held to be true: *the Slovak is not human* (*Tot nem ember*), *the German is cursed* (*A német hunczut*), *the Romanian is tanned* (*Az oláh naponsült*), and *the Jew stinks* (*A zsidó búdös*), etc. Other anonymous creations included idioms, *Hungarians have courage, German dog skin*, and a popular verse *God grant, that, as it ever was, both German and Slovak may serve the Magyar* [179 p.60]. This kind of torture was very effective, and few could stand up to it. The Vice President of the Hungarian Senate, Istvan Rakovszki (1906-1909), addressed the German deputies in plenary with expressions such as *Get out! Ass, stupid fool, coward!* and *I'll box your ears!* In order for such attitudes to be popularised, they were repeated in the newspapers [179 p.502]. *By praying in German, they were mocking God* was a slogan pushed on to the Swabians in order to achieve full Magyarization. The Swabians were often said to be *the gypsies of the Germans* [82 p.5]. Perhaps none of the many references is as all-encompassing as that of Ioan Slavici:

> The consequence of this systematic degradation was that they were looked upon as something higher, but that their neighbours also looked upon them in the same way. The Romanians, Serbs and Slovaks were ashamed of their name until more recent times; and as for the Germans, the Jews, the Ruthenians and a large part of the Slovaks, even today there is no greater insult to them than to call them what they are [160 p.692].

The terrible result of mental terror, recorded in 1871 by I. Slavici was that:

> out of 2.5 million Slovak Catholics and Lutherans [...] there are not twenty men, who represent the cause of their nation in public life; out of 1.5 million Germans there is not one in the Parliament of Hungary, and not one at the plough, from whom you can escape with an unbroken head if you call him a 'German' [105 p.702].

9.14 The Response of the Intelligentsia
to Denationalisation

With every word I put on paper, I have before my eyes
the Penal Code and behind the gendarme.
—S. Bărnuțiu

The response of ordinary Romanians to the ultra-chauvinist policy was emigration. The result of this policy was basically racial cleansing—those who did not become Hungarians were forced to leave. Romanian, Serbian, and Slovak intellectuals tried, within the depraved limits of the official framework, to take a stand against the violation of the laws, which themselves were discriminatory. Any murmur against Budapest's racist policies was punished both legally and financially. Just as there was a different electoral law for Transylvania, so there was a different press law in Transylvania than in Hungary—different countries, different laws! Here, prosecutors had discretionary powers, which they also used against the press. In 1871, three courts with juries for press offences were established in Cluj, Tg. Mures, and Sibiu. The one in Sibiu was abolished after a few years because it could not be easily controlled [179 p.295]. If a Hungarian newspaper, *Magyar Hirlap*, regretted that the heads of traitors no longer hung on the walls of the fortresses (all built by the Germans), or considered that the most appropriate punishment was to skin Slovaks alive, it was applauded; a non-Hungarian journalist could be thrown into prison just for making an allusion to the polyglot nature of the state [179. p299]. Valeriu Braniște alone (1869-1928), editor of the newspaper *Dreptatea* in Timișoara, had 72 lawsuits brought against him for articles he had published, and he was of course fined and sentenced to prison dozens of times. We do not have any studies dedicated to this particular aspect, but we have a partial inventory of the sanctions given to journalists [132 p.98].

The Nationality of journalists	Number of journalists sanctioned	Total criminal sanctions	Total fines [kroner]
Romanian	353	131 years 10 months 26 months	93.791
Slovak	560	91 years 7 months 26 days	42.121
German	14	2 years 10 months 10 days	7.720
Ruthenian	7	5 years	2.100
Serbian	4	1 year 7 months	2.500

To understand the value of the fines, let us mention that the annual property tax in Pannonia was 17.92 kroner (8.96 florins). The income of a mid-level peasant family was 20-22 florins/year [153 p.197], while that of a Romanian Greek-Catholic teacher was 70 florins/year in 1865 [153 p.23]. In 1892, 1 kg of gold was worth 3,280 kroner. The fines of Romanian journalists alone were equivalent to the taxes levied from 5,234 (wealthy-voting) citizens. Let us look at an example from the chapter *The Persecution of Romanian Publicists* in [190], the trial of retired general Traian Doda from Caransebeş. Traian Doda was elected a deputy in 1887. He published a manifesto to his electors in which *he* wrote that *he received the mandate, but did not use it*, in order to demonstrate to the monarch that *there was no place for* Romanians in the *Hungarian constitution* and that *there was something rotten* in the monarchy. For publishing this manifesto, the elected deputy was put on trial! He was tried *in absentia* only on the request of the public prosecutor who warned the magistrates that they had *a duty as Hungarians, not just as judges*. As Doda was ill, his lawyer's defence was not accepted either. He was sentenced to two years imprisonment and an enormous fine [190 p.103]. In 1890, Ioan Macaveiu was sentenced to 18 months in prison because he condemned the "monstrous dogma" of the Hungarian state in two articles. In 1906, Avram Indreica was sentenced to seven months in prison for reproducing an article from a Viennese newspaper. Young Romanian and Slovak journalists opposed this persecution with a sense of honour; for them, it was an honour to go to prison for the cause of the people in the detested feudal monarchy [179 p.197].

Another method of fighting the non-Magyar majority press was to confiscate editions. In 1907 alone, the Slovak newspaper *Ludove Noviny* was confiscated 20 times. After 1886, there were more Slovak newspapers in America than in Slovakia [179 p.202]. In 1916, the newspaper *Drapelul* (The flag) from Lugoj (Timiş County) appeared with many white spaces, as a policy of censorship no longer allowed "agitation through the press". The Hungarians were not at the front, they were in "high" position jobs: in the secret police, in the gendarmerie, and in the censor's office. Millions of people were spied on—what they said, what they thought, and what they did. The Hungarians sent non-Magyars to the frontlines.

The whole of intellectual Europe was agitating for a "way out" of the people's prison, out of the K&K Empire, which was at the mercy of the most extreme chauvinism. In 1865, the Czech historian Frantisek Palacky launched the idea of an Austrian state based on provinces with national majorities. The Romanians, stupidly loyal to the monarchy, a monarchy that had mocked them relentlessly, came up with a *United States of*

Greater Austria project in 1905 through Aurel Popovici. Aurel Popovici (1863-1917) was a lawyer who was sentenced to four years in prison for defending the cause of the memorandists and the main author of *Replica* (Rejoinder) [190]. At the same time, Seton-Watson believed that the idea of federation was utopian, as its realisation would have required a *coup d'état* [179 p.407].

The Slovak poet Jan Kollar (1793-1852) gave a novel response to the vicious chauvinism that had gripped the entire Hungarian elite. He studied at the University of Jena where he witnessed the *German Unity Movement*. Returning home to Pest as a Lutheran pastor with the goal of defending the Slovaks, so exposed to Magyarization, he laid the foundations of *Pan-Slavism*.

Another response of the Romanians, Serbs, and Slovaks to Magyarization was the formation of *The League of Nationalities* (1895) to defend their existence. In the programme adopted by the League's congress, the idea of a Magyar national state was seen to contradict ethnic and historical development, and threaten the existence of other people. The programme also expressed the hope that Germans and Ruthenians would join the League. The Germans, being among those who were hit hardest by Magyarization, did not respond. Among the German intellectuals in Transylvania, the idea that they would have no chance of survival alongside the Hungarians was weak: *besides the Hungarian nationality, no other nationality can survive without renouncing itself* [37 p12]. For the Ruthenians, there was no one to answer because they had been totally deprived of schools.

The non-Hungarian majority was aware that the minority held all the power and races that formed the majority were at the mercy of an arbitrary executive that brutally repressed even the slightest movements of the nationalities [190 p.478].

Associations

Societies and public and private clubs of any kind—religious, health, philanthropic, reading, and singing, etc.—had to have the consent of local and central government authorities; associations could be dissolved and their assets arbitrarily confiscated. Not even a village choir could be established without the approval of Budapest.

No event could be organized without being announced and specified who and what it said; the event had to be supervised. In 1887, the Serbs of Panciova (Serbia) wanted to set up a choral society and sent a request to the Minister of the Interior in Budapest, who refused to approve it. In

1899, a meeting of the Slovaks of Lipto took place at which Professor Joob was to speak. In order to prevent the word "Slovak" from being uttered, the praetor did not allow him to speak, although the professor had already replaced the forbidden word with "man" [179 p.283].

Breaking up meetings with gangs of hooligans was also a frequent solution, as in the case of a Slovak Catholic society in Trnava [179 p.277]. It was commonplace for priests to be arrested for having certain political sympathies. The Slovak deputy, Dr Paul Blaho, had a meeting with several Czech journalists at his home without informing the police; on 3.02.1908, his parliamentary immunity was removed [179 p.285]. Even in the cemeteries, the non-Hungarian majority had no right to cast a shadow on the "Hungarian political nation". No industrial enterprise could operate unless the minority wanted it to [179 p.291]. The right of association depended on the applicant: the Hungarians were allowed anything and societies with a provocative character against the Romanian-German-Serbian-Slovak majority were encouraged. The Saxons had their own associations before Dualism, which survived, but the Swabians were "denied" *in integrum* with the blessing of the Catholic Church.

On 11.02.1907, the Minister of the Interior in Budapest refused the status of the Beiuş "Singing Reunion" of the church choir because some members were in Bucharest in the summer of 1906. This aspect of police control of the citizenry should be noted.

It was not just that new associations were banned, but cultural institutions won after 1860, during the "liberal" period, were also dissolved, including:

i) the three Romanian gymnasiums established by Romanians (who provided both money and property) between 1862 and 1868 [179 p.157];
ii) Matiţa, the Cultural Association of Slovaks, founded in 1863, because *there is no Slovak nation* [179 p.166];
iii) and the Sibiu jury court in 1885, because it was not as 'Magyarizing' as was required.

The compulsory nature of enthusiasm

In opposition to the right of association of the Romanian-Serbian-Slovak-Swabian majorities was the compulsory nature of enthusiasm for the policy of Magyarization. On 11.04.1913 in Moftinul Mic (Satu Mare County), 15 peasants were arrested together with the priest Gheorghe Mureşanu because they did not want to go out to meet the vicar

Jaczkovics, who, as indicated by his name, was Magyarized. They remained in custody until the end of the trial with 39 accusers and over 30 witnesses. They were sentenced, according to their "contribution" to this lack of enthusiasm, to prison with terms of 3-18 months depending on how serious the offence was considered to have been [163 p.327].

Life at the discretion of racial hatred

After 1867, from one government to the next, regardless of alleged political orientation, the situation of the non-Magyar majority became increasingly difficult. Seton-Watson noted this very well in his work [179].

The Great War aroused patriotic enthusiasm in Vienna (including in intellectuals like Sigmund Freud) and frenzy in Budapest, while in Transylvania it brought justified fears. The Transylvanians knew they would be the ones fighting, not the Hungarians. In 1914 and 1915, thousands of civilians, after torment and torture, were hanged for their lack of enthusiasm for the Great War and for imagined acts of treason. In 1915, 55 Romanian priests were among those hanged and Serbs died by their thousands in the Hungarian extermination camps in Arad and Seghedin [38].

CHAPTER 10

FROM SAVAGE DENATIONALISATION TO RACIAL CLEANSING

10.1 Emigration

In the period 1588 to 1653, no less than six laws were passed in Transylvania to increase punishments for runaway serfs [6 vol. I p. 188]. According to some simple calculations, as the historian Gelu Neamţu noted, the number of refugees from atrocities in Transylvania in 1849 alone amounted to at least 20,000 [116 p.195]. If, in the past, we had serfdom, after 1866 we saw savage Magyarization and the obstruction of Romanians and Slovaks at all levels of social and economic life. This could not go unchallenged by the common man and between 1899 and 1914, 382,045 Transylvanians officially emigrated [141 p.214], primarily to Romania. This figure does not include illegal emigration over the mountains into Romania, circumventing the bureaucracy and official taxes of the executioner state from which people were fleeing. The most active section of the population, the young, was the one that emigrated. Even if we do not have a definitive figure for emigration, it clearly reached alarming proportions!

At that time, 1890-1918, in the country of Olt, more than 90 % of families had one or more young person who emigrated to America, some of whom never returned. The impact was visible in the 1950s in the Olt country with many houses painted light blue and all made in the same style with money from America, in contrast to the old wooden houses. For many years, we thus had a *sui generis* record of these events in every Transylvanian village, which were populated by older people whose children had gone to America around the turn of the 20th century.

10.2 Breaking up Ethnic Structures

The Romanian-Serbian-Slovak majority was being targeted and dislocated in all aspects: educational, cultural, administrative, religious, economic, and legal. Around 1880, intensive colonisation began with the aim of breaking Romanian unity in Banat, the Tisa Plain, Maramureş, Crişana, and Transylvania. At the beginning, three million florins were allocated for colonisation. The amount increased year by year, reaching 10 million florins by 1910. More than 91,000 hectares of arable land were purchased for this purpose [107 p.48]. The declared aim of colonisation was to break up the unity of the *non-Magyar* nations and, first of all, to drain the *Romanian sea*. Settlement was designed to follow the courses of the rivers Mures, Someş, and Criş. Obviously, colonisation was intertwined with all the other forms of Magyarization. At first, new villages were established (four villages with 912 families) in the counties of Arad and Torontal, which were inhabited by Romanians and Serbs. Then the tactics changed and Hungarian speakers were settled in Romanian villages. In this way, the authorities not only changed the statistics, but the settlers also better served the cause of Magyarization. In addition to the new settlers planted in purely Romanian villages, this also provided an opportunity to bring in mayors, notaries, teachers, and gendarmes, etc. The new principles of colonisation were established by the ultra-chauvinist politician and journalist Beksics Gustav, who set out the guidelines for such colonisation in his book *Program of National Policy in Transylvania and Szekler Country*, published in Budapest in 1896 [197 vol. I p.440].

In 1898 near Lugoj (Timiş County), Hungarian-speaking settlers were brought to the localities of Ţipari, Ghizela, Bethausen, Bodo, and Dumbrava [107 p.51]. In Banat, a new wave of colonisation began in 1900 with a chain of colonies organized in the Timiş valley and the aim of reaching Ilia and Dobra (Hunedoara County) where there were other recent colonies connected to the Mureş valley. In 1903, Moşniţa (Timiş County), a township of 1,280 Romanian souls with 52 Hungarian families, was colonised; then the tax office refused to lease the cattle pasture to the Romanians [132 p.52]. In addition, children from large and poor Romanian families were sent to the orphanage in Timişoara from where they were placed in Magyarized families. Here, within a few years, they forgot their mother tongue and were given a new "identity". In 1909, the Minister of Agriculture drew up a new law providing for another 10 million kroner over a period of 12 years to support colonisation. By the outbreak of war in 1914, 21 more colonies had been established in the Rodna-Prundul Bârgăului (Bistriţa-Năsăud County) area. Luduş (Mureş County), which was in the area marked for Magyarization, was also colonised. The strategies taken were, on the one hand, colonisation with "Hungarians" and, on the other, the impoverishment of the Romanians to such an extent that they emigrated of their own volition. Colonisation was combined with other educational, religious, and administrative 'methods', which were successful in Magyarizing the towns [29]. Another method of ethnic cleansing was to grant poor families land for 20 years, which they did not have to give back if they became Hungarian.

10.3 The 1910 Elections: A Real Civil War

In 1901, under a so-called liberal regime, the non-Hungarian majority (50.32 % according to Hungarian data with a correction for confession) sent only five deputies to parliament [91 p.286]. In 1905, the Romanians gave up their "passivity" and turned to *activism*, entering the parliamentary elections in Transylvania. With this decision Hungary switched to electoral terror against other nationalities. For the American Milton Lehrer, the 1910 elections were a telling example of how Hungarian governments sought to achieve their goal of racial cleansing [91]. The British historian R.W. Seton-Watson notes that Hungarian troops were present in 380 of the 413 constituencies. Criticised in the West, Budapest responded with an official statement that it used only 194 infantry battalions and 114 cavalry squadrons. In other words, the British historian notes, the government admitted a number that was equivalent to a partial mobilisation of the army. *Needing more than 173,000 soldiers to maintain order on Election Day, we can assume that something unusual is happening* [R.W. Seton-Watson, *Corruption and Reform in Hungary*, London, 1911, p.11]. The election of 1910, which resulted in human casualties, was compared to *a real civil war* [91 p.289].

10.4 An Ethnic Border

The border established at Trianon was artificial because it basically demarcated non-Magyarized and Magyarized Romanians. In March 1990, Professor Oltean from Jula (today Hungary) told me that, at that time, the villages in a strip of 15-20 km along the Romanian border towards the Tisa, despite Magyarization after 1918, still preserved certain Romanian characteristics.

The awareness of the border between the Romanians and the old Hungarians has not disappeared. Duke Ahtum (~1000-1030) of Banat smuggled shipments across the Tisa and Danube, which is why King Stephen I sent a German army against him. In 1266, King Bela IV, after engaging in war with the Voivode of Transylvania, his son Stephen, left Transylvania and returned *little by little to our country, God willing*, to the land of Pannonia [158 p.50]. In 1291, King Andrei III, regulating the customs process on the Tisa, decided that only *merchants passing from one country to another* should pay duty [148 vol. I p.90]. In 1855, the Parisian historian and jurist Elias Regnault wrote:

> *The Romanian race extends beyond the two principalities and occupies the entire country between the Tisa, the Dniester and the Danube. ... To this must be added approximately 2,000,000 Romanians scattered in groups of 50 to 60 thousand in Bulgaria, Serbia, Podolia, Hungary and Macedonia, faithfully preserving their nationality, language and customs* [152 p.V].

Fig.10.1. Map of Hungary as seen by L. Kossuth if the peoples of the kingdom were given autonomy.

The MP for Brad, Iosif Hodoșiu (Hunedoara County), clarified "on the texts of the law" in a public meeting on 21.02.1866 in the Pest Parliament that "the parts", i.e., Banat, Crișana, Ugocea, and Maramureș, were part of Transylvania, based on both the *Leopoldine Diploma* of 1691 and the *Pragmatic Sanction* of 1722, and according to the unsuccessful official attempts to incorporate them into Hungary proper in 1741 and 1792 [127 vol. IV p. 52]. In other words, Hungary as a subject of internal law in the Habsburg Empire, if one can call it that at the time, stretched all the way to the Tisa.

In his work *Kossuth and the Treaty of Trianon*, Oskar Iaszy, a university professor and Minister for Minorities (1918-1919) presents a map of Hungary drawn by Kossuth (fig. 10.1) if the autonomy of the minorities were to be respected [226]. This map shows that in the area of Sătmar (Romanians and Swabians), Romania was disadvantaged at Trianon. In fig. 10.2 we find an outline of Romania's western border as negotiated with the ambassadors of the Triple Entente in August 1916. During the First World War, almost 10,000 Romanian peasants were deported west of the Tisa and more than 3,000 Romanian intellectuals were arrested as suspects and interned in a concentration camp near the Austrian border at Sopron [112 p.41]. Among them were Emil Cioran's parents.

The Tisa was still considered to be the border between the Hungarians and Romanians at the beginning of the 20th century. Hundreds of priests exiled themselves to Romania for fear of reprisal after the withdrawal of Romanian troops in September 1916. French officers who visited Transylvania in the winter of 1918/1919 described in their reports what they found in the field; thus Lt. Col. Sangnier reported that numerous Hungarian troops *were looting and massacring* [84 p.160] and Col. Hayaux du Tilly wrote that the Hungarians were doing *quite a lot of stealing and killing* [84 p.161]. Let us add one more aspect related to the retreat of the German and K&K armies through Transylvania and the Transylvanian National Guard established in November 1918 from the Romanian contingents of the K&K army. These Romanian guards disarmed enemy troops and confiscated stolen goods. They also fought battles with changing fortunes. At Sebeş (Alba County), the Romanian National Guard *captured 31 wagons of ammunition and 24 wagons of oil from the Germans*. In Curtici (Arad County) the guards detained herds of horses, robbed from Romania. The guards at Ineu (Arad County), took from the Germans six oil wagons, one petrol wagon, one sugar wagon, two machine guns, ammunition, 116 horses, 13 chariots, and six oxen [176 p.140].

During the Communist government of Béla Kun, a strong right-wing opposition was formed by prominent ultra-chauvinist politicians, such as Ludwig von Windischgraetz, Waszony, and Horthy, and former prime ministers Andrássy and Bethlen. They organized themselves into an alternative government in Seghedin. On 10.07.1919, they appealed to the Romanian government, demanding that the Romanian army cross the Tisa and remove the Bolshevik government in Budapest. The request was addressed through the Romanian legation in Bern; the appeal ended with these words:

Only with your help will we be able to save our country and peace and order will be restored in Central Europe.

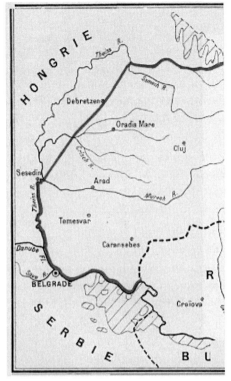

Fig. 10.2. The frontier negotiated in 1916.

The appeal asked Romania: 1) to support the government in Seghedin; 2) to favour the formation of the White Guards; 3) for the Romanian army to cross the river Tisa and defeat Béla Kun's army; and 4) to occupy Budapest and replace the Bolshevik government with a national government formed in Seghedin around Admiral Horthy [71 p.53].

In 1919, the western border was drawn by a Special Commission, made up of experts from the USA, Great Britain, France, and Italy, and based on the 1910 census, which was an exercise in Hungarian statistical malpractice. Romania had no experts and no access to such experts, nor is it certain that they had any documents proving the "Romanianness" of the recently Magyarized people. Romania did not have archaeological and epigraphic data, linguistic studies, and evidence based on folklore creation, which is inherent to an ethnic group that has developed over such a large area. There were studies by Ioan Slavici, but probably no Romanian politician had read them!

In his work *Geographie des Königreichs Ungarns*, published in Oresburg in 1770, Karl Gottlieb von Windisch established the Romanian border further west than the one drawn at Trianon.

In the *Geographical Lexicon of Hungary* of 1786, Krabinschi also mentioned the presence of Romanians in Sablociu and the plain of Crişana, further west of the present border [161 p.95]. In 1919, Bichiş, Cenad, Ugocea, Sablociu, and the lowland part of Crişana still had a large and compact Romanian population.

Who lost at Trianon?

It is obvious that if anyone lost at Trianon, it was certainly the Romanians, as well as the Germans and Slovaks. If the Swabians had wanted to, and demographics mattered, southern Pannonia could have been a German state. The Hungarians, i.e., the Magyarized people, "lost" what did not belong to them; possession alone does not make one an owner.

Eighty years ago, the modern science of genetics did not exist, but Milton Lehrer noticed that Sighet, Oradea, Arad, and Timișoara were surrounded by compact masses of Romanian peasants and concluded:

> *So, if an injustice was committed in 1920, it is the Romanians and not the Hungarians who are entitled to complain, since significant islands of Romanians were left within Hungarian territory* [91 p.178].

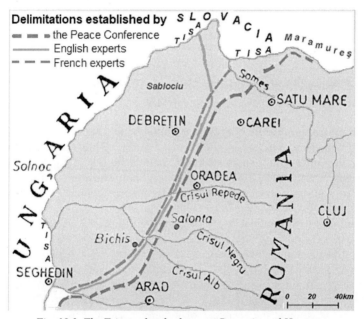

Fig. 10.3. The Trianon border between Romania and Hungary and 2 variants by British and French experts [103].

The historian Stefan Manciulea travelled on foot, along the Tisa, covering the entire area of the western border of Romania from Maramures to the Danube. In the localities on the left bank of the Tisa, he researched and studied archives and church libraries to gather archaeological, historical, demographic, and statistical documentary material on the history of the

Romanians. The result: despite the Magyarization of the Romanian population on the Tisa Plain, at the beginning of the 20th century almost the entire area was essentially Romanian! Among others, we find 300,000 "Hungarian Greek Catholics". A map of the places where the liturgical language was still Romanian at the beginning of the 20th century is given in fig. 2.20. After the Bichiș-Ciaba National Assembly, the Slovaks of Bichiș and Cenad (Hungary), 130,000 souls in total, sent a memorial signed by the intellectuals Samuel Sirka, Juray Hiabovsky, and Michal Saaz [86, 7 p.17] to the French Foreign Minister to be submitted to the Paris Peace Conference. The memorial was also supported by the Czech Eduard Benes (1884-1948) and in it they asked to be incorporated into Romania [7 p.18]:

> *The aim of oppression was the Magyarization of nationalities... On the basis of the Wilsonian principle, the Slovak people of Bichiș and Cenad demand to remain linked to the Romanian people. The Slovak people fully accept the resolution taken by the Romanians of the former Hungary in Alba-Iulia and unite with them in Greater Romania.*

10.5 Non-Magyarized People in the Middle Danube Basin After 1918

With the savage process of denationalisation under Dualism, after Trianon there remained in Hungary more than 4.5 million Hungarians with non-Magyar names [7 p.23]. In addition, there were 2 million Romanians, Slovaks, Serbs, and Ruthenians on the Tisa Plain who were aware of their identity, an assessment also made by the man of culture Raoul Sorban [166 p.101]. These final traces—the non-Magyar names—had to be erased. In 1930, the *Society for the Magyarization of Names*, headed by Dr. Lengyel Zoltán, was re-established. Lengyel noted in 1933 that no less than 4.5 million inhabitants, i.e., 50 % of Hungary's population, had non-Magyar names [7 p.44; 200 p.67]. We could describe this as phase two of the Magyarization of names, because we have already spoken of the first great Magyarization. On 13.08.1936, the newspaper *Magyarság* reported that Franz Rothen, the secretary of a German cultural organisation, had been sentenced to six years in prison for statements against the Magyarization of names. Among other things, he had said that minorities had more rights in Romania [7 p.48]. In Trianon Hungary, there were probably several hundred thousand non-Magyarized Romanians left in the territories west of the Tisa.

In 1937, Dr Denes István published the numbers of assimilated Romanians in the counties of northwestern Hungary: Berg 21,762; Haidu

19,500; and Sablociu 79,740 [7 p.64]. These figures do not include those identifiable by their membership of the Greek-Catholic confession. In the counties of Cenad, Ciongrad, Haidu, and Sablociu there were 120 townships with Romanians left in 1925 [7 p.61]. The falsification of statistics by Hungarians was well known across Europe; on 30.12.1934 the influential Deutsche Allgemeine Zeitung wrote that a large number of Germans, Romanians, and Slovaks had been registered as Hungarians. The Germans alone had lost 315,000 in the past 30 years [7 p.41]. The Germans, now a minority, still had an absolute majority in 400 localities. Looking at the map in fig. 10.6, we cannot help but relate it to the map of the Potsdam Conference (July-August 1945 where Germany was divided into three zones, as proposed by American experts). This map was seen by the author in October 1980 and revised in March 1992 at Cecilienhof (Potsdam). The American proposal envisaged a West Germany, a Prussia, and a South Germany including Budapest. In 2019, the map was no longer on display, the museographers reasoning that the exhibition was continually being updated.

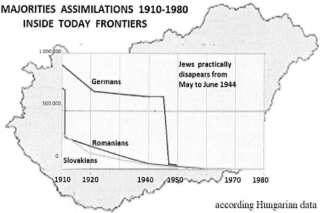

Fig. 10.4. Hungary (1910-1950), the graveyard of Romanians, Slovaks, and Germans.

On 27.11.1932, the newspaper *Kronstädter Zeitung* reported that in the town of Budaörs (Hungary) the local priest was forced to conduct the Divine Service in Hungarian, confirming the pressure of Magyarization on the Catholic Church [7. p.49]. Perpetually criminal in thought and deed, on 15.04.1932, the newspaper *Pesti Hírlap* suggested to its countrymen that in case they reoccupied Transylvania, the nationalities must adjust within

24 hours and *Dacian-Romanians must disappear from the territory* [7 p.48; 91 p.479].

Dr. Basch, the leader of the Germans in Trianon Hungary, was sentenced by a Hungarian court to three months imprisonment for giving a speech against the forced Magyarization of the Germans. The Court of Appeal increased the sentence to five months imprisonment and loss of political rights for three years [7 p.48; 132 p.50].

The fate of Franz Wesner, a Hungarian Swabian, is typical of the Germans in Hungary. He was born in 1927 in Swabian Turkey (Schwabische Turkei as the locals called the region of Branau, now southern Hungary), a desolate region colonised by the Austrians with Swabians after the expulsion of the Turks from Pannonia (1699, Treaty of Carlowitz). Since then, the region had been German (see §8.4). The kindergarten attended by young Wesner was obviously Hungarian, although all the inhabitants were German. After kindergarten came the communal school, where he was forbidden to speak German even at break time. If any child slipped into German at recess, they were beaten.

Ungarn, ungar. *Magyarország*, Kgr. in Mitteleuropa; 117171 qkm, 10311000 E (87,9 je qkm), davon ²/₃ röm.-kath., ¹/₄ ev.; 90% Magyaren, 700000 Ukrainer, 600000 Dtsche. (Heinzen im früh. Burgenland, Schwaben vom Plattensee bis Budapest, Donauschwaben bis Fünfkirchen und in Batschka u. Arad). Tiefland (ober- und niederungar. Tiefebene, größtes europ. Tieflandbecken), Gebirge (Hegyalja, Mátra, Karpaten in der Karpato-Ukraine) und Waldplateaus (Bakony-Wald) im N u. NW, im W der Plattensee (Balaton): 591 qkm, der größte See Mitteleuropas. Schwemmland an der

Fig. 10.5. Hungary after the Vienna Diktat (1938) in Knaurs Lexikon 1940.

After primary school in the village, he went to school in Fünfkirchen (1942-1944) where he was educated in the same "Hungarian" spirit. He was 17 when the Red Army appeared and he was deported to Russia along with other Germans from Hungary. The motto of the Hungarians was "only Swabians"! In Russia, in a labour camp, he met other Germans from Romania and from Yugoslavia. They seemed to the young Franz to be Imperial Germans—they had their own schools, speaking and studying in

German! The Pannonian Swabians were all Catholics. The Catholic Church in Pannonia was led by the Swabian Bhem and the Magyarized Minzenti. This cardinal worked with Count Teleki to organize the *Movement of Devout Swabians*, which had the goal of assimilating the Swabians. In the Carei area, three Swabian villages Wahlei, Merk, and Saiten, remained in Hungary after Trianon, but they had no chance of surviving as German villages. In the Romanian Swabian villages, the Germans also fought a battle for survival, with their own Catholic Church, i.e., with their own Magyarized and Magyarizing Catholic hierarchy [229 p.63].

Fig. 10.6. The mayor of Bichiș-Ciaba offering bread and salt to King Ferdinand (1919).

10.6 The Magyarization of the Germans in Sătmar

We have mentioned the Magyarization of the Swabians, especially in the paragraph in which we analysed the emergence and development of the culture of hatred. *The History of the Germans in the Satu Mare Region* [82], written by Dr. Ernst Hauler, throws more light on the matter. We have several testimonies from Professor Alfons Brauchle in a manuscript entitled *The struggle of the German nationality in Satu Mare* [18]. A copy was deposited in the Library of the Academy in Cluj-Napoca. After 1918, the Swabians from Satu Mare in Romania awakened to national life with the help of the Saxons and the Banat Swabians. They began to rebuild their German consciousness, demand German schools, and listen to sermons in their own language. The greatest resistance came from the hierarchy of the Catholic Bishopric of Satu Mare, which was largely made up of Magyarized Swabians from the period of savage Magyarization. The schools were denominational, i.e., Catholic, and were run by the local Catholic hierarchy. When in 1925 the *German-Swabian Community of Satu Mare* was founded and the revival of German consciousness among the Swabians was felt, the clergy reacted with anger—they refused to introduce preaching and teaching in German instead of Hungarian. The Swabians said: *Everyone woul d be a Swabian in our country if it weren't for the priest being against it!* In 1931, a Banat-Swabian, Stephan Fiedler, ascended to the bishop's seat after Bishop Boromizsa (a name with a Dacian ring to it). This change did not ease the pressure of the chauvinist policy on the Swabians. When a delegation from the village of Homorod asked the bishopric to teach them in German, they were greeted with the response *May God not help you and your families.* What a message to hear from a bishop to his parishioners!

After the pupils at Ciumeşti started to pray in German, the priest harangued them: *Children, you are mocking God if you pray in German!* The priest Kuliffay of Tiream told members of the school and parish councils that *teaching in German would make them stupid*, while the priest Schwegler told the children: *This German language is the ugliest, the most stupid language in the world. With it you remain as stupid as your parents.* The priest Bottlinger blackmailed his parishioners in Ardud, who had petitioned him to set up a German section in the denominational school: *I will keep the petition. There will come a time when you will regret it!* Bottlinger often said, I *am ashamed that I was born a Swabian!* From the pulpit he was all politics, preaching that *God and the Mother of God, only understood Hungarian* [18].

An illegal Hungary in Romania

Here are some significant excerpts related to our topic from an interview with Professor Ernst Hauler, a Swabian from Satu Mare born in 1917 in Meitingen (Moftinu-Satu Mare County) where he also attended a Hungarian school. In Meitingen, there were only Swabians just as in the rest of the county (those registered as 'Hungarians' were actually Magyarized Swabians). In 1992, when Prof. Hauler looked through the Meitingen school archives, he was astonished to find that he had attended a German school [229 p.69-75].

Of course, you don't understand what I mean. So [...] we, the Satu-Mare Swabians, were annexed to Romania by the Treaty of Trianon, but Satu-Mare was 10 km from the border with Hungary, and the Romanian government of the time noticed that Magyarization was continuing in Satu-Mare, and that the irredentist movement was gaining momentum. For this reason it was decreed that here, in Romania, Magyarization should end, and that the Swabians should be educated in German. This decree was issued in 1920 and sent to the bishop, because all the Swabians were studying in confessional Roman Catholic schools. The Romanian Ministry informed the Bishop of Satu-Mare—because he was the head of the confessional schools—that from 1921, German would be the language of instruction in the schools where the Satu-Mare Swabians were taught. The bishop rejected this, continuing to teach in Hungarian, even though we were in Romania. The Romanians caught on and the Minister of Religious Affairs, Angelescu, decreed that Germans were not allowed to be taught in Hungarian, and if they did not agree, the school would be closed. The church, and therefore the teachers, did not want this and so the school in Meitingen was closed. The state did not even allow a Romanian school to exist in Meitingen, only a German one. For two years 210 children were left without schooling. After two years the school was reopened, but it was done in such a way as to make it look like it was taught in German. ... Bishop Fiedler, who came from Banat, being uninformed and a very pious man, could not believe that the priests he led could be so perfidious and capable of such things. Those priests were so perfidious that they hid ammunition in the library of theology. This ammunition was discovered in 1939 by the Romanian authorities. For this reason, the bishop had to resign. [...] At the heart of it was the irredentist movement. [...] after 1945, as in Northern Transylvania, there was a Hungarian proletarian dictatorship. Before 1940 one could speak of an illegal Hungary, and after 1945 of a Hungarian proletarian dictatorship [...] I did not learn German in Meitingen, but in Timişoara.

CHAPTER 11

FROM RACIAL CLEANSING TO A SECOND GENOCIDE

11.1 Racial Cleansing During the First World War

Lt. Octavian Tăslăuan, commander of the 11th Company of the 23rd Territorial Regiment, witnessed the racial cleansing of Transylvania during the 1914 campaign in Galicia. One of the many passages in his diary refers to the racial cleansing practiced by the Hungarians:

> *We stop in front of Staremiasto. The 5th Regiment of Seghedin's rabble, all Hungarian natives with tricolour ribbons on their caps and chests, arrives. They hadn't been in any combat. From Halici to here we met only Romanians; they had moved from Transylvania to Galicia. Now I saw for the first time a Hungarian regiment, intact. Tisza, together with the Austro-Hungarian army leadership, was also practising a policy of extermination against nationalities on the battlefield. It could not have been mere chance that Galicia, crossed by us, was teeming with Romanians* [173 p.119].

We have already seen the percentages of survivors in the 11th Company of the regiment and the whole 23rd Regiment (§3.3) and we will see the same practice enacted in the Second World War [101 p.232].

The Red Terror and the White Terror were both experienced in Hungary. Oskar Iaszi, who lived through that time, wrote:

> *The most abject atrocities of the red guards are attributed to half-beasts or totally debased social elements* [71 p.132].

After the Red Terror of 1919, unleashed by the Hungarian Bolsheviks and institutionalised by the Hungarian Soviet Republic, which liquidated all "bourgeois" resistance, came the "White" Terror organized by Horthy, no less terrible than the first. The removal of the Bolshevik regime, which also had the absurd Leninist idea, literally, of attacking Czechoslovakia and Romania, was carried out by the Romanian army. On August 1, 1919, the Romanian army obtained its surrender at Budapest.

In his book *Inside Europe*, published in 1934, the American John Gunther wrote about Horthy's officers in Siofok (Hungary). On 10.08.1919, he notes how they spoke in blood-thirsty terms about the Bolshevik horrors commented upon by Horthy with the following words: *Words, always only words! And never deeds!* The officers took action and immediately killed 60 Jews and communists [64 p.193]. Also in 1919, the actions of Horthy and his officers were questioned by the journalist Bela Somogy in an article entitled *Hard Core*. One evening in a Budapest casino, some of Horthy's officers stated the opinion that *someone needed to take a bath in Budapest*. Shortly after, Horthy intervened, saying *now there is no need for so much talk, now there is a need for action*. The journalist and a friend of his were subsequently taken to the banks of the Danube, where they were shot and thrown into the water. [64 p.194] According to John Gunther's opinion, Horthy created as early as 1919 *the cruellest, the most terrible dictatorship in Europe* [64 p.194]. Hungary's hatred of Jews, its economic National Socialism, and its strangulation of anyone with an opposing opinion outstripped all other 20th century dictatorships. Oscar Iaszi filled tens of pages detailing the atrocities committed by the white guards, concluding that the intellectual and moral authors belonged to Horthy's close circle of friends [71 p.133]. In 1920, Horthyst Hungary passed Europe's first anti-Jewish *numerus clausus* law. In 1933 in Budapest, a coffin floated on the Danube with the inscription: *Here lie the sons of Israel. You will be destroyed one by one* [64 p.233]. The warning describes well the atmosphere of the first Hungarian state, but as David Prodan judged:

> *Horthyism was, in no way, an accident. It was the exacerbated mentality consciously cultivated from top to bottom, from the leading intellectuals to the majority opinion. An overrated proverbial self-pride, consciously cultivated, of the Magyar people, a self-pride which is second to none, an overinflated hatred against the rising peoples, an unmatched hatred against the Romanian people, the first of which, by its large population, is an obstacle to its domination.*

11.2 The Culture of Hatred in the Interwar Period

The historian Petre Țurlea had the courage to call a spade a spade in this regard, the first among Romanian historians to do so [175], as if telling the truth was not the only duty of the historian. But while others "fabricate" histories based on fantasies coming from the culture of hate, ours do not tell the truth in order not to upset the former. Since 1919, the hierarchs of the Hungarian churches in Romania had engaged in the most despicable racist actions, starting with the bishops G. Májláth and St. Friedler, this latter being part of a terrorist network. When Romania was brought to its knees, partly with the help of its own Greek-Catholic politicians in the matter of the privileges *of the Catholic Status*, the Vatican showed no restraint, nor Christian goodwill: the Vatican was totally hypnotized by the culture of hatred from Budapest. The words of Senator Elemer Gyarfas, the President of the Hungarian Community in the Romanian Senate regarding the *Catholic Status*, apologetically hinted at their lies. He minimized the contribution of Hungarian Catholicism to the feudal oppression in Transylvania and diminished the value of the Roman Catholic status, which in all the succeeding states was the property of these states, but not in Romania [175 p.94]. Gyarfas claimed that they could appeal directly to the Vatican, bypassing the sovereignty of King Ferdinand, etc. All the miseries invented by the Catholic hierarchs in Transylvania, but which had the red thread of the culture of hatred, were supported by the Vatican hierarchies in the pontificates of both Pius XI (1922-1939) and Pius XII (1939-1958), although even in the bosom of the Vatican there were still people who had qualms of conscience, such as Cardinal J. Ritter [175 p.300].

11.3 The Second Genocide: Continuing Genocide

The Hungarian-administered genocide began after the first Vienna Diktat in 1938 in Slovakia. Löränt Tilkovszky presented the types of genocide practiced there in his book *Revision of Borders and Hungarian Policy on Nationalities* (Budapest, 1967). Among others, the educated middle classes of the Slovaks, Ruthenians, and Romanians were liquidated [182 p.127].

On August 30, 1940, Hitler and Mussolini forced Romania to cede northwestern Romania to Hungary. What followed was racial cleansing through mass murder and assassination, namely, a second genocide in Transylvania. A few days after the Diktat, the Hungarians (army and locals) committed abominable crimes everywhere: Ciumârna, Nuşfalău, Zalău, Ip, Trăznea, Huedin, Cluj, Lazuri, Aita Seacă, Surduc, Mureşenii de Câmpie, Cosniciu, Marca, Sărmaş, Leordina, Kameneţ-Podolsk, Moisei, and Aghireş, etc. Murders and expulsions were the result, which resumed on a different scale in December 1989 and continue unabated, depending on the circumstances.

The intellectual Tudor Bugnariu, enlisted for the front in the 2nd Hungarian Army, observed the army of which he was part at the Gherla railway station:

> *I have never seen so many people gathered here; thousands of peasants, all Romanians [...] The company commander told me that my real function would be that of translator and that I would have to help him [...] Writing down the names of those mobilized, I was surprised to find that, although they were spelled in Hungarian, the vast majority of them were Romanian, Serbian or Ukrainian [...] Romanian dominated the barracks. From the very first day I realized that, fulfilling Keitel's request, Horthy intended to send to the eastern front troops of minorities, [...] They were hastily trained to be sent to the front [...] On the whole territory occupied by the units of the Division, Romanian soldiers were gathered. I had no idea there were so many of them. It was clear that Horthy, in order to fulfil his obligation to the Reich, wanted to sacrifice the minorities [...] 20.11.1943. Leaving Bielița (Ukraine), we meet a compact group of Maramureș [...] the soldiers did not know, and the officers did not want to know, that the Second* [Hungarian] *Army had been sent from the beginning to be sacrificed* [166 p.231].

In a postcard sent home from the front dated 15.11.1943, Lt. Vasile Păltineanu, from Rășinari (Sibiu County), wrote that on the front in Ukraine, more than half soldiers in the Hungarian army he met were Romanians from Northern Transylvania [166 p.234]. We should not forget that, in addition to the Second Army, since 1941 there were labour and demining units in the front area made up of Romanians, Jews, and Ruthenians. In WWII, Hitler's ideological forerunner, Horthy, sent hundreds of thousands of Romanians to their deaths. It is known that after the protocol of 1.02.1942, the Swabs in Hungary and the annexed territories were integrated into German military units. Miklós Kallay, Prime Minister of Hungary (1942-1944), confirmed the genocide in his answer to the parliamentary committee on the defeat of the 2nd "Hungarian" Army at Don:

> *We lost 100,000 people, but don't panic, they were not Hungarians* [82 p.69].

Raul Sorban, having lived through the Hungarian occupation of Cluj, also notes that from the occupied area, more than 150,000 other uneducated Romanians were taken to work on demining at the eastern front, precisely with the aim of liquidating them. In December 1942, Transylvania was made "purer" by the absence of 500,000 young Romanians who had been sent to the front in Russia, never mind those already murdered or expelled.

11.4 We Exterminate them All

We exterminate them all, we drive them out wrote Prime Minister Pal Teleki to Miklos Horthy the day after the Vienna Diktat [182 p.127]. The strategy of the Horthyst occupation of northwestern Transylvania was summed up by Baron Aczél Ede of Budapest, head of a paramilitary gang and Horthy's envoy to Stalin:

> *We must extirpate these Wallachians, the oppressors, and kill them as our enemies [...] The priests preach the love of the people, but this is only bait, because God only helps brute force, and this brute force we must all use to kill and exterminate these Wallachians. Religion, through its ten commandments, says: don't kill, don't steal, don't covet another man's woman because these are sins. Is this* [our note: killing the Wallachians] *a sin? It is not a sin! It will really be a sin if we don't exterminate this gang of oppressive Wallachians. We will also organize a night of Saint Bartholomew [...] and we will also kill babies in their mothers' wombs* [2 p.56].

This was the "philosophy" of Kossuth and Petőfi; of all Hungarians.

At the entrance to the commune of Trăznea (9.09.1940), the Horthyst troops shot children grazing cattle on the village pasture. Hearing the shots, the villagers, led by the priest Costea, went out to the centre of the village. The gathered Romanians were massacred with machine gun fire or pierced with bayonets. Houses were attacked with grenades and set on fire. The priest N. Brumar was taken from his home with his wife and two daughters and slashed with bayonets. The other priest hiding in the parish house was set on fire and burned alive. The teacher and his wife were caught trying to escape and brought back to Trăznea where they were crucified alive on the church door.

On the morning of 10.09.1940, the protopope Aurel Munteanu went to officiate the funeral service of a believer. When he arrived at the centre of Huedin (Cluj County), a gang of 21 local Hungarians surrounded him and hit him with clubs, beating him around the head until they knocked him to the ground, bleeding profusely. They beat and maimed him for four hours. One of them, Buday János Gyepü, shoved an iron bar through his mouth and out through the back of his head. Gheorghe Nicula was also beaten and killed. The gang of murderers threw them into a pit and covered them with earth. Sixty days later, the wife of the protopope found out where they had been disposed of. The "royal" court of Cluj found that the acts committed by the accused were due to the *strong emotion caused by the happiness of their release* and they were sentenced to 23 months suspended imprisonment [192 p.25]. On the same day, the mayor Dr. Andrei was arrested and disappeared, Prof. Gheorghe Herdea was shot in the back, Vasile Popa and Ion Negru were hanged, and E. Moga, N. Socolici, A. Creț, P. String, and I. Furcovici were all beaten and arrested. Local gangs also devastated the houses of Romanians. For comparison, in 1941 the same "royal" court sentenced the publicist Gh. Dăncuș to two years and six months imprisonment and three years loss of service for publishing the poem *Decebal to the People* by G. Coșbuc in a magazine in Cluj [166 p.217].

In the village of Lazuri (Satu Mare County), Hungarian soldiers stripped the deacon Gheorghe Buze naked, placed him on the floor in the middle of the church and placed a burning candle on his abdomen, which burned down to his skin. Then, the Hungarian soldiers made him dislodge the large wooden cross that was planted in front of the church and forced him to carry it on his shoulders to a place where they burned it. Finally, they savagely defiled the church [71 p.123]. The historians Bodea, Suciu, and Pușcaș, quoting contemporary documents, write that at the time of the entry of the Hungarian army into Cluj, groups of Hungarian citizens armed with sticks and stones broke the windows of Romanian houses and those caught in the streets, children, women, and men, were all beaten. The murders, arrests, and mistreatments continued under the nose of the Pannonian army [13 p.276]. Things changed suddenly, said Prof. Ovidiu Moțiu (1930-2004). A disabled man, who begged mercy from his fellow citizens in order to survive, was wrapped in barbed wire and dragged, bleeding, by a horse around the German Dome in the centre until he died. A minor but significant fact for the culture we incriminate: in front of the National Bank headquarters in Cluj, the manhole covers of the water network were inscribed with the name of the Cluj Water Company. In September 1940, "Hungarian" citizens polished the Romanian language inscriptions until they were rubbed off; in 1990, a former employee of the water company showed me the polished and still functioning covers in downtown Cluj. At the Cluj Water and Canal Company in August 1940, there were 57 Romanians and 11 Hungarians; a year later, there were no more Romanians [16].

The events in Muresenii de Câmpie (Cluj County) represent the normality of hate. Muresenii de Câmpie was 5 km from the border dictated by Hitler on 30.08.1940. A group of soldiers under the command of Sublieutenant Csordaș Gergely of the 19th Hungarian Regiment from Nyiregyhaza (Hungary) were stationed in the village. On 23.09.1940, the soldiers gathered before 22:00 at the house of the priest Andrei Bujor. The following people were present in the house: Andrei Bujor, priest, 52 years

Fig. 11.1. Rodica Petrea just before the arrival of Hitler's ally in Transylvania.

old; Lucretia Bujor, clerk, wife of the priest, 48 years old; Lucia Lucretia Bujor, graduated in letters and philosophy in Paris, 24 years old; Maria Bujor, student of letters and philosophy in Cluj, 22 years old; Victor Bujor, 8th grade student, 16 years old; Natalia Petrea (née Miron), teacher, 24 years old; Ana Miron, Natalia's mother, 54 years old; Rodica Petrea, Natalia's daughter, 5 years old; Sara Juhos, daughter of Fr. Bujor, 18; Ioan Gurzău, son of Mayor Vasilică Gurzău, 29; and Valeria Gurzău, Ioan Gurzău's wife, 9 months pregnant, 20. All of them were murdered by the Hungarian soldiers and then thrown into a pit dug behind the house over which they built a large fire. At the same time a cannonade of rifles and machine guns was unleashed on the village, which lasted for the duration of the gathering of the victims and their murder. Fifteen brave Hungarian soldiers and not a single human, Christian soul! In the morning, Slt. Csordas Gergely arrived at the scene and reported the execution of the order. The notary Zimand Gergely and the new mayor Iosif Korosi were also involved in organising the assassinations. It turned out that Slt. Csordas Gergely was instigated by the murderer Count Vass Albert from the neighbouring township of Sucutard [13 p.429]. Other murders had been committed in Sucutard by Albert Vass—a proven and convicted murderer, who today has statues in Romania! Vasilică Gurzău escaped and was not found at home on the evening of September 23, 1940, while Gheorghe Petrea, Natalia's husband and Rodica's father, had taken refuge a few days before, having heard of the atrocities committed by their Hungarian neighbours and the Hungarian army [13 p.423]. There were hundreds and thousands of such murders. The murders in Northern Transylvania raise another question: why did the Germans support the Hungarians? So that they would "fight" with five-year-old Rodica Petrea and Valeria Gurzău and her unborn child? Prime Minister Pal Teleki answers us: the assassination of Romanian leaders, teachers, and priests was the first step towards the Hungarian goal of exterminating the Romanians. A different answer to this policy was given by Johann Weidlein in a series of three studies collected under the title *Hungary's Revisionist Policy and the Decline of the German Empire* [184]. Racial hatred was manifested, sparing no one. Following an operation carried out by the Hungarian armed forces in southern Bačka (Serbia) on 4.01.1942, 3-4,000 Serb civilians were murdered. The horrific Nazi massacres at Lidice (1942) and Oradour sur Glane (1944) in revenge for the killing of Nazi commanders are on an order of savagery one unit above the hate massacres in Northern Transylvania, which reached the top of the scale. All the massacres in the territories occupied by Hitler and Mussolini or done by the new authorities, involved the army, locals, and extremist organizations, such as the *Zdrenzergarten*, the *Union of Hungarian War Fighters*, *Levente* and others. Why was there this culture of hatred and not a culture of *loving one's neighbours* among the Hungarians? At a kindergarten in Satu Mare, Catholic *nuns* forced children to sing:

> *For three dry walnuts,*
> *The Wallachians go nuts*
> *Carol we've chased away,*
> *The north has given away,*
> *Michael we'll beat black and blue,*
> *And we'll take half the country too* [195 p.149].

After the first assassinations, there followed expulsions, arrests, imprisonment, internment in labour camps, and being sent to the front. Romanian civil servants and teachers were removed almost everywhere, the use of the Romanian language was forcefully banned, and Romanian inscriptions were mocked and removed [195 p.10]. The ritual of the expulsion of Romanians was as follows: first they were beaten and tortured; those who were "unamenable" were killed on the spot by locals who thought they were descendants of Attila or by gendarmes with rooster feathers in their caps; finally, those who remained alive were forced to sign declarations that they would *willingly* leave for Romania [175 p.219]. Out of 4,700 Romanian teachers, 3,982 were expelled and those who remained were forced to teach in Hungarian. For the school year 1941/42, the communal parishes, at the urging of the non-expelled bishops, asked for the establishment of 800 parish schools, maintained by the communities. Obviously, the Hungarian regime did not approve them. All Romanian books in the libraries were collected and burned by government order [195 p.10]. Two normal schools, in Gherla and Oradea, remained quasi-

Romanian! The remaining Romanian students in the occupied territory were ordered to switch to a "Hungarian religion" or they would be excluded. The Romanian soldiers also had a choice: those who switched to the "Hungarian religion" were discharged; the others were sent to demine the first lines of the front.

Ordinance no. 1440 of 23.02.1941 abolished the entirety of the Romanian agrarian reforms of 1923 and all civil contracts could be challenged before the Horthyst courts. Expropriations for public utilities were made only at the expense of the Romanians. Communal pastures and forests were transferred to Hungarian communities. Churches were demolished, and church altars and Romanian cemeteries were desecrated. To their shame, not only the Roman Catholics and their hierarchs participated in the expulsion and seizure of Orthodox possessions, but sometimes also the Greek Catholics [175 p.218]. The horrors perpetrated by the Hungarian authorities, joyfully and bravely assisted by their citizens in northwestern Romania, surpass any horror known in modern Europe.

Horthy had called for extermination labour detachments and demanded punishment detachments, so that enemy elements, i.e., Romanians, Slovaks, Ruthenians, and Serbs, would be sent to the front [166 p.223]. All his orders were enthusiastically fulfilled. They assassinated and drove out both the intelligentsia and the peasants; banned the Romanian language; sent hundreds of thousands of young men to the "Hungarian" army and then to the front lines for demining, but their hatred was not appeased! On 13.10.1941 in the village of Meştera, Tavi, son of Isăilă was returning home in a hay wagon. The gendarmes, with rooster feathers in their caps, stopped him and made him sing the Hungarian anthem. He did not know it and so was beaten to death. A desperate woman's voice came from the hay wagon. The woman was thrown from the cart and trampled underfoot. They noticed she was with child. They used a bayonet to split her belly open and the baby was pulled out and impaled on the bayonet [178 p.28]. Protopope Professor Nicolae Vasiu reported that in Gădălin (Cluj County), in the summer of 1944, two teachers, Rasanczi Aladár and Demeny Istvan, after killing two Romanian peasants, Ioan Apahidean and Iustin Petean, had the Romanian students tied to a yoke, instead of cattle, to transport the building materials for the Reformed church [177 p.283].

Jews were murdered because they were Romanian or Ruthenian Jews. Birkenau survivor Oliver Lustig from Cluj wondered how the suffering of more than 50,000 Jews—15,000 of them from Northern Transylvania and all young—whom the Horthysts sent to Ukraine with the aim of having them liquidated, could be forgotten. According to the memoirs of the former Hungarian Defence Minister, General Colonel Nagybaconi Nagy

Vilmos, six out of every seven Jews sent to Ukraine perished of hunger or cold; alternatively they were beaten, shot, or burned alive at Doroshich [98 p.5]. Zoltan Singer, a Jew sent to the front by the Hungarians in a punishment detachment, was among the few survivors of Doroshich (Ukraine). He wrote about the unimaginable mass murders on the night of 30 April/1 May 1943. They were imprisoned in stables and in the stable he was in, there were about 800 people. The wooden stable was set on fire at all four corners and the doors were locked from the outside. Upon being set aflame, some rushed through the burning planks to get to the outside, where the military guards shot them. This hell lasted for 10 minutes and most of the prisoners burned to death. He managed to get out and was shot in the leg [166 p. 225].

Another fact of these civilizing actions is that these horrors were never prosecuted, as was the case with the Hitler regime. The whole world has heard about Lidice and Oradour-on-Glane, but about the events at Nufalau, Huedin, Ip and Trăznea, Mureseni de Câmpie, Sărmaş, Moisei, and Leordina nobody has heard. Why? The Hungarian "philosopher" Gáspár Tamás, in the newspaper *Le Figaro* (18.01.1990), gives us half an answer:

> *The Hungarian People's Alliance* (MNSz), *which had 600,000 members, Transylvanians of Hungarian origin played a crucial role in the establishment of communism in Romania.*

What the neo-Cominternist Gáspár Tamás does not say is that those who played a crucial role in the implementation of Stalinism in Romania were in fact the authors of the genocide in Northern Transylvania. They served Horthysm and then Stalinism with the same fanaticism.

Forced labour and extermination camps

The system of forced labour camps had a tradition in Hungary, some of which we have already mentioned. The Jews did not escape either. In the press and on the radio, in speeches and on posters, they screamed against the Jews. Every sentence written or spoken was a threat and a mockery of the Jews. Threats, insults, and humiliations with the goal of frightening them were accompanied by anti-Jewish laws. All this was increasingly combined with isolation and mass murder, striking terror into the Jewish population and preparing public opinion for the greatest crime. In 1935, the camps were reorganized into a *form serving the public good, higher moral goals* [14 p.27]. In 1940, after the occupation of Northern Transylvania, special camps for Romanians were established in Hungary

(Seghedin, Dobrâţin, Bichiş-Ciaba, Püpöskladany, and Loşonţ, etc). Romanians were removed from all public institutions and then forced to work in coal mines, fortifications, and factories. The command of the IX Army Corps in Cluj informed the prefectures on 9.07.1941 that the Hungarian government had decided to set up Romanian labour detachments, which would be placed at the disposal of the military and civilian authorities "to complete the policy of complete Magyarization of the Romanians". All Romanians between the ages of 24 and 60, with the exception of those under arms, had to report to the conscription centres, where they were advised to change their religion. Those who accepted were given a deadline of five days to come with a certificate from a Hungarian priest confirming that they had changed their religion. Those who changed their religion were discharged. The others were taken under military guard to forced labour camps. Those who did not fill in the form were immediately transported to the camps. Most Romanians preferred to populate the coal mines at Tatabanya, Ajka, and Felso Galla, or the metallurgical plants at Csepel (Hungary) rather.

On 6.06.1942, the Military Command of the IX Army Corps Cluj was asked to send 23 more Romanian labour companies with full manpower (almost 5,000 men) for road repairs, sewerage, drainage, military installations, ammunition depots, barracks, and forest clearing, etc., around Someşeni, Floreşti, Miercurea Ciuc, Dej, Satu Mare, Oradea, Târgu Mureş, Odorhei, Sfântu Gheorghe, Gheorgheni, Tulgheş, and Bistriţa. The expected duration of this forced labour was undefined. From April 1943 onwards, the concentration of men in labour companies took on even greater proportions, with the number of these companies increasing to 100 [10 p.32]. In addition to the labour companies, some Romanians were also sent to special internment camps, where the treatment applied was even more brutal. They worked in their own clothes, in inhumane and insanitary conditions, without sufficient food, until they were completely exhausted. These exhausted and hungry men were insulted, beaten, and mocked. The villages were deserted by the Romanians. Women, old people, and children were thrown out onto the streets without any help. The exhausted men, starving and sick, never returned from the ethnic cleansing of these Hungarian camps. [14 p.28].

Romanians were also incorporated into punishment companies that were sent empty-handed to the front line, to the minefields, to face Soviet bullets and shells. Tens of thousands of Romanians from Northern Transylvania were sent to various labour camps in Germany and to the front. Obviously among them there were no young men recruited by the "Hungarian" army, which, according to the data in the MAE archive

(Bucharest), quoted by historian Gheorghe Bodea, reached the figure of 100,000 in 1941/42 alone [14 p.36]. We also have two sources of confirmation from Bucharest concerning the mass forced labour of Romanians in Northern Transylvania for the benefit of Hungary: a telegram from the German Minister in Bucharest, Killinger, dated 26.05.1943, to the Hitlerist Foreign Ministry, in which Germany was asked to intervene to help the Romanians in Northern Transylvania; and a note from the Romanian Special Intelligence Service, dated 28.02.1944, addressed to the Council of Ministers, confirming that:

> *...almost all Romanian men in the army are permanently kept concentrated in combat and work units or requisitioned for work* [14 p.35].

In this context, forced labour camps were formed in Maramureş, on the Copilaşi Mountain, in the Borşa-Vişeu area. The term "camp" is inappropriate as the Romanians concentrated there, together with two companies of Jews, were "dumped" in the countryside where they made barracks and huts. They worked in the forest, breaking stone for military fortifications and built a retreat road for the German army. You can read more about the fate of these work detachments in §11.7. On 2.07.1942, the first Jewish labour company (240 people), Company no. 110/43, left from Reghin for the front [14 p.33].

11.5 The Final Solution

The Final Solution a year before Wannsee

In 1941, Hungary decided to review people's citizenship. Detectives from the KEOKH (Central National Office for Foreigner Control) scoured the towns and villages of the northern part of occupied Transylvania. Aided by the police, local gendarmes, and civilians, they arrested Jews by the thousand on the grounds that they could not prove their Hungarian citizenship. The Jews were hunted down by the Hungarians—they did not have Hungarian citizenship and therefore were considered enemies. All those arrested were sent to Kamenets-Podolsk in Ukraine. On 28.08.1941 at Kamenets-Podolsk, 36,000 Jews from the new territories occupied by Hungary were exterminated by the Hungarian army under the pretext that they were enemies of the state [166 p.228]. Other sources speak of 20,000 Jewish victims at Kamenets-Podolsk! This is not necessarily a contradiction, but the reports have different references: one of them refers to all Jews deported by Hungary and another only to Jews from Transylvania, Crişana, and Maramureş. At Kamenets-Podolsk the Hungarians did not wait for the plans of the Final Solution to be decided a year later in Wansee. Thus, the first mass extermination of the Jews, prior to the implementation of the Final Solution was carried out by the Hungarians.

The Final Solution

Endre Laszlo, the Secretary of State at the Ministry of the Interior in Budapest, in a radio broadcast (March 1944) that was picked up by the entire Hungarian press, derided the idea that Hungarian anti-Semitism was political opportunism. Endre emphasized that Hungarian society was always a defender of racial purity. He stated that Hungarian anti-Semitism was not a copy or imitation of current trends and ideas, but Hungary was the first in Europe to feel the catastrophic danger of Jewish influence. Hungarians thus demanded a radical solution to the Jewish problem, i.e., the total elimination of Jews from their world [98 p.11].

Among so many civilizing deeds, the life of the Jews in Northern Transylvania, ceded to Hungary, was not forgotten either. Moshe Carmilly-Weinberger, the chief rabbi of Cluj, wrote that in the spring of 1944 the Hungarian authorities organized 13 central ghettos and 45 death trains, transporting 131,633 Jews, young and old, infants, pregnant women and the sick, to Auschwitz [186 p.8]. The organizers of the genocide of the Jews in northwestern Romania, ordered under Horthy's policy of ethnic cleansing, were Andor Jaross, Ladislau Endre, and Ladislau Baky. This was a *genocide generated by hatred*, writes Carmilly-Weinberger. Rabbi Rosen Moshes claimed that the number of those lost in northwestern Romania under the Hungarian occupation was as high as 150,000 [29 p.19]. The difference is perhaps to be found in Kamenets, Dorosici, and the Hungarian labour and extermination camps. The German authorities planned to transport 2,000 Jews (a 50-car train) to Auschwitz-Birkenau every day. SS officer Edmund Veesenmayer reported in Berlin that the Hungarians scheduled 3,000 Jews to be sent daily to Auschwitz. Outdoing the Nazis in the implementation of the Final Solution, the Horthysts, in the tense conditions of war when every wagon counted, sent four trains of 50 wagons daily. This is how it came about that not 3,000, but 12,000, sometimes even as many as 14,000 Jews were transported daily from Northern Transylvania to Auschwitz [98 p.18].

On 27.04.1944, the Minister of Public Supply by Decree no. 108.510, ordered that, by 1 May, all Jews must have communicated their personal data to the town hall of their place of residence in order to be issued with a new food card. On the basis of these lists, the ghettoization of the Jews of Northern Transylvania was organized in a matter of days. On 10 May

1944, all the Jews from the Bihor area were brought to Oradea and interned in the ghetto. In the first few days alone, approximately 27,215 Jews were brought from Sălard, Marghita, Săcuieni, Roșiori, and Aleșd; neither the sick and elderly, nor pregnant women were spared. In the ghettos, they were subjected to physical and mental torture [78 p.117]. Investigators were focused on gathering jewellery and real estate, etc.

By 20.06.1944, we note that almost 36,000 Jews from Bihor alone had arrived at Auschwitz, Birkenau, and Buchenwald, according to data provided to Prime Minister Dimitrie/Dome Sztojay (March-August 1944) [78 p.116]. Eva Heyman was a 9-year-old girl who wrote a diary at the time Horthy entered Oradea. Birkenau survivor Oliver Lustig, in his preface to Eva Heyman's *Diary* [83], *points out that* the wave of hatred and murder had a special touch—fanaticism and meticulousness in the implementation of the Final Solution, or as Eichmann's deputy Edmund Veesenmayer put it, the Hungarian gendarmes did their job with *genuine Asian brutality.* To SS officer Dieter Wisliceny, also an Eichmann collaborator, the Hungarians appeared to be truly descended from the Huns [98 p.15]. Eva Heyman wrote about the Final Solution administered by Budapest. Her sufferings, those of Oradea, in fact those of all the Jews of Northern Transylvania are condensed in the pages of her diary, *who were killed by the most ruthless program of massacre*, as remarked upon by the American historian of the Holocaust, Randolph Brahan. The first page of Eva Heyman's diary begins on 13.02.1944 with the last on 30 May when she was put on a train to Auschwitz from where she was to never return. The diary remained in the camp in Oradea. Below, we present an excerpt from Eva Heyman's diary:

> *I won't forget the moment when the Romanians left here and Miklos Horthy rode down the main street on a white horse, while I watched through the pharmacy window.* Agi [our note: Eva's mother] *was very angry when I waved at Horthy; she told me that Horthy had killed Jews at Balaton when she, Agi, was a child* [our note: early 1920s] [83 p.44].

Oliver Lustig, who experienced life in the ghetto at Cluj, transport to and triage at Auschwitz, and internment in Birkenau, was surprised by life in the Oradea ghetto. The beginning of ghettoization triggered a wave of suicides. Some foresaw the ordeal and did not feel able to go through it or sensed that entering the ghetto meant death and so all suffering was in vain. Some did not even wait to be taken to the ghetto, but, a few hours before their turn came, ended their suffering. Entering the apartment, the Hungarian policemen looked puzzled at the lifeless bodies and the broken vials lying motionless on bedside tables. Most committed suicide in the ghetto, especially after being interrogated or while waiting to be taken into the torture chamber. Dr. Dezideriu Klein, an editor, Dr. Ludovic Erczmann, a doctor, and Solomon Czitrom, a prosecutor, boarded the wagon with hidden poison and took it after the train had started moving, once they were convinced that they were not being transferred to another place, but were being deported. For those in the ghetto, the most shattering fact was not the dawning discovery of those who had poisoned themselves or hanged themselves overnight, but the surprise of the dramatic discussions between husbands and wives, parents and children about whether to endure further or put an end to their suffering. Eva captured these *struggles*:

> *That's what my grandfather said, in the dark, that here in the ghetto, many people commit suicide. There is enough poison in the ghetto pharmacy and grandpa gives it to older people if they ask for it. Grandpa also said that the best thing would be to take cyanide himself and give a dose to grandma. Hearing him Agi started crying and I heard him crawl in the dark to Grandpa's mattress and beg him crying: Father, please be patient. It can't last much longer... The most frightening was uncle Samoila Meer ... I heard his voice in the dark: Lili dear, my little girl, please again, for the thousandth time, let me have an injection, I can't wait any longer* [83 p.109].

Eva had no way of seeing what was going on in the interrogations, but one night, when the grownups thought she was asleep, she heard Agi (mother) and Bandi Kecskemeti talking:

> *They both said that people are not only beaten, but also drained. Agi told the story crying and if I hadn't heard her voice I would have thought it was all a nightmare. She said people brought to the hospital had blood coming out of their noses and mouths. Some came in with broken teeth; their feet are so swollen they can't stand. My Little Diary, Agi said something about what the gendarmes do to women, because women are taken there too, but I'm not even going to put that in your pages. I simply can't write, although you know, my Little Diary, that I've kept no secrets from you until now* [83 p.109].

In *The Jerusalem Trial*, Schoen Dezsoe points out that he had a conversation with some of the people at *Liska 06*, those who for a year, day and night, studied the Holocaust exclusively in preparation for the Eichmann trial. From these discussions, he came to the conclusion that:

> *The Hungarians were the most ruthless. Such savagery, such a lack of humanity towards the Jews, I have not seen in any other people in Europe*

[...] One of the counsellors of the German Embassy in Budapest presented himself three times to the Foreign Ministry and pointed out in no uncertain terms that it was in our common interest not to commit police excesses, which could lead to countermeasures abroad, not only against Hungarian citizens, but also against German citizens [...] In particular, he drew the attention of the Hungarian Government to the proper treatment to be meted out to citizens regarded as enemies and to their property; a summary of the German regulations in this field was forwarded, expressing the wish that the Hungarian side should not take measures that would go beyond them [98 p.14].

In hearing no. B.X.4419 on 7.01.1946, the case of Endre, Baky, and Iaross (secretaries of state and the minister of the interior), referring to the rounding up and sending to death of Jews, the tribunal stated:

There can be no doubt that the concentration and deportation across the border of 434,351 people, living in various parts of the country in only two months, was made possible exclusively thanks to the active collaboration of the Hungarian authorities who were aware of the local situation [...] At the time, several German personalities (Eichmann, Wisliceny), declared that the situation in Hungary was special, because Endre and Baky dictated a faster tempo in Jewish affairs than the Germans themselves. And, according to Veesenmayer's deposition, Eichmann Adolf, Berlin's specialist in Hungary for dealing with the Jewish problem, told him that essentially the conduct of the deportations relied on the gendarmerie and the Hungarian administration, because he had only a small command [98 p.21].

In front of the People's Court in Budapest, Baky repeated the words Horthy spoke to him when he swore him in as state secretary of the interior: *I hate Jews... Get them out of the country! Out! Out!* Finally, one of the most important political figures in World War II, Winston Churchill, in a letter to Foreign Secretary Anthony Eden stated his opinion that the most abject and greatest crime in human history was that which happened to the Jews in Hungary [98 p.20].

About the over eager performance of the Hungarian authorities in the Final Solution, let us look at the opinion of another survivor, Dr. Erno Kiraly, in a letter to a Hungarian friend in Romania:

In the spring of 1944 ... With the help of the broad masses of Hungarians the Horthyst gangs and the cock-feathered gendarmes dragged 150,000 Jews from this part of the country into the [death] factories. Of these only a part returned, the others, including our children, were slaughtered. This is the historical fact, which can neither be denied nor embellished. With a wealth of arguments and unquestionable data, I am forced to dispute the explanation that tends to prove that the entire Hungarian population kept away from this abominable massacre, data, and arguments that we will, moreover, submit to world opinion. This is the only way to explain why this beastly deed succeeded so perfectly, more perfectly than in any other country in Europe that was overrun and subjugated by the Hitlerites [167 p.292].

The statements of the former *häftling* (inmate of an internment camp) of Birkenau quoted on the Final Solution were due to the history of Transylvania, which mystified and desecrated, once again, the memory of the victims of hatred [98]. The *History* was published under the auspices of the Hungarian Academy in 1986 (Budapest: Akadémiai Kiadó). It was particularly successful in the West, both with intellectuals and historians, who were wooed by the KGB and Hungarian security services.

Would one need any further argument on what gives rise to the culture of hatred in the above testimonies of Auschwitz survivors and non-survivors? Adding the victims of the mass murders in Transylvania, Banat, Crișana, Maramureș, Hungary, Slovakia, Serbia, and Ukraine to the hundreds of thousands of young people sent to the front line for demining, the "Hungarian" troops of Romanians, Slovaks, Ukrainians, Serbs, and the hundreds of thousands of Jews sent to the extermination camps, we arrive at a total of millions.

11.6 A Final Solution of their Own

After 23.08.1944, along the temporarily imposed border the Horthyst troops penetrated to the south of Transylvania. Here all Jews, without exception, remained alive. In the township of Sărmaș (Mures County), subunits of the Horthyst army appeared on 5.09.1944. The local Hungarians took action: Biro Joszef was installed as praetor and the "national guard" was formed from all Hungarians over 15 years of age. On Sunday, September 7, in the house of the pharmacist Varga Iuliu, the *grofs* (title used by Hungarian landowners, from the German *margrave*) Bethlen Daniel, Betegh Alexandru, Kemeny Bela, Moitely Stefan, Gall Iosif, Wacsman Karoly, Wacsman Elemer, Beldy Kalman, and Beldy Francisc, who had not suffered anything in Romania, gathered and scheduled *a final solution* of their own in Sărmaș. The looting of Romanian houses had already happened and out of fear people had fled to the nearby forest. Those who had been imprudent enough not to flee or who were too sick and elderly were interned in a makeshift camp. All 126 Jews from Sărmaș were brought to this camp.

On 16.09.1944, 14 Romanians were arrested and brought to the camp in ox carts. All 126 Jews were loaded into wagons and taken to Sărmaşel. Along with the transport of Jews came two trucks and two small cars with Hungarian soldiers. The Jews were escorted with drawn bayonets to the top of Suscut Hill. As described by Mocean Ioan, hiding in a cornfield 200 metres away at two o'clock in the morning, on 17 September, there was shouting and screaming and machine gun fire [14 p.98]. The "brave" army then dug two pits. This operation was supposed to remain secret. Ioan Mocean counted 40 "brave" soldiers who participated in this operation. Of the 126 people massacred, 77 were shot (62 adults and 15 children); the rest (41 adults and 8 children) were buried alive (at exhumation they were disfigured and showed no traces of gunshot wounds) [14 p.99]. Oliver Lustig saw thousands and thousands of corpses in the camps as he passed through Auschwitz, Birkenau, Landsberg, and Kaufering. He was an eyewitness to the death of many of his comrades, who perished from hunger, cold, disease, asphyxiation, shooting, hanging, drowning, and being thrown from scaffolding, but the murders at Sărmaş seemed to him to be the height of savagery. There were women and children whose skulls had been crushed and shattered, their bones fractured [98 p.23].

The unseen face: rescuing Jews

Along the new border from Chişineu Criş (Arad County), Beiuş (Bihor County), and Feleac (Cluj County) to Brasov, Jews from Poland, Slovakia, Hungary, Ukraine, and occupied Romanian territory were helped by intellectuals (Emil Haţieganu, Raoul Şorban, and Aurel Socol to name a few) and high churchmen (the bishops Iuliu Hossu and Nicolae Bălan), as well as by many Romanian peasants on both sides of the border. The Romanian authorities participated in such rescues with the Romanian legation in Budapest alone issuing more than 51,000 transit visas for Jews after 1940 [186 p.176]. While 434,351 people were taken to Auschwitz by the Horthy regime, more than 400,000 Jews in Romania were snatched from the "flames" in those years, as Chief Rabbi Alexandru Şafran and the president of the Jewish community Wilhelm Filderman put it [164]. According to documents in the Vatican, in March 1944 the Bessarabian and Bukovinian Jews deported to Transnistria by the Antonescu regime were sent back to the country because the front line was coming to Transnistria and they risked being captured by the Germans [164 p.119]. In 1943, Chief Rabbi Alexandru Şafran drew up a list of 10 demands of the Jewish community, which was presented to Monsignor Andrea Cassulo (Vatican) by a Romanian official, Radu Lecca, from which we quote:

1. Stop deportations; 2. Transfer to northern Transnistria, under Romanian jurisdiction, deportees from concentration camps under German jurisdiction; 3. Serious measures to guarantee the lives of people living in concentration camps; 4. Repatriation of widows, decorated and wounded ex-combatants, former civil servants, war veterans and other deserving persons; 5. Abolition of ghettos; 6. Red Cross aid in the form of clothing and medicines; 7. Sending parcels of food and other goods from Bucharest, sold at official prices; 8. Freedom to exercise a profession; 9. Remuneration for any work performed; 10. Right to write and receive letters [164 p.121].

In his memoirs *A Tear from the Fire* [164], Rabbi Alexandru Şafran tells of the Jewish scholars who had the good fortune to escape from Eastern Europe to Romania and whom he met in Bucharest, including Rabbi Haim Meir Hager "Vijnitzer", Rabbi Aharon Rokeach "Belzerer", Rabbi Salomon Halberstam "Bobover", Rabbi Baruch Hager, and Philip Freudiger [164 p.135]. According to Rabbi M. Carmilly-Weinberger, between 1940 and 1944, 4,500 to 5,500 Jews were saved in Romania just in the border area around Cluj [186 p.172]. Professor Israel Gutman from Israel, in a paper entitled *The situation of the Jews in Romania against the background of Nazi-conquered or Nazi-dominated Europe*, shows that the Nazi plans to deport the Jews of Romania to extermination camps met with:

...vigorous opposition from the Romanian people and authorities, including the government and the dictator Ion Antonescu. Their refusal to surrender the Jews grew with time and this resistance is, the factor that saved the majority of Romanian Jews from the 'final solution' [98 p26].

Marton Aron, a Catholic bishop in Romania after [193] and, a notorious supporter of the mystifications about the persecution of Hungarians by Romanians since 1919, is presented today to the ignorant as a defender of the Jews during the Final Solution. However, as a racist and an advocate of Hungarian racial superiority, in the summer of 1944 he demanded that the deportations of the Jews be stopped for the reason *that these deportations would bring suffering to the Hungarian people at the future peace conference* [175 p.271]. He had no word to say, however, about the atrocities committed against the Romanians in Northern Transylvania.

A bizarre case

A Nobel Peace Laureate, born in Sighet (Maramures County) in 1928, wondered in 1992 what the Romanians of Sighet did when the Jews were taken to Auschwitz in May 1944. Had the peace laureate not heard what had happened to the Romanians in northwestern Romania starting as early as 1 September 1940? Had he not heard what happened to the Romanians in and around his town of Sighet in September 1940? In September 1940 at Săpânța, near Sighet (10 miles away), peasants were beaten with wet ropes, made to dig their own graves, then shot. In the Vișeu Valley, several villages were burned and those who were caught fleeing were then shot. Many terrified Romanians and Ruthenians took refuge in the woods [63 p.55]. Had he not heard what happened to the Jews who became *foreigners* after 30.08.1940 too? They were exterminated at Kamenets-Podolsk in July/August 1941. Did he not know who took those of the same religion to the labour camps and to Dorosici? He was 16 years old at the time when "Magyarhood" was finally resolving this issue; Eva Heyman, three years younger, knew who sent her to Auschwitz. Oliver Lustig, not only knew, but left absolutely vital testimony to the historical record. Elie Wiesel, when challenged by the writer Eugen Ionesco after a statement on French television that he had been sent to Auschwitz by the Romanians, cheerfully replied that *the French do not know history and in fact don't care* [73 p.195]!

11.7 Massacres

On the first night after Romania's exit from the Axis alliance on August 23/24 1944, 23 people were arrested at Sighet alone, while another 200 from the northern Maramureș area were deported to special camps in Slatina, Dragomirești, Ocna Șugatag, Ocna-Slatina, Teceul Mare, Carei, Kistarosa, and Kosice [14 p.79]. On the evening of August 24, around 300 Romanians were arrested in Slatina (Maramureș-Ukraine) alone! Likewise, in the whole of Northern Transylvania, tens of thousands of Romanians were rounded up. In October 1944, the Romanian front was approaching from the south; Cluj was liberated by 11 October. The Hungarian guards watching the workers at work on Mount *Copilași* (Maramureș County) were becoming increasingly agitated, while the Romanians began to escape in groups to Reghin, where they were concentrated. Thirty peasants from Reghin who escaped were caught and locked in a house without food and water: they were to be executed. Preparing to retreat, the Hungarians took the cattle of the peasants from Borșa, Vișeu, and Leordina (Maramures County), and drove them to Hungary. Two peasants who had resisted when the Hungarians were stealing their cattle, their only means of survival, were also taken to the house in Vișeu. Two or three more Jews were brought in, probably from the two forced labour companies there. On 14.10.1944, these 34-35 people were transported, forced into two houses at the exit from Moisei to Borşa and machine gunned down. Vasile Petean and Vasile Ivaşcu-Drăgan from Palatca (Cluj County), and a third person who could not be documented survived under the pile of corpses! After this massacre the Hungarian troops fled the area. It is also noteworthy that three of the Horthyst soldiers who machine gunned the Romanians at Moisei were from the same village as some of the victims [14 p.7]. The Moisei case received some notoriety, but nothing has been written about the horrific murders and burnings in Leordina. The Communist-Horthyst state, installed by the Soviets in Romania, did not investigate these cases and we only know the full story thanks to two historians working alone [14].

Massacres after the expulsion of the Hungarian army

Another kind of assassination occurred: once the Romanian troops advanced, the "local" assassins retreated with the Hungarian army for fear of judgment. But the Romanian troops were on the front lines and moved west, leaving Transylvania to be occupied by Soviet troops. Between these movements of troops, the notary Ion Ardelean returned in Imper (Harghita County), at the time a Romanian village, with his heavily pregnant wife. As the troops were leaving, instead of a Romanian administration a Soviet administration appeared! The spectre of hatred, frightened for a moment, retreated with the Hungarian troops; as things settled down with the arrival of the Russians, it returned under the protection of the Soviet administration. Several Romanians, terrified by the return of the local murderers, fled into the mountains, but the notary and his wife were not so quick. The notary was shot in the head, then a grenade was thrown at him, while his wounded wife crawled to a creek, where the assassins caught up and killed her by throwing a log onto her. The gang of killers, all local, were: Marton Ioszef, Matyas Emerik, and Vereş Adam. And here, as in other parts of Horthyst-Communist Transylvania after 1944, there were no consequences for these murderers [178 p.26].

11.8 The Horthyst-Soviet Administration in Transylvania

When the front reached Romania's western border (on the 25 October 1944, the Romanian army liberated the final town), both the government led by Szálasi (Budapest) and the provisional government of Bela Miklos (Debrecen) recommended to the Hungarians of Transylvania that they form a Communist party so that the Soviet authorities could find an ethnic

Hungarian Communist nucleus to take over the government of Northern Transylvania [159 p.96]. Indeed, many racist criminals gathered around the remaining Soviet units behind the front in Transylvania. The effervescence of ethnic chauvinism was maintained by the cadres of the Horthyst University of Cluj, propagating the idea of the formation of a "Greater Hungary" [159 p.94]. It was under these conditions that the Romanian refugees had to return home. On the return of the Romanians from the refugee camps, the Horthyst administration, with Hungarian officials brought from Hungary and local Horthysts, all of whom had become communists and brothers of the Soviets overnight, remained unchanged [177 p.372].

On 4.07.1945, units of the Soviet Army coming from the front passed through Cluj. This event was witnessed by the protopope Professor Nicolae Vasiu who described how the Hungarians were *shouting long live the Red Army as loud as they could* in the streets [177 p.366]. In the 1944/45 school year, the curriculum was still a Horthyst one in the Hungarian schools in Romania. They taught the *Honved salute*, which is an apology for the soldier who comes home to Transylvania at Christmas from the land of the Russian Federation where the Bolshevik people are deceived. Nicolae Vasiu observed that the Hungarians have developed *a real school of hypocrisy, and have benefited greatly from it in terms of territory* [177 p.366]. A uniquely two-faced people!

On 5.08.1945, Romanian troops coming from the front entered Cluj. Some Hungarians hiding behind an obelisk that had quickly been erected in honour of Soviet soldiers fired on the Romanian army. Many soldiers were wounded and Sergeant Dumitru Căciulan died on the spot. The soldiers broke ranks and fired on the assassins, killing two of them. Unashamedly, the Hungarians not only did not condemn the assassination, they turned it around. They published in *Világossag* (Light), the Hungarian National Soviet (MNSz) newspaper, the article *Maniu's fascist agents play with fire*, in which they spoke of the *reactionary hyenas feeling their doom, Maniu's paid mercenaries* [177 p.373]. In order to maintain their position, which they had gained during Horthy's time in Transylvania, they had to strike at the man who represented the hopes of the Romanians expelled from Northern Transylvania. With the Cominternists brought in to Bucharest on the Sherman tanks of the Red Army, the anti-Maniu crusade of the "Romanian" Communists started in Cluj. The houses of many Romanian refugees were occupied once again by the Hungarians [159 p.98]. At the Dermata factory and the Romanian Railway workshops, there were gangs of Hungarian-speaking workers acting under the command of former Horthysts. These gangs intervened as paramilitary commandos throughout the area, where Hungarian chauvinism, strengthened in 1940, felt threatened. The Dermata workshop moved to Cluj in 1900 from Reghin (the German Renner brothers) and by 1914 had 100 workers. From 1919 onwards it was developed with Romanian capital and production increased by 1,267 %! *Dermata*, Magyarized under Horthy, became *Janos Herbak* in 1948 through nationalisation under the Communist Horthysts! It was here that the *Dermata Guard* was formed—as the protopope N. Vasiu called it—which terrorized the Romanian townships of Florești, Someșeni, and Luna de sus (near Cluj), and also carried out the Aghireș massacre [177 p.383]. This happened in 1946, just at the time of the finalization of the peace treaties, with an attack by the Hungarian-speaking workers of Dermata on the Romanian students of the Avram Iancu dormitory, where they had barricaded themselves. The de-Horthyfication of Cluj, a process observed by the author, only finally occurred in the late 1970s through industrialisation!

11.9 An Incomplete Inventory of Hate

* The 2nd "Hungarian" Army, with 120,000 troops plus 50,000 auxiliaries, perished in the Battle for the Don: 100,000 on the spot, the rest in captivity (few would survive). Most of them were Romanians, as we know from the testimonies of Tudor Bugnariu, Vasile Păltânea, Raoul Șorban, and the Hungarian Prime Minister Miklos Kallay [82 p.69].

* 150,000 uneducated young men were sent to the front and to undertake demining.

* 100,000-150,000 disappeared in labour camps in Germany, Hungary, and military operation areas for which Romania has no archival data and studies. We have already noted the 15,000 Jews from Northern Transylvania out of the 50,000 Jews sent to Hungarian *sui-generis* extermination camps [98]. As the ratio of Jews in labour camps in relation to Romanians may be as high as 1 to 50, the estimated human losses are a minimum number.

* 18,000 Jews from historic Maramureș were shot at Kamenets-Podolsk in 1941. In 1942, the deportation and murder of Jews from Northern Transylvania and Maramureș continued and the number of those murdered is estimated at 4-5,000 [214 p.129]. Several thousand Jews were burned to death at Dorosici in 1943.

* 135,000 Jews who did not return out of the 150,000 (Moses Rosen) sent to Auschwitz. This is 135,000 out of the total of 434,351

victims of the Horthy regime established by the Budapest court [98 p.21].

* Thousands of local assassinations were motivated by the public policy *We exterminate them all, we drive them out*, as defined by Prime Minister Pal Teleki the day after the Vienna Diktat.

We have always taken the minimum numbers and have not added the number of Jews murdered after 15 October 1944 under Ferenc Szálas, which, depending on the source, varies between 75,000 and 200,000. This is because we do not know how to separate the victims geographically. So, if we add up every major case that is known, we arrive at a minimum of 573,000 people murdered in the territories ceded by Hitler to the Hungarians. Statistically, this is hard to reconcile as we do not have the census scheduled at the end of 1940 due to the breakup of Northern Transylvania, Crişana, and Maramureş, but it is not impossible. The 1941 Horthyst census can only be taken to cover the proportion of expulsions and murders after a year of occupation. If we consider the census of 1930 [210 p.376] and that of 1948 [72] for Crişana and Maramureş, we can see that the total population did not increase; here, the Hungarian speakers increased from 23.07 % to 26.28 %, even though Crişana was only partially occupied, i.e., "purified"!

Crişana and Maramureş	Total	Hungarian speakers	
1930	1,390,417	320,795	23,07%
1948	1,391,672	365,745	26,28%

If we look at the counties of Satu Mare and Maramureş, which were wholly at the mercy of racial hatred, from 1918 to 1970, the proportion of Romanians did not increase, that of the Jews disappeared, and the "Hungarians" increased by 38.21 % in Satu Mare and 53.13 % in Maramureş! In Satu Mare, the Romanians only increased by 3.8 % in 18 years! For comparison, in Muntenia, over the same period of time, the Romanians increased by 23.9 %! However, the share of Hungarians in Satu Mare County increased by 33.2 %, while that of Romanians decreased by 20.1 %. This was achieved through genocide, expulsion, and colonisation.

Satu Mare County		Total	Romanian	Hungarian speakers	
	1940	324,019	198,808	78,351	24.18%
	1948	312,391	201,569	104,419	33.42%
Maramureș County		Total	Romanian	Hungarian speakers	
	1940	181,468	105,761	11,309	6.23%
	1948	150,323	109,372	14,349	9.54%

In conclusion, if the *International Criminal Tribunal* in The Hague considered the killing of approximately 8,000 men between the ages of 12 and 77 in Srebenica in July 1995 to be genocide, and, in the words of Rabbi Moshe Carmilly Weinberger, *On April 4, 1944, the genocide indescribable in words, generated by blind hatred, began* regarding the application of the *Final Solution* in Northern Transylvania, then what could the murders in Northern Transylvania, with more than 570,000 Romanians, Jews, Slovaks, and Ruthenians, committed by the Hungarians in the name of ethnic cleansing, be called?

The Communist Party of Romania was at that time a section of the Comintern. It had no goals other than those of the Comintern to which it belonged. A good part of the total of about 700 interwar Communists were Hungarians, while the rest were Russians, Bulgarians, Ukrainians, and Jews, along with a few Romanians. In Communist-Horthyst Romania, obviously, the Horthyst agents in the leadership of the Communist Party of Romania did not prosecute these crimes. Those who could have raised their voices, the victims, were themselves liquidated by Horthyst agents in Communist prisons and camps. Hundreds of thousands of people, guilty of no more than being the Romanian elite, spent more than a decade in prison! This is how the chauvinism generated by the culture of hatred concludes, or as it was put in more subdued terms, *a preoccupied appreciation of everything Hungarian and a blind contempt for everything non-Hungarian* [160 p.689], in two genocides, the most terrible known to modern Europe!

CHAPTER 12

RACIAL CLEANSING AFTER WORLD WAR II

After the Second World War, the fate of the Romanians, Germans, and Slovaks in Pannonia was to be completely resolved by the pressure of hatred against non-Magyars and the expulsion of the Germans (1946). On 23 April 1938, Zoltán Tildy said in parliament that the Hungarians had, from the beginning, been against Bolshevism [183 p.167]. Later, having become a Bolshevik president (1946-1948), on 29.12.1945 he signed Order no. 12.330 by which the German population of Hungary was expelled. The expulsion began in 1946.

Kovagó László, in his work *Minority: Nationality* published by Kossuth Konyvkiadó in 1977 in Budapest, shows that of the 10.4 % "minorities" remaining in Hungary after World War II, 25 years later only 1.8 % still remained. Even so, from only 10.4 % in 1945, the decrease in "minorities" to 1.8 % in 1970 is a dramatic expression of the Magyarization of the Communist regime. Obviously, the minority percentage of 10.4 % in 1945 is a much reduced "Hungarian" percentage, since only in 1939 (including parts of Slovakia) according to the Knaurs/1940 Lexicon, out of a total population of 10.3 million there were only 1.3 million Germans and Ruthenians, i.e., 12.6 % minorities [198 p.1742]; to which should be added the Romanians, Ruthenians, Serbs, and Croats not highlighted in the lexicon. A minimum estimate, considering only the remaining Slovaks and Romanians, would lead to a minority of at least 20 %. But if we were to take into account the Hungarian Greek-Catholics, an aberration meant to cover one side of Magyarization, perhaps 30 % would be closer to the truth. This percentage is confirmed by the furious process of ethnic cleansing itself; it can be verified, indirectly, by the proportion of non-Magyar surnames in interwar Hungary, which exceeded 50 % of the total. The mental terror on the part of the new majority of Magyarized people was so inhuman that no minority could retain its identity. In Jula (Hungary), a former Romanian town with a small Lutheran minority (Slovak and German), which I visited in 1990, after 1910 the inscription *Hier ruhe ...* disappeared from the cemetery crosses of the Germans, after 1945 the Romanian inscription *Aici odihneşte ...* (Here rests ...) disappeared from the crosses of the Romanians.

In the only so-called "Romanian" high school in Hungary, in Jula, all subjects are taught in Hungarian, and the Romanian language is also taught in Hungarian, as I found in March 1990, when I visited the high school. Not a single pupil could carry on a banal conversation in Romanian! In comparison, Ioan Micu (Magyarized Kiss Janos), born in 1948 in the village of Bedeu (now in Hungary), told me that when he left the village to go to high school on the road, in a cart, he would ask his father how to say mouse in Hungarian!

In modern Hungary, according to the 2011 census, 54.2 % of the population are Christian. By denomination, we have: 37.1 % Catholic; 2.2 % Lutheran; 1.8 % Greek Catholic; 11.1 % Calvinist; and 1.3 % other denominations. The Magyarized Slovaks and Swabians were Catholics, while the insignificant Hungarian minority was Catholic up to a certain moment when it switched to Calvinism (a phenomenon called Turco-Calvinism) during the Pashalik of Buda (1540-1699). Over the same period, those in the Slovak territories under the Habsburgs remained Catholic. If, and only if, we assume that the 45.8 % of non-Christians came from all Christian denominations proportionally, then, with a slight margin for error, 21 % would have been old Hungarians from before 1555 (Augsburg) and 1648 (Westphalia) who switched to Calvinism. The remaining Swabians, Slovaks, Romanians, other Germans, Serbs, and Ruthenians were Magyarized after Dualism. During the savage process of Magyarization under Dualism, the names of the new converts were also Magyarized. Thus, we have cross-checked that in the interwar period, a chauvinist bloc became alarmed that more than 50 % of the citizens did not have Hungarian names.

***

If, in the Middle Ages, the religious elite was the engine of Catholic fanaticism, in modern times the engine of racial fanaticism was the aristocracy; as pronounced upon by Kossuth in the Diet on March 18, 1848: *Hungary owes its existence solely to the aristocracy* [105 p.70]. In the Communist era, the driving force was those citizens raised in a culture of hate. In post-war Hungary, it was still impossible for a native of another ethnicity (Romanian, German, Slovak, Serb, Ruthenian, and Croat) to preserve his or her identity due to mental terror.

CHAPTER 13

HORTHYSTS IN COMMUNISM

13.1 The Communist Party of Romania: A Horthyst Agent

On August 26, 1944, the government in Budapest, foreseeing the advance of the anti-German front, sent a message to the Hungarians in Transylvania that they had to organize themselves and collaborate intensely with the Russian authorities, undermining the Romanians [27 p.23]. The American historian Robert King of the Hoover Institute in his *History of the Romanian Communist Party* notes that the Communist Party worked through the Hungarian Workers Soviet (MADOSz), as 80 % of those enrolled in the Communist Party came from "Hungarian backgrounds". The consistency of minority groups in the upper and local leadership of the PCdR kept Romanians out of the party [71 p.46]. Mr. Aranyossy, an ardent advocate of Magyarhood, stated in the magazine *Esprit* (Paris) for March 1978 [p.69-70]:

> At the time of the liberation (autumn 1944) the Communist Party, according to official statistics, had barely 1,000 members and many of them were Hungarians and Magyarized Jews. They occupied the top positions. Among them Ana Pauker and László Luka, sent from Moscow, were the key personalities [...] This was the Communist Party, which was Romanian in name only [...] a Romanian Communist Party formed and partly led by the Hungarian communist majority. After liberation the number of minorities in the Communist Party increased because the membership of Romanians was very small [5 p.37].

Another piece of evidence is provided by the *Diary of the First Secretary of the USSR Embassy* in Romania, N.T. Fedorov, dated 10.10.1946. The diary records the visit of the lawyer Mathias Carp, who left him a book written by Carp and published by SOCEC in 1945 about the crimes of the Hungarians in Northern Transylvania. The book was banned by the Communist authorities in the interest of friendship between the two peoples [133 p.510]. Here, what is meant by the authorities is the Communist Party of Romania and this "friendship between two peoples" is the friendship between victim and executioner. Consequently, in postwar Romania, in which the Hungarians played the role of the founder of communism, very little was written about the period 1940-1990; on those occasions when it has been written, it has bypassed the truth. To give an example from the communist era, the Moisei massacre was supposedly caused by fascists! Which fascists in particular, is not said, i.e., it could have been the Germans. No, it was not the Germans. "Magyarhood" made the most of its essential role in the establishment of communism in Romania, both in the Stalinist era under Pauker, Luka, and Gheorghiu Dej, and later in the Ceausescu era [5 p.37-42].

Fig. 13.1. Demonstration organized by MNSz (MADOSz) in Cluj in 1945 in favour of the Soviet Army of occupation.

When the Hungarian Minister of Justice repeated his revisionist claims in London in 1946, L. Pătrăşcanu, the Romanian Minister of Justice, responded by talking about the danger of a revival of revisionism:

The necessity for the almost 300,000 or 400,000 Hungarians brought by Horthy to Northern Transylvania during the years of the Diktat to leave the country [...] I must admit that if we looked at helping the Hungarian population in Hungary with goodwill, we cannot say the same thing when it comes to that crowd, 300,000-400,000 Hungarians (from Hungary), who live, today, outside our laws, illegally in Romania. This large Hungarian population is not only here (in Romania) in search of a livelihood. The presence of these people and the permanence of this presence—people whom we have consciously excluded from citizenship rights—creates a worrying situation. Because it is precisely these Hungarians, or most of them, who cultivate and nurture revisionist tendencies and work to break up our state. In this matter our indulgence has its limits [110 p.194].

The presence of these 400,000 Hungarians from Hungary in Transylvania (including those expelled by Yugoslavia) after the war is also confirmed by the increase in the percentage of Hungarian speakers from 7.9 % in 1930 to 9.4 % in 1948, according to official Romanian data. Lucrețiu Pătrășcanu also called in his speech for the perpetrators of the crimes of Ciumârna, Lazuri, Ip, Trăznea, Nușfalău, Huedin, Mureșenii de Câmpie, Sărmaș, Moisei, and Cluj to be brought to justice, which continued to stir up spirits in Transylvania against the Romanians. Nevertheless, the Communist Party from Romania was in the hands of these criminals. Pătrășcanu was the only ethnic Romanian intellectual in the government and just being an intellectual was in itself an incriminating fact for the communists. The courage to think about the consequences of colonisation during the Horthyst period and the intention to call these murderers to account cost him his life. He was arrested in 1948 on charges of chauvinism, ironically enough, and convicted by a justice system he reorganized. He was executed in 1954. The same goal of the repopulation of Transylvania with Hungarian speakers from Hungary (1940-1945) in place of expelled Romanians was also spoken of by Protopope Nicolae Vasiu. The Hungarian National Soviet (MNSz) in Romania was exactly the right tool to support Hungarian revisionism from within. According to the census of 25.01.1948, there were 3,752,269 Romanians and 1,481,903 Hungarian speakers in Transylvania, Banat, Crișana, and Maramureș, including the 400,000 or so Hungarians brought in under the Horthyst regime to increase the Hungarian population. The Hungarians also increased their numbers by counting the Jews, the Swabians, and the Hungarian-speaking Orthodox and Greek-Catholic Romanians as their own. This also explains the small number of Germans (332,066) and Jews (30,039) recorded [177 p.415]. The influence of the Horthysts in the Communist Party was so strong that even the first census of the "communist" era was taken not according to the practice of the civilized world, but according to the Hungarian pattern and based on language. There was no question of clarifying the presence of the 400,000 Hungarians brought in between 1940 and 1945.

Absolutely all Transylvanian historians of any significance from the interwar period were imprisoned after the Horthysts, disguised as communists, took power! Many of them died in prison; they did not live long enough to benefit from the "political" pardons of 1964! And this did not only happen in the case of the Transylvanian people! The same

happened to Gheorghe Brătianu, who was one of the great worthies among
the scholars of the time. With one exception, Gheorghe Crăciun, all of the
upper echelon of the Securitate (secret police) in Transylvania were
Magyarized, including Ambrusz Coloman, Cseller Ludovic, Toma Elekis,
Weiss (Patriciu) Mihai, Sigismund Breiner, Zoltan Kling, Kalbusek
Joszef, and Iszak Adalbert. In the Cluj Regional Committee of the
Communist Party of Romania in 1950, for example, the Human
Resources, Staff Regulations, Press and Publishing, and Sport sections
were 100 % staffed with "Hungarians" [Annex F].

13.2 Hungarian Pre-eminence in the RCP

During the Horthyst occupation in the commune of Iara (Cluj county),
many Romanians disappeared; one by one. Who would the wife turn to if
her husband or child did not come home? After 1945, when the murderers
were secure in the upper echelons of the party, political police, and
prosecutor's office, you were almost as vulnerable as during Horthy's
time. The villagers had clues and suspected a family who would have
eagerly "implemented" racial cleansing. By 1960, there was talk of
building a school in the village, but to do so a shed had to be demolished,
the very shed of the family suspected of the crimes. The targeted people
and their party leaders resisted and the school was not built. In 1970, the
school was built out of necessity and a sinister discovery was made: the
bodies of dozens of people were found under the shed. The families of the
former victims demanded an investigation. The Communist Party and its
Hungarian-speaking majority did not approve the inquiry. No one has so
far dared to find out the truth (quoted in Filip Samoilă, a native of Iara).

After 1940, the German schools in Sătmar were closed and German
children were included in the Hungarian education system. After 1945,
this situation remained unchanged and the former Horthysts all became
communists. The institutions of state have remained in their hands ever
since. The establishment of the Council of Working People of German
Nationality in 1971 was a recognition of the existence of Germans in the
Satu Mare region. After this recognition, writes Prof. Dr. Ernst Hauler in
Sathmarer Heimatbriefe no. 24/5/1995, *there was an explosive awakening
of the consciousness* among the Swabians. German kindergartens, classes,
and cultural groups appeared in Satu Mare County. In 1973, Prof. Hauler
discussed with the villagers of Schinal (Satu Mare County) the possibility
of re-establishing German-language education. However, the party
secretary of Schinal, Karl Kulin, a Magyarized Swabian, was uninterested.
Kulin called on those who had the audacity to sign the application to scold

them, *how could anyone allow themselves to disturb the peace and unity of the community? And this behind his back* since here, Germanization was no longer happening, as if it ever had! The Swabians, frightened, kept silent. As a result, the party secretary replied to the school inspectorate that in Schinal only those who did not have children wanted German schooling to be available! The request of the peasants of Schinal was however sent to the Ministry of Education by the Satu Mare School Inspectorate. The Hungarian-speaking inspector general for minorities, Debreci, received it. He sent his Hungarian-speaking subordinate, Murvai, into the field to assess the situation. Murvai came to the village of Schinal and passed on following the conclusion to the ministry: *Prof. Hauler is a fascist and therefore there is no need for a German kindergarten in Schinal.* And that's how the Schinal Swabians were left without education in their own language during the Ceaușescu era! The same Murvai could also be found at the ministry in 1990 "helping" an NKVD-ist minister!

The takeover of the old, "bourgeois" institutions in Southern Transylvania in 1945 by the former Horthysts from Northern Transylvania was done with the help of clubs, chains, and metal crowbars [Annex G].

In 1973, Emil Muntean, the director of the Institute for Computing Technology in Cluj, invited his young colleague Tudor Muresan to join the RCP so that he would no longer be the only Romanian in the party organisation. All the others were "Hungarians", or, more precisely, Magyarized people. Among them were the technicians Robert, Wellman, and Kaiser.

In 1974, a teacher called Valer Voda in Odorhei (Harghita County) dared to speak Romanian with a pupil at a bus stop! A group of workers, hearing Romanian words, approached the two and hurled insults like *büdös Olah*. They also threatened them and used obscene gestures before offering a piece of advice: *This is Szekler land [...] go to Bucharest* [178 p.13].

In 1976, the Timiş Party farm, which was intended to supply only high-ranking Party members with strictly controlled ecological products through the backdoor, was run exclusively by Hungarians! The historical censuses taken by the Austrians in 1735 and 1767 found no Hungarians in Banat; data established by Fr. Griselini in a work published in Vienna in 1780 mentions them for the first time, but being so few in number they appear on the list together with the Bulgarians [56 p.30].

Acad. Ştefan Pascu told me that at a meeting of the Central Committee of the RCP in the 1980s, one of the members, a Hungarian speaker, asked: *let's stop mentioning that mercenary Michael the Brave* (1593-1601). The dictator, the "great nationalist", was also present, and said absolutely nothing! The only one to intervene was Ioan Coman, originally from Transylvania. In the Central Committee of the RCP were József Banc, János Kozma, Adalbert Kriysan, Sándor Czege, János Fazekas, Lajos Fazekas, Gyula Fejes, János Fóris, Mihály Gere, Lajos Létay, Mihály Levente, Viktor Nagy, Ferencz Nagy, Pál Nagy, István Péterfy, V. Sechel, Sándor Sencovici, Mihály Suder, Emerik Szabó, Dezső Szilágyi, Ernest Szotyori, József Uglar, Gisela Vass, N. Veress, András Barta, Géza Domokos, Emerik Füstös, Sándor Kolpádi, Emerik Molnár, András Sütő, József Szász, Lajos Takács, and István Tykodi. In the Secretariat of the Central Committee were József Banc and József Uglar. In the Political Executive Committee there were János Fazekas, József Uglár, József Banc, Lajos Fazekas, and Mihály Gere. In the State Council, István Péterfy was the vice-chairman and members Lajos Fazekas and Emil Hates, and so on and so forth [5 p.38].

13.3 Lexicon of Hungarian Literature in Romania

Among the authors of the *Lexicon of Hungarian Literature in Romania*, published by *Kriterion Publishing House* (Bucharest) in 1981, we find the Horthyst Imre Mikó, secretary of the Transylvanian Hungarian Party (1940-1944). Imre Mikó was, from 1940 to 1941, a deputy in Budapest where he initiated and voted for racist laws, including: the law for the

racial purification of Hungary; the law for the establishment of labour camps; and the law for the "lending of labour" in Germany. Mikó considered both Hitler and Mussolini to be geniuses [166 p.183]! Mikó wrote in the newspaper Ellenzék (Cluj) for 23.08.1941: *On the contrary he* [our note: King Stefan/Vajk] *had started from the idea that foreigners should be subjugated in the interests of Hungary.* On 23.08. 1944, in the same newspaper he concluded: *It must never be forgotten that in serving the cause of Transylvania we serve the universal and eternal cause of Hungary.* In September 1944, Imre Mikó founded the Communist Guards in Cluj, which were obviously Hungarian. This

Fig. 13.2. Hungarian Lexikon.

criminal [166 p.151] was an author of encyclopaedias in Ceauşescu's Romania, in which various fascists and criminals were presented as democrats, antifascists, and illegal communists. Today, in Cluj-Napoca a street bears his name! In the same lexicon of 1981, the *democratic legacy* of Daday Loránd (alias Ducso Csaba), as well as of Kosch Károly and Albrecht Dezső, of notorious Horthysts who supported the genocide, are also mentioned [166 p.143]. *The Lexicon of Hungarian Literature in Romania* has another important achievement: besides transforming Horthyst personalities and institutions into "democratic" ones, it also invents a non-existent anti-fascist resistance movement. The coordinator of the *Lexicon* in Bucharest was Balogh Edgár, a teacher from Slovakia, who maintained a chauvinist movement there: "Sickle", considered "reactionary" even in the *History of Hungary* of the Hungarian Academy [166 p.138]. The composer Nicolae Bretan, a Romanian from Năsăud, appears in the *Lexicon* as a Hungarian—Bretán Miklós! The well-known expressionist painter Hans Mattis Teutsch, a Saxon from Brasov, also appears as a Hungarian under the name Mattis Teutsch János. These are not exceptions. From the lexicon of the Ceauşescu era, the articles end up in the great Hungarian lexicon of the *Hungarian Academy Publishing House*! Then other encyclopaedias take it over. A scam of Magyarization.

13.4 Hungarian Pre-eminence in the RCP in the Last Decade of Communism

J. Fazekas, a member of the Executive Committee of the RCP, published in the *Journal of History* [no. 11/1977] a "historical" article on 1848 that was full of absurdity. The absurdity lies in the fact that it suggests that the Hungarian landowners were equally oppressed alongside (Romanian) serfs; and not only were they not oppressors, that they were also revolutionaries [150 p.200]. David Prodan, the great historian, could not reply in 1977, instead he had to wait for the fall of communism [150 p.206].

In 1983, Romulus Zaharia's novel *Ademenirea* (*The Enticement*) was published, in which an emblematic episode in the history of the early years of communism—the attack on the Avram Iancu student hostel in Cluj by Hungarian-speaking workers from the Dermata factory—is remembered.

However, hundreds of workers going and killing several dozen defenceless students is a problem that, if it did not make it to court at the time, at least deserves to be investigated and explored in the literature. This was a historical fact that definitively marked the destiny of those involved, but the book was removed from the bookshops and immediately disappeared at the request of some Hungarian intellectuals. This was done by the PCR with the reasoning that it incited ethnic hatred! Moreover, the author was persecuted and forced to emigrate in 1986. Talk about their power under Ceaușescu.

Fig. 13.3. Janos Fazekas, in front of whom the dictator Ceaușescu was silent.

In 1987, Professor Gh. Ciutrilă had a complaint lodged against him at the Party that he had "wealth". The complaint was lodged by the Hungarian Prof. G. Cs. Both professors taught at the Technical University of Cluj-Napoca. The party (RCP) sent the complaint to the criminal investigation authorities, who began their investigation. Officer Virgil Ardelean told the complainant that he was lucky that the Hungarian officer, who was a member of the team, did not come to work on the day of the investigation for medical reasons and that such complaints from Hungarians to Romanians received by the Party were very frequent—he knew how they were done! We have presented here just a few, out of thousands and thousands of other examples.

13.5 The Expulsion of Romanians After 22 December 1989

On the evening of 22 December 1989, around 8 p.m. in the village of Dealu (Harghita County), the hatred of the locals overflowed against the family of Liviu Cherchişan, the commune's police chief. He was watching the events in Bucharest on TV with his wife and two young children, when suddenly the windows were shattered by stones and pieces of wood; the animal screams made everyone freeze in fear. Liviu Cherchişan came out of the house to save his wife and children. A rain of blows fell on him and, bloody, he fell to the ground. The fallen man was beaten even more fervently! A female doctor tried to bring him back to life, but the savages armed with axes and spears returned and it was all over [178 p.31].

The revolutionaries in the commune of Zetea (Harhita County) were much more "humane", for example, Gabriel Dănăilă had his pistol snatched from him and was shot in the back of the head [178 p.32]! 39 police stations were attacked and seized in one night, according to a plan [125].

Moreover, on 22 December 1989 in Odorhei (Harghita County), the pre-planned arson of the cars of Romanians in the town took place. The conspirators were well-informed, knowing in advance the addresses and locations where the attacks were to take place. Gabor Szekely, knowing of the planned action tried to save the car of a Romanian, Nichita, but he was caught by the savage horde and for his "anti-Hungarian" action he was killed [178 p.32].

A teacher Rodica Ştefu from Baraolt (Covasna County) was driven away by her Hungarian-speaking colleagues in March 1990. Not only her colleagues, i.e., the "intellectuals" of the small town, but the majority of the citizens directly addressed the Romanians: *if you don't leave, in two days we will lynch you* [178 p.60]. Dozens of other such facts have been described by Prof. Valer Voda [178].

A statistical analysis from the first weeks after 22 December 1989 showed that the expulsion of Romanians from the Curvature Carpathians was estimated at 30,000 people [178 p.46]! Where Hungarian speakers were in the majority, Romanian historical monuments were destroyed, streets and institutions were renamed, and even cemeteries were Magyarized, as happened in Vlăhiţa (Harghita County). The new street names memorialized "personalities" of the period of the Horthyst genocide. Romanians were considered invaders in the "Szekler" area, i.e., in the Curvature Carpathians [178 p.34].

This was part of political preparation by the Hungarian communist "cadres" before the events of December 1989! On the one hand, the

Romanians were killed or threatened with death, while on the other, they were told to leave immediately, so as not to end up like Dănăilă, Cherchişan, and Coman! The heads of the Romanian state institutions in the area, all of them Hungarian communists, approved the departure of Romanian teachers only "on request"! Let there be no legal connection between assassination and expulsion.

The first thing that happened at the Central University Library in Cluj-Napoca over Christmas 1989 is that some of the heritage books were burned by the *Revolutionary Committee* that had taken over management. Among them was *Nincs Kegyelem*, a book by Dordai Lorant signed with the pseudonym Ducso Csaba, which we also mentioned in chapter 6 and which summarized the beliefs of the Magyarized people from Kossuth up to today. Another book that was given the same treatment was *The Belis Slaughter* [70] written around 1930, which investigated the slaughter organized by the Budapest Ministry of War (November 1918) against the peasants of Belis (Cluj County), when Budapest was trying to persuade the Romanians not to leave "Great Hungary". And so forth.

CHAPTER 14

HORTHYSM IN THE ORIGINAL DEMOCRACY

14.1 Hungarian Mania After 1990

Until 1989, the Hungarians maintained control through the Communist Party of Romania. Today, they express themselves openly, claiming their European identity through the Democratic Soviet of Hungarians in Romania (RMDSz). They have been in all the governments since the "original democracy" installed by the Soviet agency in December 1989.

The Bucharest newspapers cannot be used as a reliable basis for documentation in many respects, including the one under discussion. For example, in the newspaper *România liberă* for 24.02.1990, a Hungarian author stated that there was not a single Hungarian teacher in the whole country who had been appointed headmaster of a high school. The "free" newspaper did not accept a reply to this mystification. Here are the names of all the principals of Brassai High School in Cluj-Napoca from 1944 to 1990, all of them Hungarian: Gál Dénes, Szalosi Ferencz, Boda Károly, Simon Gábor, Józsa György, Péter Rozália, Székely András, and Bálint András; and the party secretaries: Doncsuly Margit, Kovács Iolanda, Balogh Gertrud, and Veres György!

In 1992, when volume V of *Documents on the 1848 Revolution in Transylvania* appeared, under the auspices of the Romanian Academy, the historian Gelu Neamțu noted that his superior, Akos Egyed, had removed notes and parts of the documents [116 p.10]. Documents too were dispossessed; it is astonishing how much they wish to obtain or conceal! Below we present three notes, omitted by Akos Egyed from this volume [116 p.11]:

(606) Baron Wesselenyi refers to the adherence of the privileged Hungarians and Szeklers in the Cluj Diet to the union and not to the general will of the majority of the Transylvanian population, which was anti-union.

(786) For the authors of the report, representatives of the conservative Hungarian nobility in Hunedoara County, the overwhelming majority Romanian population constituted the unpatriotic element, and the

Romanians, Saxons, and Serbs were foreigners.

(843) as Baron Perenyi himself admits, the new electoral law was in fact aimed at perpetuating the dominant position of the Hungarian aristocracy and keeping the Romanians politically inferior; it also reveals the efforts of these leaders to prevent a common anti-unionist front developing between the Saxons and the Romanians.

This was done under the auspices of Victor Cherestesiu, director of the *G. Barițiu Institute of History*, a collaborator of Mihai Roller, a Soviet agent! The same was done during Ceaușescu's time [116 p.13] and we are not only dealing with omissions, but also falsifications. In 1996, when the historian Gelu Neamțu published a history of the 1848 Revolution, the same historian threatened him with prosecution! All that Gelu Neamțu had done was to call out genocide as genocide.

14.2 The Disposal of Property in Transylvania After 1990

The historian David Prodan (1902-1992) spent a lifetime studying the ways in which feudal property was formed in Transylvania and trying to distinguish feudal property from property in the bourgeois sense of the word [148]. On 21.06.1854, when, finally, the demands of the Romanian Revolution of 1848 were partially and dishonestly met, the serfs were "given" their land in return for compensation! The imperial *Patent* distributing land to the peasants in 1854 was written by feudal landowners while the Alexander von Bach government only implemented it [153 p.225]. The feudal landowners received compensation for what was never theirs, i.e., the land over which the serfs had rights, but at the same time they 1) preserved the royal rights (opening taverns, milling, etc.) and 2) retained property taken by force, thus becoming owners in the modern sense of the word with allodiums (freeholds) [6 vol. II p.637]. The communal forests and pastures, or parts of them, taken over by the feudal lords and transformed into allodial land were passed on to the former feudal lords who thus became landowners. We have three types of property that were ceded, without any logical, legal, or moral sense, to racist and chauvinist Hungarian people and institutions; these properties were ceded in this way primarily due to the corruption and incompetence of Romanian judges. Obviously, the laws drafted by corrupt, but equally ignorant and incompetent politicians made the "legal operation" easier.

The first category includes properties transferred to the would-be heirs of former landowners, i.e., landowners who opted for Hungarian citizenship after 1918 and whose estates were subject to agrarian reform

(30.07.1921). Following this reform, all peasants, regardless of their ethnicity, were given equal possession of the land. The landowners and their heirs were compensated by Romania because the lawyers and politicians of the time were unable to distinguish between *confiscation for public utility* and *land division* (land reform) as *social justice.* Etienne Bartin, professor of private international law in Paris, observed that French jurisprudence had wasted half a century since 1789 disentangling feudal and purely landed property [46 p.103]. Land reform in Romania was neither lawful because it made no distinction between "nationals and foreigners" nor in fact oriented against foreign nationals. Through the Hungarian government, the landowners demanded preferential treatment and, as a result of its stupidity, the Romanian government acquiesced (1921-1930) by creating the Agrarian Fund (66.92 tons of gold), which was opened in Switzerland. Czechoslovakia and Yugoslavia did the same. When Hitler and Mussolini ceded the northwest of Transylvania to Horthy, the landowners took over the entirety of the landed estates that had been the subject of the 1921 agrarian reform, even though they had already received most of their value from the Romanian state. If the Second World War, which, like the Great War, was also the work of Hungarian chauvinism, had not started, the full payment of compensation to Hungarian nationals would have ended in 1944. In the territory ceded by Hitler to Hungary, after unimaginable crimes, expulsions, and enlistment in forced labour camps, being sent to the front line without instruction and being forced to work at demining the front lines, measures were immediately taken, among others, to liquidate Romanian agrarian reform. These measures included: a) the exclusive dispossession of the properties of Romanian peasants and Romanian churches by the military authorities; b) the expulsion of Romanian peasants who had benefited from agrarian reform; c) the establishment of "curators" where owners were missing (following expulsion) or where properties were neglected (owners had been removed to camps) on the basis of Ordinance 9370/24.12.1940; d) declaring void the mining properties and concessions granted by the Romanian State by ordinances 1630/2.03.1941 and 3400/4.06.1942, as a result of this, land, boreholes, shafts, and mining machines and construction were confiscated by the Horthyst state without any compensation; and e) the confiscation of communal lands (pastures and grazing grounds) in Romanian villages under ordinances 1890/11.03.1941 and 2790/13.04.1941. These were the immediate measures taken by the Horthyst administration. The Romanian *compossessorates* (commons) were also immediately annihilated by force and the Minister of Agriculture Daniel Banffy, great-grandson of the Romanian cnez of Haţeg, issued Ordinance 2660/1942 modifying the

Hungarian forestry regime only for the occupied territory and passing the Romanian *compossessorates* to the administration of government commissioners. We have come across this kind of legislation before, i.e., different legislation in Pannonia and Transylvania. Banffy issued the ordinance and Banffy took advantage of it: the administration of the Romanian *compossessorates* in Pratul Bradului (Mures County) was given over to Eugen Monotz, Ernest Pater, and Szortsei Geza, officials of the *Bangra Company*, which belonged to Daniel Banffy. The new administrators cut down 250 hectares of the *compossessorates* and sold the wood for nothing to *Bangra*! After analysing the situation in Transylvania, the racists issued Ordinance 970/12.01.1943, which annulled what was left of the Romanian agrarian reform, namely the retrocession of forests. Ordinance 3710/3.07.1943 stipulated that the land allocated by the Romanian agrarian reform to war widows and disabled civil servants for the construction of houses should be transferred to the Horthyst state. In Cluj County alone, 1,325 such properties became state property [221 p.182]. Finally, by Ordinance 5200/18.12.1943, the total revision of Romanian mining rights in the territory occupied by the Horthysts was ordered. Additionally, we should mention in this chapter the dispossessions carried out by the civil authorities. To give one example, among hundreds of others, 60 peasants from Corpadea and 32 from Gădălin, who had bought 175 ha. of land from the Gaal family between 1928 and 1936, had their purchase contract cancelled, without compensation, by the Horthyst authorities [221 p.196]. In the ceded territory, expropriation on the grounds of public utility made by the new authorities was made for settlements with Hungarians west of the Tisa. For example, in the commune of Crăcești (Maramureș County) the land of Romanian peasants was expropriated "for public utility", in other words, *the public utility* for the Horthysts was ethnic cleansing. This applied to settlers, to whom, we have seen, the communist minister Pătrășcanu also referred and whose number reached impressive levels.

Horthysm continued after 1945 through those who had metamorphosed into communists, but even they could no longer support the "agrarian estates" in the name of "proletarian democracy" following the new agrarian reform of 23.03.1945. *Law No 10/2001 on the legal status of properties wrongfully taken over between 6 March 1945 and 22 December 1989* also retroceded the properties of landowners compensated in the interwar period, recovered during the Horthyst occupation and again subject to the agrarian reform of 23 March 1945. However, after 1990, the Romanian state, through the courts, which were populated by *incompetent and corrupt judges*, once again ceded feudal properties to the alleged heirs, which were the subject of the agrarian reform of 1921 and 1945 and had already been compensated once or twice over.

Of the second category of properties ceded without any legal argument are those buildings built from funds collected from serfs for educational institutions—a mechanism established during the time of Maria Theresa and Joseph II. Such properties also existed in Austria, Hungary, the Czech Republic, Slovakia, Serbia, Croatia, Slovenia, and Italy, where they remained in the public patrimony. The funds for schools and cultural institutions were built up by contributions from the serfs and once the school, theatre, or philharmonic hall had been built they were given to Catholic and Calvinist churches. Even in the successor states of the Habsburg Empire, the administering churches did not become owners.

Of the third category of Romanian properties lost and not recovered right up to today are those in which the Horthyst murderers settled in 1940, some of them in the homes of the Romanians killed in what we have called the *continuous genocide*, a genocide of which the Final Solution was part. If any Romanian survivor had been left alive after 1944 who dared to claim the family property, he was declared Manist (a supporter of Iuliu Maniu), reactionary, and sent to Sighet, Gherla, or Aiud, also by the Horthysts, who administered public affairs (land register, courts, militia, prosecutor's office, and party) as "communists".

14.3 Today's Romanian Political Class

Many of today's Romanian political rulers are, without any doubt, shameful. They are corrupt, ignorant, and lacking in determination, have no progressive national policy and are incapable of overcoming their individual or group interests. Most of them were former members of the Communist Party or of the political police, the Securitate. Most of them lacked a profession since communist activity was not a profession and therefore did not have a solid professional career. Now the transfer between generations is taking place, in the sense that former communists and Securitate agents die off and their sons enter the political scene, just as corrupt and incompetent, only greedier.

The political class continues to increase Romanian problems, rather than pulling the people out from the lethargy into which it was thrown by communism.

The confusion in the Western world as to the situation of Hungarian-speaking citizens in Romania, financially supported, directly, by Budapest, is deepened by the Romanian political class, which is completely ignorant in matters of national history and unwilling to persevere in any serious and profound investigation. The press in Bucharest also blurs the matter by unsound, sporadic, and self-contradictory approaches, as well as by contempt towards centuries of oppression inflicted upon the Romanians living in the "frontier" zone.

Paradoxically, Romanians, the most tolerant people of Europe, always compliant to the will of their southern, eastern, northern, and western neighbours—those neighbours who have situated themselves throughout history on the opposite side of tolerance. Romanians are discriminated against today at the insistent requests of those very neighbours.

CHAPTER 15

THE CIRCLE OF IGNORANCE

15.1 Resolution 147 of the 98th US Congress

Getting back to the ignorance of leaders, this time the target is the US Congress, which had its strings pulled by the Hungarian and Russian secret services. In Transylvania, Banat, Crişana, and Maramureş, the first census of 1930, meticulously and accurately undertaken, recorded 1.35 million Hungarians. Supposedly there were 3.19 million people who declared themselves to be Romanian. After the expulsions of Romanians and Horthy's colonisations (1940-1945), and following the Stalinist period (1945-1964) administered through the hands of those who were in the minority, the last census before Resolution 147, i.e., the census of 1977, in Transylvania, Banat, Crişana, and Maramureş declared that there were 5.2 million Romanians. Thus, the number of Romanians had increased between 1930 and 1977 by 63 %, while after Resolution 147 the number of Hungarians would have supposedly increased by 86.5 %. Therefore in *dark Transylvania*, Hungarians, who used to hold and still held key positions in the Party, the security services, the prosecutor's office, and the police, who spoke their own language, whitewashed their war criminals, published what they wanted and blocked Romanian books, were supposedly discriminated against precisely by the regime they had forged. It was indeed a feat for Congress to be at the discretion of communist intelligence agents to the point that even logic no longer worked!

15.2 The Position of Great Personalities Against Ignorance

In a letter written by Leo Tolstoy (1828-1910) to the Budapest magazine *A Hír* in 1907, the great writer denounced:

> *What is sadder is that abroad Count Apponyi has the reputation of a pacifist, while in Hungary he does not even recognize the non-Magyar people as human beings. Every sane person must tear off this man's lying mask from his face, to show the whole world that he is not a benefactor but*

a bird of prey [91 p.311].

To this, we may add the words of other great writers and personalities of the age.

Unpardonable are those unscrupulous persons who, for personal 'reasons', encourage in England Budapest's revisionist policy and attempt to disrupt the established order, an attempt fostered by people who have proved themselves to be intolerant, oppressive and lawless in their dealings with other nations.

George Bernard Shaw (1856-1950).

In my youth, when the Hungarian nation was oppressed, I used to love it and admire it a lot, and I shed bitter tears for it. But later, when I studied the situation more closely, I became convinced of the injustice that was being done to other nationalities in Hungary, and I started hating Hungarian chauvinism. I am certain that there is nobody outside Hungary who does not share these feelings—and believe me, these injustices sooner or later will lead to Hungary's downfall.

Bjoernsterne Bjoernson (1859-19420, writer.

The Hungarians pursue a blind and violent policy against the nationalities which are the subject of the Hungarian crown, against the Romanian in particular.

Lord Edmond Fitzmaurice (1846-1935),
member of Gladstone's Cabinet.

By arbitrary stipulations which were introduced into the electoral law, the Romanians no longer enjoy any political rights. The electoral census is ten times greater for the Romanians in Transylvania than for the rest of Hungary. The Romanians, who... should have 75 of the total of 417 deputies in Parliament, have, in fact, none.

G. Clemenceau (1841-1929), French Prime Minister.

Persecution has been carried so far that it is almost impossible to find a Romanian newspaperman who writes for a political newspaper, and who has never been in jail, charged with a political crime ... Until Hitler eclipsed modern tyrannies by his contempt for justice, tradition and humanity the Hungarian conception of HERRENVOLK was the most exaggerated and must be revised as what happened under Hungarian rules would be revealed.

R.W. Seton-Watson (1879-1951).

The Hungarians are people who, by their violent method of governing, have created the Romanian problem.

Leon Gambetta (1838-1882), French Foreign Minister.

The cultural life of Hungary has no part of merit. As the fiery spirit... on both sterile.
Otto Hauser (1876-1944), in *Weltgeschichte der Literatur* [91 p.420].

Fig. 15.1. O. Hausser's History of Universal Literature in two volumes from 1910.

Hungarians are not worthy of Italy's sympathy, because they oppress in the most barbarous mode three million Brothers
Menoti G. Garibaldi (1840-1903).

Austrian colonialism, which prevented Hungary from undergoing its natural development? On the contrary, the Austrian state protected the Magyar nobility's colonialism; a safe shield by its omnipotence and tax exemption, of the whole system of exploitation and anachronism.

Horthyism was, in no way, an accident. It was the exacerbated mentality consciously cultivated from top to bottom, from the leading intellectuals to the majority opinion. An overrated proverbial selfpride, consciously cultivated, of the Magyar people, a selfpride which is second to none, an overinflated hatred against the rising peoples, an unmatched hatred against the Romanian people, the first of which, by its large population, is an obstacle to its domination.

David Prodan (1902-1992).

Fig. 15.2. David Prodan, the great historian of Transylvania in whose work not even a single comma can be challenged.

CHAPTER 16

INSTEAD OF A CONCLUSION

16.1 The Key to Understanding Magyarmania

Things can no longer be regarded as simply as they were in the time of Hermann Cornring (1606-1681), the greatest German polymath until Leibniz (1646-1716), who in his *Thesauri Rerum publicarum pars quarta* considered the Hungarian inhabitants of the kingdom of Hungaria to be of notorious cruelty and savagery [182 p.27]. Such a reputation must be explained, as observed by Ioan Slavici:

> *In the bizarreness of the Hungarian character there is something very interesting ... The Hungarian is indeed wild (szilaj) in all forms of his life* [160 p.712].

The one who has appropriated the Hungarian spirit is extreme in everything. At the same time, he sees himself as a straw fire—*A magyar szalma tüz*! Neither Slavici nor the intuition of Iorga's genius could see what genetics knows with absolute precision. The philosopher of culture Lucian Blaga (1895-1960) observed in his Messianic neighbours *the ridiculous illuminations and the grimaces pitifully devoid of the spirit of self-irony.*

There is no single idea of culture... that originated with the Hungarians says the writer Franz von Löhrer (1818-1892) in *Magyaren und andere Ungarn* [182 p.20]. There is one idea that originated with the Magyarized people: hatred of everything that is not "Hungarian". But Löhrer probably correctly intuited the dichotomy in the title: *Hungarians-Magyars.* "Hungarians" here means the Romanian-German-Slovak majority in the Catholic state called *Hungaria*, while the "Magyars" refers to as many as were left of the 16 or 17 Magyar-Cuman clans that remained in the 13th century. The total proportion of today's Turanian-Ugric-Cumaean-Turk-Mongols has been resolved through genetics.

Where is that famed racial superiority they claimed to possess? Let us get over the nicely packaged racial idea, accepted by the academic world in the West, and repeat the question of the historian David Prodan: what is the purpose of the superior race to Magyarize the inferior races of Germans, Romanians, and Slovaks [150 p.157]?

In 1993, the Chief Rabbi of Budapest, Gyula Landeszmann, in an interview with the magazine *IGEN*, said that *if we tear* Jewish values *out* of Hungarian culture, *nothing remains* [64 p.218]. The rabbi was immediately removed from office.

Having unravelled the history of the peoples of the middle Danube basin through: 1) the prism of traditions, some pre-Christian and other folkloric creations; 2) the evolution of the Romanian language; 3) the artefacts of early Christianity and the linguistic evidence of Christianity; 4) written documents; 5) genetic studies; and 6) decoding the culture of hate, we are able to understand the domination by a tiny minority of an overwhelming majority. We believe that understanding this unique phenomenon can only be done culturally.

16.2 Equal to the Culture that Produced them

Many works, some centuries old, such as Sebastian Brandt's *The Book of the World* (Tübingen, 1534), have argued that Hungary has a people *who do not keep their word and are fickle* [182 p.26]; but the fickleness of the inhabitants is only the projection of the fickleness of the clans who ruled Hungary. Uncertainty became a value for the newly Magyarized people.

Ludovic Kossuth (1802-1894), a Slovak, disowned his nationality and identified with the Magyarized people, just as the Magyarized people identified with this *agitator* (as Mihai Eminescu and Seton-Watson considered him). Kossuth's former friend, Count Batthyányi, wrote of him that he bowed like a reed to any stronger breath, being a worthless character. Karl Marx (1818-1883), a contemporary of his, considered him an upstart and a man utterly without character, *changing his opinions as easily as his audience*. When he visited America, he declared himself pro-slavery in the south and against it in the north [177 p.406]. Bartholomew Szemere, Kossuth's Minister of the Interior and later Minister-President, wrote of Kossuth that he was *a real disgrace* [53 vol. V p.98].

In the 1920s, on the one hand, they were the forerunners of National Socialism and German revisionism, and on the other, they "cooperated" with the (anti-revisionist) League of Nations [161 p.77]. The hypocrisy of the Magyarized people reached its peak when, allied with the "Aryans", after the Japanese victory at Pearl Harbour in 1942, they suddenly advocated Turanism and "Hungarian scholars" loudly confessed their belief that:

...it is only a matter of time before the world empire will be realized: the Japanese-Manchurian-Chinese-Mongolian empire through which all the Turanian states, side by side, will be able to harness their global political and economic will [177 p.279].

There is nothing sacred, in the Christian sense, for the Magyarized people. For them there is no God, but a Hungarian God; the Blessed Virgin was also Hungarian and as such crowned with Hungarian insignia etc. [175 p.157]. If they have nothing they hold sacred, then Hungarian religious organizations are only an instrument, among others, of a culture of hatred and chauvinism. The fact is that of the dozens of Romanian churches destroyed, one even with a cannon, and dozens more turned into stables, warehouses, etc., after the Vienna Diktat (1940), most were in the vicinity of Hungarian churches [175 p.183]. It is also hard to decide which was worse: the civilians transformed by hatred who terrorized and killed their own, or the Hungarian army, which, professing *a holy race war*, killed en masse.

After the first Vienna Diktat regarding Slovakia (1938), Horthy and his henchmen directed a campaign against Germany in which they spoke of *Germany's infamy*. The anti-German campaign was used by Horthy and his government as a powerful argument for Berlin to accept other Hungarian fantasies. On the evening of the second Vienna arbitration, the Hungarians shouted outside the German embassy in Budapest: *Arad, Timişoara, Braşov—the painter has deceived us* [184]. This is the same strategy they had practiced in 1867 to force feckless Austria to sign up to Dualism. Such considerations must have led the great scholar Nicolae Iorga to consider them an *operetta people*. Besides, they did not take themselves seriously either, since they themselves said *the Hungarians are a fleeting fire*. The participation of a fascist, the chief of a gang of assassins, Baron Aczél Ede, as Horthy's envoy in March 1944 in the talks with the Soviets thus seemed perfectly logical.

Referring to Miklos Horthy, in 1935 Adolf Hitler said: *he had been a National Socialist before the advent of German National Socialism* [166 p. 236]; in 1939, he called Horthy *cowardly and spineless* [161 p.169]. All the more, then, does Johann Weidlein's observation that Horthy used Hitler for revisionism and not the other way around stand up [184].

Horthy wrote to Hitler on 3.11.1939: *We were faithful comrades... We are a grateful people* [162 p.127]. He wrote to Stalin in September 1944, flatters him with the invented title of *Field Marshal* and concludes *I take this opportunity to assure you, Marshal Stalin, of my highest respect. Yours sincerely Horthy* [133 p.298]. He was still Hitler's ally, since Hitler had given him parts of Serbia, Romania, and Slovakia, but he wrote to

Stalin that for a thousand years the fate of the Hungarians had been influenced by the German colossus; under the influence of this colossus they were involved in this unworthy war with the Soviet Union; the Hungarian people had many similarities with the Russian people, and so on [133 p.298]. This letter of Hitler's ally is disgusting in itself being a mixture of lies and flattery. The letter was carried by a delegation consisting of Gen. H. Farago, Geza Teleki, D. Szent-Ivani, and Aczél Ede, which arrived in Moscow on 1.10.1944.

For those driven by hatred against everything that is not Hungarian, it is a "virtue" to be with Hitler, Stalin, or Putin, if under each of them you can ensure the purity of the supposed Hungarian race!

16.3 A Legitimate Question and an Explanation

What good is a state without its own ethnic substance, organized and structured solely and only on the ideology and culture of hatred towards other peoples? A state that has elevated intolerance to a principle and a raison d'être. A state that perpetrated the first genocide in modern Europe. A state that was the first National Socialist one, the first fascist one, yet crueller than any other. An anti-Semitic state whose bestiality astounded even the Nazis. A state that was, of its own volition, the first Bolshevik state. A state that printed and placed counterfeit currency in the West. A state that committed the most *bestial* crimes of the Second World War and applied the Final Solution in full. A state of racial hatred and absolute intolerance and two ethnocides!

The scholar Johann Weidlein has revealed the contribution of the culture of hate to the outbreak of World War II in a series of articles [184]. If the scourges of the 20th century are global problems, in Romania, no assessment has been made for a European problem: that of the contribution of the culture of hatred to Stalinization. By subterfuge, Russian Jewry is blamed for the Stalinization of Romania, without noticing that when the Hungarian-speaking Jews were liberated from the Nazi camps, all the institutions in Transylvania were in the hands of the Horthysts: police, prosecutor's office, security services, universities, prefectures, and town halls. These Horthysts suddenly became full-blooded Stalinists. The Magyarized people, as minorities, as Stalin's instrument, played first fiddle, by far, in the communization of Romania; hence the communization, in a distinctive manner, of Romania, which had not known native communists, except at the level of a few dozen people [29].

How did a tiny minority manage to dominate the peoples of the middle Danube basin? An explanation was offered by Baron Wesselényi (1796-

1850):

> *For a small number of Hungarians to have succeeded in dominating* [...]
> *the overwhelming majority of the other races, this was only possible thanks*
> *to the fact that this imposing majority equalled zero in Hungary* [91 p.222].

We know the opinions of Hungarian-speaking people of culture about Germans, Romanians, and Slovaks. They were, according to case, place, and circumstance: Turcophile and anti-German, Germanophile and anti-French, Francophile and anti-English, Germanophile and anti-Russian, and vice versa, Japanophile and anti-American, and also Americanophile! After all, for them the Americans were no good either. For Alexander Lukács, American women were lazy, dirty, primitive and *untidy creatures* [91 p.389]. They have fooled all German governments from Bismarck [179 p.171] until today! Their hypocrisy, their lack of scruples, did not work only in the face of great values, as briefly shown in §15.2.

16.4 A Matter of Saving Nationalities

If the Slovaks, Germans, and Romanians of the middle Danube basin could be Magyarized, mutilated by the culture of hatred, why should cultures that are clearly superior in terms of their contribution to universal culture not be able to recover their "lost sheep"? And we are not referring to the opinion of Chief Rabbi Gyula Landeszmann [64 p.218], who was referring to the positive aspects of the contribution of the Magyarized people, i.e., the Jews, but to the fundamental aspect of the culture of the Magyarized people, of hatred against everything that is not Hungarian.

The correct and effective way to defend the nationalities of Central Europe, Romanians, Germans, Ruthenians and Slovaks, etc., is to denounce the culture of hatred and de-Magyarize the Hungarians. As a minimum, immediate measure of protection for the Swabians in Romania and Hungary, it is necessary to remove them from the chauvinism of Hungarian Catholicism and create a Catholic diocese of Satu Mare and Banat that would be properly Germanic. The Lutheran Transylvanian Saxons, also subjected to savage Magyarization during Calvinization and then during Dualism, held out incomparably better than the Swabians [193 p.91]. The Satu Mare Swabians, victims of "Catholic universality", were "smashed" by Hungarian intolerance. But if the Germans were Magyarized, why would German culture and civilisation not recover them? Can a Herder, a Goethe, a Schiller, a Hölderlin, a Heine have an honourable counterpart in a culture of hate? Can Bach, Mozart, Beethoven and Kant, Hegel, Schopenhauer, and Heidegger not be a reason for

Magyarized Germans to return to their original cultural roots? If they have been Magyarized with the stick, with repugnant iniquities and then drawn into a culture of absolute intolerance, only ignorance can keep them in the darkness of hatred!

A luminous, humane, and significant culture that has given unique people of culture to the world, such as Petru Movilă, Cantemir, Haşdeu, Eminescu, Blaga, Eliade, Enescu, Brâncuşi, Dimitrie Paciurea, Liviu Rebreanu, Nicolae Iorga, Mihail Sadoveanu, Constantin Noica, Eugen Ionesco, I.D. Sîrbu, Emil Cioran, Paul Goma, Radu Mărculescu, Ioan Ioanid, Hans Bergel and Eugeniu Coşeriu, with brilliant scholars like George Emil Palade, Ştefania Mărăcineanu, Ştefan Odobleja, Nicolae Paulescu, Ştefan Procopiu, Emil Racoviţă, Octav Onicescu, Stefan Lupaşcu, Alexandru Proca, Petru Căpiţă, Gheorghe Benga, and Laurenţiu Popescu, and engineers of genius such as Alexandru Ciurcu, Traian Vuia, Aurel Vlaicu, Henri Coandă, Elie Carafoli, George Fernic, Ioan Paulat, Nicola Tesla, Augustin Maior, Gogu Constantinescu, Hermann Oberth, D. Hurmuzescu, L. Edeleanu, A. Saligny, Ion Bazgan, A. Aslan, and E. Grebenicov; why would it not be able to recover its Magyarized descendants?

In the legal and political field, Aurel C. Popovici proposed a federal state at the centre of Europe. After all, what Popovici was proposing one hundred and ten years ago, namely a union of the peoples of the middle Danube basin in which each nation would develop its culture and social life according to its own ideals, was an incipient form of the union of European states, a huge step towards political modernity instead of the union of two autocracies, one of them primitive and feudal. A.C. Popovici was not the only one, a similar proposal came from that prince of the spirit (the appreciation belongs to Tomas Masaryk), the one who had proposed in 1918 a customs union of the successor states of the K&K Empire, the philosopher and economist Mircea Vulcănescu, with his *Economic Project of Eastern Europe* [193 p.225].

Here are some important Romanian scientific achievements:

Year	Invention	First author	Other authors	Nobel Prize
1886	Jet engine	Alex. Ciurcu, Just Buisson	1910, H. Coandă	
1887	Polyphase generator, power transmission, asynchronous motor	Nicolae Tesla*		
	Power transmission via waves	Nicolae Tesla		

1898	Radio transmission, remote controlled robot	Nicolae Tesla	1901, Marconi 1902, Braun	1909, Marconi, Braun for "wireless telegraphy"
1907	Multiplexing frequency signal carriers	Augustin Maior	1908, E. Ruehmer	
1913	The magnetic moment of the electron; the measurement of the magnetic moment of the electron entailed a very good knowledge of the atomic structure.	Ștefan Procopiu		1923, R. Millikan "elementary charge determination" 1955 P. Kusch "the measuring of the magnetic moment of the electron"
1914	Theory of sonics	Gogu Con-stantinescu		
1921	Insulin	Nicolae Paulescu	1923, Fr. Banting J. Macleod	1923, Fr. Banting J. Macleod
1923	The theory of interplanetary flight	Hermann Oberth	1569 Conrad Haas	
1924	Artificial radioactivity	Ștefania Mărăcineanu		1935, Irene and Fr. Jolliot Curie
1935	Proca's equations is a relativistic wave equation a massive spin-1 field of mass m in spacetime Minkovski.	Alexandru Proca	1935, H. Yukawa	1949, H. Yukawa
1938	The principle of Cybernetics	Ștefan Odobleja	1948, N. Wiener	
1947	The dynamic logic of contradictory elements	Ștefan Lupașcu		
1974	Ribosomes			George Palade, A.Claude, Chr. De Duve
1986	Water channel protein	Gheorghe Benga	1988, P. Agre	1988, P. Agre and R. MacKinnon
2010	Telocytes	Laurențiu Popescu		

Note:
Nicolae Tesla came from an Orthodox family from Croatia. In a discussion with general Constantin Coandă he admitted that his family was Romanian.

ANNEXES

Annex A: Excerpt from the report of Bishop Napragy of Alba Iulia to Emperor Rudolf II in 1602

1. The Saxons [...] Among the numerous duties imposed on the Saxons is the obligation to keep the prince and his court fed and watered over the winter. These princes, accustomed to spending the winter eating and drinking, at the expense of others who work, are the prototype of the Hungarian noble. [...] 2. The Szeklers, who once were all nobles and free, have now become stripped of their rights and enslaved like the Romanians. 3. The Hungarians were scattered [...] they lived according to the laws of the Hungarian kingdom. They were therefore strangers to the country [our note: Transylvania], they lived by foreign laws and were scattered like all exploiters. 4. The Romanians scattered throughout the country [...] are subject partly to the princes, partly to the nobles. They are useful, because they are good for all services [160 p.131].

Annex B: What the feudal lords understood by "revolution" in 1848

From the statement of the sixtieth witness in the trial of the priest Ioan Pop from Budiul de Câmpie (the father of Alexandru Papiu Ilarian), vice-judge Kovacs Sandor: I heard the villagers talking loudly:

Well, the priest from Budiu is a true man because he does not side with the Hungarians, but with the Romanians. The other Romanian priests, who side not with the Romanians, but with the Hungarians, should all be impaled.

In the meantime, the Honourable Mr. Viscount Bojer Simon, who had stopped at the court at Bethlen, called the priest and the people of the village in front of him. I, the Honourable Baron (Bethlen), Captain Count Kleber, and the court officials were all standing in the porch of the mansion, as well as the priest; we all took off our hats, but the Romanian priest stood there with his hat on next to the Honourable Baron and said ... all sorts of words in a harsh tone [33 p.76].

Annex C: Page from The Formation of the National State and its Minorities by Oskar Iaszi

5. MAGYARORSZÁG MAGYAR ÉS NEM-MAGYAR ANYANYELVŰ
NÉPESSÉGÉNEK MEGOSZLÁSA:

	1720-ban		1787-ben	
Összes lakosság	2,583.000	%	8,003.000	%
Magyar	1,161.000	45.0	2,322.000	29.0
Nem-magyar	1,421.000	55.0	5,681.000[79]	71.0

	1850-ben		1869-ben :	
Összes lakosság	11,364.000[90]	%	13,579.000	%
Magyar	5,000,000[11]	44.0	6,027.000	44.4
Nem-magyar	6,364.000	56.0	7,552.000	55,6

	1880-ban		1890-bén	
Összes lakosság	13,750.000	%	15,163.000	%
Magyar	6,404.070.	46.6	7,358.000	48.5
Nem-magyar	7,346.000.	53.4	7,805.000	51,5

	1900-ban		1910-ben	
Összes lakosság	16,722.000	%	18,265.000	%
Magyar	8,589.000	51.4	9,698.000	53.1
Nem-magyar	8,133.000	48.6	8,567.000	46.9

mat nyer itt. A 18. századvégi nagy népvándorlás kaotikus hullámai óta évről-évre folytatódik, sőt a kapitalizmus erőteljesebb behatolása óta, mondjuk a 70-es évektől kezdve, egyre gyarapszik a magyar kultura magába olvasztó ereje. A fenti számitás szerint 1787-től 1900-ig körülbelül 2,800.000 idegen anyanyelvü ember olvadt be a magyarságba. Még pedig 1787-től 1850-ig (vagyis abban az időszakban, melyben egy intézményileg magyarositó politika alkotmányi és materiális eszközei, sőt ideológiai erőforrásai csaknem teljesen hiányzottak) körülbelül 1,700.000 és 1850-től 1900-ig az uj alkotmányos rend megszilárdulása korszakában, a sovinista-magyarositó jelszavak idején körülbelül 1,120.000 ember olvadt be a mi számitásaink szerint. Vagyis egy állandó, kikerülhetetlen folyamattal állunk itt szemben, mely független a korszakok uralkodó áramlataitól. Természetesen, ismételjük, a fenti számitásainknak csak valószinüségszámitás jelentőségét tulajdonitjuk. Ilyen volt maga a kiindulási pont s ilyen a további levezetés. Igy pl., mint már emlitettük, a

161

Annex D: Excerpt from Older Notes Referring to the 1848 Revolution in Transylvania by David Prodan

The consequences of the Hungarian thesis regarding the 1848 Revolution are quite serious. The axiomatic sophism is quite simple: the Hungarians are the revolution and Austria is the counter-revolution. As the Romanians are on the Austrians' side, they are on the side of the counter-revolution, of the reaction. Or, to use social terms; *here is the revolutionary Hungarian nobility* and *the reactionary Romanian serfs*. After such a preposterous accusation, Hungarian historiography had to make efforts to diminish this serious contradiction. Though such efforts would not be necessary at all, a mere change of words would suffice, and things would be cleared up immediately.

What is revolution? The replacement of one social order by another one, in our case the removal of feudal relations. When did this happen? In 1848. Were the Romanians, particularly the Romanian serfs, against the abolition of serfdom, just so as to call themselves "reactionary" and "counter-revolutionary?"

In 1849, the political conclusions of the revolution were drawn nationally. And this is where the order of things was inverted. Under the national banner, the nobility managed to come off victorious. It lost its subjects, but preserved its economic and political power, its first-rank political role under bourgeois circumstances too. Under the new circumstances, it put forward the idea of a *one-nation Hungary*. Thus, the national issue, which had been much more acute now, regressed a lot. Up to then, one could at least talk about nations, about nations expressing political desires, about a State belonging to Transylvania alone. The peoples of Hungary rose against the state of one nation. So, they changed irrevocably from "revolutionary" (as they had been up to that time) into "counter-revolutionary" peoples [150 p.207].

Annex E: The kind of documents "omitted" from publication after 1990

The fights that the Szekler and Hungarian soldier brothers and the Hungarian women guards of Aiud (Alba County) made with the Romanians of Obreza and Mihalţ are great and unspeakable; for the Szekler and Hungarian soldier brothers killed fifty Romanians, one hundred mortally. The number of those who made men, babies, women jump into the water is unknown. The women were raped by them, and thus raped, they pierced them with bayonets through childbirth ... Sibiu, 5.06.1848, Hungarian Archive, Budapest, fond C.P. nr. 11074/1848.2 [116 p.18].

Annex F: Who Set up Communism in Transylvania?

by Octavian Căpăţînă, translated by Emma Tămâianu

We receive a candid answer from Mr. Gaspar Tamas, deputy in the Parliament of Budapest, native of Transylvania, and someone with a good understanding of the realities that exist here. We quote:

> *On souligne aujourd'hui a l'envi la faiblesse du parti communiste roumain d'apres guerre (15,000 de membres) mais on oublie le parti frere de Transylvanie, L'Alliance populaire hongroise, qui comptait 600,000 membres. Les transylvaines d'origine hongroise ont joue un role crucial dans l'implantation du communisme en Roumanie.* (Today we emphasize the weakness of the post-war Romanian Communist Party (15,000 members), but we forget the sister party of Transylvania, the Hungarian People's Alliance, which had 600,000 members. Transylvanians of Hungarian origin played a crucial role in the establishment of communism in Romania) [*Le Figaro*, Jan. 18, 1990].

[…] As the Communist Party had, before the war, about 700 members, ethnic Romanians represented only a small minority; Hungarians were the ones who consolidated the Communist Party in Romania and especially in Transylvania. At this time, the Hungarian fascists were trying to hide their past under "new democratic" activities. The Hungarians were the instruments of the Soviet Army in order to introduce communism to the country.

We have some suggestive data from September 4, 1950 in the State Archives of Cluj-Napoca [Fund 13, File 527] with the list of the Communist Party's Regional Committee:
- Out of four secretaries, three were Hungarian;
- In the party's cabinet, 72 % were Hungarian;
- In the Regional Committee's sections, such as Statutory Affairs, Press and Editing, Human Resources, and Sport, 100 % were Hungarian.

In the region of the town of Cluj, where, according to the 1956 census, there were 20.4 % Magyarized persons from a total of 1,153,076 inhabitants, the composition of the Communist Party in Romania in December 1945 was as follows:

Hungarians	Romanians	Jews	Germans
2490	288	195	8

[State Archives of Cluj: Fund 1, File 1, page 13].

The Hungarians took advantage of their privileged position in the Communist Party in order to occupy all the leading positions in the "Securitate", the prosecutor's office, and the police in Transylvania. Here are some well-known examples in the region of Cluj: Breban Joszef, Peres Sandor, Criszan Gyula, Nagy Wilhelm, Iakab M., Kulcsar L., Istvan E., Kiraly A., Pall Fr., Szekely M., Dombodi L., Fele L., and Barany E. All of them were chiefs of departments or bureaus.

In order to understand more clearly the strange situation that Romanians experienced in the period when communism was being set up, we quote from official documents of the Intelligence Office at that time [21]:

> *Three days ago, in Tg. Mures, armed Hungarian civilians attacked in war formations the military troops* [our note: Romanian] *stationed in town. Because it was ascertained from an official source that the arming and organization of these civil formations' actions were achieved with the tacit knowledge of the Tg. Mures commander's office* [our note: Soviet]*, the battalion commander (Romanian) requested details* [from telegram no. 452/Nov. 16, 1944].

> *Generally speaking, in this region as well as in other parts of the country, Romanian public opinion is clearly hostile to the new domination* [our note: communism] *that is being established. ... The Hungarian delegation which left for Moscow has the mission not of closing an armistice, which has in fact been closed since 1942, but to perfect the majority of Hungarian requests approved through the secret Treaty of 1942. According to this agreement, immediately after the Soviet Union would have forced the passes in the Carpathian Mountains, Hungary would have entered behind the German-Romanian battlefront in order to open the way towards Vienna and Berlin. According to this agreement, Hungary and the whole of Transylvania would be independent Republics under the suzerainty of the Soviet Union* [Act no. 503/Dec. 31, 1944].

An important moment in the "democratization" of Romania is represented by the elections of November 19, 1946. From the same sources we give a few excerpts:

> *The arrests that take place in the whole country do not have as a main task only preventing the opposition to submit lists. The arrests will continue through November, December, and January. More than 90,000 Romanian intellectuals will be arrested. ... The regime that they will have during the winter will be a very hard one and many will die because of disease* [act 396/Oct. 23, 1946].

We are informed that in Dermata 'shock teams' [our note: Hungarian] *are prepared to assure the 'liberty' of elections. These teams will guard the elections in villages. They are armed with machine guns, automatic weapons and hand-grenades* [act 64/May 23, 1946].

In Chiuesti, the County of Somes. At the opening of voting, a group of Hungarians working as guards, dressed as guards in soldier uniforms together, with a group of policemen took the ballot box by force and left quickly for the town of Dej. ...The peasants gathered around the election station followed the wagon of the thieves. They sent messengers to all villages calling armed people to Dej. On Thursday, November 21, 1946, the town of Dej was completely isolated, being surrounded by about 50-60 thousand peasants. ... Gâlgau, the County of Somes. Even if in the villages that voted there live only 1-2 % Hungarians, the ones who remained after the colonisation made by Horthy, it is said that the Hungarian list included a couple of hundred votes [act 411/Nov. 21, 1946)].

In the organization of the new state the greatest role is reserved for the Magyar Popular Union, which, it is said, has the confidence of the domination as a reward for services rendered [act 397/Oct. 23, 1946].

Annex G: How Was Communism Set up in Romania?

by Octavian Căpăţînă, translated by Carmen Borbely

After the second Vienna Diktat and the occupation of Northern Transylvania by fascist Hungarian troops, suddenly and overtly, almost all the Hungarian and Magyarized population became Horthyst, that is, more than both fascist and Nazi put together. Hundreds of Romanians were assassinated by the Hungarian army and their neighbours, merciless Christians (*nincs kegyelem*). Hundreds of thousands of Romanians fled or, if they had failed to understand the "suggestion" of the assassinations, they were subjected to forced evictions in freight and cattle wagons. From a family of 10 children from Călăţele (the family of Boboş Viorica from the Computer Technology Institute in Cluj-Napoca), only one returned home after the expulsion of the occupant, while the rest, boys and girls, who had fled to southern Romania in the autumn of 1940, never returned home. Hundreds of thousands of young Romanians were enrolled in the Hungarian Army and sent to their deaths as auxiliary forces, cleaning the front line of mines. This was one of the favourite practices of the government in Budapest: racial purification. Thus, the Hungarian Prime Minister Kallay informed the parliamentary committee of the loss of 100,000 people on the eastern front, saying "do not be frightened, they were not Hungarians" (see the work of Johann Weidlein)! The Jews were also not forgotten, since, as the Hungarian Secretary of State Endre Laszlo said on Radio Budapest on 31 March 1944, "Hungarian society, defender of racial purity, has unanimously urged for nearly 25 years the solving of the Jewish problem". The Hungarian Council of Ministers on 29 March 1944 adopted the first measures of the *Final Solution* and, in just a few days, more than 150,000 Jews from Northern Transylvania arrived in the death camps. Romania and the Romanians, to their credit, did not respond in the same way, which was also noticed by some Hungarians, who had remained in the parts of Transylvania that had not been occupied by the Horthysts.

From Braşov, some Magyarized Szeklers, not forced in any way by the Romanian majority, but quite enthusiastic about the racial purification practised north of the provisional Horthyst border, withdrew into the Szekler Land in the autumn of 1940. Their jobs were occupied by Romanians who had been forced out of Northern Transylvania. As a consequence, some young refugees from Maramureş were hired by the rubber factory in Braşov, where they acquired qualifications and secured, in the following years, a respectable situation for themselves through their diligence and skill. They married, had children, and developed an attachment to their new place of residence. At that time, the rubber factory was headed by Octavian Stoichita and one of the union leaders was Luca Capatina. However, on 25 October 1944, the last locality in Northern Transylvania was freed from the horthysts and Germans and by Romanian troops. Suddenly, all the Hungarians and Magyarized people became communists and were organized in an association called MADOSz, on racial grounds, Romania being under the occupation of Soviet troops. Of course, this instant metamorphosis, as yet unencountered in history, also had pragmatic reasons: rather than face prosecution for crimes committed as Horthysts against the Romanians, better to be communist accusers and prosecutors of the "undemocratic" Romanians. And so, in October 1944, the *sui generis* Bolshevisation of Transylvania started with the former Horthysts. Since the Romanians were not communists, the party of the communists, about 700 members, had consisted, until then, of Hungarians, Bulgarians, Ukrainians, Russians, Slovaks, and Serbs, and was called, accordingly, the Communist Party in Romania. By February 1945 in Braşov, MADOSz was already organizing large demonstrations to intimidate the supporters of the National Peasants' Party (NPP) and the local Romanian newspaper, *Avantul* (The Elan), which opposed Bolshevisation. Besides invectives addressed to the Radescu government and the National Peasant Party, the protesters also had more "democratic" slogans, such as: *We'll shoot Radescu, We will kill Maniu,* and *Down with the King* (see

Avantul, 19 February 1945). MADOSz also started a newspaper in Romanian, *Drum nou* (New Way). Shortly thereafter, the "bourgeois" newspaper *Avantul* was liquidated and only one opinion of their new way was to be broadcast. The former workers who had left the rubber factory in 1940, as enthusiastic Horthysts across the border, came back as communists, organized by MADOSz, and reclaimed their old jobs. The trade union from the factory refused to endorse, before the factory management, the firing of the workers from Maramureş to make room for the Szeklers. This is what the trade unionists had been waiting for! But the newspaper *New Way* reported that:

> *The situation from the rubber factory did not escape the vigilance of the democratic authorities in Braşov, as well as of the conscious working class, who will know how to put an end to the hooligan provocations sponsored by Capatana.*

And indeed, the communist Horthysts racially grouped together in MADOSz would know. Several truckloads of workers armed with clubs and iron crowbars came from the Szekler Land and descended on the workers of the rubber factory in Braşov, who were in a union meeting at which they had just discussed the challenges that were presented by the new "democratic forces" now on the rise. They were severely beaten and left almost breathless in the meeting room. Their families gathered them in cars and carts. However, the workers and clerks who had been "cautioned in worker-like fashion" returned to the factory the next day, suffering, injured, bandaged, some with splints; they resumed work, but would not leave the factory to accommodate the new communists! In no time, hordes of the new ethnic communists were back in more trucks, better equipped with clubs, iron crowbars, knives, and chains, more determined and more hateful. They invaded the factory, all the Romanians being removed with blows of clubs onto the pavement in front of the factory, where they were beaten unconscious, until they could no longer move, with blood streaming from their noses and mouths! Their human and Christian resistance (people and spirit) to defend their jobs and make a living for themselves and their children was, this time, gathered by the police, and placed at the service of the "people". Here is how, on 12 December 1945, the self-same communist-Horthyst sheet reported, under the title "*A Factory Purged of Saboteurs and Reactionaries*," and subtitled with phrases such as "Hooligan Methods" or "Manist Arguments: Iron Crowbars and Knives", the results of the intervention made by the fresh communists: "The hooligans proved to be well trained, iron crowbars and knives being found on some. They were all disarmed and those found guilty of conspiracy were surrendered to the police, which drew up documents for their arrest". And, indeed, those mutilated, bloody bodies were arrested.

This is how communism was established in Transylvania!

BIBLIOGRAPHY

1   P. Anonymus, 1996, *Cronica notarului Anonymus*, Bucureşti, ISBN 973-9182-34-8
2   Ion Ardeleanu, 1985, *Teroarea horthisto-fascistă din nord-vestul României*, Bucureşti
3   Adolf Armbruster, 2002, *Romanitatea românilor*, Bucureşti, ISBN 978-973-45-0660-6
4   Nicolae Arnăutu, 1996, *12 invazii ruseşti în România*, Bucureşti, ISBN 973-9200-34-6
5   G. Badea-Lătuceanu, 1995, *In the name of the truth*, Furstenfeldbruck
6   George Bariţ, 1993, *Părţi alese din istoria Transilvaniei*, Braşov
7   Petre Bărbulescu, 1991, *The Drama of National minorities in Hungary*, ISBN 973-49-0021-8
8   Mathias Bernath, 1994, *Habsburgii şi începuturile formării naţiunii române*, Cluj-Napoca, ISBN 973-35-0353-3
9   Ligia Bîrzu, Şt. Brezeanu, 1991, *Originea şi continuitatea românilor*, Bucureşti, ISBN 973-15-0011-2
10 Lucian Blaga, 1966, *Gândirea românească în Transilvania în secolul al XVII-lea*, Bucureşti
11 Lucian Blaga, 1972, *Izvoade,* Bucureşti, ed. Minerva
12 N. Bocşan, R. Gräf, 2003, *Revoluţia de la 1849 în Munţii Apuseni*, ISBN 973-610-231-9, Cluj-Napoca
13 Gheorghe Bodea, şa, 1988, *Administraţia militară hortistă*, Cluj-Napoca
14 Gheorghe Bodea, Vasile T. Suciu, 1982, *Moisei*, Tg.Mureş
15 Ioan Bolovan, 2000, *Transilvania între Revoluţia 1848 şi Unirea din 1918,* Cluj-Napoca, ISBN 973-577-240-x
16 Ioan Bolovan, 2021, *Valeriu Anania şi mişcările studenţeşti de la Cluj din 1946,* revista Oraşul, nr. 53-54, ISSN: 1841-9704
17 Valeriu Branişte, 1980, *De la Blaj la Alba-Iulia,* editura Facla, Timişoara
18 Alfons Brauchle, 1935, *Lupta naţionalităţii germane din Satu-Mare*, mss, Stetten, Biblioteca Academiei Cluj-Napoca
19 Gheorghe Brătianu, 1980, *Tradiţia istorică despre întemeierea statelor româneşti*, ed. Eminescu, Bucureşti
20 Gheorghe Brătianu, 1942, *Cuvinte către români*, Bucureşti

21 Gheorghe Brătianu, 1939, *Acțiunea politică și militară a României în 1919*, București
22 Gheorghe Brătianu, 1988, *O enigmă și un miracol istoric*, București
23 Gheorghe Brătianu, 1943, *Origines et formation de l'unite roumaine*, București
24 Stelian Brezeanu, 2007, *Istoria imperiului Bizantin*, ISBN 978-973-7839-20-6
25 Eugen Brote, 1895, *Cestiunea română în Transilvania și Ungaria*, București
26 Augustin Bunea, 2010, *Stăpânii Țării Oltului*, Cluj-Napoca, ISBN 978973-647-736-2
27 Emil Burzo, 2010, *Transilvania de Nord la răscruce de drumuri*, Orașul, nr. 48-49, ISSN 1841-9704
28 Dan Busuioc von Hasselbach, 2000, *Țara Făgărașului în sec. al XII-lea*, Cluj-Napoca, ISBN 973-577-244-2
29 Ocravian Căpățînă, 1995, *The Towns of Transylvania*, Cluj-Napoca, ISBN 973-9683010
30 Octavian Căpățînă, 2019, *Cum un fals istoric devine adevăr*, Orașul, nr.49, ISSN-1841-9704
31 Cecilia Cârja, 2009, *Românii greco-catolici și Episcopia de Hajdudorogh. Contribuții ...*, ISBN 978-973-610-946-1, Cluj-Napoca
32 Ioan Chindriș, 2003, *Transilvanica*, Cluj Napoca, ISBN 973-9414-74-5
33 Ioan Chindriș, G. Neamțu, 1995, *Procese politice antiromânești ...*, București, ISBN 973-9172-25-3
34 Tiberiu Ciobanu, 2002, *Oștile romane și cruciadele antiotomane*, Timișoara, ISBN 973-592-070-0
35 Ioan Ciolan, 1982, *Official Magyar and foreign documents confirm that Transylvania ...*, Edizioni Europa, Italia
36 Emil Cioran, 1937, *Schimbarea la față a României*, București
37 George Cioranescu, 1996, *Românii și ideea federalistă*, București, ISBN 973-45-0186-0
38 Roman R. Ciorogariu, *Zile trăite*, 1926, Oradea
39 Ion Clopoțel, 1926, *Revoluția de la 1918 și unirea Ardealului cu România*, Cluj
40 Sorin Paliga, Alex. Comșa, 2018, *Tracii*, București, ISBN 978-973-728-703-8
41 Leontin Constantinescu, 1997, *Chestiunea Transilvaniei*, București, ISBN 973-97732-2-2

42   George Coşbuc, 1979, *Opere alese, vol. IV*, ed. Minerva, Bucureşti
43   Eugenio Coşeriu, 1994, *Limba română în faţa occidentului*, Cluj-Napoca, ISBN: 973-35-0346-0
44   Ela Cosma, 2009, *Cronologia anilor 1848-1849 în Transilvania*, Anuarul Inst. Istorie al Acad. "G. Bariţiu" Nr. XLVIII, Cluj Napoca
45   Ela Cozma, *Armatele imperiale austro-ruse şi românii la 1848-1849*, Cluj-Napoca, ISBN 978-973-109-383-3
46   Mircea Coşofreţ, 2018, *Reforma Agrară din România şi optanţi unguri*, Iaşi, ISBN 978-606-13-4484-0
47   Hadrian Daicoviciu, 1994, *The ethnogenesis of Romanians*, Cluj-Napoca, ISSN 1220-8833
48   Ioan Budai-Deleanu, 1950, *Ţiganiada*, Bucureşti
49   Ion Budai-Deleanu, 1991, *De originibus populorum Transylvaniae*, Bucureşti
50   Nicolae Densuşianu, 2002, *Istoria militară a poporului român*, Bucureşti, ISBN 973-9418-37-6
51   Ion Dimitriu-Snagov, 1996, *Monumenta Romaniae Vaticana*, Bucureşti, ISBN 973-567-135-2
52   Silviu Dragomir, 1968, *Avram Iancu*, ed. Ştiinţifică, Bucureşti
53   Silviu Dragomir, 1944, *Revoluţia românilor din Transilvania, în anii 1848-1849. Documente din arhive...* Bucureşti
54   Nicolae Drăganu, 1933, *Românii în veacurile IX-XIV pe baza toponimiei şi a onomasticii*, Bucureşti
55   Virgiliu N. Drăghiceanu, *707 zile sub cultura pumnului german*, Bucureşti, ISBN 978-973-8455-44-3
56   Johan J. Ehrler, 1982, *Banatul de la origini până acum – 1774*, ed. Facla, Timişoara
57   Mircea Eliade, 1986, *Istoria credinţelor şi ideilor religioase*, Bucureşti
58   Mircea Eliade, 1980, *De la Zamolxis la Genghis-han*, Bucureşti
59   Mihai Eminescu, 1997, *Transilvania sub dualismul austro-ungar*, ISBN 973-9211-60-7
60   Mihai Eminescu, 1989, vol. XV, *Fejer Codex Diplomaticum*, Bucureşti
61   Mihai Eminescu, 1990, *Basarabia*, Bucureşti
62   Pal Engel, 2006, *Istoria Ungariei medievale*, Cluj-Napoca, ISBN-10 9737867-63-7
63   Mihai Fătu, 1985, *Biserica românească din N-V ţării sub ocupaţia horthistă*, Bucureşti
64   Jergus Ferko, 2019, *Maghiarii sub semnul autoamăgirilor*, Cluj-Napoca, ISBN 978-973-109-181-5

65   Johann Filstich, 1979, *Încercare de istorie românească*, Bucureşti
66   Vlad Georgescu, 1995, *Istoria românilor*, Bucureşti, ISBN 973-28-0548-x
67   Ovidiu Ghitta, 2002, *Iosif de Camillis: Un vicar apostolic la porţile Transilvaniei* http://diam.uab.ro/istorie.uab.ro/publicatii/colectia_auash/annales_6bis/8%20 ghitta.pdf
68   Constantin C. Giurăscu, 1967, *Transilvania în istoria poporului român*, Bucureşti
69   Constantin C. Giurăscu, 1942, *Istoria românilor*, ed. a 4-a, Bucureşti
70   Aurel Gociman, 1995, *Măcelul de la Beliş din 1918*, Cluj-Napoca, ISBN 973-555-077-6
71   Traian Golea, 1988, *Transilvania and Hungarian Revisionism*, Miami Beach, ISBN 0-937019-08-9
72   Anton Golopenţia, D.C. Georgescu, 1948, *Populaţia R.P.R la 25 ian. 1948*, Probleme economice nr 2, Bucureşti
73   Paul Goma, 2004, *Săptămâna roşie*, Bucureşti, ISBN 973-645-097-x
74   Nicolae Gudea, 2002, Ioan Ghiurco, *Din istoria creştinismului la români*, Cluj-Napoca, ISBN 973-647-074-1
75   Nicolae Gudea, 1986, *Porolissum res publica municipii septimii porolissensium*, Bucureşti
76   Nicolae Gudea, 2011, *Christiana minora*, Cluj-Napoca, ISBN 978-606-543-126-3
77   Nicolae Gudea, 2016, *Porolissum*, Cluj-Napoca, ISBN 978-606-543-738-8
78   Ion Teodor Guţ, 2002, *Revizionismul şi Dictatul de la Viena*, Cluj-Napoca, ISBN 973-85148-3-5
79   Ladislau Gyemant, 1986, *Mişcarea naţională a românilor din Transilvania între 1790 şi 1848*, Bucureşti
80   Bogdan Petriceicu Haşdeu, 1984, *Istoria critică a românilor*, Bucureşti
81   Bogdan Petriceicu Haşdeu, 1984, *Cuvente den bătrâni*, Bucureşti
82   Ernst Hauler, 1998, *Istoria nemţilor din regiunea Sătmarului*, Satu-Mare, ISBN 973-971-56-6-4
83   Eva Heyman, 1991, *Am trăit atât de puţin*, Bucureşti. ISBN 973-9011-02-0
84   Gheorghe Iancu, 1997, *La presence francaise en Roumanie pendant la Grande Guerre 1914-1918*, Cluj-Napoca, ISBN 973-9261-54-x

85   Take Ionescu, 2005, *Amintiri, Discursuri*, Bucureşti, ISBN 973-8434-66-1

86   Nicolae Iorga, 1984, *Studii asupra evului mediu românesc*, Bucureşti

87   Nicolae Iorga, 1915, *Istoria românilor din Ardeal şi Ungaria*, Bucureşti

88   Nicolae Iorga, 2013, *Istoria românilor. Oamenii pământului*, Bucureşti, ISBN 978-973-45-0674-3

89   Nicolae Iorga, 2014, *Istoria românilor. III. Ctitorii*, Bucureşti, ISBN 978-97345-0671-2

90   Milan Kundera, 2019, *Gluma (Zert)*, Bucureşti, ISBN 978-606-779-484-7

91   Milton G. Lehrer, 1991, *Ardealul, pământ românesc*, Cluj-Napoca, ISBN 973-29-0010

92   Paul Lendvai, *Ungurii*, Bucuresti, Bucureşti, ISBN 973-50-0206-x

93   Ignaz Lenk von Treuenfeld, *Siebenbürgens geographisch, topographisch, statistisch Lexikon*, vol. 3, Viena

94   Ioan Lupaş, 1988, *Din istoria Transilvaniei*, ed. Eminescu, Bucureşti

95   Ioan Lupaş, 1928, *Lecturi din izvoarele istoriei române*, Bucureşti

96   Ioan Lupaş, 1992, *The Hungarian Policy of Magyarization*, vol. I, nr. 1, Cluj-Napoca, ISSN 1220-8833

97   Ioan Lupaş, 1977, *Scrieri alese*, ed. Dacia, Cluj Napoca

98   Oliver Lustig, 1987, *Denaturări şi falsificări care jignesc şi profanează memoria victimelor terorii horthiste*, Magazin istoric nr 5, Bucureşti or 1996, Hallandale, Florida, USA

99   Alexandru Madgearu, 2001, *Românii în opera notarului anonim*, Cluj-Napoca, ISBN 973-577-249-3

100   Liviu Maior, 2006, *Habsburgi şi români*, ed. Enciclopedica, Bucureşti, ISBN 973-45-0535-1

101   Liviu Maior, 2018, *De la Marele Război la România Întregită*, ISBN 978-606-006-140-3

102   Liviu Maior, 2008, *In the Empire Habsburg and Romanians*, Bucureşti, ISBN 978-973-7784-17-9

103   Ştefan Manciulea, 1994, *Graniţa de vest*, Baia Mare, ISBN 973-9083-84-6

104   Ştefan Manciulea, 2002, *Aşezările româneşti din Ungaria şi Transilvania*, Cluj-Napoca, ISBN: 973-99109-9-0

105   Karl Marx, 1964, *Însemnări despre români*, Bucureşti

106   Dumitru Mărtinaş, 1985, *Originea ceangăilor din Moldova*, Bucureşti

107   Ştefan Meteş, 1977, *Emigrări româneşti din Transilvania în secolele XIII-XX*, Bucureşti

108   Ioan Mihaly de Apşa, 2009, *Diplome maramureşene*, Cluj-Napoca, ISBN 978-973-8274-32-7

109   Teodor Misaroş, 1990, *Din istoria comunităţilor bisericeşti ortodoxe române din Ungaria*, Budapest

110   Mihai Munteanu, 2002, *Provincia Dacia pe monedele Romei imperiale*, Cluj-Napoca, ISBN 973-9357-14-8

111   Thomas Nägler, 1992, *Aşezarea saşilor în Transilvania*, Bucureşti, ISBN 973-26-0229-5

112   Gelu Neamţu, N Cordoş, 1994, *The Hungarian Policy of magyarization in Transylvania. 1867-1918*, Cluj-Napoca, ISSN 1220-8833

113   Gelu Neamţu, 2010, *"Religia română" în Transilvania*, Cluj-Napoca, ISBN 978-973-109-249-2

114   Gelu Neamţu, 2009, *Documente pentru viitorime privind genocidul antiromânesc din Transilvania*, Cluj-Napoca, ISBN 978-97310 9169-3

115   Gelu Neamţu, 1996, *Revoluţia românilor din Transilvania, 1848-1849*, Cluj-Napoca

116   Gelu Neamţu, 2013, *Falsificarea istoriei revoluţiei de la 1848-1849*, Cluj-Napoca, ISBN 978-973-109-815-9

117   Mihai Netea, 2022, *Istoria genetică (incompletă) a românilor*, Bucureşti, ISBN 9789735075712

118   Vasile Netea, 1900, *O zi din istoria Transilvaniei*, Bucureşti

119   Virgil Oniţiu, 1894, *Limba română*, ed. Librăriei N. Ciurcu, Braşov

120   A. Onofreiu, Bolovan, 2012, *Contribuţii documentare privind istoria reg. grăniceresc năsăudean*, Cluj-Napoca, ISBN 978973 109324-6

121   Manfred Oppermann, 1988, *Tracii între arcul carpatic şi Marea Egee*, Bucureşti

122   Ovidiu, 1968, *Epistole din exil*, Bucureşti

123   Ştefan Pascu, 1990, *Transilvania,* Cluj-Napoca

124   Cătălin Pavel, 2021, *Tălmaci la daci*, Bucureşti, Dilema veche, https://dilemaveche.ro/sectiune/tilc-show/articol/talmaci-la-daci

125   Tudor Păcurar, Florin Bichir, 2021, *Târgu Mureş 1990: Zori însângerate*, Bucureşti, ISBN, 978-606-94060-6-9

126   Victor Păcală, 1915, *Monografia satului Răşinariu*, Sibiu

127   Teodor V. Păcăţian, *1904-1915, Cartea de aur*, Sibiu

128 Zenobius Pâclişanu, 1985, *Hungary's Struggle to Annihilate its National Minorities*, Miami Beach, ISBN 0-937019-00-3

129 Vasile Pârvan, 1911, *Contribuţii epigrafice la creştinismul Daco-roman*, Bucureşti

130 J. Perenyi, 1969, *Le developpement de la conscience nationale en Europe orientale*, Paris, cod UNU303543

131 Dorin Petresc, Ioan Lăzărescu, 2004, *Istoria regimentului k&k nr 64 Orăştie*, ISBN 973-622-154-7, Deva

132 Titus Podea, 1936, *Transylvania*, Bucureşti

133 Tatiana Pokivailova, Tofik Islamov, 2014, *Documente din arhivele ruseşti*, Cluj-Napoca, ISBN 978-973-757-922-5

134 Ioan-Aurel Pop, 1998, *Naţiunea română medievală*, Bucureşti, ISBN 973-45-0264-6

135 Ioan-Aurel Pop, 1996, *Romanians and Hungarians from the 9th to the 14th Century*, Cluj-Napoca, ISBN 973-577-037-7

136 Ioan-Aurel Pop, 1994, *Observaţii privitoare la structura etnică şi confesională a Ungariei şi Transilvaniei medievale*, Cluj-Napoca, ISBN 973-9132-73-1

137 Ioan-Aurel Pop, 2011, *Din mâinile vlahilor schismatici*, Cluj-Napoca, ISBN 978-606-600-112-0

138 Ioan-Aurel Pop, 2018, *Din mâinile valahilor schismatici*, Cluj-Napoca, ISBN 978-606-797-116-3

139 Ioan-Aurel Pop, 2019, *Românii, Eseuri dinspre unire*, Cluj-Napoca, ISBN 978-606-797-382-2

140 N. Bocşan, I. Lumperdean, I-A Pop, 1996, *Ethnie et confession en Transylvanie*, Cluj-Napoca, ISBN 973-577-014-8

141 Ioan-Aurel Pop, I. Bolovan, 2013, *Istoria Transilvaniei*, Cluj-Napoca, ISBN 978-973-7784-85-8

142 Ioan-Aurel Pop, 2022, *De la romani la români*, Bucureşti, ISBN 978-606-33-8378-6

143 Ion Pop Reteganul, 1986, *Poveşti ardeleneşti*, ed. Minerva, Bucureşti

144 G. Popa Lisseanu, 2010, *Continuitatea românilor în Dacia*, Bucureşti, ISBN 978 973 642 239 3

145 G. Popa-Lisseanu, 2020, *Fontes Historiae Daco-Romanorum*, Cluj-Napoca, ISBN 978-606-17-1702-6

146 G. Popa-Lisseanu, 1934, *Românii în Descriptio Europae Orientalis*, Revista istorică, an XX, aprilie-iunie, Bucureşti

147 Adrian Poruciuc, 2017, *Rădăcini preistorice ale unor tradiţii româneşti şi sud-est europene*, Bucureşti, ISBN 978-973-642-371-0

148   David Prodan, 1967, *Iobăgia în Transilvania în secolul al XVI-lea*, ed. Academiei, București
149   David Prodan, 1991, *Din istoria Transilvaniei*, București
150   David Prodan, 1992, *Transylvania and again Transylvania*, Cluj-Napoca, ISBN 973-9132-52-9
151   Sextil Pușcariu, 1977, *Brașovul de altădată*, ed. Dacia, Cluj-Napoca
152   E. Regnault, 1855, *Histoire politique et sociale des Pricipautes Danubiennes*, Paris
153   Simion Retegan, 1979, *Dieta românească a Transilvaniei*, ed. Dacia, Cluj-Napoca
154   Ion I. Russu, 1998, *Les Roumains et les Sicules*, Cluj-Napoca, ISBN 973 577 185 3
155   Ion I. Russu, 1973, *Dacia și Pannonia Inferior*, București
156   Ion I. Russu, 1981, *Etnogeneza românilor*, București
157   Alain Ruzé, 1994, *Latinii din Carpați*, București, ISBN 973-44-0117-3
158   Tudor Sălăgean, 2007, *Un voievod al Transilvaniei Ladislau Kan*, Cluj-Napoca, ISBN 978-973-109-070-2
159   Marcela Sălăgean, 2002, *Administrația sovietică în nordul Transilvaniei*, Cluj-Napoca, ISBN 973-577-258-2
160   Ioan Slavici, 2007, *Opere, vol. VIII, Scrieri istorice și etnografice*, București, ISBN 978-973-637-158-5
161   Romulus Seișanu, 1987, *Rumania*, Miami Beach, ISBN 0 937019 07 0
162   Aurel Simion, 1996, *Dictatul de la Viena*, București, ISBN 973 24 0404 3
163   Vasile Stoica, 2016, *Suferințele din Ardeal*, București, ISBN 978-60694182-4-6
164   Alexandru Șafran, 1996, *Un tăciune smuls flăcărilor*, București, ISBN 973 97375 6 0
165   Gheorghe Șincai, 1970, *Cronica românilor și a mai multor neamuri*, București
166   Raoul Șorban, 2001, *Chestiunea maghiară*, București, ISBN 973-95092-4-x
167   Raoul Șorban, 2003, *Invazie de stafii*, București, ISBN 973-33-0477-8
168   Virgiliu Ștefănescu-Drăgănești, 1987, *Romanian continuity în Roman Dacia*, Miami Beach, ISBN 0-937019-04-6
169   Ion Taloș, 2019, *Istoria și semnificația unui toponim: prat și prat de Traian sau câmpul lui Traian (pușcariu/ewrs 1369, meyer-*

lübke/rew 6732), Caietele Sextil Puşcariu IV, Cluj-Napoca, ISSN 2393-526X

170   Ion Taloş, 2021, *Otgerius rex Daciae catilene româneşti din vremea lui Carol cel Mare?*, Astra Clujană, an XVII, 1-2/2021, ISSN 2284-5321

171   Ion Taloş, 2021, *Împăratul Traian şi conştiinţa romanităţii românilor*, Cluj-Napoca, ISBN 978-606-797-739-4

172   Octavian C. Tăslăuanu, 2019, *With the Austrian army in Galicia*, first published in 1919, New Delhi, ISBN 4 444000 340739

173   Octavian C. Tăslăuanu, 1915, *Trei luni pe câmpul de război*, ed. 2, Bucureşti

174   Şerban Turcuş, 2011, *Antroponimia în Transilvania medievală*, Cluj-Napoca, ISBN 978-606-543-191-1

175   Petre Ţurlea, 2020, *Catolicismul şi revizionismul maghiar*, Bucureşti, ISBN 978-606-15-1322-2

176   Gheorghe Unc, A. Deac, 1979, 1918. *Gărzile naţionale române din Transilvania*, Bucureşti

177   Nicolae Vasiu, 2015, *Consideraţii asupra evenimentelor naţionale...*, Cluj-Napoca, ISBN 978-606-690-104-8

178   Valer Vodă, 2015, *Un român alungat se destăinuie*, Sfântu Gheorghe, ISBN 978-606-8695-09-0

179   R.W. Seton-Watson, 2012, *Racial problems in Hungary*, Midleton, De, USA, ISBN MOD 1005462344

180   Larry L. Watts, 2014, *Aliaţi incompatibili*, Bucureşti, ISBN 978-606-609-542-6

181   Larry L. Watts, *Misapprehending Romania: The Impact of Cognitive Bias, Organizational Pathologies and Disinformation on US assessments of Romanian policy and behavior during the Cold War*

182   Johann Weidlein, 2002, *Imaginea germanului în literatura maghiară*, Cluj-Napoca, ISBN 973-577-257-4

183   Johann Weidlein, 1990, *Untersuchungen zur Minderheiten politik Ungarns*, Schorndorf

184   Johann Weidlein, 1962, *Hungary's Revisionist Policy and the Decline of the German Empire, suite of articles from Der Donauschwabe* şi *Südostdeutschen Vierteljahresblättern*, Munchen

185   Johann Weidlein, 1979, *Pannonica*, Schondorf

186   Moshe Carmilly Weinberger, 1994, *Istoria evreilor din Transilvania*, Bucureşti, ISBN 973-45-0090-2

187   A.D. Xenopol, 1985, *Istoria Românilor din Dacia Traiană*, vol. I, Bucureşti

188   ***, 1968, *Apulum, Semicentenarul Unirii*, Alba Iulia
189   ***, 1996, Analele Institutului de Istorie G. Bariţiu, nr. 35, Cluj Napoca
190   ***, 1892, *Replica, Cestiunea Română în Transilvania şi Ungaria*, ediţia a II-a, Viena, Budapesta, Graz, Cluj
191   ***, 1877, *Foaia Asociaţiunii transilvane pentru literatura şi cultura...*, Braşov, 1 iunie 1877
192   ***, 1980, *Transilvania, ultima prigoană maghiară*, Roma
193   ***, 2013, *The Encyclopaedia of Outstanding Romanian Personalities*, Cluj-Napoca, ISBN 978-973-53-0993-0
194   ***, 2010, *Istoria românilor*, ed. Enciclopedică, ISBN 978-973-45-0611-8
195   ***, 2005, *Cinci ani de luptă românească în Ardealul de nord*, 1940-1944, Tg. Mureş, ISBN 973-0-04210-1
196   ***, 1992, *The History of Transylvania. A Historical Reply*, Romanian Cultural Foundation, Cluj-Napoca
197   ***, 1898-1904, *Dicţionarul ASTRA*, ed. W. Krafft, Sibiu
198   ***, 1940, *Knaurs Lexikon*
199   ***, 1993, *Armata Română şi Marea Unire*, Cluj-Napoca, ISBN 973-95712-5-5
200   ***, 1992, *The Romanians in Hungary*, Bucureşti
201   ***, 1997, *Nobilimea românească din Transilvania*, ISBN 973-97339-6-4
202   ***, 1901, *Osztrak magyar monarchia, Delkeleti magyarorszag*, Budapesta
203   ***, 1911, *Revai Nagy Lexikona*, Budapesta
204   ***, 1896, *Pallas Nagy Lexikona*, Budapesta
205   ***, 1985, *Civilizaţie medievală şi modernă românească*, ed. Dacia
206   ***, *Recensământul 1857. Transilvania*, ed. Staff, Cluj-Napoca, ISBN 973-967-961-7
207   ***, *Recensământul 1880. Transilvania*, ed. Staff, Cluj-Napoca, ISBN 973-9679641
208   ***, *Recensământul 1900. Transilvania*, ed. Staff, Cluj-Napoca, ISBN 973-96796-9-2
209   ***, *Recensământul 1910. Transilvania*, ed. Staff, Cluj-Napoca, ISBN 973-99122-1-4
210 *** *Recensământul 1930,* vol. IX, partea 5, Bucureşti
211   ***, 1941, *Documenta Historiam Valachorum in Hungaria*, Budapesta
212   ***, 1975, *Fontes Historiae Daco-Romanae*, vol. III, Bucureşti
213   ***, 1989, *1918 la români. Documentele unirii*, Bucureşti, ISBN

973-29-0062-6
214 ***, 2015, *File din istoria evreimii clujene*, Cluj-Napoca ISSN 2360-350x
215 ***, 1941, *Problema Transilvaniei*, Astra, anul 72, nr. 1, martie
216 ***, 1936, *Fraților Alexandru și Ion Lăpedatu*, București
217 ***, 2012, *Profesioniștii noștri, Ioan Ranca*, vol. III, Sf. Gheorghe
218 ***, 2015, *Românii în Marele Război. Anul 1915*, București, ISBN 978-973-32-0996-6
219 ***, 1997, Istoria României. Transilvania, vol. 1, Cluj-Napoca, ISBN 973-97902-0-2
220 ***, 1878, *Colecția Foii Asociațiunii, Transilvania*, anii1877/1878
221 ***, 1997, *Raport despre bestii,* Brașov, ISBN 973-97582-9-0
222 ***, *România 100*, București, anul I, nr.9, ISSN: 2601-4750
223 ***, 2007, *Comparison of maternal lineage and biogeographic measurements of ancient and modern Hungarian populations*, 2007, American Journal of Physical Anthropology, 1343
224 ***, 2008, *Y chromosome analysis of ancient Hungarian and two modern Hungarian-speaking populations from the Carpathian Basin,* https://pubmed.ncbi.nlm.nih.gov/18373723/
225 I-A Pop, 2016, *Transilvania starea noastră de veghe*, fragment translated from Hofkammerarchiv Wien, 1547, fol.93
226 Oskar Iaszy, 1933, *Kossuth and the Treaty of Trianon* https://www.foreignaffairs.com/hungary/kossuth-and-treaty-trianon
227 Daniel Roth, 1895, *Von der Union und nebenbei ein Wort über eine mögliche dakoromänische Monarchie unter Oesterreichs Krone*
228 ***, 2008, *Redobândirea hegemoniei maghiare, București*, ISBN 978-973-8931-77-0
229 *** *1999, The Romanians and the Hungarians, Interviews with Franz Wesner*, Hallandale, Florida, USA
230 David Prodan, 2020, *Județul, orașul Cluj*, ISBN 978-606-020-225-7